The Poverty of Slavery

Robert E. Wright

The Poverty of Slavery

How Unfree Labor Pollutes the Economy

palgrave
macmillan

Robert E. Wright
Augustana University
Sioux Falls, South Dakota
USA

ISBN 978-3-319-48967-4 ISBN 978-3-319-48968-1 (eBook)
DOI 10.1007/978-3-319-48968-1

Library of Congress Control Number: 2016962214

Cover design by Fatima Jamadar

Printed on acid-free paper

This Palgrave Macmillan imprint is published by Springer Nature
The registered company is Springer International Publishing AG
The registered company address is: Gewerbestrasse 11, 6330 Cham, Switzerland

Previous Publications

Also authored, co-authored*, edited, or co-edited** by Robert E. Wright

Bailouts: Public Money, Private Profit
*Broken Buildings, Busted Budgets: How to Fix America's Trillion-Dollar Construction Industry**
*C.Q. Guide to U.S. Economic Policy***
Corporation Nation
*Financial Founding Fathers: The Men Who Made America Rich**
First Wall Street: Chestnut Street, Philadelphia, and the Birth of American Finance
Fubarnomics: A Lighthearted, Serious Look at America's Economic Ills
*Genealogy of American Finance**
Hamilton Unbound: Finance and the Creation of the American Republic
Higher Education and the Common Weal: Protecting Economic Growth and Political Stability with Professional Partnerships
*History of Corporate Finance: Development of Anglo-American Securities Markets, Financial Practices, Theories and Laws***
*History of Corporate Governance: The Importance of Stakeholder Activism***
*Knowledge for Generations: Wiley and the Global Publishing Industry, 1807–2007**
Little Business on the Prairie: Entrepreneurship, Prosperity, and Challenge in South Dakota
Money and Banking
*Mutually Beneficial: The Guardian and Life Insurance in America**

One Nation Under Debt: Hamilton, Jefferson, and the History of What We Owe
Origins of Commercial Banking in America, 1750–1800
U.S. National Debt, 1787–1900
*Wall Street Journal Guide to the 50 Economic Indicators That Really Matter: From Big Macs to "Zombie Banks," the Indicators Smart Investors Watch to Beat the Market**
Wealth of Nations Rediscovered: Integration and Expansion in American Financial Markets, 1780–1850

Acknowledgments

Pray God you never feel the lash of the scourge, the unwanted pressure of a tumescent penis penetrating your body, the stigma of having been sold naked on the block along with cattle, or any of the thousands of other pains suffered by those enslaved (Skinner 2008: 133). Remember always that there but for the love of God go I. But remember, too, that even if you are not directly victimized by an enslaver, you are being indirectly victimized by all enslavers. So if you can't bring yourself to help save enslaved persons, at least help to save yourself and join the antislavery non-government organization (NGO) that makes the most sense for you. If you are an historian, that may well mean Historians Against Slavery, where you can meet with some of the brightest antislavery minds around: Jim Stewart, Stacey Robertson, Zoe Trodd, Matthew Mason, Tailtha LeFlouria, Elizabeth Goldberg, Randall Miller, Jason Allen, Michael Landis, and Stephen Rozman, among others. They all helped me to think about slavery and antislavery more deeply through direct criticism of drafts or indirectly through board conversations and dinner time debates, but I would be remiss if I did not point out that Jim and Randall were especially generous with their time.

Praise also be to the others who helped me to formulate the important message of this book. Foremost, I thank the students in my interim courses on global slavery who helped me with this book, Augustana University history graduates Gabe Dunn and Dan Jansen, "Augie" economics major Cephas Mampuya, St. Thomas economics major Nicole Niedringhaus, and Augustana Civitas (honors) students Lynette Apio, Alexis Bakalakos, Ajla Becirovic, Tyler Beck, Jacob Fenner, Sara Fisher, Halelua Hamito, Asel Kaldybaeva, Kat

Klumper, Jordan Lindberg, Daniel Matzner, Bezawite Mekonnen, Rachel Nevin, Tori Remington, Haley Schoenecker, Sophia Silverman, Tinker Srour, and Rediet Tewold. In addition, Augie history professor Matt Pehl and two additional classes of Civitas students helped me to hone the freedom index in a course called the Clash of Capital and Class.

The National Underground Freedom Center in Cincinnati hosted two important HAS conferences where some of the ideas in this book were further developed. Former Procter and Gamble chief executive officer (CEO) John Pepper has given liberally of his time and purse to help historians to connect with activists at those conferences. The Mercatus Center at George Mason University allowed me to bring important antislavery speakers to Augustana University (then College) in the Spring of 2015. One of those speakers, John Majewski, inspired me to stay with this project when other commitments beckoned, loudly. Liverpool's Andrew Smith also offered several key insights and sources. Thanks also to Laura Murphy and her Modern Slavery Research Project at Loyola University of New Orleans for allowing me to present a synopsis of the argument one lovely Friday afternoon right after Mardi Gras 2016.

Of course any errors of fact or interpretation herein remain my sole responsibility. I spent years working on this project, and risk my scholarly reputation bringing it forth sooner rather than later, because understanding the ubiquity and seriousness of slavery renders "it intolerable to passively live with it any longer" (Barry 1979: 6).

Bibliography

Barry, K. 1979. *Female sexual slavery*. New York: New York University Press.

Skinner, E. B. 2008. *A crime so monstrous: Face-to-face with modern-day slavery*. New York: Free Press.

Contents

CHAPTER 1

Yet Another Half Untold

This book's title encapsulates its thesis: wherever and whenever people enslave other people the entire economy suffers on net, and pretty much to the extent that enslavement occurs. No ifs, ands, buts, maybes, exceptions, or other qualifications. Note, however, that the thesis is *not* about enslavers' (slaveholders') "profits" or the relative "(in)efficiency" of slave versus other types of labor. It is a claim about the total economic effects of enslavement (slavery) on economic growth (output per capita) and development (capacity, as measured by human and physical capital, such as education and infrastructure). More enslavement means less output or, in extractive economies like the Old South or Arabia, less development. Less enslavement (more liberty or freedom one might say) means more output and/or development.

"The time has come when we must study slavery as an economic institution without regard to its ethical or political aspects" (Stone 1908: 779). Economic growth and development are technical concepts created by economists that can be widely applied across time and space. Direct comparisons of growth or development across vast expanses of time need to be calculated carefully and are not attempted in this book. Rather, economic growth and development are used here because they are more empirically grounded and more widely applicable than fuzzier concepts like "capitalism" and the "Industrial Revolution" are. The former term can mean just about anything and the latter presupposes a model of development that unduly ignores other important economic, political, and social

R.E. Wright, *The Poverty of Slavery*,
DOI 10.1007/978-3-319-48968-1_1

transformations, including "revolutions" in governance, finance, transportation, and agriculture (Baumol, Litan, and Schramm 2007; Wright forthcoming).

As a work of history, this book is deeply rooted in the past, even delving into prehistory, and describes change over time. One thing that has not changed, however, is the fact that always and everywhere, slavery hurts the overall economy. I consider that thesis an empirical regularity rather than a universal truth or law and lay no claims to its novelty. It is an important claim nevertheless, because slavery's effect on the overall economy has too often been conflated with its effects on enslavers' profits or its efficiency (total output per unit of input) compared to other labor systems (Dal Lago and Katsari 2008). They are not the same economic phenomena. Most importantly, profits and efficiency do not necessarily lead to growth and development, which are what ultimately matter to human comfort and longevity ("happiness" in the older, Jeffersonian sense of the term[1]). As political scientist Joel Quirk argues, organizing the economy around free labor may be advantageous overall but individual employers may nevertheless prefer other types of laborers (2011: 120). Quirk's claim that economic tools for understanding and evaluating different labor regimes are limited, however, requires rethinking. Negative externalities, or costs imposed by enslavement not accounted for in the market for slaves, explain why private profits and even economic efficiency do not add up to economic output.[2]

Making clear that slavery stymies growth and development is also important because enslavement, after a period of quiescence (but not, as discussed below, disappearance), appears to be on the rise. Certainly awareness of the continued existence of slavery has increased in the public generally and in scholarly circles. In 1980, hardly anyone knew that slavery still existed but by the end of the century, most Westerners acknowledged the fact although they did not appreciate the size of the problem (Miers 2003: xii). In 1987, historian David Eltis claimed that slavery "did come to an end eventually on both sides of the Atlantic" (1987: 223) and nobody seriously questioned the assertion. Ditto two years later when economist historian Robert Fogel, in a book subtitled the rise and fall of American slavery, mentioned that "many decades passed before Indian slavery was finally ended" (1989: 236) after Parliament made slavery illegal in India in 1843. About the same time, economic historian Patrick Manning claimed that in Africa "slavery ended in the early twentieth century" (1990: 24) despite ample evidence to the contrary (Miers 2003). In 1996, editor Michael Bush argued that "slavery was often no more than a legal construct, with only a change in the law required for its obliteration," and cited "the Americas" (p. 8) as an example even though other contributors to the same volume noted that slavery persisted in the contemporary world (Turley 1996: 196). By 2011, eyes rolled when Robin Blackburn wrote that "the Atlantic slave trade and the slave systems it created in the New World were destroyed through definite acts of legislation and resistance" (p. 277, but see also p. 456) and the following year when Paul Lovejoy announced that "by the 1930s, slavery largely ceased to exist or was well on the way to extinction almost everywhere" (p. 266).

Skepticism surrounding claims of the "destruction" of slavery arose due to the efforts of a growing number of activists and scholars who showed two things. First, traditional forms of servitude continued in many places throughout the globe (Klein 1993: 26). Vestiges of slavery were always known to have persisted, in isolated pockets, in lawless places like parts of Africa, even though outlawed (e.g., as in Ethiopia in 1942) (Quirk 2011: 78, 158–59, 168). Second, and more importantly, they showed that canonical chattel slavery did not end so much as it splintered, transmogrifying into a dizzying and disheartening array of slave-like labor forms, the victims of which go by names like children soldiers, convict laborers, debt peons, forced prostitutes, bonded workers, indentured laborers, and so forth. Instead of ending slavery, the great emancipations of the nineteenth century merely changed the nature of enslavement, rendering it more difficult to define or identify and, hence, to extirpate. At best, legal abolition is a first step toward truly ending slavery rather than the end of the story (Quirk 2011: 113, 145–49; Lovejoy 2012: xiv).

Similar patterns have appeared numerous times throughout history. Roman slavery, for example, begat debt peonage and eventually serfdom. In the Spanish Empire, abolition of the outright enslavement of Amerindians simply changed the ways in which elites economically exploited the natives (Gallay 2002: 47, 66; Resendez 2016). In the British Empire, Indian "coolies" (hereafter, except in quotations, indentured laborers) supplanted African chattel slaves after the latter's emancipation (Kara 2012: 189–91). In the United States, Chinese bonded laborers, debt peons, and convict laborers replaced former slaves. Even in Africa, internationally traded slaves were re-branded as *engages a temps* (in French), *libertos* (in Portuguese), or apprentices, pawns, peons, or serfs (in English) (Lovejoy 2012: 146, 191, 204, 221, 227, 232, 254, 276–77).

In recent decades, slave-like labor conditions appear to have become more common throughout the globe, as measured by the total number of people enslaved to others. That is not to say that abolitionists have not improved matters over time, just that there remains a long way to go before all workers can be considered "free" in any meaningful sense of the term, of which more is explained in Chap. 2. Clearly, the traditional story of slavery, emancipation, and freedom needs to be jettisoned in favor of a more nuanced and less teleological and self-congratulatory narrative. The world is a more civilized place than it was a century or a millennia ago, but it is still a brutish place for far too many millions of workers (Quirk 2011: 18–20). And slavery is still dragging on the world's economies, even serving to anchor some of them in the dangerous shallows of low growth and limited development.

Few people today deny that slavery is an unmitigated evil, even a crime against humanity (Quirk 2011: 23). Freedom from slavery is a natural human right, a subject no longer up for debate or negotiation (van den Anker 2004: 15). Abolitionist William Channing was right when he wrote that "we are poor judges of another's happiness," (1839: 30) but we can be sure that nobody wants to be enslaved. The immorality of slavery should never be forgotten or downplayed, but it would be immoral to ignore the economic side of the institution. That is all this book will say about the immorality of slavery. To steal a line from antebellum antislavery author Hinton Rowan Helper, other "writers have already done full and timely justice" to the "humanitarian or religious aspects" of slavery, so "I have considered my subject more particularly with reference to its economic aspects," which are far from fully understood (1860: v).

In 1996, Michael Bush opined that "no likelihood exists of reviving a belief in the virtue or even usefulness of either slavery or serfdom" (p. 17). Since Bush wrote, however, modern forms of slavery have continued to grow in importance and at least one Muslim extremist group has revivified ancient proslavery sentiments. Moreover, a disturbing number of scholars have claimed that enslaving others creates economic benefits. This book counters that slavery is as economically bankrupt as it is morally reprehensible. Morality and economics are not as distinct as often implied (Davis 1966: 28). In fact, part of what should morally repulse us about slavery is that it victimizes everyone to some degree, not just those unfortunate enough to suffer direct enslavement. As sociologist Orlando Patterson argued, slavery is like a parasite. The enslaved suffer the most, but we all host enslavers, losing a little blood (as well as some of our souls) to their voracious appetites.

As previously mentioned, the claim that slavery hurts economic growth and development holds for slavery everywhere, in all its various guises, and in all periods. While analysis of antebellum US chattel slavery, which serves as the canonical type of slavery for many readers, forms a major component of this work (due both to the author's early scholarly interests and the state of slavery historiography [Zeuske 2012]), the thesis is not limited to it. When the book references an "enslaved person" or a "slave," it refers to any person who has been enslaved, regardless of his or her age, creed, ethnicity, gender identity, nationality, race, sexual orientation, or other group affiliation. Yes, this book is relevant to African-Americans but also to "white" Appalachians, to Amerindians but also to Saami (indigenous people of northern Scandinavia traditionally known in English as Lapps), to Dalits ("untouchables") but also to Brahmins. We are all humans and, hence, we all react to oppression and injustice in similar ways. So John Wesley (1703–1791), a founder of Methodism, was correct when he noted that "the dreadful consequence of slavery is the same amongst every people and in every nation where it prevails" (Benezet and Wesley 1774: 58). Moreover, given the ubiquity of slavery throughout human history (a point established in Chaps. 3 and 4) and the frequent sexual relations between slaves and their masters, it is unlikely, could we trace everyone's genealogy back through the ages, that we could find a single human alive today who is not descended from at least one slave *and* at least one slaveholder.

That claim holds even if "slave" is defined narrowly to mean a chattel slave. If the definition is broadened just a bit, the link between us (people alive today) and them (ancestors linked to bondage) becomes even clearer and closer. For me, the connection is quite close: early in the twentieth century, my maternal grandfather was a coal miner in a company town in western Pennsylvania. He was not a chattel slave but as a debt peon—think Tennessee Ernie Ford's song "Sixteen Tons"[3]—his freedom index score (discussed below) was pretty pathetic. Because of his experiences, related to me in the 1970s when he was very old and I was very young, I am an antislavery activist today, a board member of Historians Against Slavery, an non-government organization (NGO) dedicated to "using history to make slavery history." I am also a libertarian, though a pragmatic one far from anarchist wing of the movement. That background means that I am predisposed to view limitations on human liberty skeptically, but that does not mean that I am biased in the sense of having prejudged the matter, as I hope the copious references to a wide variety of primary and secondary sources will attest. And although this book's thesis may seem to some readers to be a politically correct slam dunk, it actually appears that it will be rather contentious.

Traditionally, advocates of slavery argued that the slave trade, and/or slavery itself, constituted an important sector of the economy, so any move to weaken either would only benefit competitors with fewer scruples (Blackburn 2011: 165, 331). That is why antislavery author Hinton Rowan Helper, a North Carolinian fed up with slavery, railed that "the value of cotton, to the South, to the North, to the nation, and to the world, has been … grossly exaggerated. … So hyperbolically has the importance of cotton been magnified by certain proslavery politicians of the South," he continued, "that the person who would give credence to all their fustian and bombast, would be under the necessity of believing that the very existence of almost everything, in the heaven above, in the earth beneath, and in the water under the earth, depended on it" (1860: 54). Antislavery and abolitionist thinkers, by contrast, almost never explicitly conceded that slavery was good for the economy, even if they quietly believed it (Eltis and Engerman 2000: 123).

The odd thing is that today, people who purport to be on the side of morality and against slavery claim that enslaving others is, has been, or at least can be, economically beneficial. The odd combination of a proslavery argument coming out of the mouth of critics of slavery first forcefully hit me in early 2014, when I attended a summit called "Justice Against Slavery" hosted by Republican Kristi Noem, South Dakota's representative in the House of Representatives, who is genuinely concerned about the uptick in forced labor in the United States and other developed economies (Noem 2014). During the question and answer period that followed, I listened in horror as a member of the audience suggested that the South Dakota state government had a vested interest in sex trafficking because prostitution boosted tourism, especially that associated with hunting, and hence state tax revenues. Another concurred, noting that tourism, and by extension slavery, was good for the state's economy. After several years of painstaking research, I have concluded that slavery is *never* good for an *economy.* More precisely, coercive forms of labor are bad for the economy in direct proportion to the number of people enslaved and the degree of their enslavement. Claims to the contrary are rooted, sometimes knowingly and sometimes innocently, in false or incomplete models of economic growth.

Take, for example, historian Ed Baptist's claim that slavery was a "rocket booster to American economic growth" in his otherwise excellent *The Half Has Never Been Told* (2014). "African-Americans," he claims, toiled "under the hot sun for the profit of the rest of the world." That slavery made capitalism and that "enslaved African-Americans built the modern United States" he believes to be a self-evident "truth" (pp. xix–xxiii). One might be tempted to label this extraordinary call to faith a Baptist theology but the claim can be traced back to social theorist Karl Marx, who wrote in 1846 that "without slavery you have no cotton, without cotton you have no modern industry."

Robin Blackburn has also recently claimed that slavery "was responsible for an extraordinary boom in output, and eventually for great changes in the power and prosperity of the West in relation to the rest of the world" (2011: 1). Patrick Manning also argued that "slavery brought material benefit—growth, if not equitable distribution—to the New World" (1990: 5). In 2006, antislavery historian and activist Matthew Mason claimed that "the Atlantic slave trade was a key contributor to economic growth ... especially in New England" (p. 10). That same year, David Waldstreicher, a very well respected mid-career scholar of colonial America, argued that slaves catapulted the American colonists into "a position where they could even imagine national self-sufficiency" (p. 184). In that same volume, Seth Rockman, another mid-career historian of note, wrote, approvingly, that scholars are "connecting the rapid economic devel-opment [sic] of the thirteen North American colonies to the array of compulsory labor regimes that made the New World 'the land of the unfree'" (p. 335). According to Harvard historians Sven Beckert (2014: 22–28, 54–95, 272) and Walter Johnson (2013a, b), without slaves there would have been no cotton and hence no Industrial Revolution or modern economic miracle. Historian Calvin Schermerhorn also recently argued that the evil institution "quickened the march of American development" and even that "slavery businesses" charted "the progress of nineteenth-century American capitalism more strikingly than any other enterprise"(2015: 1).

Perhaps because such arguments, scrubbed of racist intonations, are eerily reminiscent of the views of nineteenth century proslavery commen-tators like Thomas Carlyle (Neff 1924), George Fitzhugh (Wiener 1979), and J.D.B. DeBow (Kvach 2013), earlier scholars tended to be more circumspect in their claims while still implying that slavery aided growth or development. Doyen David Brion Davis, for example, wrote that "with-out exaggerating the economic significance of Negro slavery, we may safely conclude that it played a major role in the early development of the New World and in the growth of commercial capitalism" (Davis 1966: 10). Of course many factors played a "major role" in growth, so perhaps Davis did not intend to say any more than legal historian Richard Kilbourne did when he wrote that "most of the nation's economy, even late in the antebellum period, was directly affected in some way by slave agriculture" (2006: 149).

The most nuanced view of the matter may be that of Catherine Hall, Nicholas Draper, Keith McClelland, Katie Donington, and Rachel Lang, who recently wrote: "We do not ... contend that slavery alone, still less slave-ownership, formed modern Britain. Slavery was embedded in a wider series of historical changes that transformed Britain and then [sic] the world in this period. ... There is no single number we—or anybody else—can provide in answer to the question 'how important was slavery to Britain's wealth?'" (2014: 251). Those authors also correctly understood that even the investments that, in fact, originated in the slave labor camps (plantations) of the New World might have been financed anyway, from other sources (p. 11). I will go a step further to assert that they *would* have been financed even if slavery had not existed in the New World.

The argument of Baptist (and the others to varying degrees) is laudable in the sense that it is designed to uplift African-Americans today and to pave the way for reparations payments (Van Bueren 2004: 242, 246). I believe, however, that we have a moral obligation to end slavery today before we can ethically begin to consider reparations for the descendants of deceased slaves. As Kevin Bales argued, we can *End Slavery Today* (see also Chap. 8) but reparations appear to be a non-starter economically, politically, and even morally. The African World Reparations and Repatriation Truth Commission thinks that $777 trillion would be sufficient compensation (Van Bueren 2004: 245) but that exceeds most estimates of the value of the entire planet. Privately owned real estate in the United States, for example, is valued at just $15 trillion.

Even if a more realistic figure could be negotiated, who should pay whom? Would an impoverished North African whose ancestor captured and enslaved a European sailor in the sixteenth century have to pay reparations to the sailor's wealthy descendants? Would an impoverished Nigerian whose ancestor was a prince, and an active slave trader, owe millions of dollars to the thousands of African-Americans descendants of the slaves he sold to European slave traders? Apparently not. The Movement for Black Lives (2016), for example, wants Euroamericans, even those whose recent ancestors lived in near-slave conditions, to make payments to African-Americans, on the supposition that the ancestors of the latter improved the overall economy for the ancestors of the former. Not only is the call morally suspect (why should people alive today pay for the sins of their ancestors? For the sins of people with whom they share nothing but skin color?), the notion that slavery aided the economy is demonstrably false. The time to pay reparations is immediately upon emancipation and payments should be made directly from the enslaver to the enslaved, with a reasonable cut for the government (see Chap. 8).

Ironically enough, in addition to containing numerous fundamental logical and empirical flaws (Anon. 2015), Baptist's book misses half the economic story, the half where slavery creates social costs that exceed the profits it creates for enslavers.(It also conflates slavery with globalization but that would entail another book to disentangle. See Fogel [1989: 22].) Missing the other half, as Baptist has to admit, is a major problem because enslavers have a long history of using economic arguments to try to cover their sins. Proslavery forces, for example, used Thomas Malthus's famous essay on population to justify the slave trade although Malthus himself argued strenuously against both slavery and the use of his population formula in support of it (Emmett 2014). Similarly, Europeans subsisting in Canada in the early eighteenth century argued that they could forge prosperous economies like those of New York and New England by importing African slaves (Davis 1966: 126).

If slavery does spur economic growth (which emphatically it does not) enslaving others would still not be morally justifiable. "Be it so," as Scottish enlightenment jurist George Wallace put it, "would it from thence follow, that the bulk of mankind ought to be abused, that our pockets may be filled with money, or our mouths with delicates?" (Wallace 1760: 264). Obviously not, but the rhetorical argument today goes like this: if slavery (child labor, pollution, etc.) made the wealthy world rich, then it is incumbent on the wealthy world to allow slavery (child labor, pollution, etc.) in poor countries today, so they can catch up. Using the mistaken notion that slavery spurs economic growth to justify heinous violations of human rights is not just a threat, it is very much a reality, and has been for a long time. University of Birmingham sociologist Louise Brown, for example, reported in 2000 that places like Thailand and the Philippines view the sale of their females as a development strategy (p. 28. See also Bishop and Robinson 1997). In his seminal *Disposable People*, Bales noted that governments often tacitly allow child labor and other forms of slavery because they believe them to be "essential to economic growth" (2012: 112).

One way to explain how slavery cannot possibly improve an economy is to recall a hoary and universally accepted concept, but one too often forgotten—opportunity costs, or the simple observation that one cannot have (in the sense of possess, not consume) one's cake *and* eat it too. When invoked in the policy realm, the concept is often referred to as "guns or butter," implying that with a given dollar the government can purchase military weapons or consumption goods but not both. The concept's applicability to economic growth was famously elucidated by French political economist Frederic Bastiat in his 1850 essay, "That Which Is Seen, and That Which Is Not Seen." In the essay, Bastiat notes that people are apt to praise a child who breaks a shopkeeper's window because the act creates employment for glassmakers and window repairmen. Bastiat grants that those groups benefit from the careless child, noting that "All this is that which is seen." But what is unseen, Bastiat explains, is that the shopkeeper now cannot afford to buy dinner, or a bottle of wine, or new shoes, or a book. Destruction of the window, therefore, does not increase the economy's total output, it merely shifts it from some industries (say, wineries and publishing) to others (glass manufacturing and window installation).

People inherently understand the gist of Bastiat's story, which for shorthand is often referred to as Bastiat's window, which is why we (usually) do not bash in our windows when recession threatens or even when depression hits. But they still cling to the old myth that World War II saved America from the Great Depression even though it is now clear that what kept the national economy from generating jobs were certain aspects of the New Deal, including the National Recovery Administration (NRA) and its high wage policies (Taylor 2014). It is true that wars stimulate aggregate demand and hence output but the gains are fleeting and wiped out by inflation (or rationing, as in the USA during World War II) and the destruction of capital, physical (e.g., windows) and human (Higgs 2009). Wars are worth more than absolutely nothing; they may be necessary, for example, to protect home and hearth from violent outsiders. War, per se, however, is costly and hence never justified on economic grounds alone.

American chattel slavery has been likened to war, but one need not go that far to see how it, or other forms of forced labor, cannot possibly promote economic growth (Jones 1990). No slave worthy of the appellation ever reached his or her full potential. Frederick Douglass created more value as a civil rights leader than he ever would have, or could have, had he remained enslaved; Solomon Northup created more value as a free musician than as a slave who was occasionally forced to make music. The opportunity cost of slavery to an economy is the sum total of the difference between each slave's actual total output and each slave's potential output under a less oppressive labor regime. So when scholars like Baptist and Blackburn claim that slaves made major contributions to the economy, they are not wrong per se, they are merely emphasizing that which is seen. The other half, that which is not seen, however, must be accounted for if we are to understand the whole picture, which is that slaves would have produced much more if they had been freer to pursue their own interests (whether they perceived those interests to be individual, familial, or as part of some collective).

Why, then, did slavery arise, probably in prehistory, and why has it been so ubiquitous and so difficult to extirpate (Blackburn 2011: 9)? Because under certain circumstances, often achieved, slavery is profitable *for enslavers* and their sundry paid enablers and helpers (Naim 2005: 98). After all, slavery is, at its heart, the systemized theft of human labor, and little is more lucrative than robbery, especially when the theft has the de facto sanction of legal authorities. Some of the profits (or rents as economists say) of that thievery accrues directly to the enslaver in the form of direct services: an emptied commode, a tended garden, a well groomed quaff and face, a polished shoe, a satisfied manhood. Much of it, however, is indirect: slaves work in armies, brothels, fields, factories, fisheries, and mines to produce goods that enslavers sell for cash.

I am hardly the first person to consider slavery an economic scourge: many have considered enslavers *hostis humani generis* (enemies of all humankind) but few have explicitly linked slavery to a type of market failure known as negative externalities. Economist Jeffrey Hummel, though, has recently shown that slavery causes so-called deadweight losses, losses that no one else gains, and economic historian John Majewski has persistently uncovered and elucidated some of the specific negative externalities caused by slavery without calling them such. In a footnote, Davis mentioned that "although slavery may well have been profitable for individual planters, it would appear that the system helped to prevent the growth of a balanced and healthy economy," but if he understood the full implications of that insight he failed to elaborate on them (1966: 157 n63).

In any event, a market is said to fail when it does not do what markets are supposed to do, which is to allocate resources as efficiently as possible. A successful market is Pareto optimal: after all trades have been made, nobody can be made better off without making someone else worse off. A market that is competitive (many buyers and sellers), deals with a private good (i.e., something from which a profit can be made), provides both buyers and sellers with equal information, and does not impose costs on, or provide benefits for, people outside of the market, will be allocationally efficient and

Pareto optimal. Such markets do exist and they are responsible for much of humanity's physical well-being today.

For a variety of reasons, some political and some inherent in the nature of the goods themselves,[4] some markets are subject to one or more failures. Insurance markets, for example, are inherently prone to asymmetric information because potential insureds know more about their habits and intents than insurers ever could, while insurers know more about their willingness and ability to pay claims than insureds do. So the market for, say automobile insurance, is inefficient because insurers are subject to adverse selection (the fact that those who most need auto insurance, the ones with the worst driving habits, will be the ones most eager to obtain it) and moral hazard (the fact that insureds will drive more recklessly than they would if uninsured knowing that they will be partially compensated should an accident occur). Both insurers and the government know about adverse selection and moral hazard and try to mitigate their effects, for example, by forcing all drivers to be insured or by imposing deductibles or co-insurance. Nevertheless, mitigation is always costly and often ineffective (e.g., the worst drivers do not obtain mandatory insurance) so insurance markets remain somewhat inefficient.

Externalities are another form of market failure and can be positive or negative. A positive externality occurs when the market for a good creates *benefits* that are shared by people not directly involved in the market. The market "fails" because less of the good will be produced than socially optimal because the buyer of the good has no incentive to benefit other people. Education is a prime example of a positive externality because more highly educated people, all else equal, are better employees, neighbors, friends, and so forth. But why should someone go to school another year (or decade) to be a better dinner party host? Why not obtain just enough education to meet their personal income and other goals? Governments try to mitigate the failure by subsidizing education, essentially providing buyers (students) an incentive to get more education than they otherwise would so that society experiences less crime and is composed of more active citizens.

Negative externalities are an even more pernicious type of market failure that occurs when the market for a good creates *costs* not included in the price of the good, that is, outside of the market transaction. Pollution is the classic example of a negative externality: the factory owner supplies, and the consumer demands, more of a manufactured good when the costs of production are put off onto people downstream or downwind of the plant. Ideally, governments should minimize or eliminate the externality by allowing the factory owner and the victims of the pollution to negotiate a solution or, barring that, by forcing the factory owner to reduce or eliminate pollutants, or to pay for their cleanup. That will raise the cost of the good and hence, *ceteris paribus* (all else equal), its price, while of course lowering the total quantity of the good produced (i.e., shift the supply curve leftward).

Slavery (not the enslaved, but the enslaving of others) is essentially a form of pollution. The costs that slavery imposes on society are real, large, and discernible, although unfortunately not as obvious as smoke belching from a stack or raw sewage being dumped in a river. I say unfortunately because if the costs that slavery imposed on the non-enslaved were more salient, people would be much more abolitionist-minded as they would understand that the enslavement of others hurts them just as surely as uncontrolled emissions of mercury, lead, and sulfur do. Slavery would still exist (as pollution does) but it would be much less common than previously and have no basis of support, economic or moral.[5]

As noted above, almost everyone today admits that enslaving human beings is immoral, case closed. (Even Mauritania finally abolished slavery, for the fourth time, in 2007. See Turley [1996: 195] for more on slavery in that African nation.) The morality debate therefore hinges on defining slave labor, a discussion taken up in Chap. 2. Rather than rigidly defining the boundaries of slavery, as many previous approaches have done, Chap. 2 ranks labor forms by how much autonomy or freedom workers retain and argues that the more unfree a labor form is, that is, the more like chattel slavery it is, the more negative its impact on the economy will be. Chapter 3 surveys the history of slavery, the world over, from prehistoric times until the great emancipations of the nineteenth century. Chapter 4 takes up the history of slavery since emancipation. The next, Chap. 5, shows that enslaving others is a profitable pursuit for enslavers, but carefully differentiates between profit, efficiency, and economic growth and development. Chapters 6 and 7 show that the proposition that slavery is in any way beneficial to the overall economy does not follow from enslaver profitability or slave efficiency. Enslavers profit from using unfree laborers, who are poorly incentivized to work productively, because slavery creates negative externalities or "pollution," costs borne by everyone in the entire economy, which are detailed in those chapters. Finally, Chap. 8 offers policy perspectives, the most important of which is that the costs of slavery are pervasive and not limited to victims and their immediate families. So when conducting cost-benefit analyses of policy alternatives, policymakers need to factor in the "pollution" losses created whenever and wherever enslavers are allowed to turn human capital into anything resembling chattel. In democratic nations, voters conscious of the negative spillover effects of slavery (as well as its basic immorality) can induce policymakers to act quickly and decisively to make slavery truly illegal by raising the expected costs of enslaving others above the expected benefits. The technical aspects of reducing the profitability of slavery are far from trivial but the problems will never be solved until they are seriously attended to.

Notes

1. "Good fortune or luck in life generally or in a particular affair; success, prosperity. [Usage] now rare." "Happiness," 1a, *Oxford English Dictionary*.
2. Some scholars have intuited this without fully explicating its implications. See, for example, Lovejoy (2012: 243).
3. Miners loaded 16 tons of coal and in return got only older and deeper in debt. Even death did not bring relief as miners felt as if they owed their very souls to the store owned by the coal mining company.
4. Goods are anything (including "services") that people will pay to acquire, as opposed to bads, or anything people will pay to avoid.
5. For additional discussion of market and other failures, see Wright (2010).

Bibliography

van den Anker, C. (2004). Contemporary slavery, global justice and globalization. In C. van den Anker (Ed.), *The political economy of new slavery* (pp. 15–36). New York: Palgrave Macmillan.

Anon. (2015). Roundtable of reviews for The Half Has Never Been Told. *Journal of Economic History, 75*, 919–931.

Bales, Kevin. (2012). *Disposable people: New slavery in the global economy*, Rev. ed. Berkeley: University of California Press.

Baptist, E. E. (2014). *The half has never been told: Slavery and the making of American capitalism*. New York: Basic Books.

Baumol, W., Litan, R. E., & Schramm, C. J. (2007). *Good capitalism, bad capitalism, and the economics of growth and prosperity*. New Haven, CT: Yale University Press.

Beckert, S. (2014). *Empire of cotton: A global history*. New York: Knopf.

Benezet, A., & Wesley, J. (1774). *The potent enemies of America laid open: Being some account of the baneful effects attending the use of distilled spirituous liquors, and the slavery of the negroes*. Philadelphia: Joseph Crukshank.

Bishop, R., & Robinson, L. S. (1997). *Night market: Sexual cultures and the Thai economic miracle*. New York: Routledge.

Blackburn, R. (2011). *The American crucible: Slavery, emancipation and human rights*. New York: Verso.

Channing, W. E. (1839). *Remarks on the slavery question in a letter to Jonathan Phillips, Esq*. Boston: James Munroe and Company.

Dal Lago, E., & Katsari, C. (2008). The study of ancient and modern slave systems: Setting an agenda for comparison. In E. D. Lago & C. Katsari (Eds.), *Slave systems ancient and modern* (pp. 3–31). New York: Cambridge University Press.

Davis, D. B. (1966). *The problem of slavery in Western culture*. Ithaca, NY: Cornell University Press.

Eltis, D. (1987). *Economic growth and the ending of the transatlantic slave trade*. New York: Oxford University Press.

Eltis, D., & Engerman, S. (2000). The importance of slavery and the slave trade to industrializing Britain. *Journal of Economic History, 60*, 123–144.

Emmett, R. B. (2014). *Malthus, the slave trade, and the civilizing effect of the preventive checks*. Social Science Research Network. Retrieved August 11, 2016, from http://papers.ssrn.com/sol3/papers.cfm?abstract_id=2449035

Fogel, R. (1989). *Without consent or contract: The rise and fall of American slavery*. New York: W. W. Norton.

Gallay, A. (2002). *The Indian slave trade: The rise of the English Empire in the American South, 1670–1717*. New Haven, CT: Yale University Press.

Hall, C., Draper, N., McClelland, K., Donington, K., & Lang, R. (2014). *Legacies of British slave-ownership: Colonial slavery and the formation of Victorian Britain*. New York: Cambridge University Press.

Helper, H. R. (1860). *The impending crisis of the South: How to meet it*. New York: A. B. Burdick.

Higgs, R. (2009). *Depression, war, and Cold War: Challenging the myths of conflict and prosperity*. Stanford, CA: Independent Institute.

Johnson, W. (2013a). *River of dark dreams: Slavery and empire in the cotton kingdom*. Cambridge: Harvard University Press.

Johnson, W. (2013b, March 31). King Cotton's long shadow. *New York Times*.

Jones, N. T. (1990). *Born a child of freedom, yet a slave: Mechanisms of control and strategies of resistance in antebellum South Carolina*. Middletown, CT: Wesleyan University Press.

Kara, S. (2012). *Bonded labor: Tackling the system of slavery in South Asia*. New York: Columbia University Press.

Kilbourne Jr., R. H. (2006). *Slave agriculture and financial markets in antebellum America: The Bank of the United States in Mississippi, 1831–1852*. London: Pickering & Chatto.

Klein, M. (1993). Introduction: Modern European expansion and traditional servitude in Africa and Asia. In M. A. Klein (Ed.), *Breaking the chains: Slavery, bondage, and emancipation in modern Africa and Asia* (pp. 3–36). Madison: University of Wisconsin Press.

Kvach, J. (2013). *De Bow's Review: The antebellum vision of a new South.* Lexington: University of Kentucky Press.

Lovejoy, P. E. (2012). *Transformations in slavery: A history of slavery in Africa* (3rd ed.). New York: Cambridge University Press.

Manning, P. (1990). *Slavery and African life: Occidental, oriental, and African slave trades.* New York: Cambridge University Press.

Miers, S. (2003). *Slavery in the twentieth century: The evolution of a global problem.* New York: Rowman & Littlefield.

Movement for Black Lives. (2016). *Reparations.* Retrieved August 11, 2016, from https://policy.m4bl.org/reparations/

Naim, M. (2005). *Illicit: How smugglers, traffickers, and copycats are hijacking the global economy.* New York: Doubleday.

Neff, E. (1924). *Carlyle and Mill, mystic and utilitarian.* New York: Columbia University Press.

Noem, K. (2014). *Argus Leader: Social media factor in driving sex trafficking, speakers say.* In the News. Retrieved August 11, 2016, from http://noem.house.gov/index.cfm/2014/2/argus-leader-social-media-factor-in-driving-sex-trafficking-speakers-say

Quirk, J. (2011). *The anti-slavery project: From the slave trade to human trafficking.* Philadelphia: University of Pennsylvania Press.

Resendez, A. (2016). *The other slavery: The uncovered story of Indian enslavement in America.* New York: Houghton Mifflin Harcourt.

Schermerhorn, C. (2015). *The business of slavery and the rise of American capitalism, 1815–1860.* New Haven, CT: Yale University Press.

Stone, A. H. (1908). Some problems of Southern economic history. *American Historical Review, 13*, 779–797.

Taylor, J. E. (2014). The Great Depression and its aftermath. In R. E. Wright & T. Zeiler (Eds.), *CQ Press Guide to U.S. Economic Policy* (pp. 45–60). Washington, DC: Sage.

Turley, D. (1996). Slave emancipations in modern history. In M. L. Bush (Ed.), *Serfdom and slavery: Studies in legal bondage* (pp. 181–196). New York: Addison Wesley Longman.

Van Bueren, G. (2004). Slavery as piracy: The legal case of reparations for the slave trade. In C. van den Anker (Ed.), *The political economy of new slavery* (pp. 235–247). New York: Palgrave Macmillan.

Wallace, G. (1760). A system of the principles of the laws of Scotland. In *The annual register, or a view of the history, politicks and literature of the year 1760* (3rd ed., pp. 263–265). London: R. and J. Dodsley.

Wiener, J. (1979). Coming to terms with capitalism: The postwar thought of George Fitzhugh. *Virginia Magazine of History and Biography, 87*, 438–447.
Wright, R. E. (2010). *Fubarnomics: A lighthearted, serious look at America's economic ills*. Amherst, NY: Prometheus.
Wright, R. E. (2017). Financing U.S. economic growth, 1790–1860: Corporations, markets, and the real economy. In P. L. Rousseau & P. Wachtel (Eds.), *Financial systems and economic growth: Credit, crises, and regulation from the 19th century to the present*. New York: Cambridge University Press.
Zeuske, M. (2012). Historiography and research problems of slavery and the slave trade in a global-historical perspective. *International Review of Social History, 57*, 87–111.

CHAPTER 2

Various Degrees of Liberty

"Slavery is essentially the lawless, unrighteous tyranny of man over man. The forms are many" (Anon. 1903). Everybody knows that slavery is about ownership and extreme exploitation but what exactly do people mean by those terms? One scholar's claim that "the definition of slavery is contested" (van den Anker 2004: 1) is a major understatement of the situation as the twentieth century was replete with attempts to (re)define the term, though to date no single definition commands the field (Quirk 2011: 141–57). Images of cotton and sugar plantation workers in the early nineteenth century cloud many peoples' views of slavery. For them, slavery means *Roots* and *Uncle Tom's Cabin* and only *Roots* and *Uncle Tom's Cabin*. For other readers, any diminution of liberty whatsoever constitutes slavery. So factory workers are "wage slaves" enslaved by corporations, wives are "sex slaves" enslaved to their husbands (Meriwether 1881: 186–87), children are enslaved to their parents (or even parents to their children in wealthy nations), and so forth. For yet others, slavery applies to entire social systems, not just individual laborers, so for them Apartheid and colonialism are forms of enslavement (Quirk 2011: 139, 153). In extreme cases, people have conjured up slavery to describe ants (Dublin 1927: 71), explain addiction to cigarettes (FJ 1918: 18), and castigate policies that make English the official language of the United States (Anon. 1917: 456). Dilution of the concept of slavery serves no one (Bales and Soodalter 2009: 112), but Robert C. Davis's completely undiluted assertion that "slaves are slaves, after all" is almost as unhelpful as equating slaves and insects (2003: xxvii).

R.E. Wright, *The Poverty of Slavery*,
DOI 10.1007/978-3-319-48968-1_2

For anyone with a social scientific bent, absolutist definitions of anything as important and diverse as slavery ultimately fall flat, although definitions with fairly clear litmus tests make more sense than empirically vague formulations. So attention should be paid to definitions like that proffered by the historian of Roman slavery William Warwick Buckland, who argued that a freeman can do anything until his lawful "incapacity" to do so is "proved," and that the "reverse is the case with a slave" (1908: 437). But like all absolutist definitions, Buckland's is bound to a time and place and is of no help at all where slavery exists illegally or extralegally. Many other definitions of slavery, including the notion that slaves have no rights and/or no civic duties, are also time and culture bound, as Buckland himself noted (p. 2). For example, David Brion Davis's expansive definition of slavery in *The Problem of Slavery in Western Culture* has also been questioned. "His person is the property of another man," Davis wrote, "his will is subject to his owner's authority, and his labor or services are obtained through coercion" (1966: 31). That definition, medieval historian David Pelteret countered, was satisfactory in general but inadequate, and even inaccurate, when applied to actual instances of enslavement over time, space, and culture (1995: 1).

One often used definition is that of the 1926 League of Nations Slavery Convention, which asserted that slavery is "the status or condition of a person over whom any or all the powers attaching to the right of ownership are exercised" (United Nations). Sociologist Orlando Patterson accepted the notion that slaves are property but argued so persuasively that focusing on property rights is misleading that many scholars began to concentrate on control rather than formal ownership (Miers 2003: 415). That legal abolition of slavery had encouraged the creation of slightly different forms of exploitation helped to prepare the ground (Derrick 1975: 15), as did the inherent fuzziness of the concept of property. As Johannes Fahrenfort explained in 1960, property conveyed a range of notions from an absolute to a weak right to dispose of the good.

Patterson's definition of slavery as "the permanent, violent domination of natally alienated and generally dishonored persons" (1982: 13), however, missed temporary forms of bondage, like the British apprenticeship system, which was defended in the House of Lords as a state of "preparation and transition" and a "limited state of freedom, to prepare [former slaves] for the unqualified exercise of their civil liberties" (Barrow 1838: 3,146). It also overemphasizes socioeconomic variables. Society's most vulnerable and dispossessed are indeed more likely to end up working in slave-like conditions, but membership in a dishonored or minority group and slavery are not coeval: not all slaves are minorities and not all minorities are slaves. Some high-caste women in Nepal, for example, are forced into prostitution due to economic pressures (Brown 2000: 3, 47).

In 1930, the International Labour Organization (ILO) created a distinction between "slaves" as chattels and "forced labor," which it defined as "all work or service which is exacted from any person under the menace of any penalty and for which the said person has not offered himself voluntarily" (Article 2). Those working for low wages it did not count as forced laborers unless they worked against their will. Enslavers under the ILO framework could include individuals, illicit organizations, legitimate businesses, and governments, although to the chagrin of many it carved out exceptions for compulsory military duty and other civic obligations (International Labour Organization 2014: 3–5). A bigger difficulty with the ILO definition was the notion of voluntary will. Was *ex ante* (i.e., before beginning work) acceptance of a contract, position, or situation sufficient to avoid the "forced labor" appellation or was *ex post* (i.e., after being on the job) acceptance necessary too? If the latter, could workers leave at any time, or only after the termination of their contracts?

Recently, human rights scholar Siddarth Kara defined slavery as "the process of coercing labor or other services from a captive individual, through any means, including exploitation of bodies or body parts" (2009: 5. But see also 2012: 31). This definition is more serviceable than most, though one might wonder what Kara meant by exploitation of body parts. As it turns out, some people have organs involuntarily harvested from their bodies, and Kara wanted to include them in the definition of slavery, though many find their inclusion a stretch (Miers 2003: 416). Such definitional gymnastics are not unusual. In the past century or so, slavery has become an epithet throughout much of the world, and people who wish to attack something they perceive as unjust (as involuntary organ harvesting certainly is!) often latch onto the term to score rhetorical points and put their opponents on the defensive.

As Africanist Suzanne Miers showed, the term slavery has long been used as a political football to attack a wide range of practices, a veritable wild card that could be played, or not, depending on the situation. The definition was changed to serve various purposes, including indicting pornography, sweatshop wages, child marriage, and much more (2004: 12–13). "Slavery," she claimed, "is arguably the most misused word in the English language. It has become a metaphor for extreme inequality, for subordination, deprivation and discrimination. It is bandied about in all manner of contexts," (p. 1) an insight also articulated by Kevin Bales (2012: 5), Julie O'Connell Davidson (2015: 28–54), Laura T. Murphy (2014: 16), Benjamin Skinner (2008: 105), and others (van den Anker 2004: 7; Anderson 2004: 108). The definition became so expansive, Joel Quirk complained, that it became difficult to find anything exploitative, from children living in the street, to female genital mutilation, to the honor killing of Muslim women by their relatives, to organ harvesting in China, that had not been deemed slavery by somebody (2011: 157). Even mortgages and taxation have been called slavery (Bales 2012: xix). The logic behind such hyperbolic uses of the term seems to be that "all slavery is bad" and "all taxes are bad," ergo "all taxes are slavery," a *non distributio medii* (fallacy of the undistributed middle) if there ever was one!

At the same time, again because of slavery's overwhelmingly negative connotations, governments often contest applying the appellation "slavery" to practices that most people would consider enslavement (Quirk 2011: 4). Unsurprisingly, elites have a long history of manipulating definitions of slavery to suit their own political goals. So, for example, the same practices that constituted slavery under native rule suddenly became perfectly acceptable non-slavery practices when under the control of European imperial administrators (Quirk 2011: 95). Fearful of arousing the ire of powerful local elites, or of being forced to care for freed slaves, British and other imperial powers renamed slavery a form of mild serfdom (Miers 2004: 10)! In a similar vein, Lord Cromer (Evelyn Baring, 1841–1917) once saw fit to define compulsory labor "when employed for private profit" as "slavery," but when "employed for recognized and indispensable purposes of public utility" it was suddenly a perfectly acceptable form of in-kind taxation (Harris 1920: 126). Other colonial administrators were also happy to coerce locals into laboring for purportedly public purposes, even when those public purposes were of dubious public popularity or merit (Quirk 2011: 104–5).

Other European powers were even more unscrupulous. Imperial Portuguese capitalists eager to grow cloves on Zanzibar and cocoa on the islands of the Gulf of Guinea, for example, claimed to "redeem" slaves from slave traders, at going market prices, in Angola, Dahomey, and Gabon. They then forced the allegedly freed slaves to sign five-year contracts that renewed automatically. "Employers" who owned too many "contracts" sold the contracts, not the people who had signed them, or so they rationalized. The contracts stipulated the payment of wages, but the very low wages were often paid in kind or in plantation scrip, promissory notes worthless outside of the plantation store (Clarence-Smith 1993: 156–57).

"The problem," wrote Quirk in his perceptive study of antislavery thought, "is not that there are no answers to these types of questions, but that there are many competing answers of varying quality and credibility" (2011: 4). That, one could argue, is because no theory of slavery exists, as anthropologist Leland Donald confidently asserted in 1997 (p. 312). Due to its atheoretical nature, the study of slavery is inherently comparative and historical. But that does not mean that the study of slavery cannot be rendered more precise if not actually quantitative. Measuring the various modern forms of forced labor poses numerous challenges, the ILO in Geneva, Switzerland, recently lamented, but the first step in the process of counting how many people are unfree is to think about how enslaved people toiling in different labor situations actually are (2014: 3).

In other words, instead of arguing about who is a slave and who is not, why not try to discern how much a given person is enslaved (or free)? Instead of imagining a bright-line test, why not create a scale of (un) freedom? (Dal Lago and Katsari 2008: 29). Then scholars can precisely say that A.B. is enslaved in ways X, Y, Z but not in ways M, N, O, or P. Maybe A.B. is representative of an entire class of workers or maybe A.B. is an outlier, a chattel slave with a lenient master as freedman Isaac Johnson claimed to have been when he recalled that "Marster allowed his slaves lots of freedom" (Hurmence 1984: 23).

Classics scholar M. I. Finley asserted that the compulsion used in "debt bondage, clientship, peonage, helotage, serfdom, chattel slavery, and so on … is fundamentally different from that lying behind hired labour, which implies the conceptual abstraction of a man's labour power from the man himself. The wage-labourer also surrenders some of his independence, when he accepts employment." Finley conceded, but then asserted that "such loss cannot be classed with that suffered by slaves or serfs" (1980: 68). But why cannot they be classed together? Why cannot we concede that many wage laborers have little or no say in how they do their jobs? Can we not admit the possibility that wage laborers have more freedom than chattel slaves but less than their bosses? Or the self-employed?

In Roman law and traditional Western thought, a person was either slave or free (Buckland 1908: 1). But reality is rather more complex and subtle than that (Quirk 2011: 114). Other scholars are coming to appreciate this crucial point as well (Brass 2013). Jonathan Derrick, a careful student of African labor in the 1970s, noted that it was often difficult to discern the difference between a slave, a serf, and a debt peon (1975: 14). Shortly after, economist Yoram Barzel argued that serfdom and indentured servitude were "simply one step down in the severity of the 'slave contract'" (Barzel 1977: 106). In the mid-1990s, Michael Bush noted that "some serfs ... could resemble slaves, and some slaves ... could resemble serfs" (1996a: 17). About the same time, historian Ehud Toledano admitted that scholars should be "dealing with a continuum of various degrees of servility rather than a dichotomy between slave and free" (1993: 42). About a decade ago, economists Jonathan Conning and Michael Kevane argued that "the bright line between involuntary and voluntary labor arrangements is better redrawn as continuous shading" (2007: 136).

Even canonical chattel slavery—like that practiced in the nineteenth-century America and Brazil—was not a monolith but rather characterized by, as economist historian Gavin Wright (no relation) put it, "an extremely wide variety of labor relationships" (2006: 5). The exact condition of slaves was of course largely dependent on the dispositions of their respective masters (Finley 1980: 93). Consider, for example, the management practices of Virginian Charles Dabney (1745–1829), a Revolutionary war hero who was as equally uneasy with slavery as he was with the thought of manumission. Instead of whipping his slaves, Dabney, who was said to possess "a thorough knowledge of human nature," credited them money for good work and deducted money when they slacked or otherwise misbehaved. Every Christmas, he settled balances in cash, and they were always in favor of his slaves. His descendants castigated that practice, claiming that it was a failure, but Dabney's records show that his farm produced prodigious quantities of foodstuffs for decades. Unlike many other slaveholders, Dabney was not afraid to experiment with new crops or techniques and even heated his home with coal instead of wood long before his neighbors made the switch (Wright 2008: 224–25).

Defining freedom or liberty in a short compass is no easier than defining slavery, so the backdoor, defining slavery as non-freedom, is another non-starter. Both slavery and freedom, however, have core meanings that are not completely time or culture bound and that are implicit in the definitional squabbles described above. That core content is most easily seen, I believe, when expressed as a series of 20 questions phrased in terms of freedom. Workers who could truthfully answer in the affirmative to fewer questions are/were closer to what people mean by the term slave, while those with a higher number of affirmative responses are/were closer to what people mean by the term free. What ultimately matters are the answers to these 20 questions, not what we call people who provide a specific pattern of responses. After all, what's in a name? That which we call a slave (or a debt peon, or a wage laborer) by any other name would be as exploited.

The questions used to differentiate free from coerced laborers are listed below, grouped under three headings, direct methods of control, working conditions, and personal life, in no particular order.[1] Brief explanations of and rationale for each question follow in parentheses. All 20 questions I believe are of equal weight or importance, though some researchers might want to weight the answers to questions 5 and 10 in this "scale of freedom" more heavily.

Direct Methods of Control:

1. Is the laborer paid primarily in cash or other liquid asset (e.g., company stock)? (Payment entirely in kind or in company scrip can be used to limit worker mobility or otherwise ensure his/her dependence on the employer.)
2. Can the laborer own property on the same terms as his or her employer? (Preventing laborers from owning property serves the same purpose as paying him or her entirely in kind as it prevents the worker from selling assets when s/he wishes to move to a new employer.)
3. Is the laborer free from physical restraints? (Punishment should be termination of employment, not being beaten.)
4. Is the laborer free from psychological constraints? ("Invisible" or psychological chains can be as potent as iron ones.)
5. Is the laborer not legally required to work? (Vagrancy or compulsory labor laws contain, as a newspaper put it in 1922, "the essence of slavery" [Anon. 1922b] because they reduce each worker's option to remove himself or herself from the labor force, thereby reducing the attractiveness of strikes, subsistence lifestyles, or self-employment.)
6. Is the laborer inalienable (unsalable or otherwise nontransferable to another employer without his or her consent)? (Sale of labor services is also another characteristic of slavery, though of course not the only one.)
7. Is the laborer incapable of owing his/her employer significant sums or of being listed as collateral security for an advance or other loan payable to his/her employer? (When an employer is also a major

creditor to his/her/its workers, the employer possesses too much economic power over them, which can lead to debt bondage.)

8. Has the worker not been subjected to "seasoning" designed to break his/her will to find other employment? (This is another standard sign of enslavement.)
9. Does the laborer have freedom of movement in order to search for other employment? (Employers that prevent laborer movement can effectively stop laborers from moving to employers willing to offer better terms of employment.)
10. Can the laborer quit without monetary or other loss? (This question appears key to many.[2])

Working Conditions:

11. Can the laborer control his/her work schedule? (If not, s/he can be prevented from having a personal cultural, economic, political, or social life outside of the workplace.)
12. Can the laborer control the total hours s/he works? (Ditto.)
13. Can the laborer control the tempo of his or her work? (If not, s/he can be driven to work at a pace that injures his/her well-being, as well as his or her ability to have a personal life outside of work.)

Personal Life:

14. Is the laborer not legally dead, socially dead, or otherwise alienated from the formal or dominant social order? (If dead to society, the laborer has no basis for a personal life outside of work.)
15. Does the laborer not belong to a group that has been dishonored? (Ditto.)
16. Can the laborer determine his/her own name? (If not, his or her identity is controlled by another.)
17. Can the laborer determine what to consume and where to buy consumption goods? (Employers can lower wages into negative territory by selling laborers goods at monopoly rates and can prevent laborers from purchasing goods that might aid in their resistance.)
18. Can the laborer choose his/her place of residence? (If not, a major component of the laborer's personal life is outside of his/her control.)

19. Is the laborer able to marry on the same terms as his or her employer? (Ditto.)
20. Does the laborer control his or her own children on the same terms as his or her employer? (Ditto.)

The freedom scale can be applied to specific individuals or to canonical labor types like chattel slave, apprentice, and wage laborer. If the answer to a question is no, then the freedom score for that question is zero. If the answer is yes, then the score is one. If the answer is "sometimes" or "to some extent," then the score is 0.5. If the answer is consistently "it depends," then the type of laborer needs to be more tightly defined.

In most instances, the freedom score for a chattel slave who worked in the gang system on an antebellum US cotton plantation, who no one would consider anything other than a slave, was zero, the lowest score possible. That accords with most descriptions of antebellum US chattel slavery (Franklin and Moss 1988: 114–15), the victims of which might also be termed "absolute slave(s)" (Deane 1886: 27). The freedom score for an executive (highest-ranking leaders of a business corporation) in the West in the early Third Millennium AD is 20, the highest score possible. As I showed in *Corporation Nation* and many others have argued, CEOs (chief executive officers) are not even beholden to shareholders, much less enslaved to them (2014). They were also not enslaved to their customers, markets, regulators, and so forth in anything other than the loosest, most colloquial sense of the term. Most proprietors (business owners) would also score 20, which is why Kelly Miller in 1905 argued that "the man who works for himself is of more service to any community than the man whose labour is exploited by others" (p. 15). It also explains why ancient Greeks preferred to be self-employed rather than employees, and to work for a piece rate rather than by the hour, day, week, month, season, or year (Rihll 2008: 130–31).

The freedom scale allows scholars to carefully assess claims that situation X was "as bad as" or "worse than" situation Y across time, space, and perhaps even culture. Abolitionist Rachel Lazarus, for example, claimed that while "the Slave System" consisted of many "evils, … the condition of the Irish poor" was "worse than that of the slave" in America and even "in the Islands" (1827/1977). Lazarus must have referred to the material condition of the Irish rather than their freedom because nobody can be less free than a chattel slave. The same goes for the author of the poem, "The Black and the White Slave," which strongly implied that chattel slaves were better off than child industrial workers. While black slaves labored in the "fruitful, bright, and shining fields" in the sun and took lunch "where the blue stream played," the poet asserted, "yon poor sickly child" had only her own tears for a stream and a "strap" applied to "the infant o'er the face, The neck, the trembling breast." The black slave was whipped too, the poet knew, but he "was a huge and hardy man, And well that lash might bear" (Thompson 1833: 39).

Henry Whiteley, a young man sent to Jamaica in September 1832 "by a respectable West India house in London, under the patronage of a relative" (1833: 1), confessed that, for a time, he believed the poet. "I was, in fact, one of those individuals who believe that there is more real slavery in England than in any of her colonies," and he was convinced that "all things considered, the condition of the negro slave was much preferable to that of the factory child" (p. 1). Once he saw the reality of chattel slavery, however, his view revolved 180 degrees. He saw negro slaves with manure running down their faces, flogged, on the word of a driver alone, for minor offenses or lapses in work discipline, until "the blood" began "to spring at every stroke" (p. 2). He saw them then sent immediately back to work (p. 3). He noted that not one managed to avoid being flogged and that some were whipped merely to obtain revenge against their white friends (pp. 7–8). The slaves were not allowed religious instruction and those who dared to learn the word of God were kept in stocks at night and worked all day, every day, to break their wills (pp. 9–11). After being personally roughly handled by enslavers who forced him leave Jamaica under threat of bodily harm, Whiteley realized that "between the cases of the factory child and the plantation slaver there can be no just comparison. The former is very bad: the latter is INFINITELY WORSE" (p. 15).

Labor leader Samuel Gompers (1850–1924) once claimed that compulsory arbitration was slavery of the worst kind. While compulsory arbitration in labor matters certainly decreased worker freedom somewhat, it did not make union members worse off than chattel slaves, a point one newspaper editor made when he retorted "we have known slavery in this country, in which a workman had no wages, was fed and clothed as the master chose, was whipt if he did not work to suit the master, was caught and whipt if he ran away, was not allowed lawful marriage, was not allowed to learn to read, and he or his wife or children could be sold where he could never see them again" (Anon. 1913a: 389).

By contrast, the black "mammy" who worked all day, every day, except every other Sunday afternoon, and could not even sleep in her own house, with her own children, and earned a paltry $10 per month was living an existence much closer to chattel slavery, especially when white men used her body for sex, and referred to her and her coworkers as "their niggers" (Negro Nurse 1912: 196–201).

Modern marriage, it turns out, is usually not very much like chattel slavery. In some specific instances and in some cultures, however, marriages can be quite unfree: when the wife is kidnapped or tricked into marriage, held (sometimes in a foreign land) against her will, beaten for insubordination, raped (sometimes by men other than her husband, but with his consent), and so forth, as in the case of Miriam Ali's daughters (Brown 2000: 62; Ali and Wain 1995).

The freedom scale can also help scholars to make sense of seemingly trivial claims of enslavement. The claims of slavery made by white-collar clerks were clearly exaggerated. Clerks could quit and move on, could not be lawfully beaten, and so on, so their freedom index score was considerably higher than that of a chattel slave. What the clerks meant, though, was that they were not as free as they thought they should be because employers treated them with disrespect. They felt psychologically violated during their employment interview and application process, especially by being assigned employee numbers and forced to follow certain workplace rules (Ex-Slave 1932: 242).

The great iconoclast economist Thorstein Veblen even claimed, apparently with a straight face, that professors were enslaved. Baseball, basketball, and other highly paid professional athletes have also played the slavery card (Anon. 1922f: 4), as have the debtors of loan sharks (Theiss 1908: 1053). The last mentioned is easily disposed of as rhetorical because the borrowers were not employed by the lenders. The others represent situations similar to that of the clerks: their situations did entail a loss of one or more of the freedoms on the freedom scale, but, of course, they retained many freedoms (like professors' academic freedom) not enjoyed by slaves, peons, convict laborers, and so forth.

Note that whether a worker agreed to employment in the first instance is not one of the questions in the freedom scale because initial acquiescence has proven itself a relatively insignificant issue (Quirk 2011: 123). What matters is the ability of a worker to leave a situation that has proven itself disagreeable, not the worker's pre-work conceptions, which can be easily manipulated by employers or their agents. The ability to walk away from a bad situation, even if alternatives also appear bleak, is crucial to ameliorating other aspects of the work environment because it exposes the employer to competitive pressures (Brass 2013: 6).

The ability to leave an employment situation even applies to so-called voluntary slaves,[3] people who allow themselves to be enslaved during drought or famine or to save themselves or their families from death after losses in battle or other extreme situations (Donald 1997: 117; Lovejoy 2012: 69; Engerman 2000). In a fair and free market, how could a mere subsistence ever cost an individual's autonomy *in perpetuity*? People may prefer a low freedom score to death, or one type of enslavement over another, but society should not force them to make the choice (Kara 2012: 65). As British political theorist John Locke argued long ago, one can sell oneself into drudgery but not into slavery (Locke 1690/1952: 15–16). People hard pressed to earn subsistence today should not have to pay for it forever. Room and board is an absolute, physical "minimum wage." Any payment less than that—as in debt peonage where workers are paid negative wages—cannot be bargained for legitimately in any society that purports to be antislavery, pro-civil rights, or even pro-property rights. The matter is really one of finance. When in 1922 mechanic Charley Jones offered himself into slavery in exchange for $1500 to pay for his mother's medical procedure, he was essentially looking for a loan and offering an infinite rate of interest (assuming his heirs were to be enslaved in perpetuity) and his body as collateral (Anon. 1922e: 9).

When answering the freedom scale's questions, it is important to keep in mind that to be *constrained* by external forces is to be human, not to be enslaved (Engerman 2007: 81; Kloosterboer 1960: 2). There is a categorical difference, economists Carol Ann Rogers and Kenneth A. Swinnerton have explained, between being physically or psychologically forced to do something against one's will in favor of a specific enslaver and being forced by circumstances (2007: 33 n.). In the United States today, for example, wage laborers are free laborers in the sense that they can quit with notice, even if some workers may not do so for fear that they will not be able to obtain other employment. Such workers are *constrained* by the current condition of the local labor market, but they indeed have the freedom to leave their employer *should they see fit*. That is vastly different from not being able to leave one's employment regardless of alternatives, including the alternative of not working at all (Quirk 2011: 234).

Proslavery theorists like George Fitzhugh liked to conflate external constraints with a dearth of freedom in order to render slavery less onerous-looking. "The free laborer," he wrote, "is more of a slave than the negro, because he works longer and harder for less allowance than the slave, and has no holiday, because the cares of life with him begin when its labors end. He has no liberty, and not a single right." He could not sleep due to worry, while slaves, thankful that their masters looked after them, slept contented (Fitzhugh 1857: 30). Karl Marx apparently also had external constraints in mind when he called wage labor "economic bondage," "external forced labor," and even "slavery" (Miles 1987: 24). When social theorist Henry George (1839–1897) argued that wage slavery was worse than chattel slavery because it offered workers none of the attenuating circumstances of slavery (i.e., paternalism and the safety net it promised), he was simply forcing his subjective value judgment, that security was more important than freedom, on others (Steele 1987).

Perhaps the best way to see through the external constraint distraction is to note that even the owner of a large, successful butter and poultry producer claimed to be enslaved, specifically to business and economic conditions. "I eat my early breakfast and get to my desk six mornings a week at half-past-seven. I am so busy I scarcely move from my chair till noon. . . . I am too tired to go to a show at night. . . . I am no more free than the poorest laborer in my employ. ... Here I am like an animal in a treadmill—I can not stop because there is too much machinery to keep going. My money will not buy my freedom" (Anon. 1921: 7). Of course as the owner he was much more free than his workers and infinitely freer than any chattel slave.

Another way to think about the freedom scale is to identify the extent to which people are denied the basic human right to make their own decisions. The questions help researchers to sort out which decisions are denied in specific cases.

The scale of freedom approach to the definition of slavery can be judged empirically because most people, almost all of the time, will prefer higher states of freedom to lesser ones.[4] As Scottish Enlightenment political economist John Millar put it, "no man would choose to be a slave if he could earn nearly the same wages by living in a state of freedom" (1771/2006: 275–76). Slaves who enjoyed a relatively high degree of freedom, like the rice and long staple cotton slaves in low country South Carolina and Georgia, became extremely militant after emancipation because they found themselves trapped in labor agreements that actually decreased their freedom scale score (Foner 1983: 74–107; Hodkinson 2008: 303–4). Similarly, wage laborers feared becoming slaves and CEOs have expended fortunes to avoid becoming convict laborers. The labor movement in America was as much about improving the conditions of work (increasing workers' freedom score) as it was about increasing wages. Enslavers were not the only employers who sought to limit their workers' freedom index score because freedoms created monetary costs that diminished their profits (Quirk 2011: 119).

The freedom scale also helps explain many other historical facts, like why in Africa and preindustrial England "freeman" and "freeholder" (outright owner of land) were synonymous and how antebellum US slaveholders could call wage laborers "wage slaves" (Eltis 1987: 19, 23). Wage and "free" laborers are both paid monetary wages, but they can be distinguished by their response to question 10, that is, the ease with which they can quit (Tinker 1993: 243). Contract wage laborers were not (and are not) as free as free laborers because they cannot quit without considerable cost. And neither type is as free as freeholders or other types of sole proprietors. Both are, in fact, closer to being slaves than are those who own their own farm or shop. As economic historian David Eltis suggested, "ownership of an individual could be seen as one end of a spectrum of servitude, the beginning of which was wage labor" (Eltis 1987: 19). The freed slaves who refused to sign labor contracts in October 1865 in Virginia because they believed the contracts "a sort of slavery" were not far off as the contracts bound them to work for an entire year and contained other onerous provisions (Smith 1985: 31). The freedom scale, however, would have helped the freed persons to see that wage laborers are freer than chattel slaves in several important ways.

The scale also helps us to understand variations of freedom within broad categories of labor, like wage labor. "Regulations to be Observed by All Persons Employed by the Lawrence Manufacturing Company," for example, shows that early wage laborers were less free than most wage laborers today because in 1848 workers had "to board in one of the boarding houses of the company," attend "public worship on the Sabbath," and work a full "12 months" before they could quit, giving "two weeks' notice of their intention to their overseer" (Anon. 1848).

The freedom scale also provides policymakers with some guidance regarding the magnitude of economic problems caused by the use of different types of unfree labor. A few outright slaves will not have much economic effect compared to millions of quasi-slave convict laborers. A given quantity of debt peons is better for the economy than the same number of slaves, but better still would be to help the peons to achieve wage labor status.

A certain degree of unfreedom comes with most forms of employment. Principals want specific results, even in non-profits, and in order to achieve those results, they need to mandate some degree of order or regularity. Consider, for example, the Powderhorn Food Community Cooperative in Minneapolis, Minnesota. Established by nine young, idealistic college students in the early 1970s (some contemporary observers might have called them "hippies"), Powderhorn soon discovered that a "do as you please" attitude toward workers spelled retail disaster, with customers disappointed that the foodstuffs they sought were "out of stock" or expired due to poor inventory control and overall ineffective management. Powderhorn ended up compensating experienced full-time workers better than its for-profit competitors did, but ultimately at the expense of new, part-time, and temporary workers. Its overall employment policies (e.g., seniority scheduling, vacation time, maternity leave, evaluations, termination) were typical of the era. It even gave detailed instructions to its "boycott coordinator," which was a strictly "voluntary" (i.e., unpaid) position created to help the co-op to track products on its shelves that somebody wanted to boycott. By the early 1990s, just before Powderhorn's dissolution, co-op employees griped of "pay inequity, unfair hierarchy, and scheduling difficulties," and organized a "personnel committee" to seek redress (Powderhorn 1974–1995).

Note that the freedom scale does not mention wages or other forms of remuneration because high pay and good benefits are in the eye of the beholder. Deborah Cohen found that Mexican migrant workers to the United States under the Bracero program, 1942–1964, felt proud and not victimized by their experiences. They earned more in the program than they could have in Mexico and built more human capital too (Cohen 2006). Note, too, that the freedom scale does not concern itself with the (il)legality of slavery. In one sense, slavery was never really legal because it was an abomination unto the Lord and natural law (Spooner 1845; Tiffany 1849). In another sense, slavery is legal, or, to be more precise, de facto extralegal, in most places today because most governments have yet to render the expected costs of enslaving others greater than the expected benefits. In that sense, little has changed over the last ten millennia.

Notes

1. Some of these resemble the questions that Anna Rodriguez suggests that law enforcement officials ask when investigating possible slavery cases (Batstone 2010: 251–52). Others are similar to those used by the ILO and Anti-Slavery International (International Labour Organization 2014: 32; van den Anker 2004: 18). Some are implied by various definitions of slavery, debt bondage, and so forth, in the academic literature. See, for example, Kara (2012: 31); Miers (2004: 1–2); Pelteret (1995: 2); Bales and Soodalter (2009: 163–64); Bales (2012: 158); Engerman (1996: 18–41); Murphy (2014: 142, 148, 156, 238, 287–88); Lovejoy (2012: 1–2); Skinner (2008: 221); Brown (2000: 98); Buckland (1908: 3); Patterson (1982: 5–6, 10).
2. See, for example, Kloosterboer (1960: 2); Derrick (1975: 15); Steinfeld (2001: 1–2); Miers (2004: 3); Ali and Wain (1995: 277); Bales and Soodalter (2009: 13); Tinker (1993: 83).
3. At certain margins, the distinction between free choice and coercion blurs anyway (Kara 2012: 7, 36).
4. Kara makes a good case that ex-slaves are "near-unanimous" in their preference for "freedom, self-respect, and self-sovereignty" over "coercion and abuse" (2012: 31). Exceptions include people who suffer from Stockholm syndrome and those too old, unsupported, or beaten down by enslavement to enjoy, or even countenance, a higher state of freedom. See, for example, van den Anker (2004: 25).

Bibliography

Ali, M., & Wain, J. (1995). *Without mercy: A mother's struggle against modern slavery*. New York: Warner Books.

Anderson, B. (2004). Migrant domestic workers and slavery. In C. van den Anker (Ed.), *The political economy of new slavery* (pp. 107–117). New York: Palgrave Macmillan.

Anon. (1848). *Regulations to be observed by all persons employed by the Lawrence Manufacturing Company*. Lawrence, MA: Lawrence Manufacturing Co.

Anon. (1903, July 16). The new slavery. *New York Observer and Chronicle*.

Anon. (1913a, February 20). What is slavery? *The Independent: Devoted to the Consideration of Politics, Social and Economic Tendencies*.

Anon. (1917, September 20). A worse thing than slavery. *Life*.

Anon. (1921, December 10). Where is slavery? *Indiana Farmer's Guide*.

Anon. (1922b, February 18). Are we ready for industrial slavery? *The Independent and the Weekly Review*.

Anon. (1922e, April 6). Offers self as slave for funds to save mother. *Columbus Daily Enquirer*.

Anon. (1922f, April 14). Only slave country. *Bellingham Herald*.

Bales, K. (2012). *Disposable people: New slavery in the global economy* (Rev. ed.). Berkeley: University of California Press.

Bales, K., & Soodalter, R. (2009). *The slave next door: Human trafficking and slavery in America today*. Berkeley: University of California Press.

Barrow, J. H. (Ed.). (1838). *The mirror of Parliament for the first session of the thirteenth Parliament of Great Britain and Ireland, in the first and second years of the reign of Queen Victoria*. London: Longman, Orme, Brown, Green, & Longmans.

Barzel, Y. (1977). An economic analysis of slavery. *Journal of Law and Economics, 20*, 87–110.

Batstone, D. (2010). *Not for sale: The return of the global slave trade and how we can fight it* (Rev. ed.). New York: HarperCollins.

Brass, T. (2013). Debating capitalist dynamics and unfree labour: A missing link? *Journal of Development Studies, 50*, 1–13.

Brown, L. (2000). *Sex slaves: The trafficking of women in Asia*. London: Virago Press.

Buckland, W. W. (1908). *The roman law of slavery: The condition of the slave in private law from Augustus to Justinian*. Cambridge: Cambridge University Press.

Bush, M. (1996a). Introduction. In M. L. Bush (Ed.), *Serfdom and slavery: Studies in legal bondage* (pp. 1–17). New York: Addison Wesley Longman.

Clarence-Smith, W. G. (1993). Cocoa plantations and coerced labor in the Gulf of Guinea, 1870–1914. In M. A. Klein (Ed.), *Breaking the chains: Slavery, bondage, and emancipation in modern Africa and Asia* (pp. 150–170). Madison: University of Wisconsin Press.

Cohen, D. (2006). From peasant to worker: Migration, masculinity, and the making of Mexican workers in the U.S. *International Labor and Working-Class History, 69*, 81–103.

Conning, J., & Kevane, M. (2007). Freedom, servitude, and voluntary contracts. In K. A. Appiah & M. Bunzl (Eds.), *Buying freedom: The ethics and economics of slave redemption* (pp. 108–140). Princeton: Princeton University Press.

Dal Lago, E., & Katsari, C. (2008). The study of ancient and modern slave systems: Setting an agenda for comparison. In E. D. Lago & C. Katsari (Eds.), *Slave systems ancient and modern* (pp. 3–31). New York: Cambridge University Press.

Davidson, J. O. (2015). *Modern slavery: The margins of freedom*. New York: Palgrave Macmillan.

Davis, D. B. (1966). *The problem of slavery in Western culture*. Ithaca, NY: Cornell University Press.

Davis, R. C. (2003). *Christian slaves, Muslim masters: White slavery in the Mediterranean, the Barbary Coast, and Italy, 1500–1800*. New York: Palgrave Macmillan.

Deane, C. (1886). *The connection of Massachusetts with slavery and the slave-trade*. Worcester, MA: Charles Hamilton.

Derrick, J. (1975). *Africa's slaves today*. London: Allen & Unwin.

Donald, L. (1997). *Aboriginal slavery on the northwest coast of North America*. Berkeley: University of California Press.

Dublin, L. I. (1927, January 27). Are ants civilized? *Youth's Companion*.

Eltis, D. (1987). *Economic growth and the ending of the transatlantic slave trade*. New York: Oxford University Press.

Engerman, S. (1996). Slavery, serfdom and other forms of coerced labour: Similarities and differences. In M. L. Bush (Ed.), *Serfdom and slavery: Studies in legal bondage* (pp. 18–41). New York: Addison Wesley Longman.

Engerman, S. (2000). Slavery at different times and places. *American Historical Review, 105*, 480–484.

Engerman, S. (2007). Slavery, freedom, and Sen. In K. A. Appiah & M. Bunzl (Eds.), *Buying freedom: The ethics and economics of slave redemption* (pp. 77–107). Princeton: Princeton University Press.

Ex-Slave. (1932, April). White-collar slavery. *Forum and Century*.

Finley, M. I. (1980). *Ancient slavery and modern ideology*. New York: Viking Press.

Fitzhugh, G. (1857). *Cannibals all! Or, slaves without masters*. Richmond: A. Morris.

FJ. (1918, December 14). Slavery. *Indiana Farmer's Guide*.

Foner, E. (1983). *Nothing but freedom: Emancipation and its legacy*. Baton Rouge: Louisiana State University Press.

Franklin, J. H., & Moss Jr., A. A. (1988). *From slavery to freedom: A history of negro Americans* (6th ed.). New York: Alfred A. Knopf.

Harris, J. H. (1920). *The chartered millions: Rhodesia and the challenge to the British Commonwealth*. London: Swarthmore Press.

Hodkinson, S. (2008). Spartiates, helots, and the direction of the agrarian economy: Toward an understanding of helotage in comparative perspective. In E. D. Lago & C. Katsari (Eds.), *Slave systems ancient and modern* (pp. 285–320). New York: Cambridge University Press.

Hurmence, B. (Ed.). (1984). *My folks don't want me to talk about slavery: Twenty-one oral histories of former North Carolina slaves*. Winston-Salem, NC: John F. Blair.

International Labour Organization. (2014). *Profits and poverty: The economics of forced labour*. Geneva: International Labour Organization.

Kara, S. (2009). *Sex trafficking: Inside the business of modern slavery*. New York: Columbia University Press.

Kara, S. (2012). *Bonded labor: Tackling the system of slavery in South Asia*. New York: Columbia University Press.

Kloosterboer, W. (1960). *Involuntary labor since the abolition of slavery.* Amsterdam: E. J. Brill.
Lazarus, R. M. (1827/1977). Letter to Maria Edgeworth, January 6. In E. E. MacDonald (Ed.), *The education of the heart: The correspondence of Rachel Mordecai Lazarus and Maria Edgeworth* (pp. 109–114). Chapel Hill: University of North Carolina Press.
Locke, J. (1690/1952). *The second treatise of government.* New York: Macmillan Publishing.
Lovejoy, P. E. (2012). *Transformations in slavery: A history of slavery in Africa* (3rd ed.). New York: Cambridge University Press.
Meriwether, E. A. (1881, August). Are women slaves? *Shaker Manifesto.*
Miers, S. (2003). *Slavery in the twentieth century: The evolution of a global problem.* New York: Rowman & Littlefield.
Miers, S. (2004). Slavery: A question of definition. In G. Campbell (Ed.), *The structure of slavery in Indian Ocean Africa and Asia* (pp. 1–16). London: Frank Cass.
Miles, R. (1987). *Capitalism and unfree labour: Anomaly or necessity?* New York: Tavistock Publications.
Millar, J. (1771/2006). *The origin of the distinction of ranks: Or, an inquiry into the circumstances, which give rise to influence and authority, in the different members of society.* Indianapolis: Liberty Fund.
Murphy, L. T. (2014). *Survivors of slavery: Modern-day slave narratives.* New York: Columbia University Press.
Negro Nurse. (1912, January 15). More slavery at the South. *The Independent: Devoted to the Consideration of Politics, Social and Economic Tendencies.*
Patterson, O. (1982). *Slavery and social death: A comparative study.* Cambridge: Harvard University Press.
Pelteret, D. (1995). *Slavery in early mediaeval England: From the reign of Alfred until the twelfth century.* Rochester, NY: Boydell Press.
Powderhorn Food Community Co-op Records. (1974–1995). *Minnesota Historical Society.* Minnesota: St. Paul.
Quirk, J. (2011). *The anti-slavery project: From the slave trade to human trafficking.* Philadelphia: University of Pennsylvania Press.
Rihll, T. (2008). Slavery and technology in pre-industrial contexts. In E. D. Lago & C. Katsari (Eds.), *Slave systems ancient and modern* (pp. 127–147). New York: Cambridge University Press.
Rogers, C. A., & Swinnerton, K. A. (2007). Some simple analytics of slave redemption. In K. A. Appiah & M. Bunzl (Eds.), *Buying freedom: The ethics and economics of slave redemption* (pp. 20–36). Princeton: Princeton University Press.
Skinner, E. B. (2008). *A crime so monstrous: Face-to-face with modern-day slavery.* New York: Free Press.
Smith, J. D. (1985). *An old creed for the new South: Proslavery ideology and historiography, 1865–1918.* Athens: University of Georgia Press.

Spooner, L. (1845). *The unconstitutionality of slavery*. Boston: Bela Marsh.

Steele, E. S. (1987). Henry George on chattel and wage slavery: The American social philosopher condemned both forms as immoral, irrational denials of equality. *American Journal of Economics and Sociology, 46*, 369–378.

Steinfeld, R. J. (2001). *Coercion, contract, and free labor in the nineteenth century*. New York: Cambridge University Press.

Theiss, L. E. (1908, November 5). Loan slaves and their emancipation. *The Independent: Devoted to the Consideration of Politics, Social and Economic Tendencies*.

Thompson, W. G. (1833, May 26). The black and the white slave. *Weekly True Sun*.

Tiffany, J. (1849). *A treatise on the unconstitutionality of American slavery*. Cleveland: J. Calyer.

Tinker, H. (1993). *A new system of slavery: The export of Indian labour overseas, 1830–1920* (2nd ed.). London: Hansib Publishing Limited.

Toledano, E. (1993). Ottoman concepts of slavery in the period of reform, 1830s–1880s. In M. A. Klein (Ed.), *Breaking the chains: Slavery, bondage, and emancipation in modern Africa and Asia* (pp. 37–63). Madison: University of Wisconsin Press.

van den Anker, C. (2004). Contemporary slavery, global justice and globalization. In C. van den Anker (Ed.), *The political economy of new slavery* (pp. 15–36). New York: Palgrave Macmillan.

Whiteley, H. (1833). *Excessive cruelty to slaves. Three months in Jamaica, in 1832: Comprising a residence of seven weeks on a sugar plantation*. Philadelphia: n.p.

Wright, G. (2006). *Slavery and American economic development*. Baton Rouge: Louisiana State University Press.

Wright, R. E. (2008). *One nation under debt: Hamilton, Jefferson, and the history of what we owe*. New York: McGraw-Hill.

Wright, R. E. (2014). *Corporation nation*. Philadelphia: University of Pennsylvania Press.

CHAPTER 3

A Not So Peculiar Institution

Slavery in the antebellum United States was referred to as the peculiar institution. If by peculiar one means somewhat different, slavery in the United States was a mite peculiar. But in no sense was it an outlier. As Davis noted in *The Problem of Slavery*, "slavery in America was not unique in its central characteristics or in its underlying contradiction" (Davis 1966: 29–31, 60). If by peculiar one means something unique or unusual, American slavery was not peculiar at all but merely just another example of the popular Roman proverb (later adopted by Thomas Hobbes and Sigmund Freud), *homo homini lupus* (man is wolf to man) (Patterson 2008: 33; Kolchin 1993: xi). In fact, acceptance of the near universality of slavery in human history is nearly universal (Dal Lago and Katsari 2008: 3). "Slavery . . . is a weed that grows in every soil" (Burke 1775/2000: 129).

In the early seventeenth century, antislavery author Jean Bodin noted that "servitude seemth to have taken the beginning thereof immediately after the generall deluge" (1606: 34). Over a quarter of a millennium later, French historian Augustin Cochin (1823–1872) claimed that "in all places, in all latitudes, under the shelter of all religions, is the same spectacle of one half of humanity held in bondage by the other; slavery is as ancient as war, as ancient as human nature" (Cochin 1863: 289–90). "The condition of slavery," a newspaper editor in 1846 conceded, "has existed from the remotest ages, and assumed different shapes under different circumstances, in all countries" (Anon. 1846: 244). "The sin and shame of slavery," another newspaper man wrote in 1903, "is as old as the time of the dwellers before the flood. It has existed in all lands and among almost all peoples"

R.E. Wright, *The Poverty of Slavery*,
DOI 10.1007/978-3-319-48968-1_3

(Anon.: 79). The nineteenth-century French historian Numa Denis Fustel de Coulanges also believed that slavery was primordial, and began with the first society (Finley 1980: 67). Scholarly sentiment, if anything, has hardened on the issue ever since. "From the dim moment when the first scribe started to scratch symbols in the first mud table," antislavery activist Kevin Bales recently wrote, "there were slaves" (Bales 2007: 2). "Humans keep slaves; we always have," he claimed, along with coauthor Ron Soodalter, two years later (p. 5). "Slavery," economist historian and leading expert on the economics of slavery Stanley Engerman argued, "has been among the most frequent human institutions, existing in almost all societies in the past and in most parts of the world" (Engerman 2007: 79).

In the early nineteenth century, abolitionist Henry Brougham bristled at the claim "that Slavery has in all ages of the world existed, and that no country has ever been discovered in which traces of it might not be found" because he thought enslavers would leverage it "to justify an atrocious crime" (1807: 23). But proof of the ubiquity of slavery was too overwhelming to ignore, so abolitionists soon shifted ground and argued instead that the ubiquity of slavery was no justification for its continuance (Davis 1966: 409). Paraphrasing Voltaire, weasels have eaten our chickens for millennia but that does not stop us from destroying the voracious little predators whenever we can (Cochin 1863: 363).

In his ice age novel *Dance of the Tiger*, Finnish paleontologist Bjorn Kurten depicted the use of slaves in Northern Europe some 30,000 years ago but admitted that his invocation of slavery was completely conjectural (1980: 199–218, 262). Others have postulated, based on no real physical evidence, that Homo Sapiens enslaved Neanderthals before driving them to extinction. Scientists know from DNA analysis that modern humans and Neanderthals successfully mated, but of course they cannot discern if the couplings were voluntary or not (Boas 2014). We may never know when the first human was enslaved, but the best guess is that the worst forms of bondage arose in tandem with animal domestication (Campbell 2004: xii). Perhaps the concomitant rise of animal domestication and slavery explains why slaves were often equated with animals in real life and in fictive works about slaves and slavery like Apuleius's *Golden Ass* (McKeown 2007: 119–20). It might not be coincidental that the words "dog" and "slave" in Iroquoian share the same roots and are almost synonymous and that the word for enslaving a human and domesticating an animal are identical (Starna and Watkins 1991: 48–49). Perhaps, too, the close linkage between husbandry and slavery explains the widespread custom of enslaving children born of slaves (Wergeland 1916: 23). Pastoralists would not turn their calves, kids, and lambs out into the wild, so why would they allow the offspring of their domesticated humans to roam free? The idea of castrating male slaves almost certainly came from pastoralists accustomed to controlling the reproductive processes of their flocks.

Hunter-gatherers, Karl Marx's patron and collaborator Friedrich Engels argued in *The Origin of the Family*, had little use for slaves, a conclusion reached by numerous other scholars (Engerman 2000). According to this view, only once there was a crop or a flock that grew faster than the family did it make sense to turn captives into laborers (Blackburn 1996: 164). Economist historian Robert Fogel did not even find pastoralism compatible with slavery, asserting that slavery began at the dawn of civilization and rudimentary agriculture (Fogel 1989: 17). The first slaves likely came by way of raids, however, so it is not clear why a victorious hunter-warrior would not find it in his best interest to kill the vanquished band's men while appropriating/assimilating/impregnating its women, who could gather for themselves and help to process and eat big game, which suddenly became overabundant after a successful hunt (Campbell 2004: xiii).

Moreover, it would presumably have been profitable to incorporate adults (no need to raise them first) into social units and limit their consumption if some technology were available to minimize the costs of controlling the slaves and preventing their escape (Blackburn 1996: 166–67). Apparently, such technology was not widely available to hunter-gatherers as George P. Murdock's sample of 800 societies worldwide revealed that only 3 percent of hunter-gatherer communities countenanced slavery, compared to 73 percent of the communities practicing pastoralism (Blackburn 1996: 165; Blackburn 2011: 9).

Of course Murdock studied existing societies in the mid-twentieth century, not defunct, ancient ones, so his famous sample is hardly definitive proof of a dearth of prehistoric enslavement. Unfortunately, slavery does not often leave clear material evidence of its existence (Taylor 2001: 28). If one believes that deceased slaves were discarded rather than given standard burials, or that skewed sex ratios arise only due to slavery, the evil institution may have begun sometime between 1500 and 500 BC on the northwest coast of North America. But the dead could have been killed by accidents when hunting or foraging alone, so they remained unburied, and war could account for skewed sex ratios. The 185 males for every 100 females unearthed in one skeletal sample is more difficult to account for and certainly could indicate that the 85 "missing" females were slaves and, hence, not buried (Ames 2001). Or it could mean that female infanticide was practiced for whatever reason.

Archeological sites with differential room or dwelling sizes or barrack-style living arrangements along with more private ones, especially if the lesser living spaces were located near known places of work, like rice husking platforms, may indicate slavery (Chanana 1964: 17). Defensive rock shelters found in southeast Kenya, different cultural customs, like cranial deformation, found in the same location and the same time; different lifetime activities that leave evidence on skeletons, like different diets, work routines, healthcare after injury, and so forth; as well as different grave or burial treatment, might indicate slavery (Kusimba 2004; Donald 1997: 202–3).

Such evidence, however, is open to wide ranging interpretations and skepticism. "No artifact known to me," Leland Donald wrote, "can be shown to be exclusively associated with slaves" (1997: 202) and John Alexander argued that it is nearly impossible to recognize slavery using archeology alone (2001). Late in prehistory, however, iron shackles and gang chains began to appear and they seem to many to be pretty unambiguous evidence of some sort of bound labor. Few examples of shackles have been found but that does not mean that slavery was rare as iron can be, and often was, recast rather than jettisoned. Shackles also appear in prehistoric iconography and art (Taylor 2001: 28–29). Linguistic evidence also adds credence to the view that slavery predated writing (Donald 1997: 205–9). (If related languages have the same word for slave then slavery is likely at least as old as when the languages split.) Oral origin legends often included references to slaves, suggesting that myth creators did not know of a period before which slavery existed and that they did not consider the causes of slavery an important question (Donald 1997: 45).

Moreover, slave trading possesses unusual economic characteristics that suggest it should have been relatively commonplace. Unlike most other goods, slaves can move themselves as well as other articles of commerce. Unlike pack animals, slaves invariably become more valuable as they travel away from their homes because they became easier to control. It would be astonishing, therefore, if slave trading was not among the earliest forms of long-distance trade (Lovejoy 2012: 102).

Regardless of the precise outlines, slavery was certainly a well ensconced social institution in many parts of the world when writing finally appeared (Finley 1980: 9). The Greeks and the Romans both accepted the notion that in some distant past, perhaps just prior to the movement of the first tribes into Greece and Italy, men had lived free, without slavery (Vogt 1975:

27–28). But those days were long gone as slavery was well entrenched in Greek society by the time the first written evidence became available (Rihll 2008: 90).

Even those somewhat skeptical of the importance of slavery in human history concede that it was ubiquitous across human societies by the time writing was invented (Starr 1958). In fact, the Ur Nammu tables, created circa 2300 BCE in Mesopotamia, are the first known legal documents referring to the sale of slaves (Campbell 2004: x). Apparently, anyone in ancient Mesopotamia could become a slave by war or debt. Some sold themselves into slavery in order to finance their emigration while others sold unwanted children (Roberts 2011: 16–17). In ancient Babylon, marriages between male slaves and free women were common and the children of such "mixed" marriages may have been considered free (Davis 1966: 47). So slaves in the ancient Middle East may have been slightly freer than the canonical slaves of the Old South, but not by much.

More disturbing to abolitionists was the slavery of ancient Greece and Rome. As Cochin wrote during the US Civil War, "we must have the pain of repeating once more, to the shame of the human family, that, if all the greatest minds agree to-day in condemning slavery, all the greatest minds formerly agreed in justifying and practicing it" (1863: 285). Slavery in Homeric Greece, circa 700 BCE, was apparently small scale and relatively unstructured. By about 500 BCE, however, Greece had developed into a slave society (Rihll 2008: 89–90). Around the time of the Peloponnesian War (so about 450 BCE), Athens was home to about 172,000 citizens, 28,000 Metics (resident aliens), and 115,000 slaves, or about a third of the population (Vogt 1975: 4). Surplus land may have induced elites to try to control laborers rather than real estate (Klein 1993: 4; Reid 1993: 65).

While scholars' view of Greek and Roman slavery is much clearer than their view of more ancient slaveries, many details remain shrouded due to a dearth of good primary sources (Rihll 2008). Apparently, the institution was characterized by much variability not only over time and place but also at any given moment in any given city state or region of the Empire. Instead of a sharp dichotomy, a continuum between slave and free appears to have existed (Pelteret 1995: 2). "There were men in many inferior positions which look almost like slavery," Buckland asserted, but they were not considered a *res*, a thing (non-human), or a *res mancipi*, a thing that could be sold (1908: 10–11). In addition to the helots (slavish and serfish but ultimately without modern equivalent [Hodkinson 2008]) were other types of ancient bondsmen with a variety of limited freedoms (Vogt 1975: 3).

But chattel slaves were certainly part of the ancient spectrum of unfree labor types and the ancients even had their own proslavery ideology (Buckland 1908: 3). Most importantly, Aristotle argued that some men were slaves by nature, an argument that impressed many observers up to French philosopher Auguste Comte (1798–1857) and beyond (Davis 1966: 20–21, 70). Few ancient thinkers opposed slavery on any grounds (Taylor 1983: 40; McKeown 2007: 43; Quirk 2011: 18; Davis 1966: 62). An exception were Sophists, like Hippias of Elis (late fifth century BCE), who saw slavery as an infringement of natural law, a concept he helped to develop. But antislavery thinkers were few and their ideas remained marginal though some philosophers were themselves slaves (Buckland 1908: 7). Slavery was so ingrained that even utopian plays did not dispense with slaves except to mock radical utopias run by communistic women (Vogt 1975: 29–32, 40).

In the ancient world, people became enslaved when they were captured in war; born to a slave mother; or convicted of a capital crime, of failing to pay taxes or civil debts, or of evading military duty. Only newborns could be sold by fathers but older children could fall into bondage as well if their parents "exposed" them to confiscation. The ancients did not question the righteousness of enslaving conquered peoples but the Athenians, alone of the Greek city states, for a time outlawed bondage for civil debt. The Athenians also allowed slaves to sue their masters for barbarous treatment (Buckland 1908: 397–98, 401–7, 420–21; Vogt 1975: 3; Millar 1771/2006: 255).

Most of those enslaved by the Romans were owned by individuals but some were owned by Imperial or local governments. Individual Roman masters had broad powers over their chattel slaves but their control was not absolute. For example, without approval from a magistrate they could not punish a slave by making him fight with beasts. If a slave grew ill but received no aid from his or her master, s/he was freed by the government upon his/her recovery. It was illegal to castrate slaves but it was done anyway because it increased their market price. The Roman slave trade was conducted on a large scale by unscrupulous men. Roman slaves could also be mortgaged and they were without families under the law. How frequently slave families were broken up will never be known with any degree of certainty but it was certainly within the master's power to do so

(Buckland 1908: 36–39, 281–86; Vogt 1975: 94; McKeown 2007: 25; Finley 1980: 76; Roberts 2011: 210).

Those enslaved by the Romans could own property (*peculium*) but only with the consent of their masters. *Peculium* could range from small sums of money, trinkets, and so forth, but it could be valuable and take any form, including other slaves. The master, however, retained legal title to the property. Rape was common as, apparently, was corporal punishment. Many agricultural slaves suffered from malnutrition and exposure because it was typically cheaper to buy new slaves than to adequately feed and clothe them (Buckland 1908: 187–206; McKeown 2007: 34, 37; Finley 1980: 93; Roberts 2011: 209). For centuries, Rome's successful expansion provided a large supply of new slaves and hence relatively low slave prices (Phillips 1996: 74).

Many Roman slaves were mistreated severely enough to induce them to run away, despite the fact that they were usually branded (Vogt 1975: 44). Despairing successful escape, some even took their own lives (Buckland 1908: 267–68). Others resisted with physical violence directed at private property or even the master, while others, fearful of the brutal punishments the Romans doled out at the first sign of insubordination or insurrection, engaged instead in malicious gossip or forgery and fraud (Roberts 2011: 209; McKeown 2007: 46–47, 57, 69, 78–79). Conditions for slaves working in the *latifundias* (plantations) or mines improved when market prices rose (Phillips 1996: 73–77). Slaves engaged as domestics, as agents in mercantile networks, or who possessed valuable manual or administrative skills, also typically fared better (Vogt 1975: 46, 104–21). Roman masters tried to cajole work and obedience out of slaves by promising them manumission or employing the tools of paternalism (McKeown 2007: 35, 38, 115). Slaves made a clear distinction between a loving *pater* (father) and a *dominus* (master) who ruled by force. Domestic slaves were more likely to encounter the former than were slaves who worked in agriculture or mining or who were used by the government to power galleys (Saller 1996: 112, 128–29).

For complex reasons not yet fully understood, slavery slowly died in Western Europe following the demise of the Roman Empire as agricultural slaves transformed, over generations and unevenly over space, into serfs, or workers bound to particular pieces of real estate called manors rather than to individuals. The shift may have begun as trade contracted when the Empire was on its last legs (Phillips 1996: 77; Pelteret 1995: 3). That may have induced the owners of agricultural slaves to give up the high costs of monitoring slaves' daily activities in exchange for a share of the crop (Blackburn 1996: 171, 177; Davies 1996: 225).

Due to incursions from Viking and Muslim slave raiders and a thriving trade in Celtic peoples, in the millennium following the fall of Rome chattel slavery continued in Western Europe but after about 1000 A.D. it was not nearly as potent a force as serfdom (Phillips 1996: 78–79; Davies 1996: 226, 233, 239–41; Pelteret 1995: 15). Slavery and serfdom coexisted and overlapped to such an extent that medieval jurists often confused the two conditions. So the classical word for slave, *servus*, formed the root for serf, while Slav formed the root for slave. While it is commonly assumed that serfs were not as bad off as slaves, in the early Middle Ages matters were too dynamic to make such judgments with confidence (Davis 1966: 33, 52).

The Germanic tribes that laid Rome low held slaves, as almost all warrior cultures did. Their slaves were articles of property without personal rights or any place in society, aside from their respective connections to a master, who had complete authority over them. For centuries, Germanic peoples continued to hold such chattel slaves, even as serfdom evolved (Wergeland 1916: xi–xii, 26). Some scholars believe that slaves in Europe had a relatively easy time of it due to the influence of the Christian church, which made it illegal or sinful to sell family members, to enslave Christians, and so forth, but that might be wishful thinking (Cochin 1863: 336–45). After all, slaves could not vote, hold offices, serve on juries, and so forth, rendering them legally powerless to combat domineering masters regardless of prevailing religious mores (Bloch 1961: 443).

After the fall of Rome, slavery continued in the British Isles as well, including England proper, and the institution was somewhat invigorated through contact with Scandinavians and the Danelaw. Those enslaved by the British were under the complete control of their masters, except they could not be lawfully sold out of the country to pagans or be forced to work on Sundays and certain religious holidays (Pelteret 1995: 1, 41, 181, 242–45). The enslaved also had the right to marry, even free people, but it remains unclear whether the status of any offspring followed that of the mother or the father, although some enslavers spoke of owning other people along "with their offspring" (Pelteret 1995: 181). When founding Thorney Abbey in 972, Bishop Aethelwold treated the slaves in his accounts no differently from the rest of his "stock," including herring and bean seed (Pelteret 1995: 12, 71, 76, 180). There is evidence of an extensive slave trade within the British Isles and from the British Isles to Rome and other parts of Italy, as well as to Scandinavia and possibly Spain (Bromberg 1942).

(Slavery was so endemic in Italy that *ciao*, currently an informal greeting/ parting term, is thought to derive from *schiavo*, literally "I am your slave" [Frankopan 2016: 119]). In Bristol in the 1080s, observers witnessed young people of both sexes bound together for sale abroad as prostitutes or laborers. The supply of slaves came from the traditional sources: abandonment of children by parents or death of parents, birth, conviction of a crime, debt, raids against allegedly inferior indigenous peoples such as the Irish, Welsh, or Scots, and wars, like those between the Mercians and Northumbrians (Pelteret 1995: 12, 32–34, 42, 44, 71, 77, 111; Bloch 1961: 270).

As late as the compilation of the Domesday (1086 A.D.), such chattel slaves accounted for between 10 and 25 percent of England's population (Davis 1966: 38). Although they provided needed domestic and agricultural labor, and even some skilled labor such as goldsmithing, they disappeared less than a century thereafter. Some undoubtedly died and were not replaced while others were reclassified as serfs at the same time that many propertyless but technically free men also became tied to the manors. The slave trade, however, remained legal in England until the 1102 Council of Westminster (Pelteret 1995: 4, 7–8, 78, 124, 183–240).

Even as it transmogrified into serfdom in the northwest, slavery remained strong in Eastern Europe, where Slav literally became synonymous with slave. Christians (like Jews and Muslims) were not supposed to enslave fellow believers, but Orthodox Slavs and Bogomil heretics were not considered such, so they were eagerly sought by enslavers with access to Eastern European markets (Blackburn 2011: 15, 32; Taylor 2001: 35; Pelteret 1995: 43; Resendez 2016: 26).

Feudal relationships were both variable and dynamic, rendering any generalizations precarious (Bloch 1961: 255). At its heart, however, feudalism was akin to a protection racket: feudal lords promised to protect peasants (if only from themselves) in exchange for their labor and loyalty and over time came to have almost complete control over the serfs tied to the manors they owned (Conning and Kevane 2007: 114). "The feudal system," historian Marc Bloch wrote, "meant the rigorous economic subjection of a host of humble folk to a few powerful men" (1961: 443). He may have been right when he concluded that slavery ended when the supply of slaves dried up as demand grew or remained steady. Unwilling to enslave fellow Christians or to engage in expense wars against distant heathens, and increasingly secure in their land ownership, Western European elites found a convenient loophole and exploited it as hard as they could, tying workers to the land instead of to themselves. The same loophole, the ability to tie workers to the land, could also be conveniently used to ensnare free men (Pelteret 1995: 252; Bloch 1961: 260; Cook 2007: 181; Bush 1996b: 200). As shown in Chap. 4, this would not be the last time that erstwhile enslavers created new forms of bondage to avoid sanctions against outright slavery.

Serfs in Western Europe enjoyed some customary protections typically not afforded to slaves. They could marry, but only a person from their manor. Unlike slaves, serfs were not easily transferred to other manors so their family structures were relatively secure and serfs could own personal and real property in some places (Bloch 1961: 256–60, 271; Dyer 1996: 284; Bush 1996b: 211). Typically, lords did not micromanage serfs' activities on their own plots, but they did hire bailiffs to supervise the services serfs supplied on the lords' lands and they retained the right to intrude upon serfs' personal activities if they saw fit (Fogel 1989: 25). As one master said of his serf, "he is mine from the soles of his feet to the crown of his head" (Bloch 1961: 265). Physical punishment, akin to that doled out to slaves, was thought necessary to earn decent profits (Bush 1996a: 13). It is therefore not surprising to learn that serfs, like slaves, never received their full marginal product (Cook 2007: 188). Clearly, then, the freedom scale would place serfs close to chattel slaves, though the latter were clearly less free because they generally enjoyed no identity under the law as a person (Bush 1996a: 2). So a serf circa 1300 AD enjoyed more rights, in general, than a slave had two centuries prior (Pelteret 1995: 240).

Serfdom did not take as firm a hold in Iberia, where thanks to the *Reconquista* there were plenty of Moors to enslave. Until the nineteenth century, slaves were imported into Iberia to work in mines and so forth. In Central and Eastern Europe, access to Slavs also kept slavery viable longer than elsewhere in Europe. There, a class of compulsory day laborers called *Tageschalken* lived in a condition of subjection that was servile to the last degree (Bloch 1961: 266–68; Davis 1966: 41, 45).

Although economic and religious pressures tended to favor abolition, countervailing forces, like the social destabilization caused by Viking raids, worked in the opposite direction. Slowly, however, slavery began to wane as slaves won rights, like property ownership, incompatible with slavery and urban and commercial elites carved out "free air" zones that not only banned slavery but protected runaways. In the Germanic areas, the notion developed that *Stadtluft macht frei*, or city air makes you free. Later, free air became a common law precept in Britain. The great jurist William Murray,

First Earl of Mansfield, held that slaveholders' power was so odious that it could only be supposed to exist where it was explicitly sanctioned by law, which it was not in England. In France, all men were free, in the sense of not being slaves anyway, by 1608 (Pelteret 1995: 85, 119, 139, 242–43, 251; Davis 1966: 46, 106; Bales 2012: 107; Wright 2006: 35–36; Blackburn 2011: 134).

Unfortunately for millions of Amerindians and Africans, the spread of the free air doctrine was simply an ideological manifestation of economic trends and a misleading version of Christianity, and not due to modern antislavery sentiment. Western Europe was shorn of its de jure slaves but the enslavement of non-Christians remained perfectly acceptable in European colonies (Pelteret 1995: 14, 234; Blackburn 2011: 89–91).

Serfdom also eventually petered out in Western Europe as serfs evolved into free peasants, first de facto and then de jure. At the same time, however, serfdom strengthened in Eastern Europe, enforced by the iron fist of autocratic government. Serfs could not leave the manor without their lord's permission. They had little legal recourse against their lords and were forbidden to enter into holy orders or otherwise improve their situation. Like the earlier, Western European serfdom, serfdom in the East was highly variable. In some places, like seventeenth-century Bohemia, serfs were harshly oppressed, but in other places, like on manors where they worked their own land and just paid dues and rent instead of providing labor on the lord's land, serfs could accumulate resources that helped them to improve their lot (Bush 1996a: 13; Bush 1996b: 211–14).

In Russia, outright slavery prevailed, especially in Muscovy, from about 1450 until 1725. Most were household rather than agricultural slaves and they represented about 10–15 percent of the population in Moscow in the seventeenth century. At the institution's height, slaves constituted the second most important labor group in Russia after peasants (Hellie 1982: 679–720). As slavery waned, however, serfdom waxed. It became increasingly difficult over successive generations for peasants to move to new land. Once enserfed, the peasants were subjected to the extraction of monopsony (buy side monopoly) rents (excess profits) by landlords, so they earned far less than their marginal product, that is, what they would have been paid in a competitive market (Conning and Kevane 2007: 122). But even in Eastern Europe, economic and social change rendered serfdom increasingly anachronistic. By 1870, an Enlightened Europe, awash in cheap labor, freed itself of serfdom for the first time in over a millennium (Bush 1996a: 14). The task was accomplished in Russia by forcing the serfs to buy their own freedom and overcharging them some 37 percent for the privilege as economist historian Alexander Gershchenkron estimated in 1965 (Cook 2007: 194).

Given the widespread presence of slavery in the ancient Mesopotamian and Mediterranean worlds, it is not surprising to find its widespread acceptance in the Old Testament. Most infamously, Noah cursed Ham and his descendants to lives of slavery, an act that made slavery seem like a just punishment for sin or a defective soul. Jews were later enslaved to the Egyptian state but that experience did not turn them into abolitionists (Cochin 1863: 290–303; Davis 1966: 64, 90). If a Jewish master took a slave's eye or tooth, the slave was automatically manumitted. The master was not punished, however, for accidentally killing his slave "for he [the slave] is his [the master's] money [property]" (Millar 1771/2006: 255). Jews were later scapegoated as the most important players in the transatlantic slave trade, but such claims do not bear empirical scrutiny (Hall et al. 2014: 57; Faber 1998).

Although slavery ran counter to the overall message of Jesus, the early Christian church also accepted slavery and even tried to ensure the security and control of masters (Davis 1966: 89). If slavery was unacceptable, early Christian apologists wondered, "then why had God authorized it in Scripture and permitted it to exist in nearly every nation" (Davis 1966: 92)? Martin Luther was repelled by the notion that Christ opposed slavery and John Calvin saw little wrong with the institution (Davis 1966: 106; Blackburn 2011: 88).

The world's third major monotheistic religion, Islam, also offered little reprieve for the enslaved. According to William Clarence-Smith, "a libertarian whiff accompanied the birth of the new faith in early-seventh-century Arabia, but the legitimacy of slavery was only ever contested by scattered sects" (2006: 6). Islam was not proslavery, but like Judaism and Christianity, it was not antislavery either and the explicit restriction on enslaving fellow Muslims seemed to justify the enslavement of infidels (Klein 1992: 35). Manumission, especially of those slaves who converted to Islam, was considered a pious act and Islamic law tried to ensure the humane treatment of those who remained enslaved (Clarence-Smith 2006: 22). Slaves were chattels, but where the law was strictly followed, slaves were well treated and self-purchase was allowed. Freed slaves, however, were still tied to their masters' families in perpetuity as so-called clients (Miers 2004: 4).

Enslavement was ultimately seen by ulama as divine punishment for non-belief, so it is not surprising to learn that Muslims carried on slavery on a large scale for over a millennia (Clarence-Smith 2006: 1–2, 28). Indeed, the Sokoto Caliphate (Northern Nigeria, 1809–1903) was likely the second largest slave society in recent history (Hogendorn and Lovejoy 1992: 49). The Ottoman Empire, which at its height claimed the Balkans as well as Asia Minor and large parts of the Middle East, was another large Islamic slave society. Military slavery had played a major role in the Abbasid Caliphate in the ninth century and the Ottomans built upon that precedent with its *kul* system of military-administrative servitude, which coexisted with other types of slavery, including harem, domestic, and agricultural slavery, none of which were particularly alluring (Toledano 1993: 39; Quirk 2011: 26–27).

By contrast, slaves of the *Kapi Kullari*, or slave institution, filled every civil post from cook to prime minister (Grand Vizier). Composed of Christian children raised to fulfill official functions, these slaves of the sultan were forced to convert to Islam and forbidden to have families or own property. Free of distractions, the unsullied youths could devote themselves to the state and its leader, on whom they were entirely dependent for money and other necessities (Tuchman 1984: 384). The sultan could raise them to high posts without creating envy and could have them killed without danger because they had no families. While many probably found working as a valued administrator better than slaving away in some field, they were slaves nonetheless because they were dishonored people who could have their lives taken or their possessions seized at any time (Patterson 1982: 8; Toledano 1993: 39–42).

During the Tanzimat period (reform era from the 1830s to the 1880s), Ottomans continued to import slaves, around 12,000 per year, across the desert from Chad, down the Nile, and from Persian Gulf ports and the Caucasus. Abolitionist sentiments from the West, along with indigenous stimuli, brought change, especially in the *kul* system. First, the Ottomans outlawed slave trading by degrees in different areas and the elite began to switch to hired servants, thereby voluntarily decreasing their slaveholdings. Reforms, though, were slowed by the belief that Ottoman slavery was almost benign and certainly humane. Slavery, though, was clearly on the decline in much of the Empire when the new Turkish republic finally abolished it completely (Toledano 1993: 38–44, 50–52).

Islamic slavery was extremely heterogeneous. Some rulers relied so heavily on slaves in administrative and military roles that they were able to seize power. A small percentage of slaves in Muslim societies were given power over free people and could even become richer than their own masters and possess slaves of their own. But the vast majority suffered as manual drudges, cannon fodder, or eunuchs, branded or scarred to mark their slave status (Clarence-Smith 2006: 2–4, Miers 2004: 5).

By the nineteenth century, Muslim-owned slaves produced a wide range of agricultural commodities, including cloves, coconuts, coffee, cotton, dates, millet, sesame, and sugar, as well as copper, gold, pearls, salt, and tin. Slaves also served as porters, sailors, servants, and weavers. Many were owned by small and middling proprietors. The number of people enslaved by Muslims ran into the tens of millions. Millions were dragged from Asia Minor and Central Asia. Muslims also obtained slaves from India, Iran, and Southeast Asia, and untold millions hailed from Eastern Europe and the Caucasus (Clarence-Smith 2006: 10, 14–16). Vikings happily sold them Irish lads and lasses as well as Franks, Slavs, and whoever else they could lay their hands upon. The young were needed for Muslim harems, the females as concubines and the castrated men as eunuch guards or mercantile helpers. Slavs, in particular, were thought to become more intelligent and skillful if their reproductive organs were removed. Others in thrall to the Vikings were bound to labor in Scandinavia (Frankopan 2016: 114–18; Pelteret 1995: 71).

About one million slaves under the control of Muslim masters hailed from Western Europe. In the seventeenth century alone, tens of thousands toiled in Algiers while over 100,000 were held throughout North Africa. At one point, slaves in Algiers were so numerous that it was said that one could trade a Christian for an onion. Into the nineteenth century, North Africans continued to enslave Western Europeans whenever they could. Corsairs seized many western Europeans at sea, a fact borne out by insurance premium and claim records. More boldly, Muslims also raided coastal villages as far north as Iceland. Some raids were major affairs but others entailed picking off a fishing family here or a granary there. At times in the early 1600s, Muslim raiders sailed up the Thames to raid English fishing villages but most raiders concentrated on the easier pickings to be found along the Italian, French, and Spanish coasts. According to one scholar, western Europeans living along the Mediterranean coast were enslaved in the sixteenth century at a rate comparable to the African Diaspora at the same time (Davis 2003: xviii–xix, 3–7, 10, 23, 133; Clarence-Smith 2006: 11–13).

Many Christian slaves did light duty while awaiting ransom payments but others were forced into construction, farming, logging, quarrying, prostitution, or, worst of all, galley rowing. Galley slaves slept little, were shackled to the oar, dehydrated and underfed, and often expired at the oar during days of uninterrupted rowing. Those who lived but proved unable to row any longer were thrown overboard. Muslim slaveholders threatened to sell recalcitrant slaves to a corsair captain in much the same way that antebellum US slaveholders threatened to sell their uppity chattels down the river. To avoid galley service, some slaves with means were forced to pay 20 Spanish dollars per voyage (Davis 2003: 25, 69–78, 88).

Profit, whether derived from ransom payments or hard labor, was paramount, but the raids also took on almost a jihad-like character and were considered payback for the reconquest of the Iberian peninsula. Enslavement of Western Europeans helped spur antislavery sentiments there (though not as much as one might presume) by helping some Europeans to see slavery's horrors and even to empathize with sub-Saharan Africans, who bore the brunt of the Islamic slave trade. In his last public act, for example, Benjamin Franklin parodied the rationale used by Barbary pirates to justify the enslavement of Christians (uncivilized, better off as slaves, opportunity to learn the one true religion) in order to shame American slavery apologists (Davis 2003: xxiv–xxv; Blackburn 2011: 153; Quirk 2011: 25; Houston 2008: 202, 216).

Muslims also obtained millions of slaves from sub-Saharan Africa. The trade of slaves across the Sahara and along the east coast of Africa was larger and older than the Atlantic slave trade. It originated in the early medieval period at the rate of about 5000 to 10,000 slaves per year and lasted even after suppression efforts by Britain after explorer David Livingstone described its extent and its horrors. Muslims did not part with slavery easily even though the West and the Druze sect pushed for abolition. Not until the 1980s was slavery legally abolished in all Muslim countries, and even today it continues clandestinely (Lovejoy 2012: 25, 27, 61; Fogel 1989, 236; Clarence-Smith 2006: 11, 16–21).

The great Asian civilizations have also countenanced slavery for millennia and up to the present. Slavery in China rapidly expanded during the Former Han Dynasty (206 B.C. to 25 A.D.). Its class structure held officials at the top, followed by the nobility, then commoners, then convicts, and finally slaves. The legal code was very detailed, apparently to increase the size of the convict class, who were essentially enslaved during their period of punishment to the government, which also owned some lifelong or hereditary slaves. Privately owned slaves arose from economic distress (self-sale or sale of children), foreign conquest, or birth and could be sold or otherwise transferred to new owners. The market for slaves was often active enough to support brokers, dealers, and slave traders (Wilbur 1967: 11, 33, 41, 64–66, 72, 121–26, 177).

Together with convicts, Chinese slaves numbered in the hundreds of thousands and perhaps even one million, and their numbers swelled during famines, droughts, floods, frosts, and wars. As late as the 1920s, destitute Chinese families sold their children to avoid starvation. Chinese law long forbade forcible kidnapping and enslavement by guile but kidnapping was common during civil wars and other periods of instability (Wilbur 1967: 85–86, 89–92).

The Chinese government sometimes exchanged slaves with private individuals and sometimes obtained slaves through confiscation or taxation. When the domestic supply proved insufficient, Chinese enslavers imported foreigners, including Korean girls for sex and Turkic, Tibetan, and Uighur slaves captured in raids or sent as tribute by frontier governments, including the tribal areas of what is now southern China. Arab traders also exchanged Iranian dancing girls and even Africans for Chinese wares (Wilbur 1967: 92–96, 118; Davis 1966: 51).

Slaves owned by individual masters did domestic chores and agricultural work while the government's slaves toiled on public works, including dams, dikes, canals, and, of course, the Great Wall. Chinese masters could apparently kill their slaves but only after obtaining permission from the proper government official first. Slaves could not bear witness against their masters except for rebellion or other forms of high treason. Intermarriage between slaves and free people was eventually restricted and the children of slave women were usually enslaved. Sons sired by masters, however, could attain free status (Wilbur 1967: 152, 156–60, 164, 178–203, 222–26).

Some scholars assert that slavery was not important in China but its population was always so large relative to that of the world's population that even if only a small percentage of the total population was enslaved it still constituted a major slave country (Schottenhammer 2004). And for several centuries late in the first millennium AD its western territories were part of a massive "slave road" system that traversed the spine of Asia, the center of the world, along with the better known "silk road." Societies that commanded gold and silver coin traded it away for the excess populations of societies that could not otherwise obtain the precious stuff. Slavers in the latter then sent some of the coins back in exchange for luxurious textiles and spices produced by their own former countrymen (Frankopan 2016: 114–31)!

Some parts of that extensive slave road system lay in what is today India and Pakistan. Other slaves entered or exited greater India, where slavery is at least as old as the Harappa period (2600–1900 BCE) at Mohenjo-Daro (now Pakistan), via Indian Ocean trade routes. Many other slaves, though, were both sourced and worked wholly within the subcontinent and each of its great cultural, political, and geographical divisions. Caste, gender, tribe, and economic fortune interacted in complex ways to create a continuum ranging from slaves for life to coerced laborers who enjoyed some freedoms. In ancient India a *dasa* was someone who was not the master of himself, so he or she depended on another and did not enjoy freedom of movement. A master could beat and even kill a *dasa* with impunity. On the other extreme, a *bhujissa* or *attano santako* was an independent person without a master who could act as he or she pleased within the law. Slaves were absolute or qualified. Absolute slaves could be sold or killed by their masters and their children were automatically slaves. Qualified slaves could buy their freedom or were promised manumission upon the master's death (Kara 2012: 17, 187–88; Chanana 1964: 64).

Absolute slaves in ancient India had no legal rights or protections, could not own property, and were under the complete control of their masters. "A slave, enjoying himself on a festival-day," explained one ancient text, "leaves everything and goes running where he is told to go (by his master) on hearing that something urgent has got to be done, and that he must go there at once, failing which his hands, feet, ears or nose may be cut" (Chanana 1964: 54, 57).

In the earlier Vedic period, slaves had darker skin than their masters but by the time the sage Gautama Buddha ("The Buddha") arrived in India, circa 500 BCE, slaves could not be physiologically or racially distinguished from free people. Dress, hair, name, and demeanor marked them. Buddha forbade his followers from living on income derived from the slave trade but ultimately he rationalized slavery as a physical necessity and Buddhist monasteries owned large numbers of slaves. Slaves originated from slave raids and wars fought for general purposes of state (Chanana 1964: 53, 74–82, 105; Klein 1993: 14–15; Fogel 1989: 201).

Legal slavery continued in India through the British Raj until 1843 and included child sex slavery. In the 1830s, as many as 16 million Indians remained outright slaves and many millions more toiled as something more akin to serfs and debt peons. Uniformity, in law or practice, was unknown. After formal abolition, millions remained forced laborers, subject to local customs, caste restrictions, and a precarious subsistence. In colonial Kerala, for example, *adima* (male slaves) and *adimai* (female slaves) were bought, sold, mortgaged, confiscated, and even killed by their masters. In other areas of the subcontinent, agrestic laborers, much like medieval European serfs, could not be sold apart from the land they worked (Fogel 1989: 235; Temperley 1996: 150–51; Kumar 1993: 113, 117).

India and China were but the two largest players in the grand slave system of the Indian and Pacific Oceans (IPO). Older, more complex, and just as large as the transatlantic system that brought Africans to the New World, the IPO slave trading system moved slaves from East Africa to Muslims in the Middle East and Indians to the Middle East as well as Indonesia, South Africa, and Mauritius. Eastern Europe and Caucasus slaves ended up in Muslim slave marts, while Indochinese and Korean slaves were sold in China. Eventually, Chinese slaves were sent to western North America. Some of the IPO routes, which were both overland and maritime, lasted 4000 years and captured between 20 and 50 percent of the population of some Asian countries in its insidious web. In parts of Southeast Asia, for example, slaves were so common that wage labor, except for hired out slaves, was virtually unknown (Campbell 2004: ix; Reid 1993: 67; Turton 2004: 72).

Korea, too, had a slave system that thrived between the seventh and nineteenth centuries AD. Called *nobi*, it was not abolished until 1894, although it had eroded into insignificance (just 1.5 percent of population) by the mid-nineteenth century. Earlier, though, *nobi* had been quite significant, ensnaring up to 40 percent of the population in a public, private, feudal-like system of forced labor. Japan also had a feudal system, replete with paternalism, that tied peasants to the land in exchange for protection. In Asia, serfs were considered as free as a chicken rather than as free as a bird because they were tied to the land and essentially domesticated by their lords (Blackburn 1996: 178; Kim 2004; Genovese 1972: 663–64; Miers 2004: 8; Turton 2004: 88).

Throughout the IPO trading system, other types of unfree laborers, like debt peons, worked side by side chattel slaves. Some slaves and other unfree workers toiled in New World-style plantations in European enclaves like Mauritius and in Muslim cash crop plantations in East Africa. Others were pressed into the sex and entertainment trades. Young girls typically sold at premiums over men and older females in the IPO and eunuchs were also highly prized, suggesting that the sex trade dominated demand. Some slaves served mainly for elites anxious to improve their social status. But even those purchased as signs of wealth must have worked because few slaveholders were financially ruined by their slaves. Many were probably part of a letting out system that allowed slaves to work for wages and remit 50–75 percent of their earnings to their owner (Campbell 2004: x–xi, xiii, xix–xx).

At some times and in some places, slaves enjoyed some rights. They could marry in Korea, for example, but that did not prevent them from being involuntarily sold to new masters, who could punish them with violence to keep them in line. As in other slave systems, however, there were practical limits to the master's power given each slave's ability to run away, disable him or herself, or even commit suicide. Chinese indentured laborers were known to throw themselves overboard or simply die of despair (Campbell 2004: xiv; Alpers 2004: 59; Meagher 2008: 165).

IPO slaves were often hereditary, literally outcasts (outside of the caste system), and social pariah. In Southeast Asia, racial differences led to slaves being considered as animals, not as men. The rise of more powerful states in the region ended easy/cheap slave raids, dampening supply and raising prices (Campbell 2004: xvii; Delaye 2004: 132; Reid 1993: 132).

In Indonesia, routes to slavery included inheritance, debt, capture in war, and condemnation in court. Slavery there was often described as "mild." One Portuguese slaveholder who lived in the region even claimed that Indonesians pampered their slaves. Mild treatment may have been a way to keep slaves happy in a society where the government was too weak to protect slaveholders or to return runaway slaves. That a form of serfdom and sharecropping was also found there suggests that Indonesian slaveholders indeed found it difficult to control their chattels. Slavery in Indonesia had become less important by the time it was legally abolished, yet it remained in existence long after being outlawed (Reid 1993: 67–69).

In Thailand, slaves were sometimes hereditary but owner-sired slaves were freed and masters faced restrictions on how they punished their slaves. During wars, government-owned slaves entered the army and during peace they toiled on public works. Slaves also worked in artisanal workshops and royal courts. The need for slaves declined in the nineteenth century as peace became more common than war and an increasingly monetized economy allowed for the development of labor markets and cash tax payments. Diplomatic pressures helped, too (Feeny 1993: 89, 92, 96, 98–99).

At the western end of the IPO lay Africa, which for centuries fed the IPO system, its own domestic demand for slaves, and the Transatlantic slave system. As elsewhere in the world, slavery in Africa stretches at least as far back as the historical record goes and hence existed well before European or Asian slave traders arrived. Some scholars argue that domestic slavery was less cruel than the Asiatic or New World varieties because the Africans had more open societies in which slaves were assimilated and not treated as outsiders. (The same claim is made of indigenous North American slavery as well, as detailed below.) While some African slaves may have found themselves integrated into family, kin, or tribal networks, it is not clear that the median African slave was to be envied, if for no other reason than that he or she could be easily sold into the Transatlantic, IPO, or Muslim trading systems, each of which condemned the slave to arduous travel, harsh working conditions, and the likelihood of early death. Moreover, in certain areas of Africa, slaves were eventually put to hard labor on farms and plantations, some under the control of powerful states like Segou, Futa Jallon, and Sikasso, and others under the control of Muslims looking to earn commercial surpluses. By 1300, Negro slaves grew sugar on Cyprus, which served as a prototype for the colonies of the West Indies (Manning 1990: 19; Meillassoux 1991: 43–49; Klein 1993: 171, 173; Campbell 2004: xviii; Davis 1966: 42).

Even after the great emancipations of the nineteenth century finally killed the Transatlantic and IPO slave trading systems, domestic demand continued and even increased as African economies transitioned toward commercial farming of crops like palm oil, cloves, gum arabic, and kola. Slaves, usually children, traded hands, often under the noses of imperial officials too incompetent or complicit to stop it. In fact, French officials often returned escaped slaves to their masters and even became enslavers themselves through so-called liberty villages, which locals referred to, without exaggeration, as *villages de captifs* or *les villages des captifs du gouvernement* (slave villages or government slave villages)(Lovejoy 2012: 161, 175, 179, 185, 210, 223; Klein 1993: 181; McDougall 2007).

From independent Ethiopia (Abyssinia) came slave raiders, aided with American made weapons and ammunition, who seized slaves from neighboring European colonies with near impunity. Such raids persisted well into the interwar period. By 1975, slavery in Africa was uncommon but it persisted in local pockets for various reasons, many cultural. The pockets were allegedly a residue of traditional slavery and not due to the Transatlantic or IPO slave trading systems but to its victims that mattered but little (Anon. 1922f: 3; Klein 1993: 190–91; Derrick 1975: 10–11).

Slavery also existed in North America before European contact but apparently on a smaller scale than in the Old World. The members of most tribes native to North America were not hunter-gatherers but rather horticulturalists who, to a greater or lesser extent, merely supplemented their diets by hunting and gathering. Not as densely populated or powerfully organized as the empires of Meso or South America (Zapotec, Maya, Azetc), North American tribes enslaved others but in what many believe was a mild, domestic form of bondage. Before contact with Euroamericans, Indian slaving to some extent involved the capture of people who became wives or other relatives or status symbols rather than laborers. Slaves, like a peacock's feathers, presumably showed that the master was wealthy enough to keep them alive. But the fact that Amerindian slaveholders also sometimes killed slaves, ostensibly to prove that they could bear the loss, indicates that slaves were considered assets, not liabilities (Resendez 2016: 3; Davis 1966: 168; Donald 1997: 38–40, 89). So enslaved Amerindians no doubt worked, as almost all members of such societies did, but perhaps, in some instances, mostly for their own subsistence.

Iroquoian speaking tribes in the northeast said that they adopted captives to replace deceased relatives, implying that the captives enjoyed all the claims, obligations, powers, privileges, and status of those who they replaced in kinship networks. Some scholars, however, believe that at least some adoptees were really slaves who were never equal to others in their putative kin group. Talk of kin ties, according to proponents of this view, was essentially a paternalistic attempt to reduce control costs similar to the rhetoric employed by enslavers in other societies. What adoptees/slaves were really replacing was the labor of the person they were seized to replace. There was nothing cute and cuddly about the process, which usually entailed renaming the captive as well as amputating one or more digits as a mark of slavery (Starna and Watkins 1991: 34–57; Donald 1997: 257–68).

In the Southeast, captives could also be adopted, enslaved, or ritually executed. The enslaved were not physically bound but either maimed or taken too far from home to make escape realistically possible. The number of such slaves is unknown and unknowable, but some tribes, like the Calusa in southwest Florida, appear to have been more keen on enslavement, perhaps because their plush environment allowed for the creation of more surplus per worker than elsewhere (Donald 1997: 268–70).

On the Great Plains, at least one Amerindian group massacred another (at Crow Creek, now in South Dakota) circa 1325 AD in an apparent attempt to acquire fertile females, the remains of whom were underrepresented in the mass grave found by archeologists that contained nearly 500 dismembered and scalped corpses. According to some researchers, archeologists have underplayed Amerindian massacre sites and the young women missing from the bone assemblages and presumably seized for reproductive purposes (Pauketat 2005: 191; Willey and Emerson 1993: p. 259; Martin and Frayer 1998: 37, 97, 245, 329; Larsen 1995: 259–60).

Along the Northwest coast, from present-day Oregon to Alaska, ample evidence of pre-contact chattel slavery exists. In that region, Native American salmon farmers (formerly and erroneously thought to be mere foragers), enslaved people to do a variety of menial tasks such as carrying water or collecting firewood (Johnsen 2006). People were enslaved for life, looked down upon socially, and their children became slaves. Moreover, Northwest coast Indian slaves were frequently traded. Masters had complete dominion over their slaves, who they distinguished from non-slaves by giving them special names and slavish haircuts or other external markings, and could beat, rape, and even kill their chattels at will. Deceased slaves were often cast into the forest or water instead of buried, unless they were sacrificed in a public ceremony or after their master died (Donald 1997: 33–34, 38, 72–81, 126–28, 212–13, 318–20). All that prompted the leading scholar on the subject to conclude that by any standard definition "those held in servitude on the Northwest Coast can properly be called slaves. This places Northwest Coast slavery alongside slavery in classical Greece and Rome" and other slave societies (Donald 1997: 7). In the historical period, Northwest Coast Indians even enslaved Europeans who fell into their power. Slavery was so entrenched in their society that it did not end until the 1880s (Donald 1997: 10, 34, 74–75).

Slavery remained extant, but relatively economically unimportant, in most parts of North America until Euroamericans arrived and began exchanging manufactured goods for enslaved Indians, fueling what soon turned into a robust and important trade. By the 1670s, the Westo, possibly an Iroquoian group displaced from the north, were among the most voracious Amerindian enslavers as they cut their way south through Virginia and into the Carolinas. At first, British authorities balked at the notion of enslaving Amerindians, who they considered free peoples and deeply feared as military threats. British colonists on the ground, however, could not long resist exploiting Natives as ruthlessly as they did Africans and began buying enslaved Amerindians as eagerly as they purchased deer hides and beaver pelts. To capture the slaves and provide themselves a thin gauze of legality, the colonists directly fought some tribes while inducing others eager for European trade goods to attack their neighbors. The direct result was dizzying decades of war in the Southeast between the forces of various combinations of English, French, Spanish, Creek, Chickasaw, Choctaw, and other native groups. The number of enslaved Amerindians peaked in South Carolina at 2000 circa 1720. Amerindians also enslaved Europeans when they could, as the Apache did when Spanish authority vanished from Mexico in the 1810s. The Mexican captives they could not use were sold in the United States and were so numerous that the Treaty of Guadalupe Hidalgo banned further American purchases (Gallay 2002: 28–29, 40–42, 47–49, 57–69, 191–92; Kulikoff 2000: 104; Resendez 2016: 7, 9)!

In the West, Amerindian groups also enslaved other aboriginal peoples for their own use but especially for sale to Euroamericans, including the Spanish, French, and Americans. When Mormons appeared in the Great Basin in the 1840s, for example, Apache slavers killed any Paiute slaves that the Mormons refused to buy. Faced with an ethical dilemma of the first order, Brigham Young eventually decided to counsel his people to "buy up the Lamanite [enslaved Indian] children ... and educate them and teach them the gospel" (Roberts 1913: 83–84).

Although slavery had disappeared from much of Western Europe, Europeans did not hesitate to establish it in their New World colonies. After all, how could an institution supported and sanctioned by so many authorities and nations be unjust or opposed to nature? Proslavery thought still dominated discourse, even in Britain's northern colonies, where many believed, well after independence, that slavery was acceptable or even a positive good (Davis 1966: 115; Tise 1987).

Slavery in colonial North America varied over time and place. It was said to be quite "mild" in Massachusetts where slaves were simply servants for life who had most of the rights of free people (Deane 1886: 27–28). For example, in 1704 Madam Knight complained that colonists were "too Indulgent ... to their slaves: suffering [sic] too great familiarity from them, permitting [them] to sit at Table and eat with them ... and into the dish goes the black hoof as freely as the white hand." She claimed that a disgruntled slave was able to induce his master to submit to arbitration that eventually led to a cash payment and apology for the slave (1704/1825: 40)!

The size of the slave labor camp was an important variable. Smaller camps, like family farms focused mostly on subsistence, tended to be less rigorous than large, commercially oriented plantations. Skilled slaves working in urban environments typically enjoyed somewhat more freedom than field hands who lived in remote camps. Those who worked on the task system likewise enjoyed slightly more freedom than those who worked in gangs. What constituted a task was not a legal right, however, so they could be enlarged if the master thought he could do so without engendering too much slave resistance (Fogel 1989: 42, 179–86, 193–94).

Some limits to the power of masters developed over time. A Tennessee slaveholder who castrated an uppity slave in 1850, for example, was actually sent to prison for two years although castration had been a common punishment in the eighteenth century and continued, quietly, to be imposed by masters elsewhere in the antebellum period. Some interesting variations also developed, including slaves who hired their own time by paying their owners so much per year and keeping any surplus. Many set up as independent businessmen, especially in frontier areas (Genovese 1972: 67–68; Kolchin 1993: 58, 121; Walker 1983).

Overall, though, North American masters retained full control over their chattels, regardless of which combination of the whip, the threat of sale, or rape they used. Slaves also could be mortgaged by enslavers, that is, used as collateral to secure loans. Due to their absolute power over their chattels, enslavers could force slaves to perform like machines in gangs of 10 to 20 supervised by a slave driver (a slave himself) who whipped his enslaved fellows lest he fall to the lash of the overseer or master (Hurmence 1984: 37, 41, 55; Goldberg 2007: 135–36; Fogel 1989: 25–26; Anon. 1802–1864). "A plantation," enslaver Bennet H. Barrow confided, "might be considered as a piece of machinery. To operate successfully, all its parts should be uniform and exact, and its impelling force regular and steady" (Fogel 1989: 26).

Enslaved Africans resisted being turned into cogs in great agricultural machines, but as economist historian Robert Fogel pointed out, their resistance alone proved insufficient to topple the institution. Masters granted concessions when they believed that it was in their best interest to do so, but not otherwise. Generally, slaveholders shrewdly provided their slaves with just enough freedom, like the privilege to use small plots where they could grow their own crops, to keep them from openly rebelling but not enough to allow them to purchase their freedom or to gain the economic independence or self-confidence to runaway en masse. Instead of allowing them to sell excess vegetables for cash, for example, many US slaveholders bought the produce themselves, paying slaves in credit or scrip good only on their plantations (Fogel 1989: 187–92, 197).

The Iberians (Spaniards and Portuguese) who came to control Meso and South America, present-day Latin America, were well accustomed to slavery, which never really ended in Iberia after the fall of Rome due to the long struggle against the forces of Islam that wracked the peninsula for centuries. Desperate for workers, they thought nothing of enslaving the natives, who they found practiced both slavery and a form of serfdom before European contact. Moreover, Columbus himself had strong incentives (up to a quarter of all profits) to enlarge trade with the New World as quickly as possible. Almost completely devoid of the exotic spices he initially sought, the Caribbean yielded to Columbus and his followers its most plentiful resource, human beings, to work in gold mines, pearl beds, and cane fields (Pelteret 1995: 257; Resendez 2016: 17–26, 30–36).

Amerindians, however, proved poor slaves because they were rapidly declining in population due to the introduction of Old World diseases to which they had no natural immunity. Moreover, they could easily run away, were not easily taught agriculture, and were the object of missionary efforts and monarchical largesse, which by 1499 had prohibited their sale in Iberia (which led to some very modern-looking workaround practices). In 1542, Spanish officials decided that Amerindians were racially and culturally superior to Africans and, hence, outlawed the outright enslavement of the natives even in the New World (Klein 1986: 21–43; Resendez 2016: 46–61).

Iberian elites, however, continued to keep Amerindians in various states of unfreedom. Indians were free de jure, explained historian Andres Resendez, but they remained enslaved through loopholes, reinterpretations, and name changes that circumvented the New Laws of 1542. Simply put, gold and silver trumped God and Scripture (Resendez 2016: 4, 7, 68, 71). Indians subjected to the *encomienda* or *repartimiento* system, which was a quasi-feudal institution transplanted from Castile, scored very low on the freedom scale developed in Chap. 2, especially after separating the reality on the ground from the mandates of the law (Resendez 2016: 35–39; Quirk 2011: 195). At first, the encomienda was a sort of private corvee allotted by the government to individuals, but later it came with land rights as well. The *encomendero* did not have absolute power over his native charges but over multiple generations he did come to control them as stipulated wages, which would have given the natives some chance of escape, were seldom paid. Local officials were easily bribed to look away whenever anyone crossed a legal line (Resendez 2016: 76; Kloosterboer 1960: 80–81).

The *encomienda* system slowly gave way, however, to a corvee system where the government called all the shots. "The *corregidores*, under whose rule the Indians came when an *encomienda* expired," Dutch historian

Wilhemina Kloosterboer noted, “were notorious for their scandalous treatment of the Indians” (1960: 89–95). And the inspectors who were supposed to help the natives often did not. Incorruptible inspectors were rewarded with nothing but death threats. Natives who managed to avoid the government system typically fell into debt bondage. In California, Utah, and New Mexico, Indian slavery took the form of indentured servitude and debt peonage. Resendez recently estimated that between 2.5 and 5 million Indians were enslaved, in one form or another, in the New World in the four centuries following the arrival of Columbus (Kloosterboer 1960: 95–99; Resendez 2016: 5, 9–10, 324).

The Spanish believed that African slaves were too likely to run away or foment rebellion among the natives, so they sent white slaves from Spain or North Africa to Hispaniola in the early sixteenth century. They also sent white, even Christian, women to stock Caribbean brothels as late as 1692. They also imported small numbers of Asians. But the quantity of slaves demanded outstripped the limited supply of white and Asian slaves, forcing the Spanish to import enslaved Africans (Davidson 1961: 45–46; Resendez 2016: 111).

Thanks in part to the efforts of the Catholic Church and their own militant resistance, African slaves in Latin America enjoyed freedoms rarely granted slaves elsewhere. Masters could not lawfully murder them, their marriages were legitimated in some places, and they enjoyed some religious freedom. If they became Christian, they were guaranteed leisure on Sundays and certain religious holidays. Africans enslaved in Latin America also had some limited property rights and the right of self-purchase. In some jurisdictions, they could even pay for themselves in installments and a down payment on their freedom meant they could not be sold to another master (Davis 1966: 241; Fogel 1989: 38; Klein 1986: 190–95).

Except in Brazil and the West Indies, African slavery never really took hold in Latin America. The institution gradually disintegrated in Mexico over the seventeenth and eighteenth centuries thanks in large part to voluntarily manumissions. As early as 1592, one in four blacks in Mexico was already free. Unsurprisingly, most Spanish American republics freed their slaves soon after gaining independence. Some did so by passing laws that liberated the children of slaves while two, Chile and Mexico, opted to immediately emancipate the 4000 and 3000 persons of African descent still enslaved within their respective borders. In Central America, slaves, who were few, were emancipated with compensation to slaveholders in 1824 (Fogel 1989: 34–35, 39; Klein 1986: 250–52).

Formal abolition, however, did not prevent the rise of debt peonage. In 1900 in Mexico, a third of the population, and four out of every five agricultural workers, were termed debt slaves. The Latin republics also developed criminal justice systems designed to ensnare poor people for petty offenses so they could be sold to tobacco growers. There was even some outright kidnapping, which government officials allowed for a cut of the proceeds of the sale. Indian land, like that of the Yaquis, was also stolen and the Indians made to labor as debt peons to repay the debts incurred resisting the expropriation of their own land (Kloosterboer 1960: 99–102).

In the sugar colonies and mining areas, by contrast, slavery developed along lines similar to those in North America. The Portuguese pioneered the use of Africans in sugar production, first using them in the Canaries, Madeira, Sao Tome, and the Cape Verde archipelago before working them on New World plantations (Fogel 1989: 20). Some masters were kind but many were cruel. Practices and even laws similar to those in North America kept slaves in place. Although local laws forbid Sunday work they were no more enforced than similar laws in colonial Georgia and South Carolina were (Davis 1966: 229–43, 252). Emancipation brought not so much freedom as new forms of oppression, including forms of forced labor and debt peonage almost as bad as chattel slavery. In some places, 90 percent of the Indians, including women and children, bore the marks of vicious beatings doled out if they did not meet their near impossible quotas (Kloosterboer 1960: 79–106; Murphy 2014: 173). Much the same thing happened in the United States and other post-emancipation societies, the topic of Chap. 4.

Bibliography

Alexander, J. (2001). Islam, archaeology and slavery in Africa. *World Archaeology, 33*, 44–60.

Alpers, E. A. (2004). Flight to freedom: Escape from slavery among bonded Africans in the Indian Ocean world, c. 1750–1962. In G. Campbell (Ed.), *The structure of slavery in Indian Ocean Africa and Asia* (pp. 51–68). London: Frank Cass.

Ames, K. M. (2001). Slaves, chiefs and labour on the northern northwest coast. *World Archaeology, 33*, 1–17.

Anon. (1802–1864). Negroes miscellany. Society Miscell. Collection, Box 11A. Historical Society of Pennsylvania, Philadelphia, PA.

Anon. (1846, October). Slaves and slavery. *United States Magazine and Democratic Review*.

Anon. (1922f, April 14). Only slave country. *Bellingham Herald*.

Bales, K. (2007). *Ending slavery: How we free today's slaves.* Berkeley: University of California Press.

Bales, Kevin. 2012. *Disposable people: New slavery in the global economy*, Rev. ed. Berkeley: University of California Press.

Blackburn, R. (1996). Slave exploitation and the elementary structures of enslavement. In M. L. Bush (Ed.), *Serfdom and slavery: Studies in legal bondage* (pp. 158–180). New York: Addison Wesley Longman.

Blackburn, R. (2011). *The American crucible: Slavery, emancipation and human rights.* New York: Verso.

Bloch, M. (1961). *Feudal society.* Chicago: University of Chicago Press.

Boas, F. (2014). *Neanderthals.* Quite Interesting. Retrieved October 9, 2014, from http://qi.com/infocloud/Neanderthals

Bodin, J. (1606). *The six bookes of a commonweale* (R. Knolles, Trans.). London: Impensis G. Bishop.

Bromberg, E. (1942). Wales and the mediaeval slave trade. *Speculum, 17*, 263–269.

Brougham, H. (1807). *A concise statement of the question regarding the abolition of the slave trade* (4th ed.). London: Longman, Hurst, Rees, and Orme.

Buckland, W. W. (1908). *The roman law of slavery: The condition of the slave in private law from Augustus to Justinian.* Cambridge: Cambridge University Press.

Burke, E. (1775/2000). Mr. Burke's speech on moving his resolutions for conciliation with the colonies. In D. Browich (Ed.), *On empire, liberty, and reform: Speeches and letters of Edmund Burke* (pp. 66–134). New Haven, CT: Yale University Press.

Bush, M. (1996a). Introduction. In M. L. Bush (Ed.), *Serfdom and slavery: Studies in legal bondage* (pp. 1–17). New York: Addison Wesley Longman.

Bush, M. (1996b). Serfdom in medieval and modern Europe: A comparison. In M. L. Bush (Ed.), *Serfdom and slavery: Studies in legal bondage* (pp. 199–224). New York: Addison Wesley Longman.

Campbell, G. (2004). Introduction: Slavery and other forms of unfree labour in the Indian Ocean world. In G. Campbell (Ed.), *The structure of slavery in Indian Ocean Africa and Asia* (pp. vii–xxxii). London: Frank Cass.

Chanana, D. R. (1964). *Slavery in ancient India as depicted in Pali and Sanskrit texts.* New Delhi: People's Publishing House.

Clarence-Smith, W. G. (2006). *Islam and the abolition of slavery.* New York: Oxford University Press.

Cochin, A. (1863). *The results of slavery.* Boston: Walker, Wise, and Company.

Conning, J., & Kevane, M. (2007). Freedom, servitude, and voluntary contracts. In K. A. Appiah & M. Bunzl (Eds.), *Buying freedom: The ethics and economics of slave redemption* (pp. 108–140). Princeton: Princeton University Press.

Cook, L. D. (2007). The end of serfdom in Russia—Lessons for Sudan? In K. A. Appiah & M. Bunzl (Eds.), *Buying freedom: The ethics and economics of slave redemption* (pp. 181–199). Princeton: Princeton University Press.

Davidson, B. (1961). *The African slave trade.* New York: Atlantic Monthly Press.

Davies, W. (1996). On servile status in the early Middle Ages. In M. L. Bush (Ed.), *Serfdom and slavery: Studies in legal bondage* (pp. 225–246). New York: Addison Wesley Longman.

Davis, D. B. (1966). *The problem of slavery in Western culture.* Ithaca, NY: Cornell University Press.

Davis, R. C. (2003). *Christian slaves, Muslim masters: White slavery in the Mediterranean, the Barbary Coast, and Italy, 1500–1800.* New York: Palgrave Macmillan.

Deane, C. (1886). *The connection of Massachusetts with slavery and the slave-trade.* Worcester, MA: Charles Hamilton.

Delaye, K. (2004). Slavery and colonial representations in Indochina from the second half of the nineteenth to the early twentieth century. In G. Campbell (Ed.), *The structure of slavery in Indian Ocean Africa and Asia* (pp. 129–142). London: Frank Cass.

Derrick, J. (1975). *Africa's slaves today.* London: Allen & Unwin.

Donald, L. (1997). *Aboriginal slavery on the northwest coast of North America.* Berkeley: University of California Press.

Dyer, C. (1996). Memories of freedom: Attitudes towards serfdom in England, 1200–1350. In M. L. Bush (Ed.), *Serfdom and slavery: Studies in legal bondage* (pp. 277–295). New York: Addison Wesley Longman.

Engerman, S. (2000). Slavery at different times and places. *American Historical Review, 105,* 480–484.

Engerman, S. (2007). Slavery, freedom, and Sen. In K. A. Appiah & M. Bunzl (Eds.), *Buying freedom: The ethics and economics of slave redemption* (pp. 77–107). Princeton: Princeton University Press.

Faber, E. (1998). *Jews, slaves, and the slave trade: Setting the record straight.* New York: New York University Press.

Feeny, D. (1993). The demise of corvee and slavery in Thailand, 1782–1913. In M. A. Klein (Ed.), *Breaking the chains: Slavery, bondage, and emancipation in modern Africa and Asia* (pp. 83–111). Madison: University of Wisconsin Press.

Finley, M. I. (1980). *Ancient slavery and modern ideology.* New York: Viking Press.

Fogel, R. (1989). *Without consent or contract: The rise and fall of American slavery.* New York: W. W. Norton.

Frankopan, P. (2016). *The silk roads: A new history of the world.* New York: Alfred A. Knopf.

Gallay, A. (2002). *The Indian slave trade: The rise of the English Empire in the American South, 1670–1717.* New Haven, CT: Yale University Press.

Genovese, E. (1972). *Roll, Jordan, roll: The world the slaves made.* New York: Random House.

Goldberg, E. S. (2007). *Beyond terror: Gender, narrative, human rights.* New Brunswick, NJ: Rutgers University Press.

Hall, C., Draper, N., McClelland, K., Donington, K., & Lang, R. (2014). *Legacies of British slave-ownership: Colonial slavery and the formation of Victorian Britain.* New York: Cambridge University Press.

Hellie, R. (1982). *Slavery in Russia, 1450–1725.* Chicago: University of Chicago Press.

Hodkinson, S. (2008). Spartiates, helots, and the direction of the agrarian economy: Toward an understanding of helotage in comparative perspective. In E. D. Lago & C. Katsari (Eds.), *Slave systems ancient and modern* (pp. 285–320). New York: Cambridge University Press.

Hogendorn, J., & Lovejoy, P. E. (1992). Keeping slaves in place: The secret debate on the slavery question in northern Nigeria, 1900–1904. In J. Inikori & S. Engerman (Eds.), *The Atlantic slave trade: Effects on economies, societies, and peoples in Africa, the Americas, and Europe* (pp. 49–76). Durham, NC: Duke University Press.

Houston, A. (2008). *Benjamin Franklin and the politics of improvement.* New Haven, CT: Yale University Press.

Hurmence, B. (Ed.). (1984). *My folks don't want me to talk about slavery: Twenty-one oral histories of former North Carolina slaves.* Winston-Salem, NC: John F. Blair.

Johnsen, D. B. (2006). A culturally correct proposal to privatize the British Columbia salmon fishery. In T. L. Anderson, B. L. Benson, & T. E. Flanagan (Eds.), *Self-determination: The other path for Native Americans* (pp. 94–133). Stanford: Stanford University Press.

Kara, S. (2012). *Bonded labor: Tackling the system of slavery in South Asia.* New York: Columbia University Press.

Kim, B. R. (2004). Nobi: A Korean system of slavery. In G. Campbell (Ed.), *The structure of slavery in Indian Ocean Africa and Asia* (pp. 155–168). London: Frank Cass.

Klein, H. S. (1986). *African slavery in Latin America and the Caribbean.* New York: Oxford University Press.

Klein, M. (1992). The impact of the Atlantic slave trade on the societies of the western Sudan. In J. Inikori & S. Engerman (Eds.), *The Atlantic slave trade: Effects on economies, societies, and peoples in Africa, the Americas, and Europe* (pp. 25–48). Durham, NC: Duke University Press.

Klein, M. (1993). Introduction: Modern European expansion and traditional servitude in Africa and Asia. In M. A. Klein (Ed.), *Breaking the chains: Slavery, bondage, and emancipation in modern Africa and Asia* (pp. 3–36). Madison: University of Wisconsin Press.

Kloosterboer, W. (1960). *Involuntary labor since the abolition of slavery.* Amsterdam: E. J. Brill.

Knight, M. (1704/1825). Entry of October 7. In S. K. Knight & T. Buckingham (Eds.), *The journals of Madam Knight and Rev. Mr. Buckingham* (pp. 35–46). New York: Wilder & Campbell.

Kolchin, P. (1993). *American slavery, 1619–1877*. New York: Hill and Wang.

Kulikoff, A. (2000). *From British peasants to colonial American farmers*. Chapel Hill: University of North Carolina Press.

Kumar, D. (1993). Colonialism, bondage, and caste in British India. In M. A. Klein (Ed.), *Breaking the chains: Slavery, bondage, and emancipation in modern Africa and Asia* (pp. 112–130). Madison: University of Wisconsin Press.

Kurten, B. (1980). *Dance of the Tiger*. New York: Random House.

Kusimba, C. M. (2004). Archaeology of slavery in East Africa. *The African Archaeological Review, 21*, 59–88.

Larsen, C. (1995). Concluding remarks. In L. Beck (Ed.), *Regional approaches to mortuary analysis*. New York: Plenum Press.

Lovejoy, P. E. (2012). *Transformations in slavery: A history of slavery in Africa* (3rd ed.). New York: Cambridge University Press.

Manning, P. (1990). *Slavery and African life: Occidental, oriental, and African slave trades*. New York: Cambridge University Press.

Martin, D., & Frayer, D. (1998). *Troubled times: Violence and warfare in the past*. New York: Routledge.

McDougall, E. A. (2007). Dilemmas in the practice of *rachat* in French West Africa. In K. A. Appiah & M. Bunzl (Eds.), *Buying freedom: The ethics and economics of slave redemption* (pp. 158–178). Princeton: Princeton University Press.

McKeown, N. (2007). *The invention of ancient slavery?* London: Duckworth.

Meagher, A. J. (2008). *The coolie trade: The traffic in Chinese laborers to Latin America, 1847–1874*. New York: Xlibris.

Meillassoux, C. (1991). *The anthropology of slavery: The womb of iron and gold*. Chicago: University of Chicago Press.

Miers, S. (2004). Slavery: A question of definition. In G. Campbell (Ed.), *The structure of slavery in Indian Ocean Africa and Asia* (pp. 1–16). London: Frank Cass.

Millar, J. (1771/2006). *The origin of the distinction of ranks: Or, an inquiry into the circumstances, which give rise to influence and authority, in the different members of society*. Indianapolis: Liberty Fund.

Murphy, L. T. (2014). *Survivors of slavery: Modern-day slave narratives*. New York: Columbia University Press.

Patterson, O. (1982). *Slavery and social death: A comparative study*. Cambridge: Harvard University Press.

Patterson, O. (2008). Slavery, gender, and work in the pre-modern world and early Greece: A cross-cultural analysis. In E. D. Lago & C. Katsari (Eds.), *Slave systems ancient and modern* (pp. 32–69). New York: Cambridge University Press.

Pauketat, T. R. (2005). The forgotten history of the Mississippians. In T. Pauketat & D. Loren (Eds.), *North American Archaeology* (pp. 187–211). Malden, MA: Blackwell Publishing.

Pelteret, D. (1995). *Slavery in early mediaeval England: From the reign of Alfred until the twelfth century.* Rochester, NY: Boydell Press.

Phillips, W. D. (1996). Continuity and change in Western slavery: Ancient to modern times. In M. L. Bush (Ed.), *Serfdom and slavery: Studies in legal bondage* (pp. 71–88). New York: Addison Wesley Longman.

Quirk, J. (2011). *The anti-slavery project: From the slave trade to human trafficking.* Philadelphia: University of Pennsylvania Press.

Reid, A. (1993). The decline of slavery in nineteenth-century Indonesia. In M. A. Klein (Ed.), *Breaking the chains: Slavery, bondage, and emancipation in modern Africa and Asia* (pp. 64–82). Madison: University of Wisconsin Press.

Resendez, A. (2016). *The other slavery: The uncovered story of Indian enslavement in America.* New York: Houghton Mifflin Harcourt.

Rihll, T. (2008). Slavery and technology in pre-industrial contexts. In E. D. Lago & C. Katsari (Eds.), *Slave systems ancient and modern* (pp. 127–147). New York: Cambridge University Press.

Roberts, B. (1913). History of the Mormon Church. *Americana, 8*, 57–98.

Roberts, K. (2011). *The origins of business, money, and markets.* New York: Columbia Business School Publishing.

Saller, R. (1996). The hierarchical household in Roman society: A study of domestic slavery. In M. L. Bush (Ed.), *Serfdom and slavery: Studies in legal bondage* (pp. 112–129). New York: Addison Wesley Longman.

Schottenhammer, A. (2004). Slaves and forms of slavery in late imperial China (Seventeenth to Early Twentieth Centuries). In G. Campbell (Ed.), *The structure of slavery in Indian Ocean Africa and Asia* (pp. 143–154). London: Frank Cass.

Starna, W., & Watkins, R. (1991). Northern Iroquoian slavery. *Ethnohistory, 38*, 34–53.

Starr, C. (1958). An overdose of slavery. *Journal of Economic History, 18*, 17–32.

Taylor, C. C. W. (1983). A note on ancient attitudes towards slavery. *Analysis, 43*, 40–43.

Taylor, T. (2001). Believing the ancients: Quantitative and qualitative dimensions of slavery and the slave trade in later prehistoric Eurasia. *World Archaeology, 33*, 27–43.

Temperley, H. (1996). New World slavery, Old World slavery. In M. L. Bush (Ed.), *Serfdom and slavery: Studies in legal bondage* (pp. 144–157). New York: Addison Wesley Longman.

Tise, L. (1987). *Proslavery: A history of the defense of slavery in America, 1701–1840.* Athens: University of Georgia Press.

Toledano, E. (1993). Ottoman concepts of slavery in the period of reform, 1830s–1880s. In M. A. Klein (Ed.), *Breaking the chains: Slavery, bondage, and emancipation in modern Africa and Asia* (pp. 37–63). Madison: University of Wisconsin Press.

Tuchman, B. (1984). *The march of folly: From Troy to Vietnam.* New York: Ballantine Books.

Turton, A. (2004). Violent capture of people for exchange on Karen-Tai borders in the 1830s. In G. Campbell (Ed.), *The structure of slavery in Indian Ocean Africa and Asia* (pp. 69–82). London: Frank Cass.

Vogt, J. (1975). *Ancient slavery and the ideal of man* (T. Wiedemann, Trans.). Cambridge: Harvard University Press.

Walker, J. E. K. (1983). Pioneer slave entrepreneurship—Patterns, processes, and perspectives: The case of the slave Free Frank on the Kentucky Pennyroyal, 1795–1819. *Journal of Negro History, 68*, 289–308.

Wergeland, A. M. (1916). *Slavery in Germanic society during the Middle Ages.* Chicago: University of Chicago Press.

Wilbur, C. M. (1967). *Slavery in China during the former Han Dynasty 206 B.C.—A.D. 25.* New York: Russell & Russell.

Willey, P., & Emerson, T. E. (1993). The osteology and archaeology of the Crow Creek massacre. *Plains Anthropologist, 38*, 227–269.

Wright, G. (2006). *Slavery and American economic development.* Baton Rouge: Louisiana State University Press.

CHAPTER 4

Slavery Resilient

In 1853, "missionary heroine" (Dawson 1930, Chap. 3) Charlotte Tucker wrote that "the slave trade is, we hope and believe, extinct" (p. 7). She was not alone. Eminent social scientists like Auguste Comte, Karl Marx, and Max Weber all concluded that the modern industrial economy would send slavery straight to hell (Blackburn 2011: 305; Lovejoy 2012: 245). The notion that slavery in the United States ended with the ratification of the Thirteenth Amendment remains as well entrenched as the combatants on the Western Front during the Great War (Childs 2015: 4). Until recently, most scholars (and hence most people) believed that in the world's darker corners slavery disintegrated during the twentieth century. Even an Indian scholar otherwise extremely sensitive to the plight of "bonded labourers among the scheduled caste communities in Kerala" suggested that "slavery may be a thing of the past" (Saradamoni 1973: 371). The end of slavery in Africa was even pronounced, and any straggling remnants one might hear about it on the nightly news were, as anthropologist Claude Meillassoux believed, bound to disappear (1991: 314–23). So, as Martin Klein noted, "the major debate on abolition has concerned whether it was a triumph of moral principle or of economic interest" (Klein 1993: 18). In fact, it was neither! "Even after slavery was declared unlawful over the entire world, those whose interests were involved found many ways to create compulsory labour" (Fahrenfort 1960: vi).

Scholars now know what Adam Smith well understood in the eighteenth century, that the development of commercial society was no guarantee of liberty and justice for all (Salter 1996: 246). Rather than pay, as an

R.E. Wright, *The Poverty of Slavery*,
DOI 10.1007/978-3-319-48968-1_4

anonymous contributor to a newspaper put it in 1838, "wages to the highest rate competing capitalists can afford to give," employers will always look to minimize their wage bill and that means exerting control over others until the costs of such control exceeds the savings from lower wages. Enslaver employers, in other words, try to limit competitive labor agreements through a variety of strategies, including draconian labor contracts, limited suffrage or education for workers, debt-bondage, restrictions on land ownership, vagrancy and breach of contract laws, and even legal obligations to work for others (Quirk 2011: 122). South African diamond mine owners, *The Christian Observer* lamented, "want laborers, and at prices to suit themselves. The white men in South Africa demand higher wages than the owners will pay. The black men also want large wages, and further have shown themselves very skilful in concealing the jewels found" (Anon. 1904b: 2). So the mine owners imported Chinese indentured laborers under conditions little removed from slavery but soon discovered that the Chinese laborers were too costly to control (Payne 1912: 25–43, 47–69).

Interest in various forms of unfree labor has grown quickly in the last few decades. In her pioneering work *Female Slavery* (1979), Kathleen Barry cited only about 100 printed sources. Today, tens of thousands of printed sources on the topic are available (Quirk 2011: 227). Since 1996, when Howard Temperely asserted that slavery in one form or another remained an important factor in the modern world, (Temperley 1996: 157) scholars' understanding of the new forms of bondage and human trading has grown to the point that some, like Kevin Bales, believe that the great abolition movements of the nineteenth century did little but usher in "two hundred years of pretending we don't have slavery anymore" (Bales 2007: 3). One does not have to go quite that far to reject the Whiggish view of history as one of perpetual improvement (Bales 2012: 12). As economist historian Stan Engerman noted, "there was a somewhat late expansion of . . . coerced labour in the modern world, not a continuous decline in the degree of oppression and coercion from earlier periods" (Engerman 1996: 36). Once the old narrative of great emancipations and great emancipators is jettisoned in favor of a narrative that privileges the relative degree of freedom workers enjoyed, recasting related narratives becomes imperative. The US Civil War, for example, can no longer be seen as a struggle to free the slaves, but rather must be seen as a conflict over who controlled the labor of African-Americans and how that control was to be exerted. It was no accident that in areas that lacked strong leadership, members of the Freedmen's

Bureau tried, in the words of one of the Bureau's own reports, "to appropriate or control the labor of Freemen under their jurisdiction to advance their private interests" (Freedmen's Bureau 1870: 4–5).

In 1986, historian Herbert Klein argued that slavery could not have existed without the state (p. 196). He was both right and wrong about that. He was right, as Chap. 6 shows, that slavery needs multifarious government subsidies in order to thrive. In other than a narrow, legalistic sense, however, slavery does not need to be lawful in order to persist, the assertions of some very intelligent people to the contrary notwithstanding (Childs 2015: 57). Governments stripped lawful slaves away from slaveholders, but they have yet to sap the will to enslave from enslavers. The transmogrification of chattel slavery into a dizzying variety of other types of bound, coerced, and forced labor in post-emancipation societies forms the subject of this chapter.

Throughout the ages, enslavers have pretended that they were doing their slaves a favor by enslaving them, claiming that they saved their poor minions from death by the sword, starvation, or the state. In fact, however, slavery exists to enrich enslavers monetarily and/or psychosexually. That is why sociologist Orlando Patterson called slavery a type of human parasitism. Parasites, by definition, steal from their hosts just as enslavers steal the lives and livelihoods of those they enslave (Patterson 1982: 1, 5, 334–44).

In economic terms, slavery is about the extraction of "rents," of enslavers getting something for nothing. Specifically, enslavers earn monopsony rents, the extra profits to be had from "monopolizing" the labor of the enslaved through the process of enslavement, of preventing the enslaved from obtaining other employment offers. Monopsonists (monopolists on the buy side) can essentially set whatever wages they want and, not surprisingly, they generally pick the one that maximizes their utility, which typically entails some combination of leisure and lucre. When slavery is reduced, so too is monoposony, so wages increase, as they did in India when some brick molders were emancipated (Conning and Kevane 2007: 110; Robinson 1933: 281–304; Bales 2012: 190).

In short, enslaving others is profitable, a point well understood by Frederick Douglass when he predicted, correctly, that slavery in the United States would end in either compensation or bloodshed (Stauffer 2007: 221). Despite a long history of slavery giving way to closely related forms of oppression, for example, Roman slavery into serfdom and the quasi-enslavement of Amerindians into the encomienda, corregidor, and peonage systems, too few people understood that enslaving others was (and is) so profitable that enslavers had huge incentives to maintain their monopsony rents (excess profits) even after lawful abolition and the legal emancipation of the enslaved (Klein 1993: 14). One exception was social reformer Robert Dale Owen (1801–1877), who warned Americans in 1864 to guard freed slaves "against the virtual restoration of slavery, in any form, under any pretext" (pp. 228–29). "The risk is serious that ... slavery, in a modified form, may be practically restored" because former slaveholders had such a large stake in the institution (p. 226). Owen knew his history and also that most so-called free blacks in the antebellum North lived in a state of quasi-slavery (Schermerhorn 2015: 74, 201; Wright 1993: 105–6, 133–34, 144–46, 195; Davis 1966: 287). Consider, for instance, the plight of black shovers, people hired by counterfeiters to foist their bad bills onto unsuspecting marks in the dimly lit basement oyster houses of antebellum Manhattan. Even free black entrepreneurs, like Manhattan restaurateur Moses Leech, could be, and were, abused by white rogues like Fontaine Pettis, who ran up a huge bill (over $100), then reneged and beat Leech when he tried to collect "a little money to buy some necessaries for his family" (White 2014: 393–95)!

In post-emancipation societies, in other words, laborers did not move from "chattel slave" to "free" but from a condition with a freedom scale score of 0, 1, or 2, to a condition with a freedom scale score of less than 5, or, if they were fortunate, up to 7 or 8. Individual outcomes, to some extent, depended on specific circumstances but also on larger cultural, economic, and political conditions. In general, the end of slavery in sugar economies led to a large influx of indentured laborers, mostly from India, while the end of slavery in cotton economies spawned systems of debt peonage and convict labor (Beckert 2004). Emancipation was not a major break from the past, in other words, but rather created a new game with new rules for both enslavers and the enslaved (Kolchin 1996: 59).

Conditions were probably worst in Africa and South Asia. The eventual closing of the Transatlantic and Indian and Pacific Ocean slave trading systems did not end slavery in Africa or its internal slave trade. In 1906, Henry W. Nevinson portrayed in stark detail slavery as it was then practiced in Angola. By the eve of the Great Depression, the number of chattel slaves worldwide was estimated at between 4 and 6 million, most in places like the Sudan, the Horn of Africa, the Arabian peninsula, India, and Southeast Asia (Simon 1929: 1–2; Miers 2003: 47–299). In 1971, the United Nations published evidence that showed that slavery still played a major role in 17 African, 15 Asian, and 6 Latin American countries (Temperley 1996:

156). By the 1970s, slavery had been legally abolished in Arabia but various forms of labor exploitation continued unabated (Miers 2003: 352).

But the history of slavery since the age of emancipation is not as much the story of chattel slavery as it is a tale of convict and indentured laborers, debt peons, and a host of other kinds of quasi- or neo-slaves (Bush 1996: 2). Wherever slavery had existed, and as documented in Chap. 3 that was just about everywhere, new forms of exploitation, some indiscernible from chattel slavery but thinly cloaked in the garb of new words, arose. In Britain's post-emancipation sugar colonies, for example, millions of Indian and Chinese indentured laborers lived so close to chattel slave-like conditions that their entrepot in British Guiana was still called the "Nigger Yard" (Tinker 1993: 177). In the British West Indies, blacks, who knew well of what they spoke, called the Asian newcomers "Coolie Slaves" (Tinker 1993: 219). Just like African slaves, Asian indentured laborers suffered high death rates and fled their oppressors whenever they could (Tinker 1993: 303).

Before the complete victory of steam over sail to power the world's oceangoing ships, which occurred about 1900, mortality on ships carrying indentured laborers, especially on the unregulated return voyages to India, were so high that they were compared to the horrific Middle Passage. Not that many Indians made it back home. Vagrancy and identification laws, taxes, and other measures were created to render it difficult for time-expired indentured laborers to escape the estate economy (Tinker 1993: 2, 78–79, 82, 91, 107, 117–18). Lord John Russell was right when, in February 1840, he warned that importing Indian laborers into British Guiana could lead to "a new system of slavery," one based on economic necessity as well as legal compunction (Hall et al. 2014: 154).

Matters were no better in post-emancipation America (Blackmon 2008: 402). Emancipation, some ex-slaves believed, was just a way for masters to avoid the responsibility of feeding their slaves (Lichtenstein 1996: 1). "When de war was over," recalled freed slave Mary White "Granny" Ovington in 1910, "if a nigger say he was free, dey shot him down." According to a Freedmen's Bureau report, at least one recalcitrant enslaver went so far as to keep freed slaves at work on his rice plantation with "ball and chain" (1870: 8). A few years later, Reverend H. W. Pierson, the former president of Cumberland College in Kentucky and author of a Jefferson biography, discovered while doing missionary work in Georgia that whites were still beating and cheating freedmen and that they refused to sell them any land. "All we want is to live under the law," freedmen Richard Reese told Pierson, but when the law proved to be the unjust tool of enslavers, men like Reese suffered by it, as did their descendants (1870: 9–10). Indeed, decades after Pierson wrote, convict laborers in Georgia also noticed the similarities between their plight and those of chattel slaves when they sang that slavery and freedom were mostly the same, the only difference being in the name (Childs 2015: 1).

Pierson fled the South after receiving credible death threats from the Ku Klux Klan (KKK). "I have never known crime to be committed in any community with such perfect impunity," he noted. After almost being killed by a white man, Rev. Charles Ennis echoed Pierson's sentiment. "I was a slave until freed … by war, but I never received such treatment during all my life as a slave. … We have no protection at all from the laws of Georgia" (Pierson 1870: 11, 20). Freedman Thomas Hall stated the matter so clearly in an oral interview that it bears extensive quotation:

The whites have always held the slaves in part slavery and are still practicing the same things on them in a different manner. Whites lynch, burn, and persecute the Negro race in America yet, and there is little they are doing to help them in any way. Lincoln got the praise for freeing us, but did he do it? He give us freedom without giving us any chance to live to ourselves, and we still had to depend on the Southern white man for work, food, and clothing, and he held us, through our necessity and want, in a state of servitude but little better than slavery (Hurmence 1984: 52).

In many parts of the South, slave patrols were reinvented as so-called negro patrols (Schurz 1903). Slaves called the members of such patrols "pattyrollers" and rightfully feared their brutality, venality, and lust. Patsy Mitchner later admitted that "I heard them talk about pattyrollers so much I was scared so I could hardly sleep at night sometimes. I was afraid they would come and catch me" (Hurmence 1984: 1, 8, 30, 42, 76, 84, 89–90, 94). The patrollers were motivated by, in the words of German-American liberal reformer Carl Schurz (1829–1906), "the lingering hope that [chattel] slavery might yet be preserved," if not exactly replicated at least realistically simulated (1903). The same arguments used by proslavery ideologues before the war were dragged out again to support neoslavery. Most former slaveholders, and uncomfortably large numbers of other whites, still believed that slavery was a positive good. They denounced the Thirteenth Amendment and argued that blacks could reach their full potential only under servitude. If allowed freedom, they would revert to barbarism, as they allegedly did in Liberia and Haiti (Smith 1985: 6–9, 24, 47–49).

Many contemporaries, including Schurz (1903), knew that freedom was an exaggeration, if not an outright farce, in post-emancipation societies. Many believed that such conditions were temporary, part of a process by which freed slaves learned the ways of wage labor. Such paternalistic views were so pervasive that Britain's initial emancipation plan rested on an apprenticeship system that forced freed slaves to devote three quarters of their labor time to their former masters, without wages (except for overtime work) (Hall et al. 2014: 139). The Dutch pulled something similar in Java, requiring former slaves to spend two-fifths of their time in unpaid labor on Javanese coffee, sugar, and indigo estates (Reid 1993: 73).

Rather than temporary vestiges of legal slavery, however, most of the new regimes represented new long-term equilibria in a world that denounced "slavery" but coexisted, largely peacefully, with its functional equivalent. In some places, like the Banamba and Gumbu regions of French Sudan, chattel slavery ended in a process of negotiation between enslavers and the enslaved but resulted in a system of tenancy that was far from free (Turley 1996: 195). In the mid-twentieth century, Kloosterboer (1960) and others documented the existence of compulsory labor in Africa, Latin America, the United States, the East and West Indies, and Soviet Russia. The Philippines and half a dozen other places on mainland Asia could have been added as well (Simon 1929: 136–37; Reid 1993: 76). A half century later, updates by scholars like Bales and Kara showed that while compulsory labor had evolved to meet new demands, it remained a global scourge because while slavery had never really gone away, public concern with it did, especially where it managed to avoid the onerous appellation of slavery.

The new slaveries were not as much about physically seizing people and forcing them to toil, though that certainly still occurred in some contexts (e.g., the outright kidnapping of Indian laborers when harvests were good [Tinker 1993: 65, 125–27]), as it was about maneuvering people into situations where they could be easily exploited. Some maneuvers involved using the coercive power of the state to force people to work for others rather than themselves via vagrancy laws, tax structures, and anti-credit and anti-land ownership legislation (Conning and Kevane 2007: 122). Other maneuvers invoked the state to enforce lopsided or fraudulent credit contracts. Still others involved tricking vulnerable people looking for employment. By the mid-nineteenth century, it was already common practice for recruiters in India to tell marks that they were to be engaged in gardening or other innocuous occupations, or skilled occupations if they had a skill, when the workers were really slated for rubber plantations or brothels (Tinker 1993: 51, 69, 122, 231).

In the postbellum US South, illiterate freedpersons were tricked into making their mark on contracts that amounted to slavery. When the freedpersons discovered the ruse, many felt it was useless to fight back. "What could we do about it?" one former slave later recalled. "The white folks had all the courts, all the guns, all the hounds, all the railroads, all the telegraph wires, all the newspapers, all the money, and nearly all the land" (Georgia Negro Peon 1904: 411).

The new slaveries were about exploiting the lowest of the low, like former chattel slaves, Dalits (casteless "Untouchables") in India, runaway or orphaned children, abandoned, disgraced, divorced, or widowed women, and the real mother lode, entire nations, regions, or tribes stricken by disease, drought, famine, and/or war. As a colonial emigration agent in India put it, "in most cases the recruiter finds the coolie absolutely on the brink of starvation and he takes him in and feeds him and explains to him the terms of service" (Tinker 1993: 54, 119, 130).

Kidnapping, fraud, and so forth were illegal in most places but they did not quite carry the opprobrium of slavery so the police, judges, and administrators were pretty cheaply bribed. Local bureaucrats and police officers were complicit in the indentured laborer trade in India in the nineteenth century. Officers were even known to tease indentured laborers about their plight. "The police of India," an observer noted in 1840, "are ill-constituted for the duty of special protectors of the indentured laborers; that is now plain" (Tinker 1993: 67, 71, 134). When the enslaved are members of a reviled community, the police do not even need bribes to look the other way. In the North African section of Paris in the 1970s, for example, police allowed *maisons d'abattage* ("houses of slaughter") to remain in operation, though the enslaved women inhabitants were forced to sexually service 80–120 men each night, made possible by enforcing a 6-minute rule. The women never left their beds during the 12-hour ordeals (Barry 1979: 3–4).

In some instances, administrators were not on enslavers' payrolls but empathized with their plight because they emanated from the same class, race, or social milieu. Occasionally, an administrator struck by the horrors of the post-emancipation slave trade stuck out his or her neck, but most bureaucrats kept their heads down and collected their paychecks (Tinker 1993: 178, 223). Acquiescence alone, Dharma Kumar pointed out, was at times sufficient to allow enslavers to hire thugs to keep the enslaved in line (1993: 120).

Enslavers, like other businesspeople, are also adept at exploiting loopholes, exceptions in the law that allow them to enslave their workers with relative impunity. In the Thirteenth Amendment to its constitution, the United States banned slavery and involuntary servitude but created a loophole so big that Dennis Childs has called it a rhetorical trapdoor (2015: 64). Bowing to a very long tradition of enslaving criminals and popular sentiment, the amendment (as well as the Civil Rights Act of 1866 and the constitutions of all but three states in 1913) allowed the enslavement of people duly convicted of a crime. On its face, the exception seemed, and seems, eminently reasonable to reasonable people, and even natural (Childs 2015: 71, 75; Hicks 1913: 494; Tinker 1993: 44; Wergeland 1916: 11). Like Italian criminologist Cesare Beccaria (1738–1794), many believed that prisoners should repay society for the costs they imposed upon it. Hard labor also made sense to people, like famed British jurist William Blackstone (1723–1780), who sought retribution against criminals because they believed that every felon is a tainted monster and a bane to society. Slavery, for them, was a useful punishment less harsh or permanent than death (Childs 2015: 149; Davis 1966: 376–77, 412). "For there commeth more profite of theire laboure, then of theire deathe" as the great humanist Thomas More (1478–1535) explained in *Utopia*, which allowed the enslavement of criminals and other "vyle drudge" (Collins 1904: 99, 103).

When an 1886 US Bureau of Labor report claimed that "it is universally conceded that convicts should be employed at some useful labor," it was not far off the mark (Lichtenstein 1996: 18; Miers 2004: 6). Convict labor was important the world over, including in Australia, a land settled by convicts eager to enslave aborigines as well as criminals, in Burma, and in Dutch Indonesia, where convicts cleared forests and built transportation infrastructure for the government (Miles 1987: 94–117; Turton 2004: 70; Reid 1993: 73–76).

As classical economist Adam Smith pointed out, slave labor camps were a type of prison so wherever the state was too poor or impotent to build proper prisons it would find it convenient to turn convicts into slave laborers (Salter 1996: 241). Smith's contemporary, political economist John Millar, was even more explicit. "As the crimes of individuals were principally considered in the light of offences against the society," he explained, "it was agreeable to this idea that a criminal should become the slave of the public, and should either be employed in public works, or disposed of in the manner most advantageous to the revenue of the community" (Millar 2006: 252).

Americans certainly had a long history of putting convicts to work. In early Philadelphia, for example, over 3300 prisoners, mostly black or Irish, were put to work (Ignatiev 1995: 42–45). Growth in the use of convict laborers, bolstered by developments in similar markets for the hiring out of slaves, continued up through the Civil War, before blossoming as never before after passage of the Thirteenth Amendment (Zaborney 2012; McLennan 2008: 90–99; Lichtenstein 1996: 3).

Convict labor came in three major flavors: the lease system, whereby convicts were essentially turned over to private corporations and housed and fed by them, the manufacturing system, wherein manufacturers established workshops within prison walls and the related putting out or piece system, and the public account, where prisoners labored in prison-owned factories or on state projects, such as road repair, park beautification, or, as in South Dakota, the installation of internet systems in public schools (McLennan 2008: 87, 104; Lichtenstein 1996: 3, 18–19; Wright 2015: 129, 184).

The problem with the criminality exception (one is tempted to call it a criminal exception) is that it creates incentives for governments to imprison people and to turn into enslavers or slave traders (Childs 2015: 83). In the postbellum US South, those incentives combined with a widespread desire to keep freedpeople in a condition close to chattel slavery to create a particularly virulent convict labor system. Life for convicts, mostly poor blacks, on Parchman Farm in Mississippi was worse than slavery, because the veneer of paternalism and long-term self-interest were gone (Oshinsky 1997). Convicts who died (or who were released) were so easily and cheaply replaced that inmates called trusties were employed to shoot and kill runaways. Their reward for shooting a runaway, though most trusties were incarcerated for murder, or worse, was immediate release from prison (Oshinsky 1997: 194–96). Almost everyone else caught up in the system fared poorly. Convicted for vagrancy or other non-violent "crimes," unable to pay their trumped up fines, imprisoned, and then sold to corporations or plantations, the men were worked and beaten until they died, they (technically their debts) were sold to another enslaver, or their fines and fees were finally repaid (Childs 2015: 3).

During their period of incarceration, inmates were essentially worse off than chattel slaves because no one much cared if they lived or died. And incarcerated African-Americans were treated in ways eerily similar to the way chattel slaves had been treated by the worst masters. When they ran away, they were tracked down by dogs and thrown into sweatboxes. Their guard masters had almost complete control over their persons and even forced theatrical and musical performances from them. Dehumanizing spectacles akin to ancient Roman slaves fighting animals or gladiators kept the guards and their guests entertained (Blackmon 2008; Childs 2015: 8, 16–17, 99, 125). Guards also employed against their inmates the holy trinity of slave control, "the whip used sparingly, the fiddle, and the Bible" (Childs 2015: 119).

Some convict laborers were even placed on auction blocks and sold to the highest bidder (Childs 2015: 69). Early in the twentieth century, for example, Florida had "no state prison ... twelve hundred convicts and no place to put them. The state, therefore," was "compelled to speculate" in its criminals, leasing "them out to individuals who pay for the privilege" (Barry 1907).

Racist crackers, however, are not the only people who understand the profitability of enslaving others, especially when the enslavement is government sanctioned and subsidized. So the convict labor system in the United States, although deeply racially biased, affected/affects poor whites, especially members of religious and ethnic minorities, as well. While convict laborers were treated the worst in the South, as measured by mortality rates, convict labor nonetheless flourished throughout the country in the late nineteenth century. Prisoners were not the best workers but they were cheap, sober, and unable to strike. By 1887, about 45,000 people, or seven out of every 10 incarcerated individuals, were at hard labor. They produced about $30 billion worth of goods (in 2005 dollars) and 85 percent of that was outside the South. Often big businesses hired entire prisons. Oven molder manufacturer John Sherwood Perry, for example, controlled all 1300 prisoners incarcerated in New York's Sing Sing prison in the latter part of the nineteenth century. Hat and shoe makers controlled other prisons in New York, New Jersey, and even progressive Wisconsin (McLennan 2008: 88–90, 100, 108–11, 118–19).

In the twentieth century, convict leasing declined as most states decided to put their prisoners to work on state account, making bailing wire, license plates, and what not. In the last four decades, however, the rate of incarceration in America grew so quickly that it strained the state account system. The rate of incarceration now stands four and a half times higher (per 100,000 residents) than in previous periods in the nation's own history and seven times higher than in other developed nations today. State level differences are dramatic. In Minnesota, only 185 out of every 100,000 residents are incarcerated, compared to 865 in Louisiana! Eight of the ten states with the highest incarceration rates are in the Sunbelt, which is led by the "Flocatex" states of Florida, Texas, and California. The high rate of incarceration in those states practically forced prison privatization, which brought with it renewed emphasis on convict labor because the overcrowded prison system, sterilized and rechristened the criminal justice system, became prohibitively expensive (Lichtenstein 2015). Most of the victims of this new penal slavery are poor, black, native, or Hispanic young men put to labor for nonviolent drug-related offenses, which appear to be little more than new fangled vagrancy laws (Travis, Western, and Redburn 2014).

Slavery-like practices also persisted outside of the carceral state. All roads, it seems, led back toward slavery in post-emancipation societies. Where ample land was available, as in Jamaica and Trinidad, a black peasantry composed of freed slaves and their descendants developed. Aided by significant public subsidies, enslavers imported Asian indentured laborers and the peasants, as in Haiti and French Indochina, enslaved vulnerable women and children to serve as domestic drudges. Where land was scarce, either naturally as in much of the British Caribbean or due to legal barriers to acquisition as in British Guiana (where Crown lands would not be sold tracts of less than 100 acres and were so highly priced that no independent peasantry could arise), laws proved adequate to force freed slaves to work under onerous contracts. In St. Kitts, Dominica, and Barbados, elites passed ambiguous laws with harsh penalties designed to force freed slaves back to the plantations to work. British authorities struck down most such laws but the strict vagrancy laws were maintained and they proved sufficient to keep plantations supplied with penal work gangs (Tinker 1993: 2; Foner 1983: 11, 14, 17, 21, 24–26; Delaye 2004; Adamson 1972: 258).

In Brazil and Cuba, enslavers deployed European immigrants in gangs as much as they could, though similar attempts to stock post-emancipation British sugar colonies with European laborers had failed. Africans and free African-Americans could also not be lured in, not at wages planters wanted to pay. Asians, especially Indians, were a different matter. The British struggled to understand India, its caste system and religions, and its long, complex history with slavery. What they clearly understood, though, was that large numbers of Indians were desperate enough to leave their homeland, not an easy thing for anyone to do but especially difficult for Hindus, on vague assurances of work at subsistence wages (Turley 1996: 188; Hall et al. 2014: 154; Prakash 1993).

Indian, and in some places Chinese, laborers were transported from their homelands, where their labor was not needed (competitive wages were low), to places like the New World, and the Mascarene Islands, where it was desperately needed (competitive wages were high). Elites wanted to extract monopsony rents (excess profits) from the workers, so they negotiated wages and other forms of compensation with them in their homelands, where they were largely marginal, even superfluous, and hence low paid. The enslavers locked in the low wages for as long as they could via written contracts called indentures or indentured contracts (Allen 2004: 34; Quirk 2011: 12).

Indentured labor was not new. Though perhaps not as numerous or important as once thought, indentured laborers certainly did augment the population of several British colonies in the seventeenth and eighteenth centuries. During the English Civil War, Oliver Cromwell forced captured Irish and Scottish Highlander prisoners into exile on the continent or into indentured servitude on English Caribbean plantations. Later, British authorities swept the Irish countryside of priests, bards, and educators in order to break Gaelic culture and sent them off abroad, often as indentured servants (Tomlins 2006; Smith 1965: 336; Jordan and Walsh 2007). According to historian Abbott Smith, "people of every age and kind were decoyed, deceived, seduced, inveigled, or forcibly kidnapped and carried as servants to the plantations. There were many ordinary individuals of decent substance" as well as "rogues, vagabonds, whores, cheats, and rabble of all descriptions, raked from the gutter and kicked out of the country." Britain, France, Switzerland, and German principalities were the main sources. Most went to Pennsylvania and points south, while persecuted Protestants headed to New England. The term of service was usually four years for adults and longer for children, who cost almost as much to ship but who did not produce as much as adults (1965: 3–4).

Some indentured servants voluntarily emigrated to the New World to avoid religious persecution and/or with the hopes of bettering their lot. Skilled workers, for example, could often negotiate better terms, including exemption from manual or field labor or a shorter term of service. Whether the laborers were forced, tricked, or volunteers, merchants found shipping them abroad profitable and of course the rate of economic exploitation (the value of marginal product or the competitive wage minus the value of actual remuneration, including room and board and freedom dues) of indentured servants was often quite high, some £50 per worker per year in Maryland's tobacco fields, for example (Smith 1965: 4, 16–17, 27).

The experience of individual indentured servants, though, depended largely on the characteristics of their masters. Unlike chattel slaves, indentured servants in colonial America enjoyed some contractual and statutory rights that courts generally upheld. The law was clear that what masters purchased was the servants' labor, rather than their persons, so servants had access to formal courts as well as the court of common opinion regarding matters like freedom dues and proper diet, clothes, and bedding. Sometimes, the government stripped a cruel master of his servant. The courts, however, also enforced the master's rights. Servants generally were not inclined to rebel as their freedom was in sight, but of course many would break their contracts by getting drunk, running away, or getting pregnant, for which they were whipped and/or the length of their contract extended (Smith 1965: 19, 227, 235–41, 264–70, 278).

Redemptioners had an easier time of it, but still not easy. Redemptioners were people, generally from the Continent, of some means who on their arrival in the New World could borrow money, typically from kinsfolk or co-religionists, with which to buy out their contracts. If they could not raise the necessary cash before some time limit, generally 14 days, after their arrival in the New World, however, they were sold as indentured servants. The length of their servitude was a function of the size of the debt they incurred during passage minus any cash they proffered. Redemptioners, who typically came with their entire families, generally paid their own way as far as possible while regular indentured servants were generally destitute and hence had to be fed (and charged for board) from the time they signed on. Redemptioners and indentured servants alike often suffered horribly on the voyage (Smith 1965: 20–22; Grubb 2011: 59; Jordan and Walsh 2007: 222–24).

After about 1820, hardly any European emigrants needed to indenture themselves in order to finance the transatlantic passage. Passenger fares dropped, savings increased, and alternative types of financing passage arose. But when the British emancipated their slaves shortly thereafter, everyone remembered the indenture system and saw its application to impoverished Indians. The Asiatic indenture system, however, proved less benign than the European one, much more closely resembling chattel slavery (Grubb 2011: 316–71; Tinker 1993: 42–43; Temperley 1996: 156). The goal of post-emancipation planters, British imperial bureaucrat Thomy Hugon made clear, was "to weed out . . . all that tended to give the Indians greater freedom of action." Marriages between indentured laborers were not officially recognized or respected and workers who came into windfalls (usually via gambling) could not buy out their contracts (Tinker 1993: 19, 88, 172).

Until steamships finally replaced sailing ships circa 1900, the voyage from India to most destinations was longer than the Middle Passage of the Transatlantic slave trade. The 125,000 indentured laborers brought into Cuba after its abolition of slavery, for example, had to traverse half of the Indian Ocean and the entire breadth of Africa as well as the Atlantic. Early on, mortality rates were almost as high as well (Turley 1996: 188; Tinker 1993: 154).

Anti-slavery forces eventually managed to regulate the indentured laborer trade but the punishments for violating the rules were so low that they were broken with impunity. Kidnapping brought sentences of three months. One kidnapper who received a three-year sentence was more severely dealt with only because he broke caste rules! In Natal, those convicted of cruelly beating indentured laborers received only three or four months imprisonment. Other times, underlings received a few years but their bosses got off scot-free (Tinker 1993: 125, 127, 248).

As noted in Chap. 3, China knew both slavery and serfdom for thousands of years. By the late nineteenth century, its massive population was wracked by war and famine. During the Taiping Rebellion (1851–1864), which almost toppled the Manchu Dynasty, more than 20 million Chinese died while untold millions more were displaced from the 600 cities that were sacked during the conflict (Wilbur 1967; Meagher 2008: 61–62). Unsurprisingly, China became a place, as an early twentieth century author put it, "from which laborers may be drawn to perform difficult and unpleasant work at a low price" (Payne 1912: 2). Like their brethren in India, Chinese indentured laborers must have been in desperate straits to even consider leaving their homeland, which many still called the Celestial Empire. Only a small percentage (0.35) left, but that meant 1.5 million out of a total population of 430 million (Meagher 2008: 58–62; Payne 1912: 5–6).

Often, especially after the most vulnerable had already fled, highly motivated crimps (labor recruiters akin to modern day slave traffickers) tricked workers into boarding ships with promises of good jobs and/or threats of punishment for specious gambling debts. Outright kidnapping and clan wars also helped to fill out cargoes. Regardless of how they were obtained, however, the indentured laborers were treated like chattel slaves on board ship and when they arrived at their destinations in North and Latin America and eventually even places like Mauritius. The voyage to the New World compared with that suffered by enslaved Africans. Mortality on a trip to

Cuba hit almost 12 percent; voyages averaged 100 plus days. Out of 736 recorded voyages from China to Latin America between 1847 and 1874, mutinies struck almost one in ten (Meagher 2008: 21, 30–31, 74–76, 129, 149–50, 163–92)!

Matters did not improve much on dry land. As John Granville told the British Foreign Office in 1873:

The Chinese coolie is treated here precisely as a slave. He is beaten, ironed and often cruelly punished, frequently driven to suicide or crime; he can be sold or transferred like any other chattel, and at the expiring of his contract instead of receiving his liberty or release from bondage he must either leave the island, declare himself a Spanish subject or suffer himself to be dealt with as an "emancipado," *and hired out on contract after contract until he dies* (Meagher 2008: 214).

Indentured laborers had some de jure rights, like taking masters to court to seek redress of grievances, but de facto they were slaves. Hundreds of thousands of indentured laborers were traded exactly as slaves had been, stripped naked on the block for ease of inspection. Mortality rates were high, especially considering most indentured laborers were young men, as enslavers had incentives to work them to death. If they became disabled, enslavers simply jettisoned them. Like chattels, indentured laborers could be whipped for not meeting their quotas. On Peru's hot, stinky, fresh waterless guano islands, for example, indentured laborers who did not load 5 tons of bird feces per day, 7 days per week, were whipped. When questioned about such practices, enslavers retorted that they could do anything they liked to an indentured laborer, short of killing one directly. Indeed, female indentured laborers, though relatively few in number, were routinely raped just as female African slaves had been (Meagher 2008: 215–30, 233, 297–99; Tinker 1993: 192–99, 221).

As the supply of Indian indentured laborers began to recede, and Indians began to prefer serving in Natal and other places relatively close to home, demand for Chinese indentured laborers increased. Eventually they were brought to Cuba as well as Peru and Brazil, places where indigenous peoples could not be forced to work and working class Europeans rightly feared to tread (Meagher 2008: 34–39). Soon, Chinese indentured laborers became the victim of reverse racism as an ardent belief developed that, as author Leonard Way put it in the 1848 book *The Practical Sugar Planter*, no other people "can in any way be compared to the Chinese, for enterprise, energy, sobriety, intelligence, application, physical power, determined perseverance, cheerfulness, and prudent economy combined" (p. 83). The belief in the superiority of Chinese labor was remarkable given the relatively weak incentives they faced (Payne 1912: 59).

Native workers typically despised Asian indentured laborers, who they rightly believed depressed their wages. Asian indentured servants received little in return for their toil. Promised wages, low to begin with, were often withheld for months or never paid at all. Worse, enslavers fined indentured laborers for missing work via an invidious practice called the double cut. Although a few indentured laborers were able to extract themselves from servitude and attained a higher standard of living, many simply swapped one form of poverty and drudgery for another, or died trying. The suicide rate among Indian indentured laborers was astronomical by Hindu standards and much higher than in India. Conditions were so bad that indentured servitude was recognized as a new form of slavery by the Anti-Slavery Society of Britain, British bureaucrats, and others. Effective in 1874, the Portuguese banned the exportation of indentured laborers from Macau. The trade continued elsewhere but pretty much died during the Great War (Payne 1912: 5–9; Tinker 1993: 60, 186–88, 200–201, 238–39, 300, 334–40; Meagher 2008: 295–96).

China abolished most forms of domestic slavery before the Great War, including *Mui-Tsai* or the tradition of selling excess female children as domestic servants or prostitutes, but the practice of enslaving others continued, thanks in large part to the disruptions caused by the civil war and brutal Japanese incursions, including the rape of Nanking (Anon. 1910b: 295; Quirk 2011: 149). In the late 1930s, Earl H. Leaf saw his "good friend Wang purchase a very pretty twelve-year-old girl … as a wedding anniversary gift for his wife." Although illegal, the domestic trade remained quite open. "Several times during my month in this lane," Leaf reported in 1937, "a slave peddler made the rounds, calling out his wares boldly and carrying two children, a boy and a girl, in baskets slung from the pole over his shoulder. … Even in 'good times'," he noted, "slaves are bountiful in the market," especially the market for slave girls destined for "houses of prostitution." What the Chinese cracked down on were outright abductions/kidnappings and instances of "extreme cruelty" (1937: 63–68).

In postbellum America, the convict lease system could not meet all the demand for slavish labor, so other ruses developed, the most infamous of which was sharecropping combined with debt bondage. In that system, landlord elites (some former slaveholders) leased farms to tenants for a share of the crop (which varied somewhat over time and place, but most importantly, over the inputs, like seed, draft animals, or machinery, the landlord supplied in addition to the land). There is nothing inherently wrong with sharecropping per se. Contrary to widespread belief, and the writings of Adam Smith and Alfred Marshall (who concentrated solely on short-term output), sharecropping in the long term was not necessarily less efficient than fixed rent contracts or outright ownership. The system became abusive, however, when the cropper was forced to buy his dry goods and groceries from a particular store owned and/or controlled by his landlord. While the sharecropping arrangements were ostensibly free enough to ensure a competitive outcome (i.e., that tenants would be compensated with something close to their marginal product), the stores were essentially monopolies that gouged tenants on the consumption side (Garrett and Xu 2003; Foner 1983: 89–90). "In this store," one impoverished debt peon recalled, "we were charged all sorts of high prices for goods, [so that] every year we would come out in debt to our employer" (Georgia Negro Peon 1904: 411).

Mining companies perpetrated similar frauds on their workers, charging miners $2.75 for powder that cost them only $1.10. "As his debt for supplies at the company stores is taken from his pay before he gets it, and as his home is nearly always rented from the company," muckraking journalist Edwin Markham noted in 1906, "the coal barons get most of the money back" (p. 24).

Some poor whites also became debt peons, especially to turpentine and lumber corporations, the owners of which believed that whites were better workers. But according to muckraking journalist Richard Barry, the corporations were also happy to ensnare blacks in peonage. "This new form of slavery," Barry claimed, "places white and black on a plane of perfect equality, and enslaves them both with generous disregard of ancestry or complexion" (1907: 481). This was "not the wage-slavery that grinds the human undergrowth of these United States," Barry took pains to show, "but the ancient slavery, the actual, physical slavery that keeps men worse than animals" (p. 482). Such practices appear to have been temporarily put down by the sentencing of five officers of the Jackson Lumber Company to seven years hard labor for peonage plus use of "the antebellum implements of bondage—the lash and the bloodhound" (p. 482). They were sentenced harshly, Barry maintained, because they had enslaved white men, although mostly just "starving Jews, decrepit Poles, and mangy Scandinavians" (p. 483)! But others later stepped in and enslaved Florida agricultural workers through the mechanism of debt bondage and the crew leader's own hyper-expensive, mandatory store (Bales and Soodalter 2009: 51).

The number of people trapped in debt peonage in the postbellum South is debated and certainly varied over time and place. It was not, however, the only way to steal from laborers or to force them to work. Elites changed property laws in the postbellum South from open range (property owners must build fences if they want to keep others' livestock out) to private property (property owners must build fences to keep their livestock in) and also made it illegal to hunt or fish on private property without permission. Both were attempts to prevent African-Americans from scraping by hunting and ranging livestock and hence to force them into wage labor. Another way of exploiting workers was the so-called check system whereby workers could either use their paychecks to immediately obtain goods from plantation stores or to receive cash payment at some future date (Fishback 1989; Foner 1983: 64–65, 91). That was similar to the company scrip used to pay miners in remote mining towns throughout Appalachia and the Rockies. The United States witnessed a long struggle to end compulsory company stores and scrip, and to ensure that workers receive their promised pay in cash at reasonable intervals (Sawyer 2013; Pound 1909: 463, 471–74, 477, 486).

About the best that could be said of the postbellum labor regime was that some people, including some freed slaves, were able to avoid its worst excesses. In parts of low country Georgia, for example, freedmen and their descendants were able to buy a little land on which to grow cotton to pay their taxes and buy such items, like clothes and tobacco, that they could not forage from the rich surrounding countryside. "The Negroes there," one planter lamented, "will not work for wages, as they can live almost without work on fish, crawfish and oysters" (Armes 1903: 234).

Few, however, were so fortunate. With little aid from the government (blankets and "rations in bulk had been frequently . . . hauled off in carts and wagons" from Freedmen's Bureau warehouses instead of being delivered to former slaves [Freedmen's Bureau 1870: 5, 7]), freedpeople in America, like those in Africa, Latin America, India, and virtually all post-emancipation societies, were allowed to drift, easy pickings for those who wished to forge new forms of bondage (Hogendorn and Lovejoy 1992: 49–52). "Slaves," freedperson Patsy Mitchner recalled, "was turned out with nowhere to go and nothing to live on. They had no experience in looking out for themselves, and nothing to work with, and no land" (Hurmence 1984: 79). As former slave Booker T. Washington (1856–1915) argued, Southern politicians did not help matters when they yielded "to the temptation to use the negro as a means to lift themselves into political power and eminence" (Campbell 1899: 17).

In 1899, Robert F. Campbell claimed that "no one deems it either possible or desirable to re-instate the institution of slavery" (p. 19). In all likelihood, he was correct because it would have been irrational to pay the high cost of reinstituting chattel slavery when so many close substitutes were available. Freedman Jacob Manson put the matter succinctly when he recalled that "slavery was a mighty bad thing. … It's been no bed of roses since," he conceded, but nominal freedom meant that "no one could whip me no more" (Hurmence 1984: 43). Elites, however, could still exploit him economically and did so according to economist historians Roger Ransom and Richard Sutch, who noted that while freed slaves gained from emancipation, their gains were but a single step from slavery to freedom (Ransom and Sutch 2001: 2). The law saw to that. When former slaves would not work on plantations voluntarily, the government coerced them to work. Although the freedpersons enjoyed some property and civil rights, the infamous black codes prevented them from earning a competitive wage. In Mississippi, for example, the law empowered any white to arrest any black person who quit their employment. Moreover, any person who offered work to a laborer already under contract was fined $500, a hefty sum in the postbellum South (Foner 1983: 10, 49). "Every negro is required to be in the regular service of some white person or former owner," Carl Schurz told readers in 1903, "who shall be responsible for the conduct of said negro."

Without an elite sponsor, blacks and even poor whites could be scooped up, convicted of vagrancy or found to be in debt, sold to the highest bidder, and put to hard labor (Edwards 1998: 329). "According to this nefarious system, which is but a thinly disguised slavery," a newspaper reported in 1903, "a Negro would be accused of some trifling offence, such as owing a dollar or two, or of being a vagrant, whereupon he would, with or without a legal trial, be fined a sum like five dollars." Then a planter would pay his fine and have him "work it out," which might take years to do, during which time the poor victims were "treated practically as slaves." Such practices, the newspaper assured readers, existed "for the most part in obscure sections, removed from railroad centres" (Anon.).

At the same time, South Africa was developing a system called Apartheid that was designed to keep blacks in their place, separated from white society but also subjected to monopoly conditions in the labor market. South Africa's blacks were more or less geographically trapped, but by

1900 African-Americans began to leave the South for Northern cities in discernible numbers (Foner 1983: 32–33). "Already the scarcity of labor is the despair of large landowners," Charles Galloway reported in 1904, and it will get worse because there were "few negroes in ... Mississippi, the owners of property, who would not sell out at a fair valuation. Many of the thriftiest and most conservative feel, whether justly or not, that sentiment is so hostile to their race as to make all their values insecure." They left "as opportunity offers" (p. 6). Galloway argued that while whites and blacks could not amalgamate in the same churches and schools, blacks should have "the equal protection of the law" (p. 8). "It is naturally and notoriously easier to convict a poor negro of any crime," he complained, "than a white man who has influential friends and well paid counsel" (p. 14).

Debt bondage was not just the product of the postbellum US South, it was the most commonly used way of enslaving others in modern post-emancipation societies. Its grip is particularly strong in South and Southeast Asia, where it was used extensively for centuries if not millennia (Quirk 2011: 194). Much like slavery, debt bondage is a global phenomenon, and even permeates the Middle East despite religious prohibitions on the taking of interest (Clarence-Smith 2006: 76–78). In Thailand, in the eighteenth and nineteenth centuries, for example, up to half the population was bonded. India's Workman's Breach of Contract Act of 1859 rendered breaking a labor contract a legally punishable offense; enslavers used it to reduce wage laborers to debt peons (Kara 2012: 25).

"Under the guise of Peonage," Kathleen Simon wrote in 1929, "cruelties and atrocities have been committed in modern times, for which it is difficult to find a parallel even in the terrible history of slavery" (pp. 135–36). Debts are often considered hereditary so that offspring can be ensnared. Often, even poor indentured laborers, already tied down by indenture contracts and almost insurmountable physical barriers to escape, were also burdened with debts for food, travel, and interest. Their creditors made groups of indentured laborers jointly responsible for all their debts and planters jacked up prices at the plantation store, rendering escape impossible, not just improbable (Tinker 1993: 133, 179, 212). The promissory notes creditors induced indentured laborers to sign were technically illegal, but as one government report stated, it was "abundantly clear ... that the *kangany* [enslaver] considers that he has some sort of property in the labourer, and that the labourer accepts this position" (Tinker 1993: 180).

Although debt may seem voluntary, fraud runs throughout the system. People are charged for specious services without their prior knowledge or consent, charged rates of interest they do not understand or did not agree to, and so forth (Quirk 2011: 195–96). Often, debt bondage is just slavery in a new garb. Instead of buying and selling people, their debts are bought and sold, but the effect is the same (Miers 2004: 7). In late nineteenth century Britain, the sale of peon debt contracts in public was so blatant that one observer wrote of a market were where "you can buy a man—no, not a man, but a human shaped animal for £15" (Rymer 1873: 3).

Another major form of slavery in the twentieth century was, for lack of a better term, state slavery. While convicts often slaved away for the emolument of the government, state slavery was more akin to the ancient practice of corvee, the typically temporary enslavement of a nation's denizens for toil on public works like canals, dams, defensive fortifications, and so forth. Essentially a form of in-kind taxation, the corvee, like the military draft, was initially limited in both the duration and severity of the labor exacted. But governments claiming unlimited power found it difficult to stay within bounds, so soon many people preferred private enslavement to private persons over enslavement to a grasping state. In Indonesia, corvee service was so notorious that slaves refused manumission so that they would not be subjected to it and freemen willingly fell into debt peonage to avoid it. Corvee obligations were also important in Thailand circa 1800. Slaves there had to put in eight days of labor a year or pay 1.5 baht while various types of commoners owed the monarch from one month to six months labor each year, or up to 24 baht. Haiti, too, initiated a corvee system in its Rural Code of 1864 (Childs 2015: 8, 82–84; Simon 1929: 175; Klein 1993: 5; Campbell 2004: xv; Reid 1993: 79; Feeny 1993: 89; Skinner 2008: 12–13).

In Southeast Asia witches, twins, and crippled or deformed people became slaves of the state, presumably because no one else wanted them. Many of the Europeans enslaved by Muslim corsairs in the sixteenth through nineteenth centuries became public slaves owned by the divan of Algiers or Tunis and put to work on galleys or on construction projects (Delaye 2004: 132–33; Davis 2003: 12).

Not to be outdone, the totalitarian states of the twentieth century took the state-owned slave system to new heights, or rather lows. During the Great War, Germany enslaved Belgian men and set them "to work against the lives of their own people" (Noyes 1917: 146). After that war and the revolutions it engendered, the new Soviet Union's gulag system ensnared millions of comrades, and even a few Americans like John P. Littlefield and Arthur John Kujala, on the flimsiest of pretexts (Kloosterboer 1960:

174–90; Kujala 1940: 108–13). During World War II, the Japanese forced conquered Asian peoples to build fortifications, railroads, and to work in mines, and so forth, while the German Nazis enslaved Jews and other conquered peoples. The Japanese also forced some 100,000 Korean girls into prostitution for their servicemen. Many killed themselves or died literally on the job. Most survivors were so traumatized that they could not speak about the experience until almost half a century later (Sato 2004; Quirk 2011: 19; Brown 2000: 8). The Soviet gulag system continued to grow after the war while the Chinese developed for political prisoners a similar prison factory system called Re-education Through Labor (Bales and Soodalter 2009: 142). North Korea has something similar and is so repressive that practically all of its denizens could be rightly called slaves of the state (Quirk 2011: 3). Meanwhile, the Belgians in the Congo forced peasants to work on Crown or corporate lands for little or no recompense and, under Papa Doc Duvalier, Haiti's government tricked its own citizens into becoming slaves in the Dominican Republic (Anon. 1904a: 126; Skinner 2008: 16).

Post-emancipation societies also spurred the growth of so-called slaves without owners. This was not meant in the old Roman legal sense but rather was used to describe tramps, hoboes, and other types of itinerant workers (Buckland 1908: 2). By definition, these unfortunates freely traveled regions, nations, continents, and even the globe looking for work. In that sense they were perfectly free, but wherever they went they faced other forms of repression, including police beat downs. In the United States, they were subject to the Tramp Acts, which made it illegal to travel without a visible means of support, especially via the railroads. Tramps regularly received sentences ranging from one to three months and they almost never could pay their fines so they fell into the convict labor system (Harring 1977). Jack London (1876–1916), later author of *The Call of the Wild* and other classics, was one victim of the Tramp Acts, forced to work hard on a diet of bread and water on a 16-man chain gang following his conviction in a make believe trial (London 1907).

Migrant workers who managed to avoid the tramp and vagrancy traps were generally at the mercy of their employers. They could be fired at will and generally suffered poor conditions in the agriculture, agricultural processing, mining, lumbering, and construction industries. They slept in bunk houses, bachelor shacks, barns, tents, and even under the stars. And for those privileges they often had to pay agency fees for jobs and were often paid less than advertised (Higbie 2003: 25–65). And when on the job they had to follow their employers' rules. In the 1880s, on the Clover Leaf Farm of D. C. Smith in North Dakota, for example, no alcohol was allowed, lights had to be turned out at 9 p.m., and firearms could be possessed only with permission. Dancing and scuffling, Smith admitted, "are all right in their places, but the place is out of the house." Most damning of all, perhaps, Smith expected his workers to use only "proper speech" (Higbie 2003: 43).

Such workplace rules may seem innocuous and even common sense, but they did represent a diminution of worker freedom and could extend even over the personal (non-work) lives of employees. The term employee, in fact, is of relatively recent vintage. Workers, even for corporations like the British East India Company, were first called servants. The term, and the application of master-servant law and tradition, showed wage laborers that they remained servile, not free, which is why throughout the modern period to the end of the nineteenth century, the goal of most people was not wage labor but proprietorship. Almost everyone, including (and perhaps especially) former slaves, wanted their own farm, shop, or store, where they would be the boss (recall the high freedom score of the CEO) and earn competitive returns for their efforts (Edwards 1998; Foner 1983: 41; Patterson 1982: 2).

Proslavery theorists and socialists used the term wage slave too glibly as wage laborers and peasants had discernibly more freedom, de jure and typically de facto, than slaves did (Brougham 1807: 21; Channing 1839: 26). George Fitzhugh, who claimed that "the master allows the slave to retain a larger share of the results of his own labor, than do the employers of free labor," was just outright empirically incorrect (1857: 25). Advocates of slavery were certainly correct in pointing out, however, that wage laborers were far from "free," not because laborers' freedom was economically fragile and hence "an empty and delusive mockery" (p. 26), as Fitzhugh claimed, but because (in addition to onerous or intrusive workplace rules) most workers were, in fact, not legally free to tell their employers, as country and western singer Johnny Paycheck later did, to take their job and shove it (Rockman 2006: 353–56). They were bound to finish out their contracts or suffer the consequences, which in some times and places meant criminal prosecution, loss of accrued wages, and even forcible return to work. While such practices strike us as antithetical to wage labor, they were, in fact, commonplace in the Western world, having arisen from laws and customs that arose as serfdom gave way in Western Europe. Only if a landlord/employer consented could a former serf lawfully move on (Pelteret 1995: 88). Labor contracts were for long terms and criminal, not civil, affairs.

It took several centuries for free labor to evolve out of wage labor but even in the early twentieth century, when the process was more or less complete in the United States (except during wartime emergencies), vulnerable wage workers could be exploited by the unscrupulous. In some parts of the US West in the late nineteenth and early twentieth centuries, monopsonists exploited wage laborers by gaining control of local labor markets and using their market power to extract job fees and other payments from workers. Leon Skliris, for example, almost completely controlled the labor market in Bingham Canyon, Utah while his brother ran the Panhellenic Grocery store, which charged workers exorbitant prices (Steinfeld 1991, 2001; Engerman 1996: 32–33; Peck 1996: 848).

Skliris and his ilk, called padrones, essentially engaged in arbitrage, exploiting the difference between what (generally unskilled immigrant) workers would accept and what corporations would pay. They also exploited ethnic or national trust. Antonio Cordasco, for example, controlled Italian workers by promising that "there will be no tricks or schemes" (Peck 1996: 852). These labor lords did provide a service, moving immigrants from US cities or abroad to points to where they were needed, when they were needed, en masse. Ironically, the corporations could not obtain their workers themselves because they wished to avoid liability for breaking immigration laws like the Foran Act, which was supposed to stamp out the very padrone systems it actually aided and abetted. Workers suffered the system to exist if they had families to care for back in Italy or Greece. Mexican solos, however, often jumped jobs after receiving free transportation paid for by the padrones (Peck 1996: 853–55, 860).

Producerists like the Knights of Labor used the term wage slavery because owners did not allow workers to sell the fruits of their labor but rather alienated laborers from their work. Later in the nineteenth century, as the heyday of the proprietor-artisan slipped from memory, the American Federation of Labor (AFL) dropped the term. Rather than try to challenge societal structures or change industrial ownership, it increasingly concentrated on bread and butter issues like improved wages and working conditions (Hallgrimsdottir and Benoit 2007). After wage laborers became free laborers, able to quit their employment on short notice without even the loss of pay, unions became even more focused on their members' level of compensation rather than their level of freedom, which the unions themselves somewhat diminished through closed shop policies and wage constraints.

The last of the major post-emancipation neoslaveries was termed white slavery because it was thought to ensnare primarily white maidens. (The first white slaves were of course chattel slaves with light complexions born of slave mothers and their white masters [Baptist 2014: 107]. Many of the so-called fancy maids or concubines were nearly white to begin with, so when they gave birth, their offspring were often physically indistinguishable from people of entirely European ancestry [Schermerhorn 2015: 141].) In the modern sense, the term white slavery dated to 1885, when W. T. Stead, editor of *Pall Mall Gazette*, brought the child prostitution system of London to light. By the turn of the twentieth century, white slavery, in the sense of the enslavement of young females for sex, was considered widespread, though the actual extent of it is still hotly debated to this day. In fact, the white slavery of the late nineteenth and early twentieth centuries is remarkably similar to sex trafficking today (Devereux 2000; Bingham 1911). Some women, the story was, became prostitutes because they wanted to or had no other choices but many prostitutes, as a muckraking expose put it in 1909, were "forced or decoyed into the life of shame against their will" (Anon. 1909: 528). With changes to a few minor details, the rest of the article could come right out of a book on the twenty-first century by Bales or Kara:

A young Italian or Jewess in Europe has heard wonderful stories of America ... A young man of her own race makes her acquaintance; gains her confidence; promises her ... little to do and plenty to get; if necessary, wins her love and promises her marriage; in some instances has been known actually to marry her; brings her to America with him ... takes her to a house of ill fame; and there she finds herself a prisoner. Perhaps the first night of her residence she is the victim of assault, and enters on the life prepared for her very despair ... perhaps her ineffective resistance is overcome by starvation and blows.

The salacious nature of the trade rendered it rife for exaggeration and sensationalism (Anon. 1913b: 348). From the 500 or so convictions under the Mann Act, the main policy response to the white slavery scare in America, between its passage in June 1910 and late 1913, it appears that non-trivial numbers of women were, in fact, being forced into prostitution. Later, many prosecutions under the Mann Act were clearly trumped up, more about adultery (Anon. 1913a: 477), xenophobia (Anon. 1911: 567), and wild parties that happened to cross state lines (Anon. 1922e: 9) than forced prostitution. But others appear to have been legitimate cases of trafficking. In 1922 alone, a woman was sought by authorities for enticing a girl into shoplifting, apparently to get some leverage on her so that she would join a brothel (Anon. 1922i). A Jersey City girl was enticed to visit Stroudsburg, Pennsylvania where she was enslaved by a farm couple on the threat of death until her father, tipped off by one of the farmers' boarders, rescued her (Anon. 1922d: 1). A ring in Indiana bent on "the traffic of girls of the mountains of Virginia" was broken up (Anon. 1922h: 16). A woman from Norristown, Pennsylvania abducted and held by a man in Baltimore for three years finally got up the courage to run away and the police helped her (Anon. 1922g: 2). In Chicago, traffickers deliberated hooked a young girl on morphine, broke her in "a house of ill repute," and then sold her to a brothel in Manhattan (Anon. 1922c). The white slave trade even infected rural South Dakota, where in tiny Milbank a couple enticed a teenage girl from the Twin Cities for "immoral purposes." The police, with help from concerned railroad workers, reportedly saved the girl before she was despoiled (Anon. 1922f: 7).

White slavery was also a major issue in Europe, though quiescent during the Great War. The poverty that followed the peace in Central Europe, however, brought it back into the spotlight. Most stories were about unemployed Central European girls tricked by "employment agents" into going to South America where good paying jobs allegedly awaited. "When they are landed in a strange place thousands of miles from home, in a city whose language they do not speak and with not a penny of money," Milton Bronner lamented in 1922, "they realize their real plight."

Due to the Greco-Turkish War and Russian Revolution there also appears to have been a considerable traffic in Balkan and Central Asian girls to Constantinople (Anon. 1922b: 2). "I am glad," said Miss Anne Baker, secretary of the National Vigilance Association of Great Britain, "there is practically no white slavery either in Britain or the United States because both countries have such rigid immigration laws and such strict supervision over passports" (Bronner 1922). Apparently, however, that was wishful thinking on Miss Baker's part because just months earlier Ann Mason told newspapers, from personal experience, "that many girls from the United States are being forced into white slavery after being lured to Central and South America by men who sign them up in this country as cabaret and musical hall performers." After Ann learned the truth, an NGO in Cristobal called The Young Women's Christian Association (YMCA) provided her and another disillusioned young lady transportation back to New York City (Anon. 1922a: 25).

One of the great ironies of the white slave scare was that most women forced into prostitution were not white at all but rather Asian (Quirk 2011:

220–24; Mihalopoulos 2011: 117).[1] But the term white slavery helped to induce religious leaders and journalists to wage holy war against brothels, madams, and pimps with the support of many middle-class Americans and even the League of Nations (Bales and Soodalter 2009: 10–11; Lyttleton 1924: 448).

Slavery, as it exists today, is usually divided into sex trafficking and labor slavery, which includes working in a wide variety of sectors from agriculture to construction to mining and manufacturing. Both labor slavery and sex trafficking are direct outgrowths of both traditional practices and the neoslaveries that emerged in post-emancipation societies. As noted above, sex trafficking today looks a lot like the white slavery of a century ago, minus the racial connotations. Similarly, (non-sex) labor slavery is clearly an extension of the convict labor and debt peonage systems of the nineteenth and early twentieth centuries. Haitians working in Dominican Republic sugar fields and forest clearers in Para in frontier Brazil, for example, are today often paid in tokens good only at the company store as if it was 1900 in the US South or Appalachia (Kara 2012: 139–44; Ould 2004: 59; Quirk 2011: 3).

Although not typically chattel slavery, slavery today is not new in the sense of being sui generis nor is it new in the sense of being radically different from that which came before. After a quick primer on new technologies, the pimp, slave trader, or enslaver of old would have no trouble plying their dastardly trades again today. That is because slavery never went away but rather was forgotten or relegated to niches. It was easy to forget slavery, especially in Western Europe and other places that did not suffer a bout of modern chattel slavery on their home territory (Hall et al. 2014: 17). Neoslaves are also more difficult to discern unless one knows when, where, and how, to look (Skinner 2008: xvii–xviii). "When I began to write *Female Sexual Slavery* in the mid-1970s," Kathleen Barry recalled in 1979, "the subject had been so effectively buried that there was hardly a trace of evidence that women were being forced into prostitution and trafficked from one country to another. 'White slavery' had become an historical artifact" (p. xi). It never occurred to most Americans that the missing children whose pictures they put on their milk cartons should have been advertised on *leche* (Spanish for milk) cartons instead as many of the children, thanks to corrupt federales in Mexico, ended up in the sex trade south of the border and abroad (Bales and Soodalter 2009: 95).

What Barry found in the 1970s were enslavement practices virtually identical to the white slavery practices described above and by writers today. Enslavers trick young women into loving them or falling into debt to them. They use either or both as leverage to get them to travel, on their own accord generally, to places where they have no connections or even language skills. To smooth over bumps, enslavers put police officers on the payroll, and so forth (Murphy 2014: 234). "Once a procurer has drawn a young woman in by his attention to her and she commits her affection to him," Barry explained, "it is relatively easy for him to transport her to a brothel." If she resisted, then she would be raped, tortured, beaten, and/or drugged into submission (Barry 1979: 5). Clearly, little had changed a quarter of a century later when Louise Brown noted that "contrary to popular myth, large numbers of girls are not abducted, drugged and then forced into prostitution. Agents do not need to go to such lengths. … Strategies that use love and friendships as a means to procure and traffic girls," she explained, "are far more common than the use of outright force" (Brown 2000: 62, 70).

In fact, Barry's book was just one of a long line of tomes that describe slavery in the late twentieth and early twenty-first centuries (Bales and Soodalter 2009: 7–10). "I was impelled to write this book as a duty to my own conscience, as an appeal to all I can reach—and in the hope that this survey may do something to raise up liberators for the millions of slaves in the world today" (p. xi) was a sentence that could have been expressed by Bales, Barry, Brown, Kara, Skinner, or any number of other recent writers. In fact, though, those sentiments were penned by Kathleen Simon in her 1929 book *Slavery*, which listed Abyssinia (Ethiopia), Arabia, Burma, China, Liberia, Nepal, Sierra Leone, and Sudan as slavery hotspots. All remain regions of concern to this day. Her book also covered "Other Forms of Servitude" and "Forced Labour," which included peonage, contract labor, child labor, and pawning, all major concerns to this day (p. 135). According to enslavers, people are not outright sold today. Rather, they are pawned, or in other words, used as collateral for loans. In Thailand, they call it *tok khiew*, or green harvest, because it is an adaptation of the custom of pledging unharvested rice in return for a loan. In practice, though, pawning and selling amount to the same thing, the commoditization of human flesh and spirit (Brown 2000: 43, 54, 84).

Today's slaves are rarely chattel slaves whose children will automatically become slaves, but many are darn close, especially in the remote mountains of Asia (Reid 1993: 64). Siddarth Kara and Benjamin Skinner have recently shown that little has changed there or in South Asia (from Pakistan south and east) more broadly. For an initial debt of 62 cents, three generations of laborers were bonded in India. (One third-generation bonded laborer, Prakash, did not know how much debt his family allegedly owed, suggesting that a fourth generation was in danger.) Where bonded laborers are not turned into perpetual slaves it is because enslavers do not want to be tied down. Knowing that they can never justify their practices, they have no pretensions to paternalism so they jettison slaves whenever they become insufficiently profitable (Kara 2009: 64–65, 155; Kara 2012: 163; Skinner 2008: 206, 253; Brass 2013: 8).

According to Kara, bonded laborers in South Asia can be beaten, tortured, denied credit, and family members can be sold to traffickers to repay outstanding debts. Bidi rollers in India can be evicted from their huts but even then they are not allowed to stray far from their place of work (Kara 2012: 98).

Chattel slaves also exist today in Mauritania and Niger, both of which had to recently abolish slavery yet again. The lives of those poor unfortunates include torture, sexual abuse, dispossession, systematic labor exploitation, arduous work, and separation of families. Others, not technically chattel slaves, suffer similar fates. Bonded labor is so closely related to chattel slavery in practice that outsiders have difficulty telling the two apart (Quirk 2011: 168, 176–77, 193). Consider the plight of workers in Madhya Pradesh in India described by Kara as having been "forced to work and sleep in the fields for weeks on end." The workers were not allowed to gather or talk in groups and punishments included electrocution and other forms of torture (Kara 2012: 72).

Traditionally, enslavers typically preferred to enslave "the other," or in other words people of a different ethnicity, nationality, race, or tribe, or a former member of "us" who committed a crime or fell into debt. The same holds true today, but today's slavery is so globalized that it has become equal opportunity in the sense that all races, religions, and genders can become enslavers or enslaved. Today's slaves are often branded or tattooed or forced to shave their heads or wear clothes that identify them as someone's property, just as the slaves of old were, especially where slavery was not racialized (Quirk 2011: 25; Bales and Soodalter 2009: 6, 90; Resendez 2016: 62–63; Davis 1966: 49).

Outside of war zones like the Sudan, large-scale slave raiding stops wherever slavery becomes technically illegal. Enslavers instead use coercion and deception. Where slavery is illegal, and today that is essentially the entire globe, enslavers tend to focus on women and children because they are less costly to control or hide from view. Some of the women are kidnapped, others are sold by family members, others are tricked or defrauded, while still others find themselves desperately in debt (Quirk 2011: 97, 107–8, 231).

Children have always been subject to enslavement but they are probably more highly represented in slavery today than ever before. Children from poor homes traditionally sent to relatives are now sold to the highest bidder. Child slaves in Haiti, called restavecs, number in the hundreds of thousands. Beatings and sexual abuse are rampant and many turn to prostitution when kicked out at age 15, when legally they have to be paid for the first time. Yet the old myth that restavecs are part of the family keeps many at work, some all day, every day (Nizan 2004; Berlan 2004; van den Anker 2004: 24; Skinner 2008: 7, 34; Cadet 1998; Murphy 2014: 19, 42–43).

Enslavers today also take advantage of existing vulnerabilities, like deafness, that do not render the enslaved incapable of certain types of work, like prostitution or begging. If they cannot find a vulnerability, they create one, like drug addiction. Or they use sleep, food, or water deprivation to keep their victims disoriented (Kara 2009: 17; Ould 2004: 58; Skinner 2008: 124; Bales and Soodalter 2009: 120; Murphy 2014: 35, 235).

Enslavers sometimes control their victims with violence, from beatings to rape (of the victim or the victim's spouse) to murder (Kara 2012: 68, 71; Bales and Soodalter 2009: 55–56). "Traffickers shot dead four Romanian girls," Skinner reported, "when they refused to have sex with horses" (Skinner 2008: 133). The Yakuza in Japan also kill prostitutes who do not toe the line. Sometimes actual chains are used, as they were in the case of Arati, who was sold into prostitution in Mumbai when she was nine years old and chained by the ankle to the bed. Other slaves report living in fortress-like brothels, locked in rooms, and watched by guards directly or via closed circuit television (Brown 2000: 111, 114, 160–62, 181, 184, 215; Kara 2012: 71). But why pay for a bunch of big knuckleheads to sit around most of the time when slaves can be forced to monitor other slaves, for fear enslavers will seek retribution against them or make them work more or harder if one of their number resists? And the old threat of being sold "down the river," that is, to an even worse master or situation, keeps many of the enslaved in check. Just as the mere mention of Mississippi used to cow slaves in antebellum Virginia, the threat of being sold to Albanians keeps forced prostitutes in line today (Kara 2012: 12; Murphy 2014: 20, 76).

Enslavers typically kill women, and/or their families and enslaved friends, if they attempt escape. Recall that in *Uncle Tom's Cabin*, Simon Legree killed Tom due to the disappearance of Cass and Emmeline (Stowe 1852). Today, the decision to kill slaves is much more easily made as slaves are cheaply replaced and their deaths serve as a vivid example to the other victims of enslavement. Some enslavers purposely father children just to gain leverage over their slaves. Others, like fishing boat captains in South and Southeast Asia, shoot their slaves and throw them overboard at the end of the season because they are cheaper to replace than to feed and control in the off season (Brown 2000: 122; Skinner 2008: 150; Kara 2009: 192; Kara 2012: 108).

Often more common and effective, though, is the *threat* of violence to the enslaved or their families, often in graphic detail (Kara 2012: 92; Skinner 2008: 136, 192; Bales and Soodalter 2009: 21; Kara 2009: 182, 187, 196), along with sundry other "invisible chains"[2] that create "a chain around the brain" (Bales and Soodalter 2009: 24) of the slave. The chains of slavery are created by the victim's inability to see beyond his or her imprisonment (Bales and Soodalter 2009: 19). Some psychological control techniques are so successful that slaves do not consider themselves victims and hence eschew help (Batstone 2010: 189). Just as centuries ago, when a European in bondage to the Moors admitted that "in time we were so habituated to Bondage, that we almost forgot Liberty, and grew stupid, and senseless of our Slavery" (Davis 2003: 103), slaves today often become inured to their plight through various seasoning techniques (Murphy 2014: 87). (That is when slaves become zombified according to Haitian lore [Baptist 2014: 145–46; Skinner 2008: 38].) UNESCO reported in 1975, for example, that victims of the brutal *maisons d'abattage* in Paris were "passive and apathetic, unable to readjust to freedom" (Barry 1979: 4).

Sometimes, the enslaved is brainwashed or socialized into believing that his or her slavery is natural. Many feel duty bound to pay their debts no matter how trumped up, false, or fraudulent their basis. In South Asia, for example, debts are considered family obligations, not individual ones, so they transfer from one generation to the next. (This belief is apparently on the wane but enslavers are certain to do all in their power to enliven the tradition.) Sometimes, though, the enslaved person wants desperately to escape but law enforcement officials do not believe slavery or even coercion was used to detain the worker because they do not see chains or physical scars (McDougall 2007: 175; Bales and Soodalter 2009: 52; Kara 2012: 2; Quirk 2011: 208; Batstone 2010: 228).

Other times, the enslaved are simply disoriented by their new surroundings and their new names. Many victims of sex trafficking, Brown reported in 2000, argued that they could not run away because they did not know where or how to obtain help. Often, they did not know where they were and could not speak the local language (Brown 2000: 75, 122). Many slaves are afraid of local law enforcement officials, sometimes rightly so but other times due to lies fed them by enslavers or their minions. Those enslaved in the United States, for example, are shown violent television shows and movies and told they are essentially documentaries. Running away only to end up in a real life version of *Sons of Anarchy* or *The Wire* is not very appealing. Child slaves are especially prone to such brainwashing. Enslavers often give them new names and tell them that their parents sold or abandoned them (Bales and Soodalter 2009: 20, 23). Too often, such stories are true but sometimes they serve to prevent the children from trying to return home. This is all reminiscent of the psychological ops used by slaveholders in the antebellum US South when they told their bondsmen that runaways were killed when in reality they made it to Canada or that Yankee troops would shoot them on sight (Kara 2009: 148; Hurmence 1984: 8, 20).

It is not by accident that the enslaved are typically trafficked to places where they have no local language, geographic, or legal knowledge. Rural Nepali women trafficked to Indian cities fear the city more than what goes on in the brothels; most report that they have no idea how to get home even if they could escape. It is also no accident that enslavers always seize their victims' passports and other forms of identification. Insufficient food and rest are other control mechanisms that also serve to maximize the enslavers' profits by keeping expenses low and revenues high. By carefully mixing slaves from different ethnic, racial, or religious backgrounds, enslavers can get them to turn on each other and then manage by dividing and ruling (Quirk 2011: 231; Bales and Soodalter 2009: 23–24; Brown 2000: 124, 228; Murphy 2014: 91).

Prostitutes are typically moved around frequently so that they do not make friends with other prostitutes or johns. Prostitution has been called a psychological prison created by rape and its associated shame, which is strong enough to keep many prostituted girls from even thinking about returning home (Brown 2000: 98, 111, 229).

Just as ancient slaveholders did, enslavers today also exploit their slaves' spiritual beliefs, including vodoo, juju, and other forms of magic (Vogt 1975: 64; Skinner 2008: 186; Kara 2009: 10, 16). A new technique, that makes sense only where slavery is illegal, is to force the enslaved to commit crimes, even rape and murder in the case of child soldiers in Africa, so the enslaved feel like they can never leave without suffering a worse fate at the hands of the authorities. For others, the threat of eviction from their housing is a sufficient deterrent to resistance (Batstone 2010: 8–10, 46, 106, 122, 235, 249; Kara 2012: 12).

About 15,000 people are trafficked into the United States each year from Africa, Asia, India, China, Latin America, and the former USSR and its satellites. That means that more slaves flow into America today than did back in the 1600s. Some people are so desperate to get to America that they pay $5000–$8000 to get there, and then are promptly enslaved. Some work in the sex industry while others toil as fruit pickers, construction workers, or gardeners and domestics in private homes. Slaves have also been liberated from US hotels, restaurants, laundries, and factories. Most eventually escape one way or another so there are "only" about 50,000 persons enslaved in America at any one time (Skinner 2008: 265; Bales and Soodalter 2009: 6–7, 131).

Those enslaved in domestic situations were traditionally thought to be better off than those enslaved in fields, mines, or factories. Stories out of Britain, Malaysia, and Saudi Arabia, as well as America, suggest that domestics can be just as harshly treated as slaves in other settings. One domestic, for example, was forced to clean the anuses of her owners' cats. Another was sodomized by a garden tool and forced to eat dog feces. In South Asia, the wives and children of male bonded laborers must perform domestic duties, including bestowing sexual favors on the master (Quirk 2011: 3; Anderson 2004: 109; Bales and Soodalter 2009: 4–5; Kara 2012: 175).

Slaves today, like slaves of old, may receive small cash payments from their masters but such payments are made at the discretion of the owner and are not the result of bargaining. In India, enslavers pay some brick makers with "tickets," a form of scrip, instead of cash. The peons can use the tickets to purchase goods from the enslaver at inflated prices but are not allowed to purchase elsewhere or to try to sell the tickets for real money (Firmo-Fontan 2004; Kara 2012: 81).

In the Bangladeshi shrimp growing industry, lease payments are set high enough so that most people fall in debt most years, wedding them to their employers. In the Bangladeshi shrimp processing industry 18–24 hour shifts are common. Even on their short breaks, workers are never allowed to leave the premises and they cannot leave the area of the plant until the end of the season. To enforce that rule, workers are paid only at the end of the season. Similar conditions pervade the tea and construction industries and are also found in domestic households, mines, glassworks, tanneries, precious stone/gem cutting operations, fireworks manufactories, silk work, and sari embroidery shops, as well as other industries (Kara 2012: 116–18, 125–27, 143, 173, 183).

Were that not enough, enslavers typically undercount bricks manufactured, bidis rolled, tea picked, and rocks broken. Peons who resist by breaking equipment simply find its value added to their debts. No wonder many workers in the Bangladeshi tea industry are descended from slaves who arrived in the country 150 years earlier (Kara 2012: 128–30, 149, 176–77).

The sex industry today is thriving and a large part of it apparently literally rests on the backs of enslaved women and children. (Some victims are boys; in places like Pakistan, more boys than girls may be prostituted.) Some men apparently actually prefer sex with slaves, but most do not care or think about the prostitute's score on the freedom scale. Taxi drivers usually know where men can find the type of paid sexual experiences they desire and can afford (Bales and Soodalter 2009: xviii; Brown 2000: 7, 13, 19, 99; Murphy 2014: 88).

Notes

1. Some claim that all prostitution is forced but that appears not to be strictly true (Barry 1979: xi; Mihalopoulos 2011: 8; Derrick 1975: 14). What is clear is Louise Brown's claim that "the further you descend in the prostitution hierarchy the less real and the less meaningful the element of choice actually becomes" (2000: 17).
2. "The chains of slavery are not always visible to the naked eye" (Anon. 1917: 456).

Bibliography

Adamson, A. H. (1972). *Sugar without slaves: The political economy of British Guiana, 1838–1904.* New Haven, CT: Yale University Press.

Allen, R. B. (2004). The Mascarene slave-trade and labour migration in the Indian Ocean during the eighteenth and nineteenth centuries. In G. Campbell (Ed.), *The structure of slavery in Indian Ocean Africa and Asia* (pp. 33–50). London: Frank Cass.

Anderson, B. (2004). Migrant domestic workers and slavery. In C. van den Anker (Ed.), *The political economy of new slavery* (pp. 107–117). New York: Palgrave Macmillan.

Anon. (1904a, April). The Congo 'slave' state. *Baptist Missionary Magazine*.

Anon. (1904b, April 6). Is England establishing a new slavery? *Christian Observer*.

Anon. (1909, November 6). The slave traffic in America. *Outlook*.

Anon. (1910b, June 11). Slavery emancipation in China. *Outlook*.

Anon. (1911, July 15). The punishment of a white slave trader. *Outlook*.

Anon. (1913a, August 28). What is white slavery? *The Independent: Devoted to the Consideration of Politics, Social and Economic Tendencies*.

Anon. (1913b, November). Is white slavery nothing more than a myth? *Current Opinion*.

Anon. (1917, September 20). A worse thing than slavery. *Life*.

Anon. (1922a, January 11). Girls lured into slavery. *Kansas City Star*.

Anon. (1922b, February 19). Stronghold of slavery: Innocent refugee girls enticed by promises of work into traps set by procurers. *Morning Oregonian*.

Anon. (1922c, August 14). Girl bares drug ring: Revival of white slave traffic revealed. *Morning Oregonian*.

Anon. (1922d, August 28). Child 'Farm Slave' says death threat kept her prisoner. *Philadelphia Inquirer*.

Anon. (1922e, October 20). White slavery charges facing state leaders. *Fort Worth Star Telegram*.

Anon. (1922f, December 1). Held on white slavery charge in county jail. *Aberdeen Daily News*.

Anon. (1922g, December 3). Woman flees after three years' 'Slavery'. *Philadelphia Inquirer*.

Anon. (1922h, December 15). Police probe white slave ring in state. *Fort Wayne News Sentinel*.

Anon. (1922i, December 19). Girl accused in shoplifting blames woman: White slave activity here is suspected. *Fort Worth Star Telegram*.

Armes, W. D. (Ed.). (1903). *The autobiography of Joseph Le Conte*. New York: D. Appleton and Co.

Bales, K. (2007). *Ending slavery: How we free today's slaves*. Berkeley: University of California Press.

Bales, Kevin. 2012. *Disposable people: New slavery in the global economy*, Rev. ed. Berkeley: University of California Press.

Bales, K., & Soodalter, R. (2009). *The slave next door: Human trafficking and slavery in America today*. Berkeley: University of California Press.

Baptist, E. E. (2014). *The half has never been told: Slavery and the making of American capitalism*. New York: Basic Books.

Barry, R. (1907, March). Slavery in the South to-day. *The Cosmopolitan: A Monthly Illustrated Magazine*.

Barry, K. (1979). *Female sexual slavery*. New York: New York University Press.

Batstone, David. 2010. *Not for sale: The return of the global slave trade and how we can fight it*, Rev. ed. New York: HarperCollins.

Beckert, S. (2004). Emancipation and empire: Reconstructing the worldwide web of cotton production in the age of the American Civil War. *American Historical Review, 109*, 1405–1438.
Berlan, A. (2004). Child labour, education and child rights among cocoa producers in Ghana. In C. van den Anker (Ed.), *The political economy of new slavery* (pp. 158–180). New York: Palgrave Macmillan.
Bingham, T. A. (1911). *The girl that disappears: The real facts about the white slave traffic*. Boston: Richard G. Badger.
Blackburn, R. (2011). *The American crucible: Slavery, emancipation and human rights*. New York: Verso.
Blackmon, D. A. (2008). *Slavery by another name: The re-enslavement of Black Americans from the Civil War to World War II*. New York: Anchor Books.
Brass, T. (2013). Debating capitalist dynamics and unfree labour: A missing link? *Journal of Development Studies, 50*, 1–13.
Bronner, M. (1922, July 27). Unsettled conditions result in resumption of terrible traffic. *Wilkes Barre Times Leader*.
Brougham, H. (1807). *A concise statement of the question regarding the abolition of the slave trade* (4th ed.). London: Longman, Hurst, Rees, and Orme.
Brown, L. (2000). *Sex slaves: The trafficking of women in Asia*. London: Virago Press.
Buckland, W. W. (1908). *The roman law of slavery: The condition of the slave in private law from Augustus to Justinian*. Cambridge: Cambridge University Press.
Bush, M. (1996). Introduction. In M. L. Bush (Ed.), *Serfdom and slavery: Studies in legal bondage* (pp. 1–17). New York: Addison Wesley Longman.
Cadet, J.-R. (1998). *Restavec: From Haitian slave child to middle-class American*. Austin: University of Texas Press.
Campbell, R. F. (1899). *Some aspects of the race problem in the South*. Asheville, NC: n.p.
Campbell, G. (2004). Introduction: Slavery and other forms of unfree labour in the Indian Ocean world. In G. Campbell (Ed.), *The structure of slavery in Indian Ocean Africa and Asia* (pp. vii–xxxii). London: Frank Cass.
Channing, W. E. (1839). *Remarks on the slavery question in a letter to Jonathan Phillips, Esq*. Boston: James Munroe and Company.
Childs, D. (2015). *Slaves of the state: Black incarceration from the chain gang to the penitentiary*. Minneapolis: University of Minnesota Press.
Clarence-Smith, W. G. (2006). *Islam and the abolition of slavery*. New York: Oxford University Press.
Collins, J. C. (Ed.). (1904). *Sir Thomas More's Utopia*. Oxford: Clarendon Press.
Conning, J., & Kevane, M. (2007). Freedom, servitude, and voluntary contracts. In K. A. Appiah & M. Bunzl (Eds.), *Buying freedom: The ethics and economics of slave redemption* (pp. 108–140). Princeton: Princeton University Press.

Davis, D. B. (1966). *The problem of slavery in Western culture*. Ithaca, NY: Cornell University Press.

Davis, R. C. (2003). *Christian slaves, Muslim masters: White slavery in the Mediterranean, the Barbary Coast, and Italy, 1500–1800*. New York: Palgrave Macmillan.

Dawson, E. C. (1930). *Missionary heroines of the Cross*. London: Seeley, Service & Co.

Delaye, K. (2004). Slavery and colonial representations in Indochina from the second half of the nineteenth to the early twentieth century. In G. Campbell (Ed.), *The structure of slavery in Indian Ocean Africa and Asia* (pp. 129–142). London: Frank Cass.

Derrick, J. (1975). *Africa's slaves today*. London: Allen & Unwin.

Devereux, C. (2000). 'The Maiden Tribute' and the rise of the white slave in the nineteenth century: The making of an Imperial construct. *Victorian Review, 26*, 1–23.

Edwards, L. (1998). The problem of dependency: African Americans, labor relations, and the law in the nineteenth-century South. *Agricultural History, 72*, 313–340.

Engerman, S. (1996). Slavery, serfdom and other forms of coerced labour: Similarities and differences. In M. L. Bush (Ed.), *Serfdom and slavery: Studies in legal bondage* (pp. 18–41). New York: Addison Wesley Longman.

Fahrenfort, J. (1960). Foreword. In W. Kloosterboer (Ed.), *Involuntary labor since the abolition of slavery: A survey of compulsory labour throughout the world* (p. vii). Leiden: E. J. Brill.

Feeny, D. (1993). The demise of corvee and slavery in Thailand, 1782–1913. In M. A. Klein (Ed.), *Breaking the chains: Slavery, bondage, and emancipation in modern Africa and Asia* (pp. 83–111). Madison: University of Wisconsin Press.

Firmo-Fontan, V. (2004). Responses to sexual slavery: From the Balkans to Afghanistan. In C. van den Anker (Ed.), *The political economy of new slavery* (pp. 91–106). New York: Palgrave Macmillan.

Fishback, P. (1989). Debt peonage in postbellum Georgia. *Explorations in Economic History, 26*, 219–236.

Fitzhugh, G. (1857). *Cannibals all! Or, slaves without masters*. Richmond: A. Morris.

Foner, E. (1983). *Nothing but freedom: Emancipation and its legacy*. Baton Rouge: Louisiana State University Press.

Freedmen's Bureau. (1870). *Reports of Generals Steedman and Fullerton on the condition of the Freedmen's Bureau in the Southern states*. Washington, DC: n.p.

Garrett, M. A., & Xu, Z. (2003). The efficiency of sharecropping: Evidence from the postbellum South. *Southern Economic Journal, 69*, 578–595.

Georgia Negro Peon. (1904, February 25). The new slavery in the South—An autobiography. *The Independent: Devoted to the Consideration of Politics, Social and Economic Tendencies*.

Grubb, F. (2011). *German immigration and servitude in America, 1709–1920*. New York: Routledge.

Hall, C., Draper, N., McClelland, K., Donington, K., & Lang, R. (2014). *Legacies of British slave-ownership: Colonial slavery and the formation of Victorian Britain*. New York: Cambridge University Press.

Hallgrimsdottir, H. K., & Benoit, C. (2007). From wage slaves to wage workers: Cultural opportunity structures and the evolution of the wage demands of the Knights of Labor and the American Federation of Labor, 1880–1900. *Social Forces, 85*, 1393–1411.

Harring, S. (1977). Class conflict and the suppression of tramps in Buffalo, 1892–1894. *Law & Society Review, 11*, 873–911.

Hicks, F. C. (1913, August 28). Convict labor in the United States. *The Independent: Devoted to the Consideration of Politics, Social and Economic Tendencies*.

Higbie, F. T. (2003). *Indispensable outcasts: Hobo workers and community in the American Midwest, 1880–1930*. Chicago: University of Illinois Press.

Hogendorn, J., & Lovejoy, P. E. (1992). Keeping slaves in place: The secret debate on the slavery question in northern Nigeria, 1900–1904. In J. Inikori & S. Engerman (Eds.), *The Atlantic slave trade: Effects on economies, societies, and peoples in Africa, the Americas, and Europe* (pp. 49–76). Durham, NC: Duke University Press.

Hurmence, B. (Ed.). (1984). *My folks don't want me to talk about slavery: Twenty-one oral histories of former North Carolina slaves*. Winston-Salem, NC: John F. Blair.

Ignatiev, N. (1995). *How the Irish became white*. New York: Routledge.

Jordan, D., & Walsh, M. (2007). *White cargo: The forgotten history of Britain's white slaves in America*. New York: New York University Press.

Kara, S. (2009). *Sex trafficking: Inside the business of modern slavery*. New York: Columbia University Press.

Kara, S. (2012). *Bonded labor: Tackling the system of slavery in South Asia*. New York: Columbia University Press.

Klein, M. (1993). Introduction: Modern European expansion and traditional servitude in Africa and Asia. In M. A. Klein (Ed.), *Breaking the chains: Slavery, bondage, and emancipation in modern Africa and Asia* (pp. 3–36). Madison: University of Wisconsin Press.

Kloosterboer, W. (1960). *Involuntary labor since the abolition of slavery*. Amsterdam: E. J. Brill.

Kolchin, P. (1996). Some controversial questions concerning nineteenth-century emancipation from slavery and serfdom. In M. L. Bush (Ed.), *Serfdom and slavery: Studies in legal bondage* (pp. 42–68). New York: Addison Wesley Longman.

Kujala, A. J. (1940, April). An American in Soviet jails. *The Living Age*.

Kumar, D. (1993). Colonialism, bondage, and caste in British India. In M. A. Klein (Ed.), *Breaking the chains: Slavery, bondage, and emancipation in modern Africa and Asia* (pp. 112–130). Madison: University of Wisconsin Press.

Leaf, E. H. (1937, March). Oriental miscellany: I. Bootleg slaves in China. *The Living Age*.

Lichtenstein, A. (1996). *Twice the work of free labor: The political economy of convict labor in the New South.* New York: Verso.

Lichtenstein, A. (2015). Flocatex and the fiscal limits of mass incarceration: Toward a new political economy of the postwar carceral state. *Journal of American History, 102*, 113–125.

London, J. (1907). *The Road.* New York: Macmillan.

Lovejoy, P. E. (2012). *Transformations in slavery: A history of slavery in Africa* (3rd ed.). New York: Cambridge University Press.

Lyttleton, D. E. (1924, November 19). The League's big little jobs. *Outlook.*

McDougall, E. A. (2007). Dilemmas in the practice of *rachat* in French West Africa. In K. A. Appiah & M. Bunzl (Eds.), *Buying freedom: The ethics and economics of slave redemption* (pp. 158–178). Princeton: Princeton University Press.

McLennan, R. (2008). *The crisis of imprisonment: Protest, politics, and the making of the American penal state, 1776–1941.* New York: Cambridge University Press.

Meagher, A. J. (2008). *The coolie trade: The traffic in Chinese laborers to Latin America, 1847–1874.* New York: Xlibris.

Meillassoux, C. (1991). *The anthropology of slavery: The womb of iron and gold.* Chicago: University of Chicago Press.

Miers, S. (2003). *Slavery in the twentieth century: The evolution of a global problem.* New York: Rowman & Littlefield.

Miers, S. (2004). Slavery: A question of definition. In G. Campbell (Ed.), *The structure of slavery in Indian Ocean Africa and Asia* (pp. 1–16). London: Frank Cass.

Mihalopoulos, B. (2011). *Sex in Japan's globalization, 1870–1930: Prostitutes, emigration and nation-building.* London: Pickering & Chatto.

Miles, R. (1987). *Capitalism and unfree labour: Anomaly or necessity?* New York: Tavistock Publications.

Millar, J. (1771/2006). *The origin of the distinction of ranks: Or, an inquiry into the circumstances, which give rise to influence and authority, in the different members of society.* Indianapolis: Liberty Fund.

Murphy, L. T. (2014). *Survivors of slavery: Modern-day slave narratives.* New York: Columbia University Press.

Nizan, R. (2004). Child labour in Latin America: Issues and policies in Honduras. In C. van den Anker (Ed.), *The political economy of new slavery* (pp. 137–175). New York: Palgrave Macmillan.

Noyes, A. (1917, January 24). 'The Lion of Flanders': The true history of the slave raids in Belgium. *Outlook.*

Oshinsky, D. M. (1997). *'Worse than slavery': Parchman farm and the ordeal of Jim Crow justice*. New York: Simon & Schuster.
Ould, D. (2004). Trafficking and international law. In C. van den Anker (Ed.), *The political economy of new slavery* (pp. 55–74). New York: Palgrave Macmillan.
Patterson, O. (1982). *Slavery and social death: A comparative study*. Cambridge: Harvard University Press.
Payne, E. G. (1912). *An experiment in alien labor*. Chicago: University of Chicago Press.
Peck, G. (1996). Reinventing free labor: Immigrant padrones and contract laborers in North America, 1885–1925. *Journal of American History, 83*, 848–871.
Pelteret, D. (1995). *Slavery in early mediaeval England: From the reign of Alfred until the twelfth century*. Rochester, NY: Boydell Press.
Pierson, H. W. (1870). *A letter to Hon. Charles Sumner, with 'statements' of outrages upon freedmen in Georgia*. Washington, DC: Chronicle Print.
Pound, R. (1909). Liberty of contract. *Yale Law Journal, 18*, 454–487.
Prakash, G. (1993). Terms of servitude: The colonial discourse on slavery and bondage in India. In M. A. Klein (Ed.), *Breaking the chains: Slavery, bondage, and emancipation in Modern Africa and Asia* (pp. 131–149). Madison: University of Wisconsin Press.
Quirk, J. (2011). *The anti-slavery project: From the slave trade to human trafficking*. Philadelphia: University of Pennsylvania Press.
Ransom, R., & Sutch, R. (2001). *One kind of freedom: The economic consequences of emancipation* (2nd ed.). New York: Cambridge University Press.
Reid, A. (1993). The decline of slavery in nineteenth-century Indonesia. In M. A. Klein (Ed.), *Breaking the chains: Slavery, bondage, and emancipation in modern Africa and Asia* (pp. 64–82). Madison: University of Wisconsin Press.
Resendez, A. (2016). *The other slavery: The uncovered story of Indian enslavement in America*. New York: Houghton Mifflin Harcourt.
Robinson, J. (1933). *The economics of imperfect competition*. London: Macmillan & Co.
Rockman, S. (2006). The unfree origins of American capitalism. In C. Matson (Ed.), *The economy of early America: Historical perspectives and new directions* (pp. 335–361). University Park: University of Pennsylvania Press.
Rymer, N. (1873, November 8). An English slave market—A relic of barbarity. *Miners' Advocate and Record*.
Salter, J. (1996). Adam Smith on slavery. *History of Economic Ideas, 4*, 225–251.
Saradamoni, K. (1973). Agrestic slavery in Kerala in the nineteenth century. *Indian Economic Social History Review, 10*, 371–385.
Sato, S. (2004). Forced labour mobilization in Java during the Second World War. In G. Campbell (Ed.), *The structure of slavery in Indian Ocean Africa and Asia* (pp. 97–110). London: Frank Cass.

Sawyer, L. P. (2013). Contested meanings of freedom: Workingmen's wages, the company store system, and the *Godcharles v. Wigeman* decision. *Journal of the Gilded Age and Progressive Era, 12*, 285–319.

Schermerhorn, C. (2015). *The business of slavery and the rise of American capitalism, 1815–1860.* New Haven, CT: Yale University Press.

Schurz, C. (1903, January). Can the South solve the Negro problem? *McClure's.*

Simon, K. (1929). *Slavery.* London: Hodder and Stoughton.

Skinner, E. B. (2008). *A crime so monstrous: Face-to-face with modern-day slavery.* New York: Free Press.

Smith, A. E. (1965). *Colonists in bondage: White servitude and convict labor in America, 1607–1776.* Gloucester, MA: Peter Smith.

Smith, J. D. (1985). *An old creed for the new South: Proslavery ideology and historiography, 1865–1918.* Athens: University of Georgia Press.

Stauffer, J. (2007). Frederick Douglass and the politics of slave redemptions. In K. A. Appiah & M. Bunzl (Eds.), *Buying freedom: The ethics and economics of slave redemption* (pp. 213–222). Princeton: Princeton University Press.

Steinfeld, R. J. (1991). *The invention of free labor: The employment relation in English & American law and culture, 1350–1870.* Chapel Hill: University of North Carolina Press.

Steinfeld, R. J. (2001). *Coercion, contract, and free labor in the nineteenth century.* New York: Cambridge University Press.

Stowe, H. B. (1852). *Uncle Tom's cabin: Or, negro life in the slave states of America* (3rd ed.). London: C. H. Clarke and Co.

Temperley, H. (1996). New World slavery, Old World slavery. In M. L. Bush (Ed.), *Serfdom and slavery: Studies in legal bondage* (pp. 144–157). New York: Addison Wesley Longman.

Tinker, H. (1993). *A new system of slavery: The export of Indian labour overseas, 1830–1920* (2nd ed.). London: Hansib Publishing Limited.

Tomlins, C. (2006). Indentured servitude in perspective: European migration into North America and the composition of the early American labor force, 1600–1775. In C. Matson (Ed.), *The Economy of Early America: Historical Perspectives and New Directions* (pp. 146–182). University Park: University of Pennsylvania Press.

Travis, J., Western, B., & Redburn, S. (Eds.). (2014). *The growth of incarceration in the United States: Exploring causes and consequences.* Washington, DC: National Academies Press.

Turley, D. (1996). Slave emancipations in modern history. In M. L. Bush (Ed.), *Serfdom and slavery: Studies in legal bondage* (pp. 181–196). New York: Addison Wesley Longman.

Turton, A. (2004). Violent capture of people for exchange on Karen-Tai borders in the 1830s. In G. Campbell (Ed.), *The structure of slavery in Indian Ocean Africa and Asia* (pp. 69–82). London: Frank Cass.

van den Anker, C. (2004). Contemporary slavery, global justice and globalization. In C. van den Anker (Ed.), *The political economy of new slavery* (pp. 15–36). New York: Palgrave Macmillan.

Vogt, J. (1975). *Ancient slavery and the ideal of man* (T. Wiedemann, Trans.). Cambridge: Harvard University Press.

Wergeland, A. M. (1916). *Slavery in Germanic society during the Middle Ages.* Chicago: University of Chicago Press.

White, S. (2014). Freedom's first con: African Americans and changing notes in antebellum New York City. *Journal of the Early Republic, 34*, 385–409.

Wilbur, C. M. (1967). *Slavery in China during the former Han Dynasty 206 B.C.—A.D. 25.* New York: Russell & Russell.

Wright, D. R. (1993). *African Americans in the early Republic.* Arlington Heights, IL: Harlan Davidson.

Wright, R. E. (2015). *Little business on the prairie: Entrepreneurship, prosperity, and challenge in South Dakota.* Sioux Falls, SD: Center for Western Studies.

Zaborney, J. (2012). *Slaves for hire: Renting enslaved laborers in antebellum Virginia.* Baton Rouge: Louisiana State University Press.

CHAPTER 5

That Which Is Seen: Enslavers' Profits

In his epic *L'Abolition de l'Esclavage*, nineteenth century French scholar Augustin Cochin argued that enslavers were simply mistaken in their belief that slavery was profitable. He lamented convincing them. "To seek to prove to men that they are injuring themselves, is in general to lose one's trouble," he explained, "for they believe themselves good judges of their own interests" (1863: 5). The enslavers were, in fact, good judges of their own interests. They were, however, either poor judges of the root causes of economic growth and development or they just did not care that their actions served to impoverish everyone. "From this position—the profitableness of slavery under given external conditions—the inference is generally made by those who advocate or look with indulgence on the system, that slavery must be regarded as conducive to at least the material well-being of countries in which these conditions exist" (Cairnes 1862: 46).

Enslaving others can give the appearance of helping the economy (increasing real per capita GDP or aiding development) because it is, generally speaking, a very lucrative endeavor for enslavers. Slavery could linger where it was only marginally economically viable due to custom, or fear of the social consequences of emancipation, but it could not have persisted so long (Chap. 3) and so tenaciously (Chap. 4) if it did not usually provide enslavers with something extra (Cairnes 1862: 48–49; Barzel 1977: 99; Finley 1980: 91). That something was what economists call monopsony rents, which are profits (residual earnings) greater than what would be earned in a competitive labor market.

R.E. Wright, *The Poverty of Slavery*,
DOI 10.1007/978-3-319-48968-1_5

One cannot move blithely from profitability to economic growth or development, however, without first considering what economists call negative externalities, or the costs of engaging in some economic activity that do not fall on market participants. (Negative for costs, as opposed to benefits, externalities for outside of the market.) An activity, like manufacturing, might produce high profits for producers while imposing even higher costs on society, through negative externalities like pollution. (The converse is also true but even less well understood. In other words, an unprofitable enterprise is not bad for the overall economy if it creates sufficient positive externalities, like information about consumer preferences that other producers can use to improve their goods [Davis 1966: 422].) As will be shown in Chaps. 6 and 7, slavery creates massive negative externalities that essentially swamp its marginal benefit (roundly, its profitability for enslavers). Little wonder, then, that people still want to enslave others even though societies now discourage the practice. (As discussed in Chap. 8, slavery continues because most societies do not yet discourage slavery enough.) "From an economic standpoint," Siddarth Kara correctly noted, "bonded labor agreements are highly inefficient for all parties involved, including society at large—except the exploiter" (2012: 12–13).

A difficult question to answer is why it took so long for non-enslavers/non-slaves to see that slavery effectively impoverished them. Part of the answer lies in the fact that the concept of externalities was not well understood until English economist Arthur Cecil Pigou (1877–1959) popularized their study in his 1920 book *The Economics of Welfare*. As discussed below, the notion that slavery could be profitable for some but contrary to the public good was set forth by some early thinkers, including by Montesquieu (1689–1755) and German scholar Johann Gottfried Herder (1744–1803), though in truncated form, and it certainly underlay some of the economic critiques of slavery a century later (Davis 1966: 407–8; Herder 2004: 63–64). Nevertheless, until the mid-nineteenth century the point was seldom emphasized or even clearly stated and enslavers and their apologists muddied the waters yet more by essentially asserting that slavery created positive externalities, like imperial grandeur (Prakash 1993: 143; Davis 1966: 128).

Since the Civil War, the overall tendency in the scholarly literature has been to conflate profitability with growth, with the caveat that it is difficult to discern where Marxists stood/stand on the matter due to their specialized terms and heterodox economic views (Brass 2013: 8–9; Darity 1992: 259, 263–65; Meillassoux 1991: 314; Davidson 2015: 63). Even the late great economist historian Robert Fogel sometimes seems to have forgotten about negative externalities, as when he claimed that his analysis of the profitability and efficiency of slavery showed that enslavement of others "enhanced rather than diminished the wealth of the new commercial and industrial classes of Great Britain" (Fogel 1989: 216).

A second reason why externalities have remained in the background is that, as Bastiat pointed out, many economic effects are not easily discerned. Negative externalities certainly fall into that category and therefore need to be actively sought out. It is much easier to concentrate on that which can be seen, as eighteenth century British economic statistician Malachy Postlethwayt (1707–1767) did when he breathlessly asserted that "the Negroe-Trade and the natural Consequences resulting from it, may be justly esteemed an inexhaustible Fund of Wealth and Naval Power to this Nation" (Davis 1966: 150).

Finally, negative externalities can be bloody difficult to quantitatively measure, which is one reason why Pigou's solution for them, a tax (called a Pigovian or Pigouvian tax) equal to the value of the negative externality, is not always possible to implement in a responsible manner.

The creation of large (if difficult to precisely measure) negative externalities by enslavement (the lower the freedom index score, the larger the externality) also renders it impossible to move from proof that slavery, under certain conditions, was more efficient than other labor forms to the conclusion that slavery helped the overall economy. (Efficiency simply means the ratio between inputs and outputs over some time. If A.B. can produce more than C.D. can, over the same span and using the same physical capital, then A.B. is said to be more efficient than C.D.) A factory that dumps poison into a river may very well be more efficient (and/or profitable) than one that does not, but if the costs imposed on people downstream were imposed on the polluter, it would find it more efficient to stop polluting. Similarly, a hundred slaves driven in a gang system might well produce more in a season than a hundred similarly equipped free people working for wages but if the slave system creates large negative externalities, the economic effects of its relative efficiency will be muted, wiped out, or even reversed.

That is an important point because it has been shown, to the satisfaction of most economist historians and economic historians, that slavery *was* more efficient than other labor forms in specific activities, places, and times (Wright 2006: 83). Context, though, was crucial. In the late antebellum period, German family farmers in Texas and Tennessee, despite their small scale, grew cotton of higher quality and more cheaply than the average slave labor camp did (Gray 1941: 1:480; Atkinson 1861: 12). "They produce more cotton to the acre," Hinton Helper noted, "and of a better quality, and selling at prices from a cent to a cent and a half a pound lower than that produced by slave labor" (Helper 1860: 301; Fogel and Engerman 1974: 173). The key, according to textile manufacturer Edward Atkinson (1827–1905), was a process whereby unneeded seed was used as fertilizer (1861: 21). Those successes raise the question why small farms and wage labor did not appear in the cotton belt after the Civil War. Carl Schurz doubted that it was given a fair chance. His view is quoted at length below because it accords with the notion, explained in Chap. 4, that the Civil War did not so much end slavery as it created new forms of servitude:

Unfortunately, the disorders necessarily growing out of the transition state continually furnished food for argument. I found but few people who were willing to make due allowance for the adverse influence of exceptional circumstances. By a large majority of those I came in contact with, and they mostly belonged to the more intelligent class, every irregularity that occurred was directly charged against the system of free labor. If negroes walked away from the plantations, it was conclusive proof of the incorrigible instability of the negro and the impracticability of free labor. If some individual negro violated the terms of his contract, it proved unanswerably that no negro had or ever would have a just conception of the binding force of a contract, and that this system of free negro labor was bound to be a failure. If some negroes shirked or did not perform their task with sufficient alacrity, it was produced as irrefutable evidence to show that physical compulsion was absolutely indispensable to make the negro work. If negro idlers or refugees crawling about the towns, applied to the authorities for subsistence, it was quoted as incontestably establishing the point that the negro was too improvident to take care of himself and must necessarily be consigned to the care of a master. I heard a Georgia planter argue most seriously that one of his negroes had shown himself certainly unfit for freedom because he impudently refused to submit to a whipping. I frequently went into an argument with those putting forth such general assertions, quoting instances in which negro laborers were working faithfully and to the entire satisfaction of their employers, as the employers themselves informed me. In a majority of cases the reply was that we Northern people did not understand the negro, but that they (the Southerners) did; that, as to the particular instances I quoted, I was probably mistaken; that I had not closely investigated the cases, or had been deceived by my informants; that they knew the negro would not work without compulsion, and that no one could make them believe he would. Arguments like these naturally finished such discussions. It frequently struck me that persons who conversed about every other subject calmly and sensibly would lose their temper as soon as the negro question was touched (1903).

Schurz blamed the Freedmen's Bureau, but of course throughout history slavery rarely, if ever, led directly to freedom.

Clearly, though, the widespread belief that slaves were *always* less efficient than wage laborers, a belief held by Enlightenment figures like Benjamin Franklin and Adam Smith, was simply untrue (Fogel 1989: 72; Salter 1996: 226; Eltis 1987: 235; Gray 1941: 1:444–80). Specifically, slaves on larger plantations worked in a gang system completing un- or semi-skilled tasks were more efficient than other types of laborers who simply would not submit to being driven like machines (Finley 1980: 91; Fogel 1989: 72–80). Enslaving nuclear scientists, by contrast, is a losing proposition for the enslaver (Adolf Hitler tried and failed) because the master could not easily discover shirking or even sabotage as there are numerous ways of subtly destroying the usefulness of an experiment or an equation. In short, where slaves could be closely supervised and inflicting pain was enough to induce them to work, slaves could be more efficient than free laborers, but where human capital was needed or close supervision was impracticable, free laborers are more efficient (Scheidel 2008: 107).

So Smith's contemporary John Millar was closer to the mark when he argued that slaves could be more efficient than wage labors if supervision costs were low (Salter 1996: 240). Otherwise, all told, "the work of a slave . . . is really dearer than that of a free man, to whom constant wages are given in proportion to his industry" (Millar 1771/2006: 252). Recently, economists Daron Acemoglu and Alexander Wolitzky have come to a similar conclusion, phrased in the language of coercion (Acemoglu and Wolitzky 2011). That means that slaves were more efficient in a wide range of un- and semi-skilled jobs, not just growing cotton and sugar, a fact with ominous implications for post-emancipation societies (Eltis 1987: 14).

Those who believed that slaves were less efficient than other types of workers of course found it difficult to explain why slavery existed and persisted. Ben Franklin said cheap land, which worked for colonial America perhaps but not for Asia or the ancients. Millar blamed habit, a lack of insight, and the pleasure of wielding power over others being "too agreeable to be easily relinquished" (Millar 1771/2006: 252). Smith similarly argued that a love of domination and authority rendered enslaving others desirable to some men (Finley 1980: 28; Salter 1996: 241). But more than some sort of Nietzchean will to power was required to maintain slave systems, Smith realized. So slaveholders leveraged their political power to protect their property, a point developed more thoroughly in Chap. 6 (Bales and Soodalter 2009: 30; Smith 1896: 96–97).

Some scholars have claimed that sometimes slavery was more about status or signaling wealth than production (Blackburn 1996: 158–59). That may have been true in a few instances but, again, the global history of slavery suggests that status could not have been the major motivator most of the time. Slavery appears to have been profitable everywhere it was extensively practiced for long periods, including the Northwest Coast of North America (Donald 1997: 86–88).

Where slavery was legal, enslavers sometimes underestimated their profits in order to make a pathetic pitch for (additional) government subsidies (Hall et al. 2014: 41). At the same time, enslavers claimed that their allegedly barely profitable businesses were absolutely crucial to the national economy, a proposition rightly lampooned by William Channing (Eltis and Engerman 2000; Channing 1839: 44). Henry Brougham took a more serious approach, countering the claim that "the African Trade opens a wide channel for the beneficial investment of capital, and that the Abolition by suddenly throwing out of employment so great a portion of stock, would give a serious blow to the commercial resources of the country" by pointing out that "the trade does not occupy any considerable part of the national capital … and that the same capital, if excluded from this employment, would immediately and easily find a more advantageous vent" (Brougham 1807: 33). More on that crucial point is explained below.

Slavery apologists, like historian Ulrich B. Phillips, who wanted to paint slavery as a benign institution characterized more by paternalism than crass materialism, also tended to underestimate slaveholder profits (Smith 1985: 242, 248, 252–54, 258, 265–66, 274). Where slavery was illegal, enslavers kept quiet, lest they attract unwanted attention from the government or competitors. Despite those obstacles, scholars have been able to estimate the profitability of slavery to real world enslavers in several instances and agree that it was a lucrative practice when utilized by competent masters. Of course some masters, especially government ones such as those heading the British government penal colonies on Norfolk Island and Van Deimen's land, were incompetent (or venal) enough to lose money with slave labor (Blackburn 2011: 94, 306; Kolchin 1996: 48; Smith 1985: 153).

Rates of return for slaveholders in the antebellum US South ranged so widely that slavery's profitability there was debated for decades (Smith

1985: 180–83). Careful cliometric work, however, showed that slaveholder returns on large plantations growing cotton or sugar with slaves under the gang system made profits ranging from 7.5 to 20 percent per year. Profits averaged about 10 percent, which was a good return even adjusted for risk (Fogel 1989: 24; Fogel and Engerman 1974: 68–70; Huston 2003: 3). So abolitionists, like Joseph Conder, who argued that "slave-holding is as unprofitable as it is criminal, as costly as it is unjust" were easily dismissed by slaveholders and merchants who knew better (Conder 1833: 2; Eltis 1987: 147).

Such relatively high rates of return would have shocked slavery's apologists as well as proponents of Southern paternalism. (Think the Shelby family in *Uncle Tom's Cabin.*) Careful observers, however, knew differently. As "An American" put it, "it has long been a vital question to the success of the Slaveholder, to know how he could render the labor of his slaves the most profitable" (1855: 55). Whether this made slaveholders "capitalists" or not is a tired old canard, the resolution of which depends entirely on one's definition of the highly disputed term capitalism. So there is no need to vex readers with questions like whether unfree labor in capitalism is "anomaly or necessity?"[1] Enslaving others is about profiting the enslaver, be the enslaver an individual, a corporation, or a government.

Serfdom was profitable too, even on the eve of its abolition in Russia, though the data is somewhat lacking. Private landlords supervised serfs closely, minimizing agency problems. Serfs, like some slaves, were also incentivized to work harder and smarter with the promise of freedom for themselves and their families (Kolchin 1996: 46–47; Mironov 1996: 324–25, 328; Baptist 2014: 16).

Post-emancipation slaveries were profitable, too, and remain so. The ILO estimated that in 2006, private (non-state) enslavers earned $150.2 billion in profits, $99 billion from sexual exploitation, almost $8 billion from domestic work, and almost $43.5 billion from other forms of forced labor. The largest profits were earned in Asia-Pacific ($52 billion) because of the large number of forced laborers there and in the Developed Economies ($47 billion) because of the high profit per victim exacted there. The estimated annual profit per victim ranged from $34,800 in the developed economies to $3900 in Africa to just $850 for *Kamaiya*, the debt peons of southern Nepal (International Labour Organization 2014: 13–14; Kara 2012: 216).

Slavery today is a sophisticated business, a network of firms of various shapes and sizes that nimbly transforms its global supply chain to meet demand. According to Kara, it is akin to a multinational corporation with immense cash flows and steady growth (2009: 11, 17).

Bales and Soodalter claim that (in terms of total dollars generated, not rate of return) enslavement is the third most profitable criminal activity today, after only drugs and guns (2009: 3). Benita Ferrero-Waldner, foreign minister for the Europe Union, claimed in 2006 that "trafficking people is sometimes an even more profitable business than trafficking weapons" (Batstone 2010: 6). As Louise Brown explained, trafficking humans is easier than moving guns or drugs, especially when the humans have been tricked and do not yet know they are trapped (2000: 157). Whether third is the correct rank or not, it is clear that slaves today generate billions of dollars of enslaver profit annually (Shelley and Bain 2015: 140). According to Moises Naim, an expert on illicit economic activities, individual enslavers can make millions (2005: 87).

Today, slaves are very cheap in part because there are so many desperate, and hence vulnerable, people trying to improve their lot in life and/or cross guarded borders (Batstone 2010: 12; Naim 2005: 88–89). The ILO estimated that 20.9 million people toiled in forced labor conditions in 2012. Of those, 18.7 million were exploited by private individuals and enterprises. Some 4.5 million were exploited sexually and the rest were forced to work in various industries ranging from agriculture to utilities. The 2.2 million state-owned slaves labored in prisons or in military or paramilitary forces. Some 55 percent of the total were female and 74 percent were 18 years of age or older. Some 56 percent were exploited in their home countries while the rest were taken abroad. Average time as a slave was 18 months but that figure varied with different forms of forced labor (2014: 7–8).

Understanding why enslaving others is profitable is not difficult. Slaves are not necessarily more productive than other types of laborers but more of what they produce can be stripped from them. That is because enslavers do not have to pay their victims competitive wages, they have to pay them only enough to keep them physically capable of performing their allotted tasks. Punishment, or the threat thereof, does the rest. So slaves could be forced to work longer and harder than free laborers. Slaves could be forced to work at times and in places and under conditions free laborers would not consent to work, at least not for any price that employers could afford to pay (Klein 1993: 12; Eltis 1987: 231; Payne 1912: 21–24).

Enslavers not only pay their victims the smallest amount possible, they also pay in specific types of in kind goods designed to further augment their profits. Enslavers generally do not pay in cash because slaves might prefer to consume something deleterious to the enslavers' interests, like alcohol or poison. So enslavers pay prostitutes with lingerie, cotton pickers with fatback, and so forth. Or, even more deviously, they merely provide slaves with the land and time to grow their own foodstuffs (Barzel 1977: 97–98; Blackburn 1996: 170).

In some societies, enslavers clothed, fed, and housed slaves who produced less than they cost to maintain. Those slaves were effectively subsidized by much larger numbers of prime hands but enslavers still squeezed even the very young and very old for whatever they could produce. In the antebellum US South, for example, even 3–4 year olds were given minor chores to complete and the elderly, if nothing else, supervised the young ones (Fogel 1989: 52–56).

It is easy to fall into the trap of thinking that slavery and other forms of unfree labor are a response to a "shortage" of labor (Bush 1996: 4; Phillips 1996: 73). As Conder noted in 1833, free labor was generally understood to be more efficient than slave labor "so that the difficulty of securing free labour, rather than its expensiveness, is generally assigned as the reason for preferring slave labour" (p. 2). But of course that is strictly untrue because the existence of slaves, serfs, peons, and so forth shows that a sufficient number of laborers did, in fact, exist. The appearance of a shortage was a function of the desire of employers to keep total compensation below competitive levels. Instead of increasing the wage bill or employing labor saving technologies, enslavers force(d) people to toil for less and that was the root of their extra profits.

Sex slavery is especially lucrative for enslavers because sex slaves are not costly to procure or keep enslaved and they produce large revenues (Kara 2009: 24). The average annual profit of sex slaves globally is over $22,000 while domestic and agricultural work generates average profits of just $2300 and $2500, respectively (International Labour Organization 2014: 16). In the Netherlands in 2003, enslavers made an average of €193,776 per sex slave (Kara 2009: 104). Understanding sex slave profits is theoretically straightforward. Prostitution has been called the oldest occupation because sex, like fire tending, is a special type of good called a contrived good. When most goods are sold, they are no longer available to the seller, but one can sell sex (or fire or other contrived goods) and still have it. In other words, the marginal cost of selling sex (or other contrived goods) is almost zero, really just the opportunity cost of the time involved and perhaps a small amount of depreciation (Brown 2000: 157). (Granted that there is a big depreciation after the slave's first sex act, which is why enslavers have developed various ways of feigning the virginity of their sex slaves.)

Slave trading was also profitable and its profitability is also easily understood. Basically, slave traders, indentured laborer shippers, human traffickers, and the rest of their ilk engage in arbitrage, a fancy word for buying low and selling high (Fogel 1989: 10; Meagher 2008: 296–97). Specifically, they profit from the spread between acquisition costs and sale prices minus transaction costs (transportation, bribes, food and shelter, monitoring) and making allowance for risk (Davis 1966: 155). So when American social reformer Grace Abbott lamented the "terrible fact that a whole class of people exist whose object is … to supply the demand for prostitutes, because the trade is extremely lucrative" (Lyttleton 1924: 448), she was really complaining about price differentials between markets. Most slave markets involve multiple players, from raider/recruiter to final purchaser, each taking his, her, or its competitive portion of the overall profit (Inikori and Engerman 1992: 2).

The economic critique of slavery helped to bolster the antislavery crusades of the nineteenth century. For millennia, slavery's morality and its economic efficacy were largely unquestioned. The institution was backed by historical precedent, the right of capture, religious sanction, and notions of natural roles. Early abolitionists, like Samuel Sewall, the Puritan Massachusetts author of *The Selling of Joseph*, were not viewed as prophets but as men of questionable integrity and even sanity (1700). Eventually, however, slavery came to be seen, by some, who warned of a terrible retribution to come, as a sin, the willful disobedience of God's will. (Others claimed that only bad treatment of slaves was sinful because the Bible mentioned the practice on numerous occasions without negative comment.) Others called it unlawful, as in against natural law. Still others castigated slavery because it diminished individual freedom (Eltis 1987: 3–4; Fogel 1989: 203–4, 259–7, 394–98; Quirk 2011: 18, 31–32; Tomek 2011: 24–25; Mason 2006: 131).

As the moral indictment against slavery mounted in the late eighteenth century, slavery's apologists began making economic counterarguments. Until the mid-nineteenth century, few questioned slaveholders' assertions that slavery benefited the overall economy. At first, abolitionists weakly countered that reforms could be implemented without harming the nation or the economic interests of enslavers, despite the long history of claiming that certain profitable activities, like smuggling, were bad for the commonwealth (Quirk 2011: 45; Fogel 1989: 60). "The illicit Trade wch has been carryed on a long time has probably enriched the Individual," Nicholas Waln wrote to Richard Waln in 1764, "but I believe in the Event will extremely derogate from the Good & true Interest of the Colonies." A few years later, a writer in New York also noted that "a Merchant may, and often does, get rich by a Trade that makes his Country poor" (Anon. 1767: 11). In 1817, Littleton D. Teackle noted that "merchants, speculators, stock-jobbers and money changers ... may flourish and get rich though the country be ruined" (p. 7). It took decades, however, for antislavery writers to dramatically shift the national debate on slavery by pushing that same basic insight to the fore (Fogel 1989: 60).

One of the first to identify some of the negative externalities created by slavery was Jean Bodin (1530–1596), who pointed out that the profits created by slaves were offset by the fear induced by the institution in both slaves and the general population (1606: 33). Bodin's brain, David Brion Davis pointed out, was obsessed with demons, witches, and other medieval nonsense, yet on this point it was original and even modern. Bodin showed with great erudition that slavery always summoned forth "cruelty, corruption, conspiracy, and rebellion" (1606: 111–13). As Bodin himself put it, slave societies were "always in daunger of trouble and ruine, by the conspiracie of slaves combining themselves together: All Histories being full of servile rebellions and warres" (1606: 38).

Herder also clearly saw that slavery created social costs not borne by slave masters. He attributed to slavery the spread of syphilis and the devastation of three continents. His discussion of negative externalities, however, was too truncated to be of much import (Herder 2004: 63–64). The same could be said of Philadelphia abolitionist Thomas Branagan (1774–1843), who in 1805 compared slavery "to a large tree planted in the south, whose spreading branches extends to the North; the poisonous fruit of that tree when ripe falls upon these states, to the annoyance of the inhabitants, and contamination of the land which is sacred to liberty" (Mason 2006: 26).

In 1832, Charles James Faulkner said much the same thing before the Virginia House of Delegates: "Slaves are injurious to the interests and threaten the subversion and ruin of this Commonwealth" (Helper 1860: 176). Just a year later, on the other side of the Atlantic, Joseph Conder argued that free laborers cost society less than slaves did because slavery encouraged "a wasteful and deteriorating husbandry" due to its reliance on monoculture and primitive tools as well as "contingent social evils, which demand a precautionary provision." "The ultimate cost of slavery," he concluded, also included "the state expenditure which it renders necessary in order to provide against the dangers inseparable from the existence of a servile class." Conder also argued that masters deliberately limited the fecundity of slaves for fear that too great a supply would lower their prices as well as increase the likelihood of insurrection (1833: 3, 16–18, 20–25).

One of the greatest natural experiments in history, the division of the United States into free and slave states, helped observers to see the negative externalities created by slavery. As early as 1824, the economies of Pennsylvania and Virginia were compared, and the former found better and the latter laggard due to slavery (Wright 2006: 44). Several decades later, the economic differences between otherwise comparable free and slave states were even more pronounced, a point made forcefully by Cassius Clay, a Kentucky slaveholder "mugged by reality" and converted to the antislavery cause. Despite Virginia's natural advantages over New York, the latter exceeded the former in "the elements of National prosperity and glory; wealth, numbers in new countries, literature, industry, the mechanic arts, scientific agriculture, &c." Slavery, Clay concluded, was clearly to blame. "The twelve hundred millions of capital invested in slaves is a dead loss to the South," he declared, predicting, accurately, that the free North would defeat the slave South in a war (1848: 224, 347–48).

Hinton Helper, another southerner converted to antislavery, compared New York to Virginia and found the economic development of the latter lacking due to slavery. In fact, by 1856, New York City alone was more valuable than the entire state of Virginia according to Helper, who also favorably compared the economy of the free state of Massachusetts to that of his native state of North Carolina and Pennsylvania to South Carolina. The reason the North was more populous, enjoyed a higher per capita income, and was more developed than the South was because slavery created large negative externalities. "The fact is, every slave in the South costs the State in which he resides at least three times as much as he, in the whole course of his life, is worth to his master. Slavery," he wrote, perfectly, "benefits no one but its immediate, individual owners, and them only in a pecuniary point of view." "Does the slaveholder, while he is enjoying his slaves," he wondered, "reflect upon the deep injury and incalculable loss which the possession of that property inflicts upon the true interests of the country?"

According to Helper, the North was even superior to the South in agriculture, at least foodstuffs. He even claimed that the hay crop of the North alone was worth four times the cotton crop or more than all the cotton, tobacco, rice, hay, hemp, and cane sugar produced in the South

(1860: 12–21, 33, 49–53, 177, 329). It turns out he was wrong as his methodology overestimated the output of the North and underestimated that of the South, but he correctly pointed out that the North was far superior to the South by most economic metrics (Fogel and Engerman 1974: 161–69). That line of research culminated in John Majewski's magisterial *A House Dividing*, which showed that slavery limited Virginia's population, urbanization, and transportation compared to Pennsylvania (2000).

In 1862, Irish economist John Elliott Cairnes (1823–1875) laid the entire matter bare:

Those who are acquainted with the elementary principles which govern the distribution of wealth, know that the profits of capitalists may be increased by the same process by which the gross revenue of a country is diminished, and that therefore the community as a whole may be impoverished through the very same means by which a portion of its number is enriched. The economic success of slavery, therefore, is perfectly consistent with the supposition that it is prejudicial to the material well-being of the country where it is established (p. 47).

Thereafter, until recently, Cairnes and company carried the day. Only in places untouched by organized antislavery did people continue to consider slavery economically valuable (Quirk 2011: 54). Some, like Phillips, wrongly concluded that slavery had been unprofitable but Lewis C. Gray got the story right. Gray proved that slavery was a highly profitable practice but he also explained, at the very end of his mammoth two-volume study of Southern agriculture, in a short but pointed section called "Economic Disadvantages of Slavery to the South as a Whole," that overall the institution hurt the South's economy (1941: 2:940–42; Smith 1985: 274).

In their controversial book *Time on the Cross: The Economics of American Negro Slavery*, economist historians Robert Fogel and Stanley Engerman conceded the validity of Cairnes's claim but countered that Cairnes "did little to test the evidential basis of his arguments … Cairnes simply never came to grips with the basic empirical issues on which [an economic indictment of slavery] must stand or fall" (1974: 181–90). (Chapters 6 and 7 will do just that.) The duo lauded Gray's take on the profitability of slavery but were strangely silent about his critique of its overall negative economic effects (1974: 63–66, 170). "Although slavery was profitable from an individual point of view and for certain uses conferred a competitive superiority as compared with free labor," Gray wrote, "its ultimate influence upon the economic well-being of the South was pernicious" (1941: 2:940).

The antebellum US South was not poor and the North was not extraordinarily rich. Rather, per capita income in the South lagged that of the North by about 25 percent (it also lagged developmentally but that is more difficult to measure quantitatively) because of the negative externalities caused by slavery, not because slavery was unprofitable or relatively inefficient (Fogel and Engerman 1974: 247). So Robin Blackburn was flat out wrong to assert that because "modern research has shown that slave plantations were still highly profitable in the period before emancipation ... there was no purely economic reason to abolish slavery" (2011: 309).

Some scholars have linked slavery to economic growth through dubious economic theories like import substitution industrialization and changing patterns of consumer demand. Such interpretations confuse the route that happened to be taken with fundamental causes (Inikori 1992; Austen and Smith 1992; Bailey 1992: 206). Economic growth and development ultimately stem from quality institutions, what Adam Smith called, peace, easy taxes, and a tolerable administration of justice, not from top-down economic planning or particular consumption patterns (Bernstein 2004; Wright 2008). What matters are incentives to work hard and smart, not specific tariff or labor regimes.

Consider, for example, Ronald Bailey's claim that "the commercial and industrial activity related to the slave(ry) trade were essential ingredients in the process of industrialization in the United States, particularly in textiles" (1992: 206). That interpretation rests on the dubious assumption, which is directly counter to all evidence, that merchants would have sat on their hands had slaves not been available to trade. In fact, they would have traded the next most valuable commodity (Doerflinger 1986). Similarly, without cotton, nothing would have prevented New England industrialists from investing even more in flax and woolen manufacturing (Wright 2014).

Robin Blackburn argued "that the slave-based commerce of the Atlantic zone made a large contribution to industrialization, furnishing capital, markets and raw materials, tempting consumers with new drugs and stimulants, and adapting to the 'steam age' with remarkable facility" (Blackburn 2011: 3). A major problem with such views is that slavery did not lead to economic growth anywhere but Western Europe and their North American and Australian offshoots. If slavery was an important driver of industrialization, Portugal should have industrialized instead of Britain because its slave trade was much more important relative to the size of its domestic economy. The same could be said of France, or Spain (Eltis and Engerman 2000: 130–33). Everywhere outside of Western Europe, before and since, slavery and economic stagnation were handmaidens. Finally, some places, like the Netherlands, developed economically *before* becoming major enslavers (Postma 1992).

Counterfactuals, a la Jacob Price and the West Indies, have their place (Bailey 1992: 215–16). The goal here is more modest: people who believe that they will be able to enjoy the fruits of their labor discover the most profitable activities available. When that activity is blocked by war, disaster, or any other cause, businesses shift to the next best alternative. So the driver of growth is the incentive, entrepreneurs' belief that they will be able to accumulate wealth, not the particular activities that they find most profitable at a given time. The Browns, for example, manufactured handcuffs, shackles, and so forth and sold them on the African coast *because* slavery existed in Africa. If it had not, they would have made other items, not shuttered their iron works (Bailey 1992: 223). Those other items would have been less profitable to manufacture, or they would have switched to them regardless of the existence of slavery in Africa, but probably only slightly so. Similarly, if cotton was not grown in the US South, it would have been grown elsewhere, just as it was during the Civil War (Baptist 2014: 399).

Similarly, businesses prevented from using the most profitable type of labor will quickly substitute the next most profitable labor type. (This was made clear in Chap. 4; Wright 2010.) So African slaves were not critical to the New World's economy, they were merely the most profitable type of laborer actually available (Finley 1980: 47). Even some Marxists now see that slavery was not an old form of labor doomed to be overcome by wage-labor preferring capitalists (the old party line set forth by Claude Meillassoux and many others [1991: 318]) but rather just one alternative among many, and sometimes the most profitable one, even today (Brass 2013).

Economic historians largely ignored the transatlantic slave trade in their discussions of British industrialization because they possessed a deeper understanding of economic growth than their critics, like Darity (1992: 248). As Gavin Wright put it, "abolition and emancipation did not hurt the British economy" (1987: 868). The British learned from experience that they could lose a colony (even numerous colonies), lose the slave trade, and lose slavery itself without hurting their economy in any major or permanent way because the key drivers of growth and development lay elsewhere (Wright 1987: 869).

For decades, authors, especially from third-world countries, followed Eric Williams in the belief that "capitalists" first encouraged slavery and then destroyed it when they no longer needed it (Eltis 1987: 4). One problem with the infamous Williams Thesis was that Britain's domestic economy was far more important; capital flows from slavery were not significant enough to explain British industrialization (Eltis and Engerman 2000). Sugar, tobacco, and coffee were not inputs into industrial goods, and of course, Britain opposed the slave trade even as cotton grew in importance. In short, in 1800 the British should have encouraged the slave trade and slavery more generally if it was looking after its material interests *and* slavery actually aided economic growth and development (Eltis 1987: 5–7). "From the viewpoint of economic self-interest," David Eltis jibed, "British antislavery policy appears wrongheaded enough to qualify for inclusion in Barbara Tuchman's catalog of folly in government" (Eltis 1987: 7). In 1788, a British MP published a pamphlet that endorsed the slave trade on economic grounds. One of the reviewers, Arthur Young, retorted that "to offer any remarks on such [a] position in this kingdom, and towards the close of the eighteenth century, would be paying a very poor compliment to the understanding of my readers" (Eltis 1987: 3). It is therefore more plausible that the British put down slavery because they knew for sure that it was not all that important to its imperial economy.

What this means historiographically is that the British did not actually commit "econocide," or economic suicide, when they stopped the slave trade and abolished slavery, though many believed that they were doing so. It is not that Seymour Drescher's attack on the Williams thesis, a piece of Marxist drivel that should never have been cited much less adored, was wrong, it is just that, like so many before him, Drescher confused profits with economic development. Slavery hurt the British economy, just like all the others it touched (Drescher 2010).

Some British policymakers had an inkling that slavery was hurting the economy but they, too, struggled with the concept of externalities. When the British government freed Crown slaves in 1831, for example, Lord Goderich (F. J. Robinson, 1782–1859) argued that "were I to regard that interest as confined to the single question of profit and loss, I still entertain a strong belief that it would be best promoted by the enfranchisement of the Slaves." Then he went on to argue that slavery was not as profitable as supposed but he did not quite grasp that it imposed costs on non-slave, non-slaveholders (p. 15).

Other scholars are just too glib about slavery and growth and hence too casually make claims like "the formation and prosperity of the Sulu zone was based above all else on slaves" (Warren 2004: 124). For starters, the Sulu zone was not prosperous except in a temporary and relative way. Second, the prosperity was not widespread but rather limited to elites, that is, slaveholders. If anything, the existence of slavery should be used to explain the low per capita income and lack of economic development in the Sulu zone.

Ed Baptist can be forgiven for missing the other half of the economic story, that of slavery's negative externalities, but his growth narrative remains deeply flawed. Instead of seeing growth as a direct product of incentives and freedom, Baptist presents a simplified, traditional "Industrial Revolution in Britain" story (2014: 78–83). That allows him to argue that slaves created cotton and hence industrialization and the breakout from Malthusian stagnation (population growth leading inevitably to economic decline until the population declines due to famine, war, and/or disease) (2014: 82, 110). Of course it was the revolution in agriculture, specifically in the production of foodstuffs, not cotton, that allowed the West to break free of the Malthusian trap but slaves were unimportant to that story. Baptist also credits increased cotton yields to greater slave efficiency (2014: 113), even though agricultural economist historians Alan Olmstead, Paul Rhode, Franklee Whartenby, John Hebron Moore, and others showed that picking productivity leveled out circa 1840 and that much of the increase in cotton yields was due to improved agricultural techniques and a panoply of better seeds that created plants that produced bigger bolls that were positioned closer together and higher off the ground (Whartenby 1977: 54, 104–5; Moore 1988: 30–34; Baptist 2014: 127; Olmstead and Rhode 2008).

Baptist used 20-year-old GDP data instead of the latest data (available on http://measuringworth.com) because the older data fit his story better. He also distorted the US manufacturing tariff issue (2014: 316–18). His claim that "almost all commercial production and consumption fed into or spun out from a mighty stream of white bolls" was of course untrue (2014: 319). He repeatedly ignored the web of interconnections inherent in any commercial society (small world theory and the six degrees of separation theorem) to attempt to prove that "the northern economy's industrial sector was built on the backs of enslaved people" (2014: 322). All Baptist really proved is what "An American" knew in 1855: "Slavery is not an isolated system, but is so mingled with the business of the world, that it derives facilities from the most innocent transactions" (p. 37).

Scholars should follow Kara not Baptist. "The system clearly benefits those who control land, local government, assets, and means of production in the rural and informal sectors," Kara wrote, "but the economy at large and each individual laborer suffer considerably" (2012: 13). As difficult as it is, they need to tell freedperson Bayley Wyatt, who claimed credit for the "large cities in de North" which grew up "on de cotton and de sugars and de rice" that slaves made, that other people worked hard too (Foner 1983: 56). Raw materials were only the first link of a very long chain that created the wealth of the North and while slaves did create that first link they did so only to satisfy the greed of their enslavers. William Seward was closer to the truth when he claimed that New York had grown rich "by her own enterprise" regardless of the number of bales of cotton New Yorkers had purchased (Baptist 2014: 339). Slaves were neither necessary nor sufficient causes of wealth and, in fact, slavery made the world a less wealthy place.

Before moving on to describe the negative externalities created by slavery, the notion that slavery created some positive externalities must be confronted. The early Church, up through and including Martin Luther, believed that slavery brought social stability. "Masters and slaves must accept their present stations," Luther wrote, following Saint Paul, "for the earthly kingdom could not survive unless some men were free and some were slaves" (Fogel 1989: 202). In the eighteenth and nineteenth centuries, some scholars argued that slavery made possible Greek or Western civilization (Finley 1980: 90; Rihll 2008: 111). Arnold Heeren (1760–1842), for example, claimed that without slavery, the culture of Greece's ruling class could not have developed as it did (1824). Slavery was essential to both the basic Greek will to live and their devotion to the gods, Wilhelm Von Humboldt (1767–1835) claimed (Vogt 1975: 25). M. I. Finley also believed that slavery led to the Greek's many achievements (1980: 36, 39–44).

Friedrich Engels argued that slavery was a stage or step through which humanity had to pass to achieve modernity. "Without slavery, no Greek state, no Greek art and science; without slavery, no Roman Empire. Without Hellenism and the Roman empire as the base, also no modern Europe" (1894, Part II, Chap. 4). Others argued just as vehemently that slavery was a good thing because it caused the *downfall* of the wicked Greek and Roman civilizations (Finley 1980: 14, 26; Starr 1958: 19). Others thought that slavery civilized Africans lucky enough to be enslaved by Christianizing them and turning their brute power into products sold worldwide (Smith 1985: 20).

One would hope that nobody today would be persuaded by these or similar claims, which ultimately fail for the same reasons that the claim that slavery creates economic growth and development fails: they do not demonstrate that slavery was a necessary cause of civilization. As pointed out by Jean Bodin, humans engaged in the most barbarous practices, like cannibalism and human sacrifice, for millennia but that does not mean that the barbarous practices caused philosophy, writing, science, and so forth, or that they would be justified even if they did (Bodin 1606: 34–35). The best that can be said is that slavery did not utterly prevent cultural, economic, political, or social development. But it could have well stymied them. The most rapid development in human history arguably occurred after World War II, an era when slavery, though still in existence, waned in importance to arguably its historical nadir (as measured by the percentage of the world's total population deeply enslaved).

The notion that indentured laborers and the economies they left behind both benefited from servitude is likewise flawed. As David Eltis and Stan Engerman argued, "the English who went forth and multiplied (temporarily in Barbados, and eventually more permanently in the Chesapeake) would probably not have been unemployed if they had stayed at home, though they might have been less productive" (2000: 128). By lowering wages in the colonies, the indentured servants in effect squeezed out free men who might have come in their place, just as Samuel Sewall implied in 1700 (p. 2).

Recently, political scientist David F. Ericson credited slavery with helping the US federal government to develop, as part of a process that political scientists call American state development (Ericson 2011: 1–2). The problem here is that what the political scientists call development might just be statism, an ideology that presupposes that government ought to be involved in many economic activities. So for them, the national government's ubiquitous use of private agents to perform public functions signaled a lack of institutional development, while for others, the same practice was a sign of the government's sagacity. Furthermore, Ericson attributes the growth of federal power to slavery even though economist historian Robert Higgs showed that wars were the main driver of change (Ericson 2011: 168; Higgs 2009). Yes, slavery caused wars, including wars in Florida and Mexico, and of course the Civil War, but war, qua war, and regardless of its causes, was responsible for the so-called ratchet effect that Higgs documented (Fogel 1989: 337; Baptist 2014: 327–29; Cochin 1863: 366).

Arguably the worst offender was Edmund Morgan, who claimed that slavery may have given Virginians the will to rebel against the Mother

Country and establish a republic. "The presence of men and women who were, in law at least, almost totally subject to the will of other men gave to those in control of them an immediate experience of what it could mean to be at the mercy of a tyrant," he explained. "Virginians may have had a special appreciation of the freedom dear to republicans, because they saw every day what life without it could be like" (1975: 375). Of course Virginians were not especially good republicans and the daily experience of slavery did not lead to republican revolutions in the West Indies or anywhere else throughout history. And Massachusetts, Holland, and parts of Britain were very republican although they had little quotidian experience whipping minions. So, again, slavery hardly appears to be a necessary or a sufficient cause.

One cannot categorically prove that slavery never created a positive externality anywhere but surely any benefit is swamped by the many, large negative externalities it creates, the subject of the next two chapters.

Note

1. One answer was that unfree labor was "an anomalous necessity," whatever that means (Miles 1987: 196–99)!

Bibliography

Acemoglu, D., & Wolitzky, A. (2011). The economics of labor coercion. *Econometrica, 79*, 555–600.

An American. (1855). *Cotton is king: Or the culture of cotton, and its relation to agriculture, manufactures and commerce*. Cincinnati, OH: Moore, Wilstach, Keys & Co.

Anon. (1767). *The commercial conduct of the province of New York considered*. New York: n.p.

Atkinson, E. (1861). *Cheap cotton by free labor by a cotton manufacturer* (2nd ed.). Boston: A. Williams & Co.

Austen, R. A., & Smith, W. D. (1992). Private tooth decay as public economic virtue: The slave-sugar triangle, consumerism, and European industrialization. In J. Inikori & S. Engerman (Eds.), *The Atlantic slave trade: Effects on economies, societies, and peoples in Africa, the Americas, and Europe* (pp. 183–203). Durham, NC: Duke University Press.

Bailey, R. (1992). The slave(ry) trade and the development of capitalism in the United States: The textile industry in New England. In J. Inikori & S. Engerman (Eds.), *The Atlantic slave trade: Effects on economies, societies, and peoples in*

Africa, the Americas, and Europe (pp. 205–246). Durham, NC: Duke University Press.

Bales, K., & Soodalter, R. (2009). *The slave next door: Human trafficking and slavery in America today*. Berkeley: University of California Press.

Baptist, E. E. (2014). *The half has never been told: Slavery and the making of American capitalism*. New York: Basic Books.

Barzel, Y. (1977). An economic analysis of slavery. *Journal of Law and Economics, 20*, 87–110.

Batstone, David. (2010). *Not for sale: The return of the global slave trade and how we can fight it*, Rev. ed. New York: HarperCollins.

Bernstein, W. J. (2004). *The birth of plenty: How the prosperity of the modern world was created*. New York: McGraw-Hill.

Blackburn, R. (1996). Slave exploitation and the elementary structures of enslavement. In M. L. Bush (Ed.), *Serfdom and slavery: Studies in legal bondage* (pp. 158–180). New York: Addison Wesley Longman.

Blackburn, R. (2011). *The American crucible: Slavery, emancipation and human rights*. New York: Verso.

Bodin, J. (1606). *The six bookes of a commonweale* (R. Knolles, Trans.). London: Impensis G. Bishop.

Brass, T. (2013). Debating capitalist dynamics and unfree labour: A missing link? *Journal of Development Studies, 50*, 1–13.

Brougham, H. (1807). *A concise statement of the question regarding the abolition of the slave trade* (4th ed.). London: Longman, Hurst, Rees, and Orme.

Brown, L. (2000). *Sex slaves: The trafficking of women in Asia*. London: Virago Press.

Bush, M. (1996). Introduction. In M. L. Bush (Ed.), *Serfdom and slavery: Studies in legal bondage* (pp. 1–17). New York: Addison Wesley Longman.

Cairnes, J. E. (1862). *The slave power: Its character, career, and probable designs, being an attempt to explain the real issues involved in the American contest* (2nd ed.). New York: Carleton.

Channing, W. E. (1839). *Remarks on the slavery question in a letter to Jonathan Phillips, Esq.* Boston: James Munroe and Company.

Clay, C. (1848). *The writings of Cassius Marcellus Clay: Including speeches and addresses*. New York: Harper & Brothers.

Cochin, A. (1863). *The results of slavery*. Boston: Walker, Wise, and Company.

Conder, J. (1833). *Wages or the whip: An essay on the comparative cost and productiveness of free and slave labour*. London: Hatehard and Son.

Darity Jr., W. (1992). British industry and the West Indies plantations. In J. Inikori & S. Engerman (Eds.), *The Atlantic slave trade: Effects on economies, societies, and peoples in Africa, the Americas, and Europe* (pp. 247–282). Durham, NC: Duke University Press.

Davidson, J. O. (2015). *Modern slavery: The margins of freedom*. New York: Palgrave Macmillan.

Davis, D. B. (1966). *The problem of slavery in Western culture*. Ithaca, NY: Cornell University Press.

Doerflinger, T. (1986). *A vigorous spirit of enterprise: Merchants and economic development in Revolutionary Philadelphia*. Chapel Hill: University of North Carolina Press.

Donald, L. (1997). *Aboriginal slavery on the northwest coast of North America*. Berkeley: University of California Press.

Drescher, S. (2010). *Econocide: British slavery in the era of abolition* (2nd ed.). Chapel Hill: University of North Carolina Press.

Eltis, D. (1987). *Economic growth and the ending of the transatlantic slave trade*. New York: Oxford University Press.

Eltis, D., & Engerman, S. (2000). The importance of slavery and the slave trade to industrializing Britain. *Journal of Economic History, 60*, 123–144.

Engels, F. (1894). *Anti-Duhring* (E. Burns, Trans.). Leipzig: n.p.

Ericson, D. F. (2011). *Slavery in the American republic: Developing the federal government, 1791–1861*. Lawrence: University of Kansas Press.

Finley, M. I. (1980). *Ancient slavery and modern ideology*. New York: Viking Press.

Fogel, R. (1989). *Without consent or contract: The rise and fall of American slavery*. New York: W. W. Norton.

Fogel, R., & Engerman, S. (1974). *Time on the cross: The economics of American negro slavery*. New York: Little, Brown and Company.

Foner, E. (1983). *Nothing but freedom: Emancipation and its legacy*. Baton Rouge: Louisiana State University Press.

Gray, L. (1941). *History of agriculture in the southern United States to 1860* (Vol. 2). New York: Peter Smith.

Hall, C., Draper, N., McClelland, K., Donington, K., & Lang, R. (2014). *Legacies of British slave-ownership: Colonial slavery and the formation of Victorian Britain*. New York: Cambridge University Press.

Heeren, A. (1824). *Reflections on the politics of ancient Greece* (G. Bancroft, Trans.). Boston: Cummings, Hilliard & Co.

Helper, H. R. (1860). *The impending crisis of the South: How to meet it*. New York: A. B. Burdick.

Herder, J. G. (2004). *Another philosophy of history and selected political writings* (I. D. Evrigenis & D. Pellerin, Trans.). Indianapolis: Hackett Publishing Company.

Higgs, R. (2009). *Depression, war, and Cold War: Challenging the myths of conflict and prosperity*. Stanford, CA: Independent Institute.

Huston, J. L. (2003). *Calculating the value of the Union: Slavery, property rights, and the economic origins of the Civil War*. Chapel Hill: University of North Carolina Press.

Inikori, J. (1992). Slavery and the revolution in cotton textile production in England. In J. Inikori & S. Engerman (Eds.), *The Atlantic slave trade: Effects on economies, societies, and peoples in Africa, the Americas, and Europe* (pp. 145–181). Durham, NC: Duke University Press.

Inikori, J., & Engerman, S. (1992). Introduction: Gainers and losers in the Atlantic slave trade. In J. Inikori & S. Engerman (Eds.), *The Atlantic slave trade: Effects on economies, societies, and peoples in Africa, the Americas, and Europe* (pp. 1–24). Durham, NC: Duke University Press.

International Labour Organization. (2014). *Profits and poverty: The economics of forced labour*. Geneva: International Labour Organization.

Kara, S. (2009). *Sex trafficking: Inside the business of modern slavery*. New York: Columbia University Press.

Kara, S. (2012). *Bonded labor: Tackling the system of slavery in South Asia*. New York: Columbia University Press.

Klein, M. (1993). Introduction: Modern European expansion and traditional servitude in Africa and Asia. In M. A. Klein (Ed.), *Breaking the chains: Slavery, bondage, and emancipation in modern Africa and Asia* (pp. 3–36). Madison: University of Wisconsin Press.

Kolchin, P. (1996). Some controversial questions concerning nineteenth-century emancipation from slavery and serfdom. In M. L. Bush (Ed.), *Serfdom and slavery: Studies in legal bondage* (pp. 42–68). New York: Addison Wesley Longman.

Lyttleton, D. E. (1924, November 19). The League's big little jobs. *Outlook*.

Majewski, J. (2000). *A house dividing: Economic development in Pennsylvania and Virginia before the Civil War*. New York: Cambridge University Press.

Mason, M. (2006). *Slavery and politics in the early American republic*. Chapel Hill: University of North Carolina Press.

Meagher, A. J. (2008). *The coolie trade: The traffic in Chinese laborers to Latin America, 1847–1874*. New York: Xlibris.

Meillassoux, C. (1991). *The anthropology of slavery: The womb of iron and gold*. Chicago: University of Chicago Press.

Miles, R. (1987). *Capitalism and unfree labour: Anomaly or necessity?* New York: Tavistock Publications.

Millar, J. (1771/2006). *The origin of the distinction of ranks: Or, an inquiry into the circumstances, which give rise to influence and authority, in the different members of society*. Indianapolis: Liberty Fund.

Mironov, B. N. (1996). When and why was the Russian peasantry emancipated? In M. L. Bush (Ed.), *Serfdom and slavery: Studies in legal bondage* (pp. 323–347). New York: Addison Wesley Longman.

Moore, J. H. (1988). *The emergence of the cotton kingdom in the old Southwest, Mississippi, 1770–1860*. Baton Rouge: Louisiana State University Press.

Morgan, E. (1975). *American slavery, American freedom: The ordeal of colonial Virginia*. New York: W. W. Norton.

Naim, M. (2005). *Illicit: How smugglers, traffickers, and copycats are hijacking the global economy*. New York: Doubleday.

Olmstead, A. L., & Rhode, P. W. (2008). *Creating abundance: Biological innovation and American agricultural development*. New York: Cambridge University Press.

Payne, E. G. (1912). *An experiment in alien labor*. Chicago: University of Chicago Press.

Phillips, W. D. (1996). Continuity and change in Western slavery: Ancient to modern times. In M. L. Bush (Ed.), *Serfdom and slavery: Studies in legal bondage* (pp. 71–88). New York: Addison Wesley Longman.

Postma, J. (1992). The dispersal of African slaves in the West by Dutch slave traders, 1630–1803. In J. Inikori & S. Engerman (Eds.), *The Atlantic slave trade: Effects on economies, societies, and peoples in Africa, the Americas, and Europe* (pp. 283–299). Durham, NC: Duke University Press.

Prakash, G. (1993). Terms of servitude: The colonial discourse on slavery and bondage in India. In M. A. Klein (Ed.), *Breaking the chains: Slavery, bondage, and emancipation in Modern Africa and Asia* (pp. 131–149). Madison: University of Wisconsin Press.

Quirk, J. (2011). *The anti-slavery project: From the slave trade to human trafficking*. Philadelphia: University of Pennsylvania Press.

Rihll, T. (2008). Slavery and technology in pre-industrial contexts. In E. D. Lago & C. Katsari (Eds.), *Slave systems ancient and modern* (pp. 127–147). New York: Cambridge University Press.

Salter, J. (1996). Adam Smith on slavery. *History of Economic Ideas, 4*, 225–251.

Scheidel, W. (2008). The comparative economics of slavery in the Greco-Roman world. In E. D. Lago & C. Katsari (Eds.), *Slave systems ancient and modern* (pp. 105–126). New York: Cambridge University Press.

Schurz, C. (1903, January). Can the South solve the Negro problem? *McClure's*.

Shelley, L., & Bain, C. (2015). Human trafficking: Fighting the illicit economy with the legitimate economy. *Social Inclusion, 3*, 140–144.

Smith, A. (1896). *Lectures on justice, police, revenue and arms*. Oxford: Clarendon Press.

Smith, J. D. (1985). *An old creed for the new South: Proslavery ideology and historiography, 1865–1918*. Athens: University of Georgia Press.

Starr, C. (1958). An overdose of slavery. *Journal of Economic History, 18*, 17–32.

Tomek, B. C. (2011). *Colonization and its discontents: Emancipation, emigration, and antislavery in antebellum Pennsylvania*. New York: New York University Press.

Vogt, J. (1975). *Ancient slavery and the ideal of man* (T. Wiedemann, Trans.). Cambridge: Harvard University Press.

Warren, J. F. (2004). The structure of slavery in the Sulu zone in the late eighteenth and nineteenth centuries. In G. Campbell (Ed.), *The structure of slavery in Indian Ocean Africa and Asia* (pp. 111–128). London: Frank Cass.

Whartenby, F. (1977). *Land and labor productivity in United States cotton production, 1800–1840.* New York: Arno Press.

Wright, G. (1987). Capitalism and slavery on the islands: A lesson from the mainland. *Journal of Interdisciplinary History, 17*, 851–870.

Wright, G. (2006). *Slavery and American economic development.* Baton Rouge: Louisiana State University Press.

Wright, R. E. (2008). *One nation under debt: Hamilton, Jefferson, and the history of what we owe.* New York: McGraw-Hill.

Wright, R. E. (2010). *Fubarnomics: A lighthearted, serious look at America's economic ills.* Amherst, NY: Prometheus.

Wright, R. E. (2014). *Corporation nation.* Philadelphia: University of Pennsylvania Press.

CHAPTER 6

That Which Is Unseen I: Slavery's Pollution

"Slavery impoverishes Virginia, but it enriches the master" (Parker 1854: 30). As discussed in Chap. 5, enslavers create monopsony power, a type of market failure called market power. That is what the editor of the *Journal of United Labor* had in mind when he wrote in 1883 that "slavery simply consists in placing oneself in that condition where he is powerless to exact an equivalent for services rendered" (Hallgrimsdottir and Benoit 2007: 1397). Wherever slavery was outlawed, enslavers moved to contracts that tied workers to employers or to land as an alternative way of recapturing their monopsony rents. Tying, incidentally, has no redeeming economic qualities; the same or better outcomes stem from competitive markets (Conning and Kevane 2007: 109). Market power creates unseen social costs, called deadweight losses, which is why most countries try to limit it by passing laws against monopolies, monopsonies, cartels, and so forth.

Enslaving others also creates numerous significant negative externalities, or costs that enslavement imposes on the world that are not reflected in the market price. These costs, like the deadweight losses caused by enslavers' monopsony power, are difficult to discern or measure and hence they are easy to underestimate or even to miss entirely (Manning 1990: 182 n6). Their aggregate effects, however, are palpable. The economies with the least economic freedom (say, the number of workers times their freedom index score from Chap. 2) are the most impoverished, while those with the most economic freedom by the same measure are the wealthiest or most developed (Quirk 2011: 174–84). *Ceteris paribus*, of course.

R.E. Wright, *The Poverty of Slavery*,
DOI 10.1007/978-3-319-48968-1_6

Readers should note that to hurt the overall economy, the total deadweight losses and negative externalities caused by slavery need not exceed the total benefits of slavery (which largely took the form of private profits) but rather the extra benefits of slavery over its next most beneficial (profitable) alternative. This is what economists call a marginal analysis. The profitability of the second best alternative can rarely be observed directly but in most instances was likely quite close to the observed best option (slavery) so the aggregate sum of negative externalities does not need to be very high to indict slavery as an economic institution. This chapter and the next show that the total value of slavery's negative externalities far exceeds any plausible marginal benefit gained from slavery.

Specifically, slavery negatively impacts the enslaved and their descendants, the enslaved's place of origin, and even their enslavers. It also stymies the growth of population and non-slave laborers and their employers as well as the development of agriculture, education, infrastructure, and technology. Slavery also increases wealth disparities while degrading governance and institutional quality as well as public perceptions. The biggest negative externalities of slavery, though, may be the cost of protecting non-slaves from enslavement, slaves from themselves, non-slaves, and enslavers, as well as the cost of protecting non-slaves from slaves. Public control costs also loom large, as do the opportunity costs of enslavement.

Each of those costs is explained in detail in the balance of this, and the next, chapter. Because the goal of these chapters is to show that slavery always and everywhere has a negative net effect on the overall economy, they are arranged logically and topically rather than chronologically. Economists and other social scientists inclined to dismiss this evidence as too anecdotal should consult a study by Robert Smith that statistically demonstrates the negative effects of historical slavery on economic growth and development today, holding all other known major causal variables, including cultural ones, constant (2003; Bales 2007: 219). Readers also skeptical of statistics should consult the results of real-life experiments by NGOs like Free the Slaves, which reports that the local elimination of debt peonage and other coercive labor forms leads directly and immediately to substantial increases in average educational attainment, adult literacy rates, access to healthcare, livestock ownership, voter turnout, and savings as well as significant decreases in average remittances from family members living elsewhere, individual indebtedness, and interest rates, all of which portend higher productivity and incomes for all members of the local community (Sarich 2012).

The Enslaved and Their Immediate Families

"What use will freedom be to me? Can it give me back my children, or make me what I used to be" (Stowe 1852: 301)? The decision to capture a slave, whether by force or by subterfuge, takes into account only two variables, the cost of capture and transportation on the one hand and the market price on the other. Slave raiders and recruiters do not account for the negative effects on the slaves themselves, the slaves' children, or the slaves' place of origin. All those costs, therefore, are negative externalities (Manning 1990: 21).

In a recent economic model devised by Acemoglu and Wolitzky, "coercion always reduces (utilitarian) social welfare, because ... coercion hurts the agent [i.e., the enslaved] more than the additional effort it induces helps the principal [i.e., the enslaver]" (2011: 587). That is a fancy way of saying what Henry George meant over a century ago, when he argued that "the enslavement of part of their number could not increase the wealth of a people, for more than the enslavers gained the enslaved would lose" (Steele 1987: 373).

Readers are likely already convinced that enslavement is not good for the enslaved but they may not fully understand the extent and permanence of the damage. Enslavers' monopsony power means that slaves receive much less for their labor than they would where competitive wages prevailed. That exploitation ends with freedom. But the damage inflicted on the enslaved to induce him or her to toil almost completely in the interests of the enslaver is usually extensive. Slaves usually suffer, as Bales and Soodalter put it, from confusion, depression, exhaustion, fear, hunger, injury, and shame (2009: 24). Much of the damage inflicted on the enslaved is permanent, persisting even if the slave eventually finds freedom. Survivors, philosophers Kwame Anthony Appiah and Martin Bunzl explained, pay the cost of slavery for the rest of their lives (2007: 3).

Enslavement causes alcoholism and drug addiction, sickness, premature death (increased mortality rate), and a higher risk of suicide. Whenever they could, indentured laborers drank rum, took datura, a dangerous drug, and smoked ganja cannabis and opium. Slaveholders in the antebellum US South provided their slaves with alcohol strategically, like when forcing them to march to new slave labor camps in the old Southwest. In Trinidad, enslavers gave their bondspeople, even pregnant women, rum, especially during harvest, to keep their spirits up (Manning 1992: 120; Tinker 1993: 178–79, 213; Baptist 2014: 14; Fogel 1989: 146). Today, enslavers often purposely addict their slaves to powerful illicit drugs to keep them compliant and unable to escape but able to continue to work after being raped or tortured. In the carpet sector of South Asia, enslavers force enslaved children to take stimulants so that they can work 16 or more hours a day, 7 days a week. That might seem a reckless use of property but dead or damaged girls and children can always be cheaply replaced. Those not given stimulants by their masters sometimes sneak drugs or alcohol to deaden what Louise Brown called the emotional damage and rigors of prostitution (Bales and Soodalter 2009: 81, 90; Kara 2009: 2, 10, 15, 49, 87; Kara 2012: 169; Skinner 2008: 136, 217–18; Bales 2012: 161; Brown 2000: 215–16).

Like Tom in *Uncle Tom's Cabin*, a real-life slave in colonial Maryland named Antonio essentially committed 'suicide by master' by refusing to work, even under torture, until his exasperated master hung him from a ladder (Jones 2013: 1–3). According to Solomon Northup, Eliza was "round and plump" when he met her in Washington D.C. but after losing her children "grief had gnawed remorselessly at her heart until her strength was gone" and she died (Schermerhorn 2015: 196). For other slaves, a loss of self-esteem or desire to work solely for the benefit of another led to suicide, self-mutilation, or infanticide, especially (like Eliza) when being sold away from their families (Skinner 2008: 132, 152, 160, 164, 193, 196; Simon 1929: 3–4; Murphy 2014: 199; Tinker 1993: 172; Brown 2000: 225, 244; Childs 2015: 32; Schermerhorn 2015: 59). In the Soviet gulag, Arthur John Kujala "saw men who had cut off fingers so they wouldn't have to work." Others "purposely froze their feet just enough to lose the toes" for the same purpose. Kujala admitted that he "came near doing" something like that himself because the "heavy lumbering was torturous" (Kujala 1940: 111, 113). Many convict laborers in postbellum Texas hacked at their bodies in a desperate attempt to avoid being worked to death. In Alabama's mines, convict quasi-slaves ate soap or drank fetid water to sicken themselves or rubbed poison in their wounds so they would not heal (Blackmon 2008: 92, 109).

In India, debt peons have been known to shoot themselves or, where guns were not available, to kill themselves by drinking pesticides or eating dirt. Women there sometimes self-immolate after being sexually abused. Chinese indentured laborers committed suicide in droves. In the 1950s, jailhouse blues performers would sing about committing suicide. It goes without saying that people who pray daily for death are not good for the overall health of the economy (Skinner 2008: 215, 224; Tinker 1993: 11; Meagher 2008: 219, 227–28; Childs 2015: 12; Kara 2012: 147).

Due to the horrible conditions in which they survive, the enslaved tend to be less physically robust than non-slaves. The average slave teenager, Skinner reported, is 40 pounds lighter and one and a half inches shorter than the average non-enslaved 15 year old (Skinner 2008: 5). Many enslaved persons are physically scarred from overwork or overbeating (Kara 2009: 61). "There appeared on the streets of Orlando," Richard Barry wrote in 1907, "wrecks of what once were men—decrepit, with their backs scarred, their clothes in rags, shoeless, their feet splintered and swollen with the ugly wounds of the saw-palmetto. ...They were convicts, of course."

Enslavers often deliberately tattooed or scarified their slaves. In Sudan, hot irons are used to brand the enslaved lest they successfully flee their master's clutches. Some enslavers purposely blinded their slaves to reduce their ability to escape or rebel. Scythian horse dairy slaves, for example, were all blinded by their loving masters. Other slaves had their hands pierced so chains could be inserted and enslavers saved the expense of shackles. Some enslavers still use the lash but others use chemicals to deform the faces of those who resist. During the second Sudanese civil war (1983–2005), enslavers often mutilated their slaves in order to obliterate their cultural identities and smash their humanity. During that conflict, state-sponsored militiamen gang-raped young slave boys in order to destroy their gender identities (Skinner 2008: 4, 67, 73, 145, 193, 198; Taylor 2001: 38).

Some slaves today suffer such barbaric treatment that nobody will put it into print for fear of copycats. Even the quotidian stories are enough to make one wretch. In some places, sex slaves work 10–14 hours per day, 7 days a week, 365 days a year and service 20 men per day. That works out to 7300 sex partners per year. Little wonder that the 2000 or so former sex slaves in Moldova's only functional shelter for formerly enslaved sex workers have been described as severely damaged in every way (Kara 2009: 193; Brown 2000: 211–12; Murphy 2014: 235; Skinner 2008: 158).

The enslaved also suffer from a wide variety of occupational hazards. Charcoal workers in Brazil, for example, typically get black lung disease if they live long enough for it to develop (Bales 2012: 130). Convict miners in postbellum Alabama, contemporary R. A. J. Cumlie wrote, suffered "appalling" rates of mortality but also morbidity, including crippling accidents and debilitating diseases (Blackmon 2008: 76). Quarry workers in India usually get chronic lung diseases, like silicosis, because enslavers take no precautions to protect them. Others get arthritis or tendinitis or suffer from other chronic musculoskeletal conditions due to years of doing the same motions over and over and over. Faded eyesight is common in other occupations, like bidi rolling (Skinner 2008: 205–12; Kara 2012: 199). Three out of every four of the Indian indentured laborers who toiled on the Uganda Railway were "more or less broken in health" reported the Port Health Officer (Tinker 1993: 175). Edwin Markham noted in 1906 that coal miners were quickly "blunted … by a life of drudgery, hardened by years of imposition, dulled by acceptances of hardship and privation" (p. 25). Peons and convict laborers, a Georgia negro peon wrote in 1904, either died or "came away maimed and bruised and, in some cases, disabled for life" (p. 415). The youngest girls initiated into prostitution suffer from what Brown called "irreparable internal injuries" (2000: 122). Others are scarred physically by forced surgical abortions or psychologically by forced chemical abortions (Brown 2000: 217–18; Murphy 2014: 104). In 1922, an Australian woman enslaved to a Chinese family was apparently never sexually assaulted but she had almost died of starvation and an untreated leg injury before being rescued by missionaries (Anon. 1922b: 1).

Physically, most people react to the poor food, sleeping, and living conditions of enslavement in the same way, by rapidly aging (Brown 2000: 214; Murphy 2014: 75). The Janajati, Nepalese bonded laborers who eke out a living breaking river stones for paving companies, "looked ten to fifteen years older than they were," Kara noted, "which means a lot in a country where people typically look ten years younger than they are" (2012: 156). Others have noted the premature aging of slaves as well (Bales and Soodalter 2009: 166; Bales 2012: 97). After just a few months in slavery, Skinner noticed, children often look several years older. One of the slaves he interviewed, Alina, had "a sallow complexion that made her appear much older than her twenty-three years" (2008: 32, 179). According to Brown, most Bangladeshi sex slaves have to give up the sex trade by age 30 because by then they look like old women past reproductive age (2000: 230). In the antebellum US South, female slaves on average experienced earlier menopause than free white women (Fogel 1989: 148–49).

Psychologically, people over the ages have reacted to slavery in a variety of ways. Some become compliant Sambos, others cunning tricksters (some disguised as Sambos), others angry rebels, and still others runaways, while some soak in moral turpitude. Most, whether shackled by iron or by invisible chains, become survivors who learn to shirk work by becoming skilled at doing just enough to avoid punishment. From ancient Rome to the antebellum South to today's sex pits, slaves have notoriously bad reputations among their enslavers. Obviously, theft, laziness, and so forth are the natural concomitants of slavery, regardless of who is enslaved, which is what Franklin meant when he argued that slaves were "from the nature of slavery a thief" (Houston 2008: 208) and Owen meant when he noted that "men who own no property do not learn to respect the rights of property" (1864: 200). It is very difficult, though not impossible as the cases of Douglass and Washington show, for slaves or even ex-slaves to become self-actualized (Kara 2009: 216–17; McKeown 2007: 93, 108–13; Buckland 1908: 9; Appiah 2007: 257).

Most slaves today are not well fed, especially if they are in the sex trade, where in addition to malnutrition they must worry about the full panoply of sexually transmitted diseases (STDs), including HIV. In some places in India, enslavers force their victims to take bovine steroid injections to plump up their malnourished bodies so they are more attractive to Western sex tourists. One brothel owner punished runaways by putting chili paste on a broomstick and sodomizing them with it. Just as some molested children go on to become child molesters themselves, some mistreated slaves, including Haitian restavecs and regular American girls like Shamere McKenzie, themselves become enslavers, including drivers or recruiters. A 'lucky' few chattel slaves become masters and some sex slaves become madams who own and/or run their own brothels. Entire peoples, including the Apache, have managed to transform from the victims of slave raiders into slavers themselves. Even those slaves who do not learn to inflict pain on others must learn, to some degree, that violence solves problems (Dower 2004: 182; Murphy 2014: 71, 240; Kara 2009: 2, 9, 49–50, 70; Bales 2012: 60; Kara 2012: 137–38; Bales and Soodalter 2009: 84–85; Quirk 2011: 25; Brown 2000: 234–41; Resendez 2016: 7; Hurmence 1984: 39).

Eventually, enslavers discard most sex slaves because younger girls are more profitable and cheaply available. Most freed slaves then return home to a new hell, where they are shunned and even spat upon, for being a slave or bringing shame upon themselves and their families. Some of those shunned at home, realizing that they will be unable to marry or conceive, become suicidal and kill themselves outright or by selling off their organs. Others flee and, if they are still marketable, become vulnerable to re-enslavement just as slaves and former slaves in other times and places usually were. Others become street vendors, cleaners, beggars, or domestic help. Some return to prostitution, on their own account, turning more and nastier tricks for less money as they age (Kara 2009: 70–71, 76, 136; Brown 2000: 125, 180, 233, 234–42; Skinner 2008: 180; Kara 2012: 73, 92, 155; Lovejoy 2012: 112).

Of course shunning is not a new phenomenon. Indentured laborers could not return home to India, British observer D. W. D. Comins noted, because "they would be despised and mobbed in their native villages, or have to spend much money for re-admission to their caste" (Tinker 1993: 209). Re-enslavement is also a hoary problem. Slaves freed in the antebellum United States, for example, faced due to racism rather dismal prospects akin to quasi-slavery. Slaves freed by the British during the American Revolution were so impoverished in London that many agreed to be colonized on the Sierra Leone river. Even most indentured servants in colonial Virginia did not become landowners after their indentures were up (Staudenraus 1961: 6–8; Smith 1965: 298–99).

Slavery rarely produces much financial or human capital so, as the International Labour Organization argues, "people in forced labour are often caught in a vicious cycle that condemns them to endless poverty" even if they are able to escape their masters (Quirk 2011: 45, 114–15). Deliberately infantilized by their enslavers (the practice of calling male slaves boys regardless of their age began in antiquity), most former slaves are ill prepared for the labor force so they need education or training before they can become productive members of the economy. Many freed Moldovan slaves become re-enslaved simply because there is nothing else for them to do, due to a lack of economic opportunities generally and for former sex slaves in particular. Ex-slaves from many countries report a cycle of escape, rejection at home, re-trafficking, re-enslavement, escape, arrest, deportation, and another round of rejection at home (Baptist 2014: 262; Finley 1980: 96; Kara 2009: 15, 115; Skinner 2008: 159, 182). Anticipating eventual re-enslavement, many slaves, if ever released from their indentures or debts, simply renegotiate their terms of service with their former masters because they are fearful that freedom means nothing more than freedom to starve. Some become enslavers themselves (Quirk 2011: 115; Murphy 2014: 71, 194).

Post-emancipation societies are never as happy as predicted because they are filled with traumatized former slaves. Freed slaves strive mightily to have normal lives but many suffer from post-traumatic stress disorder (PTSD), the Stockholm syndrome, or similar psychological issues that make it difficult for them to make up for years of lost education, meaningful work experience, and so forth. Slaves are often illiterate in the first place and few (with notable exceptions) improve their literacy skills while enslaved because of the low benefits (no clear reason to learn) and high costs (whippings or other punishments) associated with learning to read

(Engerman 2000; Skinner 2008: 102, 118; Bales and Soodalter 2009: 15, 23–24, 39, 88; Bales 2012: 59, 61; Murphy 2014: 59, 63; Brown 2000: 225, 227, 240, 244; Ali and Wain 1995: 265).

PTSD is no exaggeration. Many former slaves exhibit the same characteristics as combat veterans, including nightmares and flashbacks. Being raped, whipped, or burned with cigarettes over weeks, months, or years will do that to a person. Others develop obsessive-compulsive disorders (OCD) like eating napkins compulsively or taking numerous long baths. Many freedpersons suffer from clinical depression and a chronic inability to trust others (Lovejoy 2012: 7; Skinner 2008: 159–60, 190, 221, 278; Kara 2009: x, xiii–xiv). Louise Brown ended one interview when the ex-slave sobbed "How do I know you won't sell me" (2000: 250)? That was not an irrational response on the part of the formerly enslaved woman because many slaves found their freedom fleeting as their enslavers track them down and return them to bondage, or worse, kill them and/or their friends and family (Kara 2009: 112, 137). Little wonder, then, that some freedpersons went insane in the postbellum period and had to be committed to state hospitals, at taxpayer expense, a clear negative externality (Hurmence 1984: 13). The sanity of some people cracked while still enslaved, of course, as was the case of a slave in antebellum Maryland who believed that everyone who approached him was infamous slave trader Austin Woolfolk come to cut pieces of his flesh from him (Schermerhorn 2015: 68). Another, a 45 year-old "white slave" named Charlotte Wyles, was rescued in 1922 emaciated, filthy, and basically insane due to seven years of captivity in the home of a Pittsburgh couple named Henry and Irene Washington. The African-American couple had somehow obtained insurance on Charlotte's life but could not bring themselves to finish the job (Anon. 1922a: 1).

Few freed slaves have ever received the help they need to fully recover from their ordeals. Time eventually heals some wounds, physical and psychological, but not all. Former slave Margeaux Gray, for example, will never recover her eyesight (Gray 2016). During the healing process, which even for children can extend for years or even decades depending on the abuses suffered, ex-slaves are much less productive members of society than they otherwise would have been. Even if their enslavement was relatively benign, most formerly enslaved children are years behind in their education (Kara 2012: 160; Quirk 2011: 211–12). "In this dim Bastille of labor," the coal mines of Appalachia, wrote Markham, "young boys are wasting away their youth; are spilling the precious energy of the critical period of their lives"

(1906: 27). All this strongly suggests that the negative externalities may be higher when children are enslaved (Basu and Chau 2007: 40).

Many formerly enslaved persons are forever ashamed to have been slaves and try not to discuss it with others, particularly their free children (Hurmence 1984: ix). Unfortunately, however, slaves and ex-slaves cannot save their children from the costs created by parental enslavement. In 1913, Frederick Hicks had the same insight when he argued that convict labor is "harmful to the prisoner and to those who are dependent on him" (1913: 494). Convict labor continues to destroy poor communities and families today (Travis et al. 2014).

Obviously, children whose parents and/or siblings are torn from them, whether by slave traders or slave raiders, will suffer for it for years, decades, even for the rest of their lives. Almost as jarring would be to see one's parents beaten, maimed, raped, or otherwise tortured, day in and day out. Because enslaved parents had no authority over their own children, slavery probably weakened family mores. Parents of the victims of slavery, like Miriam Ali of Birmingham, England, who lost two daughters to marriage slavery in Yemen, often suffer nervous breakdowns and need the support of NGOs like Lost Children International to help them to cope (Davis 2003: 145–46; Ali and Wain 1995: 123; Murphy 2014: 197; Fogel 1989: 163–68).

As Jonathan Derrick argued in 1975, "the inherited psychological effects of slavery on a large number of people cannot be assessed" (p. 10). Nevertheless, Patrick Manning argued, though not entirely convincingly, that "the rise of racism followed logically upon the end of slavery," by which he meant that "racism resulted from slavery" (1990: 6, 24–25, 164). That would mean that the free children of slaves suffered from racism *caused* by their parents' enslavement (as opposed to other causes of racism).

Slavery certainly carries a social stigma. For at least a century after slavery was abolished among the Indians of the northwest coast of North America, people who had been slaves, or who were born of former slaves, were looked down upon and prevented from rising to economic, political, or social prominence, which led them to lives of violence or underachievement. In parts of medieval Europe, the descendants of slaves were not lawfully freeborn until three generations had passed. Just as clearly, the stigma of slavery was sometimes associated with race, as in colonial Spanish possessions that barred free blacks from civic life, including owning firearms, holding public office, or even going out after dark. In the 1600s, Peruvian and Mexican officials banned blacks from attending university (Donald 1997: 245–49; Davis 1966: 55, 282).

Slaves' Places of Origin

"As long as the nations of Europe continue barbarous enough to purchase slaves in Africa, we may be quite sure that Africa will continue barbarous enough to supply them" (Malthus 1817: 3:387). What Malthus meant was that slavery degraded African society, rendering economic growth impossible, which meant that Africans would continue to find it profitable to enslave each other. As noted above, slavers do not give one whit about the effects of their activities on others because all they see is the difference between what it costs them to ensnare somebody and the price they receive for that person at market. The costs they impose on their victims' homelands, however, are palpable and substantial. That is why so many peoples, including Jews, Christians, Muslims, and the Asante, banned, or tried to ban, the enslavement of their own kind or of people in their own nations. Plato, for example, opposed the enslavement of Hellenes but was all for enslaving foreigners (Davis 1966: 48, 64–66, 99–101; Manning 1990: 35).

Slaving hurts every area it touches in direct proportion to the extent that it touches it. After a band of Northumbrians took hundreds of slaves on their drive south to Northampton, England in 1065 the areas they passed through were adversely affected for many years. Due to slave raids against them by other tribes and the preference for women and child slaves, the Arkansas tribe in North America circa 1700 suffered from a skewed sex ratio and age structure that was culturally, economically, politically, and socially destabilizing. In addition to the devastation of wars, famines, epidemics, and depopulation, slaving cost Amerindian tribes much of their cultural, demographic, economic, military, and social capital. In fact, recent research suggests that it was the trauma of forced labor, not smallpox, that started the precipitous decline of native populations in the Caribbean in the early sixteenth century. Moreover, slavery was one of the main forces that kept Indian populations down because had disease been the only source of demographic pressure, populations would have rebounded, just as they did in Europe following the Black Death. Likewise, peoples living in the hill areas of Malaya, Sumatra, Sulaweis, Borneo, and so forth were devastated by the slave trade in the sixteenth and seventeenth centuries, losing an estimated 10–20 percent of their populations. Villages in South Asia that lose people to the sex trade typically lose them permanently because they will not take back victims of sexual assault (Pelteret 1995: 72; Gallay 2002: 113, 116, 154; Rubin 2002: 118–23, 188; Resendez 2016: 6, 13–17, 45; Reid 1993: 69; Batstone 2010: 69).

Differences between places that produce large numbers of slaves and those that do not are palpable. India's Uttar Pradesh teems with people and vehicles while across the India-Nepal border in Terai, population densities and traffic levels are much lower despite almost identical climates and agricultural potential. In Nepal, members of the low-caste Tharu ethnic group are pervasive and most are *kamaiya*, or bonded laborers indebted to local landowners. The *kamaiya* work long, hard hours laboring in rice fields and cleaning private homes to repay debts at high interest rates. They have no property rights to speak of, can be beaten by their landlords, and almost never receive cash payments, all the better to keep them enslaved. Tharu who escape from the *kamaiya* system are often subject to trafficking or newer forms of debt bondage. The region, like many others, is trapped in a negative feedback loop where poverty begets slavery which begets more slavery. Parsing cause and effect from snapshots and feedback cycles can be difficult (which came first, the poverty or the enslavement?), but generally speaking areas that stop producing slaves for exogenous reasons, like intervention by a foreign government, rebound economically while areas that begin to produce slaves for exogenous reasons, like civil war, suffer. Similarly, places that receive an exogenous economic boost, like from an internationally-funded dam project, witness declines in slavery and other forms of bonded labor (Kara 2012: 52, 62; Quirk 2011: 87; Kumar 1993: 125).

In the sixteenth century, Barbary corsairs depopulated large parts of the Mediterranean coast. Not everyone was seized but enough were to induce the others to flee inland. According to one contemporary observer, slave raiders by the 1580s "ravaged and ruined Sardinia, Corsica, Sicily, Calabria, the coasts of Naples, Rome and Genoa, the Balearics, and all the coasts of Spain" (Davis 2003: 35). The effects were particularly long-lived because the corsairs carried off mostly females of reproductive age. In other areas, people responded by militarizing the coasts, which led of course to the deadweight losses associated with military expenditures. Those immediately ransomed back by the corsairs (who took a fifth of the going market price to have immediate cash without the risk of mortality, loss of space on the cramped galleys, and so forth) ironically often fell into forms of debt peonage not far removed from chattel slavery (Davis 2003: 36–37, 43–44).

Most of the historical evidence regarding the costs of slave raiding and trading concerns Africa, so that continent will form the basis of what follows (Akyeampong, Bates, Nunn, and Robinson 2014). "In Africa," Jonathan Derrick wrote in 1975, "the legacy of slavery and the slave-trade is immeasurable" (p. 10). Nevertheless, scholars have tried to quantify slavery's impact on Africa and, while the exact numbers are lost to time, the overall picture is clear enough. "The tragic experience of slavery," Patrick Manning concluded in 1990, "left Africans depleted in population, divided irremediably among themselves, retarded economically, and despised as an inferior race" (pp. 2, 23).

While parts of Africa may have benefitted from the slave trade, for example, areas near seaports that grew foodstuffs, the places where slaves originated were severely negatively impacted by the trade. For starters, slave raiding was often quite physically destructive. That is why enslavement has so often been used as a tactic of war. When the Sudanese militias raided Dinka villages, for example, they killed all the males of military age, and raped and beat the women, burned their huts, and stole their livestock. Previously thriving villages simply disappeared, the physical capital destroyed or stolen and the human capital either biologically dead or economically dead (enslaved) (Inikori and Engerman 1992: 2–3; Lovejoy 2012: 35; Skinner 2008: 72, 99, 101; Jok 2007: 149, 266; Rogers and Swinnerton 2007: 30).

From time immemorial to this day, many people believe that war somehow justifies slavery, so wars are sometimes started with the main goal of seizing slaves. War is bad for economic growth, especially in the intermediate and long terms, as it, too, creates massive negative externalities (Quirk 2011: 184–91). "It is calculated," missionary Charlotte Tucker asserted in 1853, "that there were not less than twenty thousand men in Yoruba whose sole occupation was rapine and slave-hunting." That was 20,000 men not engaged in the production of goods (1853: 14–16)!

East Africa was also devastated by the slave trade and its concomitant wars, first described in detail in English by famed British explorer and doctor David Livingston, who was shocked by the desolation and destruction caused by slave raiding. In areas where Islamic raiders sourced their victims, people moved to rock shelters in a desperate attempt to defend themselves. Famines and epidemics resulted as people moved from agriculturally productive areas to defensible ones and spent their time on lookout instead of growing crops or tending livestock (Tucker 1853: 14–15; Manning 1990: 16; Fogel 1989: 236; Kusimba 2004).

Slave raiding and trading also left large parts of Africa depopulated. The number exported was only the tip of the iceberg, though, because many died in slave raids or en route to market. In the 1830s, Thomas Fowell Buxton claimed that one African died for every African that was exported as a slave. While that figure may be too high, modern estimates suggest that at least 4 million of the 30 million people forcibly removed from their homes perished right off. That left 12 million to end up in the New World, 6 million in the Orient, and 8 million elsewhere within Africa (Quirk 2011: 87; Klein 1992: 25; Manning 1990: 15; Inikori and Engerman 1992: 6; Manning 1992: 119).

How much higher the population of Africa would have been without the slave trade cannot be known with certainty because of the Malthusian dynamic, that is, deaths due to overpopulation (Eltis 1987: 68–69), but Patrick Manning estimated that sub-Saharan Africa's population would have been up to twice what it actually was had there been no slaving, or in other words, 100 million instead 50 million (1990: 84–85). The impact on local populations, moreover, was clearly hard and Malthusian cycles would not have caused the almost complete depopulation that many areas suffered, to the great detriment of the local division of labor and, hence, economic development (Eltis 1987: 13–14, 69–71). Depopulation led to food insecurity and even famines, which led to more pillaging and slaving. During one mid-eighteenth century famine, for instance, a French commander set about 500 slaves free because he could no longer acquire enough food to keep them alive (Klein 1992: 39).

Slave raiding and trading also skewed populations. In western Africa, where males were preferred for export to the New World, male to female sex ratios dropped as low as 50–100. In eastern Africa, where women and children were preferred for export to the Muslim world, the opposite ratio occurred (Manning 1992: 120).

Many areas repeatedly raided for slaves were often so economically discombobulated, even retarded, that they became slave economies themselves. Rather than build human capital related to mutually beneficial economic activities—such as tending orange, lime, or plantain trees, or raising cotton, indigo, or sugarcane—people living in areas that suffered from large shocks to cultural, economic, political, and social stability had incentives to build human capital related to stealing other human beings. According to historian Basil Davidson, some areas even developed a monoculture in Homo Sapiens. In those places, everyone was either an enslaver, enslaved, or subject to enslavement (Inikori and Engerman 1992: 3–4, 7;

Staudenraus 1961: 49; Klein 1992: 25; Davidson 1961: 278; Blackburn 2011: 85–86). "Africa, so populous, and so rich in vegetable and mineral productions," bewailed one Quaker writer in 1784, "instead of affording all the advantages of a well regulated commerce, is scarcely known but as a mart for slaves" (Anon. 1811: 5). Slave trading/raiding led in Africa to a slave system, a slave mode of production that persisted even as the slave trades (Atlantic and Indian) died down (Manning 1990: 106–7).

Slave monoculture was not Africa's natural state, however, because areas, like Kano in northern Nigeria, thrived as long as they managed to remain outside of the slaving networks (Davidson 1961: 278–79). In other words, Scottish enlightenment philosopher George Wallace (1727–1805) was right when he argued that if Africans were set free "in a few generations, this vast and fertile continent would be crowded with inhabitants; learning, arts, and every thing would flourish among them" (Anon. 1761: 265). Many others also believed Africa was good for much more than slaves (especially, if bigotedly, if 'civilized' blacks established plantations there under the supervision/instruction/tutelage of whites) (Staudenraus 1961: 7, 49). Modern studies back up Wallace by showing that places in Africa where slaving was heavier have less schooling, less literacy, less formal employment, lower levels of economic freedom, and lower per capita output to this very day (Okoye and Pongou 2015; Wiseman 2015). (A similar study shows that the older Georgia counties that initially banned slavery *today* have higher per capita incomes and lower rates of poverty than the newer Georgia counties that allowed slavery right off [Goodspeed 2015].)

The sheer size and duration of the African slave trade has impressed most observers but skeptics note that during the long nineteenth century the slave trade took a smaller percentage of Africa's population than the percentage that left many European countries for ostensibly better opportunities in the New World (Fogel 1989: 18; Eltis 1987: 66–68). That may be true, but there is a world of difference between voluntary immigration and forced removal. Liverpool was not sacked when people left there for New England; the Dutch did not tremble in fear of their own deportation when Germans from the Palatinate left Amsterdam for Pennsylvania. While the human capital of many voluntary immigrants to the New World was below the median of the societies that they left, slave raiding is pretty indiscriminate, taking or killing the best and brightest along with people from the rest of the human capital distribution. Sometimes, slavers cream skim. For example, in 1996 in Aboke, a town in northern Uganda, rebels seized

139 girls "among the best and brightest" in the entire Kole District (Batstone 2010: 93). Slaves taken by Muslim corsairs at sea often included men of wealth and/or high human capital (Davis 2003: 50–59). According to Skinner, many families that sell their own children into slavery sell the smartest ones on the theory that they have the best chance of surviving (2008: 31).

So a good case has been made that the slave trade prepared Africa for subsequent invasion and colonization by decreasing the continent's population and weakening its economy and governance relative to Europe. Many scholars still believe that imperialism aided the economies of the imperial powers but Adam Smith was probably closer to the mark when he argued that colonies cost more than they were worth. The parallel with slavery is clear: imperialism certainly aided some businesses and men but on net, and including negative externalities, cost more than the private profits accrued. The colonial powers did not vigorously end slavery but at least they did try to curtail slave raiding, which they rightly saw as a social menace and a barrier to economic development (Manning 1990: 84–85; Davidson 1961: 287; Klein 1993: 22). Missionaries also fought the slave trade the best they could. In 1853, missionary Charlotte Tucker noted that the slave trade depopulated entire countries and demoralized "both the captors and the enslaved" (p. 6). We have seen how slaving demoralized the enslaved, their families, and their communities of origin, but did slavery really negatively affect enslavers?

Enslavers

"The habit of despotism is formed almost in infancy. The child is allowed to tyrannize over the unfortunate menial appointed to gratify its wants. Parents allow this abuse of power, without being aware of its fatal tendency" (Cary 1830: 203). When enslavers buy slaves, they exchange money for human beings, not things but sentient beings with "exquisite senses, life-lit eyes, pluck, volition," as Walt Whitman put it in "I Sing the Body Electric" (Whitman 1894: 85). Those sentient beings do not want to be enslaved, even if they agreed to serve as slaves. So they resist their slave traders and enslavers in sundry ways designed to hurt the perpetrators of their pain (Fogel 1989: 156–57; Skinner 2008: 35).

Chapter 5 showed that enslavers enslave primarily because they profit from enslaving. But that profit does not include slavery's negative effects on anyone, including the enslavers themselves. Delineating the damage that slavery causes enslavers in no way expiates their sins. They remain, as Richard Baxter astutely called them in *A Christian Directory* (1664/1665), the "common enemies of mankind" (Davis 1966: 338). The point of this section is simply to make clear that slavery creates negative externalities so extensive that they even fall on enslavers.

Parents who sell their own children are nothing more than slave traders and readers can easily see that many must have hated themselves after the dastardly deed was done (Kara 2012: 73). Undoubtedly, other enslavers hated themselves as well. According to one story, possibly apocryphal but powerful nonetheless, a Southern mistress made her runaway slave woman wear a bell that clanked whenever she moved. After emancipation, the mistress went crazy and thought she heard the bell all the time (Ovington 1910). A more recent story, definitely not apocryphal, is of a California woman who treated her slave the same as her dogs. The mistress went crazy while attempting to create a fantasy world where she owned happy pets, both canine and human (Bales and Soodalter 2009: 29). Not even committing highway robbery, John Newton claimed, had "a more direct tendency" than slavery "to efface the moral sense, to rob the heart of every gentle and humane disposition, and to harden it, like steel, against all impressions of sensibility" (Davis 1966: 390).

Granted, some enslavers were crazy or evil to begin with. Ramesh Garg, for example, was probably a monster and a serial killer before his evil brain got greedy as well (Skinner 2008: 222). Hitler and Stalin, two of the greatest enslavers of the twentieth century, were brutal psychopaths before they opened their first slave labor camps (Hochschild 2003; Von Plato et al. 2010). Other enslavers, like the infamous Mr. Vasu described by David Batstone, were not well balanced emotionally to begin with but made worse by having slaves that they could beat and rape at will (2010: 61).

But even perfectly normal people who become enslavers tend to evolve into despotic brutes, despotic because most of the time people do their bidding without challenge, and brutish because when they do run into opposition they respond decisively and violently (Mason 2006: 47). Montesquieu argued that slavery "debased one class, to the detriment of public virtue; and corrupted another with luxury and excessive power" (Davis 1966: 407). "Wherever it has been established," Augustin Cochin noted, "servitude has corrupted and debased the ruling race, and brought it back towards barbarism" (1863: 59–60). "It is no severe reproach to the man who has possessed slaves," Thomy Hugon of the Bengal service mentioned when he saw firsthand how poorly Indian indentured laborers were treated in Mauritius, “to say that he has despotic habits which he has to change entirely when he comes in control of free men” (Tinker 1993: 18). “The slaveholder lives from infancy in an atmosphere of despotism,” political economist J. E. Cairnes explained in 1862. “He sees around him none but abject creatures, who, under fearful penalties to be inflicted by himself, are bound to do his slightest, his most unreasonable, bidding” (p. 95). “The system itself makes the planters bad,” C. F. Andrews wrote in June 1915. “It gives them too much power: and there is a brute side in every man” (Tinker 1993: 337). Georg Wilhem Friedrich Hegel (1770–1831) once wrote, with great truth, that the servility of the serf costs his master his humanity (Vogt 1975: 4). According to Ed Baptist, “for many southwestern whites, whipping was a gateway form of violence that led to bizarrely creative levels of sadism” (2014: 141). It was no wonder that notorious slave trader Austin Woolfolk physically assaulted abolitionist Benjamin Lundy. William Lloyd Garrison, William Wells Brown, and Frederick Douglass also had to be protected from enslavers’ penchant for violence (Schermerhorn 2015: 62, 65).

Cruelty, Henry Whiteley argued, begat callousness and hence more cruelty, in women as well as men (Whiteley 1833: 4; Murphy 2014: 252, 260, 263). Sandra Bearden was a typical suburban housewife until she got a young slave and learned by degrees that beating and humiliating her felt good (Bales and Soodalter 2009: 4–5). Mary Prince was beaten by “a fearful woman, and a savage mistress to her slaves” (Childs 2015: 133). Ex-slave Bob Jones told of a Miss Betsy who “was crabbed and hard to get along with. She whupped the servants ... and it was her what whupped my sister Mary so bad. There warn’t but six of us slaves, but them six run a race to see who can stay out of her sight” (Hurmence 1984: 3). “One of our master’s daughters was cruel,” reported another ex-slave (Hurmence 1984: 17). “We was sold to Miz Fanny Long in Franklin county,” explained another. “That woman was a devil if there ever was one” (Hurmence 1984: 36). Ria Sorrel also recalled that her master’s “wife was a pure devil, she just joyed whupping Negroes” (Hurmence 1984: 63). Circa 1830, Virginia Cary witnessed “a young and *beautiful* female inflicting corporal chastisement *with her own hands*, and in severe measure, upon a woman older by many years than herself” (Cary 1830: 203). Wang sold a young slave he purchased for his wife as an anniversary present in China in 1937 (after slavery had been legally abolished there) because he grew “sorely disappointed that his wife, usually of a gentle disposition, displayed such a fiery temper and ill-will toward the little slave, beating her with a bamboo rod or a French-heeled slipper on the slightest provocation and scolding, even cursing, the youngster without cause" (Leaf, 1937: 63). Restavec Jean-Robert Cadet recalled that his enslaver, Florence, possessed an "unrelenting ... desire to inflict pain" upon his young body (1998: 14).

In his *Notes on Virginia,* Thomas Jefferson vaguely admitted that "there must, doubtless be an unhappy influence on the manners of our people, produced by the existence of slavery among us" (Owen 1864: 115). Lord Palmerston (Henry John Temple, 1784–1865) also believed that "slavery and the slave trade" demoralized people due to "all the degrading and corrupting influences connected with both" (Eltis 1987: 85). Contemporaries like Robert Dale Owen were happy to elaborate. In addition to "imperiousness of manner, impatience of contradiction or delay, ungovernable passion, contempt of labor," slavery also bred profligacy (1864: 116). "Female chastity," Owen continued, "is neither respected by custom nor protected by law" (p. 117). As early as 1700, it was already "too well known what Temptations Masters are under, to connive at the Fornification of their Slaves" (Sewall 1700: 2).

Some enslavers apparently became sex addicts (Fogel 1989: 327). At New Ground plantation in Jamaica in the 1830s, a visitor noted that "the overseer, book-keepers, and head carpenter, all lived in the habitual practice of gross and unblushing profligacy" (Whiteley 1833: 11). One bookkeeper had sex with a dozen different slaves within a six-month period. The ancients also complained of masters who were licentious (Finley 1980: 13, 100). When discovered or suspected by family members, as they often were, such infidelities had serious negative consequences on jealous wives and children who knew that their half-siblings remained enslaved (Cochin 1863: 83–84).

Though not common, slaves sometimes kill their enslavers, as trafficked Thai women in Japan did in the 1990s (Brown 2000: 195). Ancient masters also feared being killed or tricked by their slaves. *Quot servi tot hostes* (every slave is an enemy) stated one Roman proverb.[1] Much tension existed between slaves and masters in Rome as revealed both by elite sources and also low brow astrological handbooks and dream interpretation books (McKeown 2007: 39). Tensions pervaded other slave societies as well. When in 1765 Anthony Hunter of New York City was drowned along with "a Negro Lad ... by the oversetting of a small Skiff, about 100 Yards from the Shore off of Johnston's Ferry, at Staten-Island" was it a tragic accident or a murder-suicide (Anon. 1765: 2)? Few enslavers feared a successful slave rebellion but most felt "the most distressing insecurity individually. We are like a crowd of people," Henry Berry explained to the Virginia House of Delegates in 1832, "towards whom a single man should point a loaded gun, with the apparent intent to fire upon them. They know he cannot kill them all, but each feels that his own life is in peril" (p. 3). At the same time, slaveholders near Kumasi, the capital of the Asante Empire, trembled at the thought of a slave insurrection because they were surrounded by entire villages of slaves established to feed the army. In response, Asante leaders killed large numbers of slaves and shipped off untold others to distant plantations (Lovejoy 2012: 167, 248).

Fearful of their slaves, enslavers in the antebellum US South usually carried weapons with them at all times and that led to negative externalities like violent pastimes and customs such as dueling. Homicide rates in the South were many times that of the North. After the Civil War, men who ran farms and mines with convict laborers, poor men seized by authorities on the slightest pretense, were also a violent lot prone to excessive bouts of alcohol consumption (Fogel 1989: 327; Baptist 2014: 221; Blackmon 2008: 128–29).

Slaves also sometimes inadvertently killed their masters through communicable diseases like smallpox as well as sexually transmitted diseases (STDs) (Turton 2004: 92). The slave trade killed large numbers of slaves but also large numbers of slavers and raiders. Thomas Clarkson learned from the records of more than 300 slavers that the African trade killed proportionally more sailors than slaves (Blackburn 2011: 165; Fogel 1989: 130). In a 1787 survey out of Liverpool, sailor mortality reached close to half (Fogel 1989: 118)! Such harsh realities sometimes brought even heartless-seeming middle passage slavers to tears and occasionally action (Davis 1966: 184–85). More common, though, was the outcome in Bob Dylan's song "Tangled Up in Blue" when something inside of the singer died when he started dealing in slaves.

Even passive slaves worried their masters. "How can we be care-free," ancient Indian masters complained, "when we have to (exert ourselves to) support our parents … our slaves, servants and other dependents" (Chanana 1964: 55). That was the same sort of sentiment some antebellum Southern slaveholders expressed when they claimed that they were the real slaves because they had to take care of their negro charges (Smith 1985: 21). Not all slaves could be fed all the time; indigenous enslavers in the southeast part of North America sometimes tortured and executed their slaves when they became too difficult to feed (Donald 1997: 268).

Enslavers tend not to be religious, and when they are, their religious beliefs are skewed to justify the cruel institution (Anon. 1784: 7–8). "A professor," complained Virginia Cary, "once reproved his servant in my presence, for being guilty of using unholy language *before his earthly master*, while not a word was said of the still greater offence committed against the unseen Jehovah" (p. 204). Slavery rendered plantation owners in the antebellum US South so racist and ethnocentric that they could not adapt to changed circumstances after the Civil War (Smith 1985: 54–57).

Slavery also rendered masters and their families indolent and slothful in addition to mean, nasty, and immoral (Finley 1980: 100; Cairnes 1862: 89). Hegel pointed out that someone with total power would actually be powerless because s/he would be helpless, totally dependent on his/her minions (Patterson 1982: 2). He was right. When Diogenes freed his slave Manes, he reputedly said that "it would be absurd if Manes can live without Diogenes, but Diogenes cannot get on without Manes" (Davis 1966: 74). At least three paintings exist showing slaves in Brazil carrying their masters, grown men, about in covered hammocks, as if the masters were invalids or infants.

John Woolman noted how slaveowners' children were lazy, spoiled, and idle because they never had to develop a work discipline (Davis 1966: 484). According to Benjamin Franklin, enslavers learn to be "disgusted with Labor" and they were "educated in Idleness," leaving them "unfit to get a Living by Industry" (Houston 2008: 131). Rebecca Gratz noted that "one of the curses of slavery is the entire dependence the poor mistress is reduced to when she is rich enough to have all her wants supplied by numerous servants" (Rosengarten and Rosengarten 2002: 85). "As a general rule," Virginia legislator Henry Berry quipped in 1832, "the slaves only half work, and the masters do not work at all" (p. 7). Angelina Weld complained that South Carolina mistresses were "such fine ladies that if a shutter is to be hooked, or a chair moved, or their work handed to them, a servant must be summoned to do it for them" (Birney 1970: 87). Some former slaveholders admitted that they sold or manumitted all their slaves because they were unwilling to allow their "own children to be educated as slave-masters" (Olmsted 1856: 94).

A slave in his youth, Booker T. Washington forgave his former masters noting that "the slave system … in a large measure, took the spirit of self-reliance and self-help out of the white people" (1901: 17). Of course by the time Washington penned those words, the South's new enslavers were ruining their own capacity for work. "As formerly the people of the South were the slaves of slavery," Carl Schurz wrote in 1903, "so they are now to be made the victims of their failure to abolish slavery altogether."

Population Growth

As discussed above, slave raiding and trading reduced the population of areas forced to export slaves. The total number of slaves tells only part of the story as many were killed during raids or in transit to market and many others were killed indirectly through the loss of caregivers, the breakdown of tribal support systems, and so forth (Lovejoy 2012: 61–62). This section shows that slavery usually stunted the population of slaves themselves and the societies in which they toiled (Lovejoy 2012: 7). The most obvious instances of this occurred where slavery and genocide coincided, as they often have, as in the Armenian genocide of 1915, the Soviet, Nazis, and Khmer Rouge purges, and the Sudanese civil war in the last part of the twentieth century (Goldberg 2007: 152; Skinner 2008: 71).

Throughout history, most forms of slavery have not been hereditary, sometimes because slaves were soon manumitted or their offspring were not considered slaves, but more often because the slaves died before they reproduced (Bush 1996: 7). "Most of the indentured laborers who crossed the seas a hundred years ago or more," historian Hugh Tinker wrote, "died without issue" (1993: xiii). Benjamin Franklin noted the negative population growth among slaves and ascribed it to the fact that slaves were "worked too hard, and ill fed, their Constitutions are broken, [so] the Deaths among them are more than their Births" (Houston 2008: 131).

In the United States, in fact, the slave population did experience natural growth, though it did not grow as quickly as the free population did until after 1840, when freeperson birth rates dropped as part of the modern demographic transition (fewer births due to lower child mortality rates and increased longevity) (Fogel 1989: 116, 124; Cochin 1863: 63). Theodore Weld claimed that the older slave states purposely bred slaves for the southwestern market, where slave mortality rates were much higher and birth rates much lower due to the harsher climate as well as the harsher work regimes of new cotton and sugar plantations (Fogel 1989: 119–20; Blackburn 2011: 313; Schermerhorn 2015: 90). While there is little evidence of actually breeding slaves like horses or other livestock, the newer areas did import slaves from the East Coast in significant numbers.

Slaves in mainland North America may also have been able to reproduce themselves because America was the "best poor man's country," a region where even slaves could find sufficient food and shelter if provided a modicum of freedom (Lemon 1972). Especially after the importation of new slaves was outlawed, enslavers in the US South fed their slaves considerably better than enslavers in Cuban and Surinam fed their slaves. Unsurprisingly, US-born slaves were taller than slaves born in Trinidad, Guyana, and Cuba. They were also taller than Africans but not as tall as northern whites on average (Manning 1992: 119; Fogel 1989: 132–34, 140–41).

Elsewhere, like in Antigua, Brazil, Haiti, and most other places on the globe throughout history, slaves died off faster than they reproduced themselves. In the British West Indies as a whole the number of slaves dropped from 800,000 to 650,000 between 1808 and 1830 (Blackburn 2011: 81, 207, 310; Gaspar 1992: 306; Schulz 2008: xi; Fogel 1989: 127; Tinker 1993: 1). "What we know about the demography of slaves," anthropologist Claude Meillassoux wrote of slave societies in general, "suggests that a continual inflow of captives was necessary, as much to renew the slave population as to increase it" (1991: 78). This echoes Cochin: "It is a law of nature, that the human species (and some species of the animal kingdom share in this title of nobility) does not increase in servitude" (Cochin 1863: 61–62).

Serfs tended to regenerate but chattel slaves and debt peons held in chattel slave-like conditions did not. This had more to do with the relative freedom of serfdom than the time or place because medieval slaves were notoriously poor breeders. While one might think that enslavers would encourage their slaves to procreate, in fact, most found it cheaper to buy new slaves rather than to suffer the costs associated with pregnancy, child birth, and child-rearing (Bush 1996: 2; Pelteret 1995: 16; Fogel 1989: 118).

Because enslavers did not want to encourage fecundity, many slave societies had skewed sex ratios, which meant that many men or women were not reproductively active. Female genital mutilation and castration did not help matters. Neither did the fact that the average age of menarche for female slaves in the antebellum US South, the best fed slaves in the world, was 16, which is what it is in the poorest nations in the world today. Even in the United States, young slaves were much smaller than average and suffered from the distended bellies associated with insufficient protein intake. They suffered from low birth weight too, because their mothers often worked right up until childbirth. Even women in the last week of pregnancy picked three quarters of the average weight of cotton picked by women their same age. Breastfeeding also stopped quite early. All that spelled miscarriage and infant mortality rates for slaves that was two times higher than that for their free white contemporaries (Meillassoux 1991: 314; Skinner 2008: 73–74; Fogel 1989: 134, 142–46).

In the West Indies, birth rates were decent but infant mortality rates were even higher due to harder work, less food, and even less time spent nursing. Infant mortality was close to 100 percent, ostensibly because mothers were so close to death themselves that they could not produce milk. Out of defiance to their masters, many slaves limited their own reproductive ability through birth control, abortion, and infanticide. Others decreased or even lost their reproductive capabilities by contracting STDs from other slaves, their masters, or johns. Many enslaved prostitutes today become sub-fertile or even entirely infertile (Blackburn 2011: 82; Campbell 2004: xiv; Turton 2004: 93; Brown 2000: 218).

At all ages, slaves in the ancient world were 1–5 percent more likely to die than non-slaves. Little changed over the millennia. Mortality rates of Europeans enslaved in the Maghreb have been estimated at 10–30 percent per year depending on the age and condition of the victim when enslaved. Enslavement of Africans and Native Americans made diseases spread more quickly among the latter, leading to their demographic collapse. In Bahia in 1682 a Negro who lived for 7 years in slavery was considered long-lived indeed (McKeown 2007: 127; Davis 2003: 16–17; Manning 1990: 30–31; Davis 1966: 232).

In the late nineteenth century, the neoslaves of the Gulf of Guinea died at high rates. One in five perished in the first 18 months. Infant mortality rates there were so high that the population, though possessing close to a 50–50 sex ratio, could not reproduce itself (Clarence-Smith 1993: 157). Slave mortality rates in Pemba, Zanzibar, and Malindi in late-nineteenth century East Africa ranged from 10 to 20 percent per year (Harris 1910: 471; Anon. 1910a: 7; Lovejoy 2012: 269). Coal and other miners, especially those close to the slave end of the spectrum, suffered high mortality rates due to both "the quick freak of accident [and] the slow creep of disease" (Markham 1906: 25). Mortality on Latin American rubber plantations was also high. In the Putumayo district, the Amerindian population fell from 40,000 or 50,000 to 10,000 in the first decade of the twentieth century (Kloosterboer 1960: 104). An expert on modern Mumbai's red-light district, Manju Vyas, claims that "most victims rarely survived past their mid-thirties" (Kara 2009: 15), a fact echoed by Louise Brown (2000: 210). Many trafficked women in South and Southeast Asia develop AIDS and/or tuberculosis and then are discarded to die (Brown 2000: 1; Bales 2012).

As noted elsewhere, slaves are also more likely to kill themselves than free people are. Especially en route to their destinations, infanticide, abortion, and homicide were also unusually common (Tinker 1993: 12, 206; Simon 1929: 265).

Due to the material conditions in which they are usually kept, as well as their inability to take measures to protect themselves from pathogens, slaves are also apt to contract and spread diseases among themselves as well as non-slaves. Depots where Indian indentured laborers were collected, for example, were cesspools of stink and contagious disease (Tinker 1993: 141). As Brown pointed out, HIV/AIDS spread easily among slaves because enslaved women are not usually allowed to consult doctors, intervention programs rarely reach them, and they often cannot insist that johns use a condom (2000: 221–24).

Because slaves did not reproduce themselves in most slave societies, they had to be replenished by raid or by trade. Most Northwest Coast Indian slaves, for example, were probably war captives even though slavery was hereditary. Slave mothers committed infanticide frequently, either at behest of their mistresses, who did not want to bear the cost of child-rearing, or at their own desire not to have the child raised a slave (Finley 1980: 28–30; Donald 1997: 33, 116–17).

According to Benjamin Franklin, slavery reduced the number of free inhabitants too by reducing employment for free whites, discouraging immigration, and enfeebling enslavers. Slavery certainly discouraged immigration by non-slaves into places like the US South, which also, like other slave societies in history, lost numerous free inhabitants to emigration because, as Cassius Clay claimed, "they never had put labor on a respectable footing in slave states" (Davis 1966: 142–43; Finley 1980: 29; Eltis 1987: 14; Fogel 1989: 91; Blackburn 2011: 151, 307; Wright 1987, pp. 854–55; Clay 1848: 225). Much of the small flow of Northerners into the South was composed of individuals who sought to redeem their Southern brethren by showing them the superiority of free (well, less enslaved) labor (Smith 1945). The South's low population density, in turn, made financial services more costly there (James 1981: 447).

Interestingly, enslavers often had relatively low birth rates as well because the need to have children to work was obviated by owning slaves (Turton 2004: 92). Franklin's claim about enfeebling enslavers was discussed earlier in this very section. His claim about reducing employment is taken up in the next section.

Non-slave Laborers and Their Employers

Non-slave laborers eschewed markets where slaves were present in any significant numbers. Few voluntarily migrated into slave societies and those with the misfortune to be born in one moved away if they could. Where they could not, they sometimes threatened rebellion unless competition from slaves was decreased. Part of this reaction to slave labor was purely social: non-slaves did not want to be equated with slaves so they tended to avoid the sorts of work that slaves did, which often equated to all manual labor. As historian Randall Miller explained, Southern industrialists were forced to use slaves in some factories because the white workers would not submit to factory discipline (Ashworth 1995: 112; Finley 1980: 49; Owen 1864: 126; Fogel 1989: 328; Miller 1981; Shirley 1994: 84–93).

Another part of the reason that non-slave laborers refused to work was economic. By enslaving others, enslavers lowered the equilibrium wage rate below what would have prevailed had all laborers been free enough to create a competitive market. Kentuckian Richard Oglesby moved to Illinois because in his home state "poor white girls washed there all day over a hot and steaming tub, and under a blazing sun, for ten cents a day . . . Simply because a negro wench, equally strong, could be hired for that price. . . . I hired out for six dollars a month . . . Because a negro man, of . . . equal physical strength, could be hired for seventy-five dollars per year" (Huston 2003: 67). As Kevin Bales so eloquently put it, "slave labor anywhere threatens real jobs everywhere" (2012: 24).

Part of the wage effect is due to an increase in supply (number of hours worked) that masters forced out of slaves above and beyond what they would have supplied in a competitive market. Why pay a wage worker $1.00 cash to perform some unskilled service, enslavers reasoned, when a slave could do it for, say, $.50, with payment in kind at that? So, unless desperate, an enslaver would either not hire the wage worker at all or do so only at a reduced wage. Either way, the wage worker's total compensation would be depressed toward, if not to, the level of the slave. Depressed wages also helped enslavers by creating a group of non-slaves who could help to control recalcitrant slaves by manning slave patrols and militia units (Fogel 1989: 346; Cairnes 1862: 55).

All this is why Hinton Helper called five million of the antebellum US South's poor Euroamericans "the white victims of slavery" (1860: 32–33, 44). The idea was not new. In the eighteenth century, for example, John Martin Bolzius of Ebenezer, Georgia, argued slavery would corrupt or impoverish whites who could not compete with slaves in town trades or in farm work (Davis 1966: 149). But the notion that slavery depressed wages, reduced incentives to work, and drove the poor into sloth and vice actually stretched back into antiquity (Eltis 1987: 235; Finley 1980: 32). Modern abolitionism began in Britain when in the late eighteenth century some 400,000 artisans and laborers became aware enough of slavery's effects on their wages and social status to sign abolitionist petitions. Leading early nineteenth century British factory reformers, like Richard Oastler, also supported abolition in the belief that it would help the working poor (Blackburn 2011: 166, 305).

Mass abolitionism was also closely tied to industrialization in France and the United States. In the eighteenth century, when most Americans were proprietors who owned farms, shops, or stores, slavery seemed distant. By the middle of the nineteenth century, however, millions of Americans worked for wages and, as described in Chap. 4, were only somewhat removed from complete enslavement due to long and personally intrusive labor contracts. Little wonder they feared either being replaced by slaves or becoming enslaved themselves. A few extreme pessimists even foresaw New Englanders being forced to cultivate the tobacco fields of the South (Blackburn 2011: 368–69; Mason 2006: 57). That might seem farfetched but, as one contemporary put it, he who would enslave an African "would not spare you, if he had you legally in his power" (Mason 2006: 79). In the North, such fears manifested as support for American Republicans (nativism), Free Soilers (cheap western lands), and Republicans (Huston 2003: xiv; Fogel 1989: 309–19).

Northern wage laborers were not imagining things as their real wages decreased in the 1840s and 1850s along with their biometrics (weight and height). If the West became slave territory, immigrants and wage laborers would not go there and that would further depress wages in the East. They knew that wage laborers in Nova Scotia had almost died of starvation after the government brought in a large group of redemptioners to increase the population of Halifax for strategic defense reasons (Fogel 1989: 36–62, 371; Smith 1965: 24–25). As the Civil War wound down, abolitionist Robert Dale Owen had to reassure Northern wage workers that emancipation would not result in a "swarm" of freedpersons heading "to the North in search of work" (1864: 209).

The movement to abolish the system of penal servitude was also led by free laborers trying to protect themselves from competition. "The strongest force in this direction has been the protest of organized labor against the unfair competition of convict goods" (Anon. 1916: 374). As this quotation suggests, Northern wage laborers were also in the vanguard in the struggle against the postbellum convict labor system just as workers in the 1820s and 1830s had railed against the use of convict labor, especially in New York (Commons et al. 1918: 1:155, 432, 443).

In the antebellum South, abolitionists were quite unwelcomed. In Columbia, South Carolina, an Irish immigrant with more economic than political sense opined that slavery decreased the wages of free laborers. For his trouble, a mob tarred and feathered him on his bare skin. Nevertheless, downward pressure on wages attributed to the presence of slaves manifested itself as political pressure on Southern state legislatures to restrict the economic activities of slaves, especially in urban centers like Charleston, Norfolk, Richmond, and Savannah. Such regulations rarely worked for long, as shown by the experience of Barbados, which at first banned slaves from the higher skilled crafts and management, explicitly to reserve such occupations for Christians. Soon enough, though, slaves became drivers and skilled artisans, such as sugar boilers, because enslavers could profitably employ them in such positions (Baptist 2014: 386; Fogel 1989: 42–43).

Because, as shown in Chap. 5, enslaving others is profitable, businesses that do not use slave labor are also at a competitive disadvantage vis-à-vis those that do, a point recently made by the ILO. Slaves are compensated far less than they would be in competitive markets and enslavers spend less on health and safety equipment than they otherwise would, pretty much in direct proportion to the slave's replacement cost. Where slaves are cheap, they can literally die on the job without hurting the enslaver's bottom line. That is why young prostitutes have been allowed to die while servicing johns and why prostitutes were killed by fire while chained to their beds, a la the Triangle Shirtwaist Factory atrocity in 1911. Businesses that do not use slave labor also lament slavery's damaging effects on the overall business climate, including general levels of education, infrastructure, and technology (Quirk 2011: 124, 210; van den Anker 2004: 23; International Labour Organization 2014: 45; Brown 2000: 19, 122; Argersinger 2016).

Education, Infrastructure, and Technology

"Slavery and knowledge are incompatible" (quoted in Whiteley 1833: 13). "What we need in Brazil," a writer for *Rio News* asserted in 1888, "is a large class of small planters, tradesmen, mechanics, etc., who will be proprietors and taxpayers, and who will be deeply interested in the protection of life and property, the maintenance of schools, the creation of roads, bridges, etc., and the intelligent development of agriculture and skilled industries" (Schulz 2008: vi). Brazil did not have such a class because of slavery, and specifically the interests of enslavers. "The ignorance of the free," Cassius Clay wrote, "is the security to the holders of the enslaved" so slave societies tended to frown upon the creation of human capital, even in non-slaves (Clay 1848: 226). Or as Ralph Waldo Emerson wrote in 1844 in his "Address Delivered in Concord on the Anniversary of the Emancipation of the Negroes in the British West Indies," "slavery is no scholar, no improver; it does not love the whistle of the railroad; it does not love the newspaper, the mail-bag, a college, a book or a preacher … It does not improve the soil; everything goes to decay" (Wright 1987: 857). As "Aristides" noted, "in New-England, you can seldom find a man who cannot read and write" but in South Carolina "one-fifth part of the adult whites cannot read" (1844).

John Millar, colleague of Adam Smith at the University of Glasgow, argued that throughout history, slavery had epitomized the forces of barbarism, ignorance, and wastefulness (Davis 1966: 438). Foremost, enslavers wanted to prevent their slaves from gaining any knowledge in any manner that might suggest that a life outside of slavery was possible or desirable. For that reason, most enslavers would not openly debate the merits of abolition, just stop the circulation of antislavery materials, because merely debating the subject might put dangerous ideas into enslaved brains (Anon. 1835: 8–9). Attempts by various religious denominations to establish schools for slaves in the West Indies and elsewhere were also squelched by enslavers who believed that slave literacy and their personal security were irreconcilable (Davis 1966: 220).

Enslavers also wished to keep non-slave laborers in their proper places so they limited education and infrastructure as much as possible (Davis 1966: 158). "Of schools, roads, and welfare institutions," wrote Augustin Cochin, "the West Indies were virtually destitute" (Cochin 1863: 43–44). The antebellum US South was better, but still had many fewer schools, teachers, pupils, and libraries than the North. According to Edward Atkinson, Southern soldiers during the Civil War eventually "had learned that they were fighting for a class interest and against their own, that northern systems, schools, etc., were much better than theirs" (Williamson 1934: 18). Only military discipline kept them fighting so long, late war deserters claimed. Per capita literacy rates, even for non-slaves, were also relatively low in the South as well as in other New World slave societies like Cuba and Brazil (Blackburn 2011: 307).

To this day in Mauritania, where chattel slavery is still a major institution, slaves are rarely allowed to learn to read. In India, too, illiteracy and bondage still go hand in hand. Those enslaved as children today are typically illiterate and often have little understanding of numeracy or even time. Some do not even understand the concept of choice because their masters always told them what to do or want (Bales 2012: 3, 113; Kumar 1993: 124–25).

Slaves of course have almost no incentive to innovate, which means they do not create the positive externalities or spillover effects associated with innovation (Eltis 1987: 21; Murphy 2014: 165). As Adam Smith noted, speaking of Hungarian and Turkish miners, "slaves … are very seldom inventive; and all the most important improvements … have been the discovery of freemen" (Smith 1776/1937: 648). It was no accident that the Derosne train, which mechanized the sugar boiling process, was invented by a free man of color in Louisiana, not a slave (Blackburn 2011: 288). Only slaves who believed that they could buy their freedom by working especially hard or smart could be induced to innovate and they appear to have been few (Scheidel 2008: 112–15; Rihll 2008: 127–28). Even in "open" slave societies, manumissions were infrequent and were used mostly to bolster the institution in the long-run (Engerman 2007: 266).

As personal property, slaves were extremely geographically mobile. In fact, their mobility was one of their most attractive features for enslavers. As a result of that mobility, however, enslavers have little interest in public goods provision, including education and transportation infrastructure, which would only serve to bring in unneeded outsiders. In the antebellum US South, enslavers were "labor lords" who regularly jumped to fertile new land, leaving vast, undeveloped swathes in their rear. Crude public roads were sufficient to get cash crops to rivers (cleared of debris by federal subsidies) and hence to market once a year and they were also sufficient to carry slaves and some household goods to new lands once a decade. They were insufficient to allow for constant commercial intercourse (and its concomitant, the further extension of the division of labor), but that could be suffered because slaves could make most of what the master needed. A similar dynamic prevented African enslavers from investing in technology or permanent public goods (Wright 1987: 852, 854, 860;

Schermerhorn 2015: 15–16, 20; Clay 1848: 346; Hurmence 1984: 18, 26, 69; Lovejoy 2012: 268–69).

According to Richard Kilbourne and others, antebellum slaveholders were little more than rentiers, that is, people who collected payments from capital (to wit their slaves), but without any innovation or entrepreneurship, a claim certainly supported by the relatively few patents awarded to Southerners before the Civil War. After emancipation, Southern enslavers became landlords (to debt peons) and were forced by circumstances to become more entrepreneurial to survive. Not surprisingly, the South became somewhat more demographically and commercially dynamic though the continuance of slavery under another name continued to hold it back, compared to the North, until after the Civil Rights movement. A similar transition also occurred in the West Indies and Brazil, where after emancipation imports of machines from Great Britain almost doubled despite much increased political instability (Fogel 1989: 108–9; Kilbourne 1995: 6; Cochin 1863: 44; Wright 1987: 856, 863–70; Ransom and Sutch 2001; Lichtenstein 1996: 107; Schulz 2008: 95).

In the antebellum US North, by contrast, development proceeded steadily westward in a line broken only by geographical impediments. The North therefore built dense bridge, canal, railroad, and turnpike networks that aided market development and encouraged competition. Northerners also enthusiastically supported public education because they had strong stakes in their communities and wanted to see them thrive, which would drive up their land values. Real estate in the North was, in fact, worth much more than in the South, $35 per acre on average compared to $10 per acre according to one modern estimate (Wright 1987: 853, 858).

Northern factory owners had to recruit labor to their relatively fixed locations so they too supported public goods like schools and bridges. That made the North, in Gavin Wright's words, "a veritable demographic vacuum cleaner" that sucked up almost all immigrants to North America and many poor Southerners as well (Wright 1987: 855). The North was so much more developed than the South that the US Postal Service ran a profit in the North that subsidized postal service in the South (Helper 1860: 307), which ran at a loss because the population was, in the words of contemporary E. H. Derby, "nearly twice as dense in the free States as at the South; and at least three times as dense, if the negroes, who rarely read or write, be excluded" (1850: 8).

According to John Millar, enslavers did not notice how little work their slaves did when not carefully monitored because "this circumstance may easily be overlooked in a country where the inhabitants are strangers to improvement" (1771/2006: 249). Where improvements are few, nobody notices that slaves are laggards, "but when the arts begin to flourish, when the wonderful effects of industry and skill in cheapening commodities, and in bringing them to perfection, become more and more conspicuous, it must be evident that little profit can be drawn from the labour of a slave" (p. 249). Slave societies were, in fact, less technologically advanced than freer ones and that was just the way enslavers wanted it.

The antebellum US South, for example, had a strong economy by world standards but according to economist historians Fred Bateman and Thomas Weiss, it "could have done better than it did. Had there been more manufacturing investment, southern economic performance would have improved" (1981: 158). What prevented manufacturing from flowering there was slavery, specifically its effect on planter incentives, not comparative advantage. As the South later showed, manufacturing could flourish there, especially on the large swathes of less than prime agricultural land to be found in the uplands and pine forests (Schurz 1903).

In the antebellum South, however, as in other slave societies, enslavers had big disincentives to use new, expensive, labor-saving technologies. Worried that any change might endanger slavery, enslavers were very conservative on most matters, especially political and economic ones. Many Alabamans, for example, fought against modernization, industrialization, and railroads, and even pulled down telegraphs out of suspicion that they caused a drought. Alabama also taxed the stocks of financial and manufacturing corporations more heavily than it taxed slave and agricultural assets (Schurz 1903; Thornton 1978: 104, 291–92, 308–11, 316, 431–32).

Forced laborer management best practices gurus counseled that slaves needed to be kept busy lest they plot rebellion or steal from the master so simple tools and human power should be used instead of steam or even animal power. In the antebellum US South, slaves worked mines with crude hand tools and drained water from the holes via buckets over a century after the invention of steam engines designed specifically to pump water out of mines (Tinker 1993: 9; Blackmon 2008: 20). As Theodore Parker noted, the North "reduced iron and fire to slavery" while the South reduced "men into machines" (Cochin 1863: 45). Little wonder that Carl Schurz argued that slavery weighted down industry and commercial enterprise "like an incubus" (1903).

Slavery also created an addiction to cheap labor, by which I mean that enslavers always thought first of how to cut labor costs rather than about how to improve labor productivity. So when the slaves were freed in the South, Southern plantation owners said they wanted Northern, Irish, and German laborers to replace them to work their estates for ten bucks a month and cheap rations, which of course was well below the competitive wage. Places with a history of slavery, like Africa, expanded the use of slaves when they entered the global economy instead of investing in more capital-intensive technologies. The failure to improve productivity through technology explains why, while some slave or serf societies had a few factories, none ever experienced the set of economic transformations (improved agricultural productivity, transportation efficiency, and urbanization) associated with the Industrial Revolution while slaves still constituted the bulk of the labor force (Foner 1983: 36, 47; Quirk 2011: 85–87; Kolchin 1996: 48). (The number of workers engaged in manufacturing rose in the South 72 percent between 1820 and 1860 but over those same years manufacturing employment in the North rose 383 percent. So the North transformed but the South did not [Fogel 1989: 103].)

Basically, enslavers feared that industrialization and urbanization would end slavery (Ashworth 1995: 99; Cochin 1863: 45–46; Bateman and Weiss 1981: 161) because cities and factories both rendered slaves too independent, and, as the Louisville *Public Advertiser* put it in 1835, "insolent, intractable, and in many instances wholly worthless" (Share 1982: 90). Cities and factories, after all, harbored too many free blacks, too many ideas, and too much news. To use slaves in large-scale industry effectively, employers discovered that they had to treat slaves virtually as wage laborers by paying them allowances for room and board, incentivizing them to exert effort with cash, and giving them much freedom of choice outside of work, a fact well known to the ancients (Miller 1981; Shirley 1994: 89–90; Ashworth 1995: 109–10; Rihll 2008: 132–34). While some advanced technologies like steam engines and rails were adopted on sugar plantations, the sugar planters did not go nearly as far as they could or probably should have, partly out of fear that slaves would literally gum up the works (or worse, set them aflame). Slaves forced to design high tech goods, like some of the German super weapons in development at the end of World War II, found it easy to sabotage their work. If one mistake by a high tech slave could shut down machinery worth millions it is best not to invest in machinery worth millions, or not to use slave labor (Fogel 1989: 24; Ashworth 1995: 96–97; Temperley 1996: 148).

Awash in nearly completely enslaved serfs well into the nineteenth century, Russia was also a technologically backward and largely rural society. Its loss in the Crimean War led to introspection that probably helped to free the serfs. Thoughtful people in Russia realized that their nation urgently needed to modernize economically, industrialize, educate its people, and reform its legal and political systems, and that abolition of serfdom had to come first (Cook 2007: 189; Mironov 1996: 346).

Agricultural Productivity and the Environment

"We might continue to add proofs of the bad economy of slave [agri] culture, until our pamphlet should become a thick volume" (Atkinson 1861: 24). Textile manufacturer (and later public intellectual) Edward Atkinson, who had been a Free Soiler in 1848 (Dalton 1950: 11), so believed in the inferiority of slave agriculture that he suggested that the federal government buy all the slaves in Texas (for $90 million) and grow cotton by free labor there as a sort of grand social experiment (1861: 24–25). Family cotton farms might have worked (as mentioned above, German families successfully grew cotton in Texas without the aid of slaves) but the emancipation of chattel slaves did not usually lead to increases in total agricultural output or even productivity, a fact that needlessly embarrassed abolitionists (Blackburn 2011: 283; Fogel 1989: 407–10). The problem, of course, was that chattel slaves were, in most places, replaced by indentured laborers, peons, and other coerced laborers who were little better off, materially or in terms of the freedom index, than the slaves they replaced. Calling a slave a coolie did nothing when racism and public policies skewed toward the wealthy elite remained firmly entrenched. So the negative externalities associated with slavery continued to drag on the economy, as planters used public funds to import their new fangled bondsmen while simultaneously blocking the development of irrigation systems, healthy water supplies, roads, schools, and so forth (Adamson 1972: 255–57).

By narrowly focusing on their own short-term self-interest, however, agricultural enslavers undermined their collective long-term interests. This was perhaps most evident in Russia, which by the mid-nineteenth century had the lowest crop yields in Europe, just 17 bushels per hectare versus about 40 bushels in Belgium, 26.5 bushels in Sweden, and 21.5 bushels in Norway, where both soils and the climate were worse than in Russia. Both lords and serfs had little to no incentive to engage in more capital-intensive agriculture because of the higher monitoring costs that would have been required, so the system was an extensive rather than an intensive one. Such a system worked only when there was more arable land available to work, and more serfs available to work it. After serfdom was abolished, grain, potato, and cattle productivity jumped by 10–22 percent. Ex-serfs also grew in height, on average, and enjoyed a higher standard of living. (Those findings are unusually robust, too, due to large differences in timing of emancipation in adjacent or nearby provinces, a cliometrician's dream.) The freed serfs were hurt, however, by subsequent land reforms and, of course, by communism (Cook 2007: 188; Brenner 1996: 248–49; Markevich and Zhuravskaya 2014).

It was probably not a coincidence that the demise of slavery in England was followed by the rise of a cash economy and increased agricultural productivity (Pelteret 1995: 11–12).

As described above, slavery did not end all innovation, particularly where enslavers faced competition in the markets for their crops. So enslavers in Northern Virginia in the early Republic did successfully switch from tobacco to wheat production by following the lead of free farmers in the North. Enslavers, however, were rarely innovators, adopting new techniques with trepidation. Only after gypsum had proven its worth, for example, did enslavers start to use it, and then only when they had to stay put. Like Russian lords, they much preferred buying virgin western land to innovating (Crothers 2001; Wright 1987: 860–61). That was why Cairnes asserted that "societies based upon slavery cannot, like those founded upon free industrial institutions, take root, grow, and flourish upon a limited area ... a constant supply of fresh soils of high fertility becomes, therefore, an indispensable requisite for the permanent industrial success of such societies" (1862: 93). The fact that Northern states like Ohio supplied much of the South's foodstuffs helped to spread the impression, jumped on by Helper, that the South was not even particularly good at agriculture. Southern agricultural productivity lagged that of the Midwest well into the twentieth century, in large part because much of its agricultural labor force remained mired in slave-like peonage and convict lease systems (Kilbourne 2006: 149; Cason 1928: 33–34).

Today, enslavers still engage in extensive, rather than intensive, forms of agriculture and other extractive industries and have been known to devastate ecosystems. Already violators of both the law and human morality, enslavers have no qualms about illegally using slash and burn agriculture in rain forests, strip mining wildlife preserves, destroying reefs and coasts, overfishing, and so forth (Bales and Soodalter 2009: 143–44).

Governance, Institutional Quality, and the Distribution of Wealth and Income

"They who violate the rights of one race of men lose a portion of their reverence for the rights of all" (Owen 1864: 126). Robert Dale Owen may have gotten this zinger from colonial politician James Otis (1725–1783), who argued "that those who every day barter away other men's liberty, will soon care little for their own" (Otis 2015: 439).

Hinton Helper claimed that slavery had "sunk a large majority of our people in galling poverty and ignorance … and driven the rest away from their homes" (1860: 25). He was talking about poor whites but the enslaved could be included in that indictment as well. And, of course, slavery made a few extremely wealthy. Income and wealth distribution in the antebellum South was not completely bimodal, as Cassius Clay and others implied, but it was also not a bell curve as in the North either. In other words, people of middling incomes were harder to find in the South and most of those were enslavers, if only on the side (Clay 1848: 346–47).

Specifically, the largest antebellum slaveholders possessed an average net worth (including slaves) of just under $57,000. That same year, 1860, the average net worth of those who owned seven or fewer slaves was just $3400, while the slaveless held property worth just $1777 on average. Northern urban artisans that year owned about $2000 worth of goods, net of debts, while northern farmers averaged about $3100. Slaveholders were on average twice as wealthy as the richest northern manufacturers and merchants. Two out of every three Americans with estates exceeding $100,000 in value lived in the South in 1860. Incomes were also skewed in the South but the South's per capita income in 1860, while high by international standards, paled compared to that of the Northeast, especially when slaves are included in the denominator (as they well should be) (Fogel 1989: 82–87).

Large income and wealth disparities in and of themselves are distasteful to many people but they are also bad for economic growth. A significant percentage of people in the middle of the income/wealth distribution, if they believe that their hard work and thought will be protected from expropriation, are, as Henry Berry reminded the Virginia legislature in 1832, "stimulated by a desire to become wealthy, distinguished, independent, and powerful. All the faculties of each individual are expanded, and fully developed" (p. 8). Where the middle class is small and tenuous, fewer such strivers will emerge and the economy will be the worse for it.

A weak middle class can also stunt financial market development. While financial markets periodically cause economic turmoil, as they have numerous times from the Dutch tulip mania to the subprime mortgage debacle of the first decade of the Third Millennium, they are a crucial component of economic growth because they fund innovation by linking savers to entrepreneurs. (That is why they are so disruptive when they fail.) In addition to being poor (low income and assets), people at the low end of the income distribution generally live outside of the financial system so they cannot use it to smooth their incomes by saving for bad times or borrowing when their expenses temporarily exceed their income. That makes them vulnerable to debt peonage and other systems that force them to collateralize their bodies and freedom (Basu and Chau 2007: 43, 62; Engerman 2007: 79, 95).

The South's financial system was advanced compared to most of the world but, once again, it lagged that of the North, especially the Northeast, and again slavery emerges as the major culprit. "The operatives form a vast middle class, almost without a parallel, at the North," E. H. Derby noted in 1850, "which accumulates in savings banks, builds houses, ships, wharves, factories, and rolls up commercial capital" (p. 9). According to economists Raghuram Rajan and Rodney Ramcharan, white elites deliberately repressed the financial system of the South after the Civil War in order to limit the economic choices of poor blacks (2008).

An extremely uneven distribution of wealth distorts governance in and of itself, of course, leading to regressive tax systems and the like. But slavery in and of itself also directly distorts governance. Adam Smith believed that enslavers required weak governance so that they could manipulate governments into forcing slaves and non-slaves alike to pay them tribute. That was certainly the case in the antebellum United States, where slaveholders wanted a state that was strong enough to control their slaves but one that was not likely to use its strength to abolish slavery. They affected that delicate balance for several generations by ruling the nation, which had a constitution that could be interpreted as proslavery, antislavery, or slavery neutral, themselves (Foner 1983: 68; Salter 1996: 241; Huston 2003: 10; Ericson 2011: 11; Mason 2006: 57; Wiecek 1977: 16–19). Enslavers dominated the presidency, serving 49 of the 72 years (68%) between ratification and secession. They also held many high legislative and judicial offices: 25 of 35 (71%) presidents pro tem of the Senate hailed from slave states, as did 23 of 35 (55%) House speakers, and 19 of 34 (56%) Supreme Court justices (Ericson 2011: 14). As historian Robin Einhorn has argued, most of the Southerners did everything they could to undermine democracy in the United States (2006: 1). Where slavery was important, state and local governments were less inclusive, even aristocratic in nature. "There is no legislation," Helper argued, "except for the benefit of slavery, and slave-holders" (1860: 42). Where slavery was marginal or virtually non-existent, as in New England, governments were more competent and democratic. The superiority of governance in the North helps to explain the discrepancy in land values between slave and non-slave (or less slave) states (Einhorn 2006: 7; Mason 2006: 201; Helper 1860: 326).

From ancient times, enslavers have often controlled the government, if not completely at least enough to keep slavery strong. Manumission taxes and the outright abolition of manumission, both of which attacked property and civil rights, show how politically powerful the enslaver classes were in the societies that passed them. So, too, does the fact that while some enslavers have received public compensation for emancipation, no slave ever did (Finley 1980: 83, 98; Schulz 2008: 56).

The Brazilian government was also under the thumb of enslavers, as shown by its tax code. Their power continued even after emancipation in 1888. The monarch, Dom Pedro II, in a mad attempt to placate former slaveholders, allowed the creation of banks that lent wildly using government money. The scheme did not work and Pedro was deposed in a coup in 1889. The coup also failed because a decade of financially reckless policies that ended up in financial bamboozles, inflation, and ruin for the Brazilian economy ensued (Schulz 2008; Calomiris and Haber 2014: 418–29).

Slavery has reduced governance and institutional quality worldwide. Roman military officers were so busy slave trading with the Goths that they neglected their duties. In Africa, chiefs could sell rivals and critics into slavery, thus giving them supreme power, which of course did not bode well for the quality of their governance. Slavery there led to corruption, which begat poverty and more slavery, which begat more corruption (Finley 1980: 123–24; Davidson 1961: 284; Manning 1990: 124).

Today, throughout the world, many police officers are on enslavers' payrolls. In many places, low-level border guards who draw salaries of $10 per month drive new BMW automobiles because they turn a blind eye to illicit drugs, arms, and enslaved people crossing the border. Enslavers pay bribes of 1000–3000 rupees to get girls into India and of course add the sum to the girls' putative debts. In the antebellum US North, kidnappers tried to bribe judges so that they could conduct their nefarious practices without fear of judicial reversal or imprisonment (Kara 2009: 71; Skinner 2008: 168; Brown 2000: 79–80; Mason 2006: 142).

Matters were so bad in Romania that the European Union (EU) forced it to crack down on its police corruption/trafficking nexus before it would allow it into membership. In Transnistria, which will never get into the EU, police officers even moonlighted as slave dealers! That obscure breakaway district of Moldova was not alone. In many places, the police do not interdict traffickers and brothel owners because the police themselves are the traffickers and the brothel owners. Other times, police or other law enforcement officials are just married to brothel owners. Even UN peacekeepers and Pentagon contractors owned sex slaves in Eastern Europe (Skinner 2008: 148, 165, 176; Brown 2000: 186, 201; Kara 2009: 10).

Of course only a small percentage of police officers are enslavers but some work for enslavers as guards or even as seasoners, men who rape girls to get them to accept the sex trade as their lot. More often, however, police officers are among the johns that frequent prostitutes in places like the *tippelzones* (red light districts) of Amsterdam. According to Brown, not only are police officers among the principal clients of prostituted persons in some regions, they often press for discounted or even free sex (Brown 2000: 109, 204–5; Kara 2009: 85, 159, 167; Bales 2012: 54; Skinner 2008: 149).

Only a small percentage of police officers are on enslaver payrolls but it only takes a few well-positioned, well-compensated officers to tip off enslavers of impending raids, changes in tactics, and so forth. The Yemeni police prevented British girls sold into child marriages from returning home to Birmingham, for example, because the girls' enslavers paid them off. Where enslavers prove too greedy or dull to bribe the police proactively, officers will conduct raids in order to exact bribes. Sometimes, at enslavers' behest, police officers will arrest prostitutes trapped in debt bondage. The enslavers then pay off the police to release the girl and add the amount of the bribe to her debt balance (Batstone 2010: 55, 62, 168–69; Brown 2000: 164–65, 180, 202–208; Ali and Wain 1995: 186; Kara 2009: 51, 74). Controlling prostitutes through debt dates to at least 1811, when New York madams forced prostituted women "into a compliance with their purpose" by threatening to sue them on the many small promissory notes they forced them to sign (Anon. 1811).

In South Asia, powerful *zamindars* have such complete control of local government and law enforcement that even outsiders studying bonded labor have been harassed, detained, threatened, and surveilled by police without cause. In India, most brick kilns use bonded laborers and most kilns are owned by politicians or their relatives and they use the justice system to maintain order and profits (Kara 2012: xv, 73, 76, 86–87).

Chinese coast guard cutters suddenly disappear when boats laden with contraband take to sea. Many of the traffickers, the infamous snakeheads, are former or even current government workers. Other nefarious practices kept up the flow of Africans into the New World, including New Orleans, even after the abolition of the slave trade. Little wonder that most trafficking victims do not run to the police for help. In Albania, they cannot even run to the church because some holy men there knowingly wed women to a man known to use marriage as a ruse to trick women into sex slavery (Naim 2005: 101; Schermerhorn 2015: 83, 241; Eltis 1987: 203; Kara 2009: 14, 132).

Elsewhere, where corruption is less rampant, incompetence can prevail. Many cops are simply not very good at assessing slavery situations. Some blame their ineffectiveness on a dearth of data, but many police departments eschew reliable data because then they would be obliged to act. The fact that most brothels have strong political backers also tends to inhibit police vigilance. Even in the United States, obstruction by local law enforcement is not uncommon. Labor laws are notoriously difficult to enforce, especially in weaker states, like those of Latin America, so even when the police want to do a good job combating slavery, it still is not easy (Bales and Soodalter 2009: 75, 96; Brown 2000: 21, 158, 166–68; Carnes 2014: 6–9).

In South Asia, debt bondage laws are so weak that even if corruption was reduced, many people would still find themselves entrapped. Debts are often those contracted by others and debt totals are easily manipulated by enslavers. India's bonded labor system abolition act of 1976 is simply not enforced and the so-called vigilance committees it established are not at all vigilant (Kara 2012: 151, 193, 201; Brown 2000: 114–17).

Whether slavery is legal or not, governments never allow slaves to be good citizens. They are essentially civically dead. In antiquity, they could give evidence only under torture. In the Roman Empire, during the Christian period no less, slaves were executed for bringing accusations against their masters for any crime short of treason. Slaves were also subject to ruthless search and seizure rules to ensure that none permanently escaped. Because slaves were effectively disfranchised, elites had no accountability, no reason to protect them, much less promote their interests. So who was surprised when enslavers bribed local justices to get indentured laborer contracts extended in nineteenth century Latin America (Finley 1980: 94, 109; Meagher 2008: 218)?

In medieval England, manor lords controlled powerful institutions of coercion, like the tithings. While free men had the right to be tried in public courts, serfs were doomed to be judged by their manor lords, who unsurprisingly were rarely chastised by the courts. Such institutions, then and now, naturally breed contempt for governments and their unequal laws (Bloch 1961: 271–72; Batstone 2010: 87). ("There can be no truer principle than this," Alexander Hamilton wrote in 1787, "that every individual of the community at large has an equal right to the protection of government" [Syrett and Cooke 1962: 222].) When South Asian cops and courts routinely ignore laws against bonded labor they reveal the weakness and contemptibility of local, state, and national governments in that region. So, too, did the judicial system of the postbellum US South as it twisted logic and law to provide a steady stream of convict laborers to plantations, corporations, and the state via trumped up charges, unevenly enforced laws against vagrancy designed explicitly to entrap poor young black men in the penal slave system. The distorted decisions of the Supreme Court of the United States to uphold slavery and Jim Crow laws were perhaps even more corrosive (Quirk 2011: 204–5; Blackmon 2008; Smith 2008: 5–112).

Slavery also distorted US diplomacy and tariff policy. The young republic did not back the independence movements of its Latin American brothers, for example, because of their antislavery rhetoric and actions. The famous Monroe Doctrine, for example, sanctioned Spanish rule in Cuba, and hence, the continuation of slavery there. But even that was nothing compared to the Gag Rule in effect in the House of Representatives in the 1830s and 1840s, which ran directly counter to First Amendment protections of free speech and the right of petition. (Recently, a neo-gag rule was slapped on NGOs that argue that prostitution should be legalized.) Sugar planters were able to win protective tariffs on sugar, thus subsidizing slavery (and creating deadweight losses, including higher prices for consumers) (Cairnes 1862: 106–31; Blackburn 2011: 258, 398; Mason 2006: 217; Fogel 1989: 271; Bales and Soodalter 2009: 111; Schermerhorn 2015: 72).

The refusal of the US Postal Service to deliver antislavery pamphlets in the South was another egregious breach of the Constitution that convinced many that Southern society was thoroughly corrupted, and therefore, weak. So, too, did the slave South's numerous restrictions on the civil rights of free blacks (Anon. 1835: 8; Fogel 1989: 273). "If a free black cook can endanger the safety of Carolina," asked E. H. Derby in 1850, "where is her strength" (p. 14)? Other state and local governments were just as bad. Missouri's constitution banned the entry of free men who happened to be of African descent. That same state refused to charter banks that included any antislavery men, especially German-American ones, in the investor group. Judges in New Jersey forged the consent of New Jersey slaves to be sold South and remain slaves for life, creating a morbid southbound underground railroad in the process (Fogel 1989: 30, 180; Geiger 2010: 33–35; Mason 2006: 138; Schermerhorn 2015: 75–76, 137).

Early immediatist abolitionists were attacked by mobs that pulled down their houses and threatened to lynch them. The police saved them but then arrested the abolitionists for disturbing the peace (Anon. 1836). Apparently with consent of the mayor, Philadelphia fire companies allowed the four-day-old Pennsylvania Hall to burn to the ground because abolitionists owned the meeting place, which they nicknamed the Temple of Liberty. Local officials in Alton, Illinois failed to save Elijah Lovejoy when enslavers arrived to murder him and burn his press in 1837 (Tomek 2011: xiii; Fogel 1989: 271–72). According to historian J. Mills Thornton, Alabama was prepared at all times to grossly abridge civil liberties if necessary to preserve the slave-based social order. Abolitionists would not just be hung there, they would be hung "high as Haman" (Thornton 1978: 313). In January 1838, US Senator William C. Preston also declared that any abolitionist caught in South Carolina would be hanged (Owen 1864: 166). About the same time, William Lloyd Garrison was imprisoned for six months when he could not pay a libel suit that he lost after calling a slave trader a "highway robber and murderer" and an "enemy of the human species" (Baptist 2014: 194).

Allowing arson, lynching, and other forms of mob action of course exposed the shortcomings of the government, as in Jamaica in 1831–1832, when mobs burned a score of Baptist and Methodist chapels and attacked their preachers and missionaries on the supposition that they had encouraged a slave rebellion (Fogel 1989: 227).

Post-emancipation societies were of course not immune to the distorting influences of enslavement. According to Hugh Tinker, "the laws, the revenues, the communications—all were created for a single purpose," to keep indentured laborers in their place (1993: 3–4). Vagrancy laws were common, and commonly unevenly enforced. The governments of the postbellum US South, of course, went far beyond vagrancy laws; they allowed African-Americans to be lynched and disfranchised them too. Another major issue was black suffrage (Tinker 1993: 16–17; Campbell 1899: 19–20; Galloway 1904: 6, 9). According to Dunbar Rowland, laws designed to limit the voting rights of African-Americans were passed because "it was believed that the continued suppression of the negro vote [by violence] would promote a feeling among the whites to use the same methods on each other and promote a low tone of political morality" (1903: 11). "We cannot have a democracy for one class of our population," Charles B. Galloway noted in 1904, "and a despotism for the other" (p. 11).

State prison slave systems were further proof of government weakness. As the slave trade grew in importance in Africa, so too did crimes, like witchcraft, that were punishable by enslavement (Manning 1990: 131). A similarly perverse incentive system infected the postbellum US South and later, much of the nation. According to muckraker Richard Barry, "a vast system of corruption radiated behind" the neoslavery system of early twentieth century Florida. "This corruption," he continued, "concerns every element in the state. It corrodes politics; it blackens industry; it retards immigration; and it clogs the wheels of justice" (1907). According to Dennis Childs, the convict labor system created a racist legal structure that persists to this day (Childs 2015: 85–86).

Public Perceptions

"We are taught, both by the holy scriptures, and by the experience of ages, to believe that the Righteous Judge of the whole earth chastiseth nations for their sins, as well as individuals: and can it be expected that he will suffer this great iniquity to go unpunished?" (Anon. 1784: 3–4). Slavery was once seen as a progressive institution that represented an improvement over killing captives. But by the second half of the nineteenth century, slave societies and enslavers had become objects of pity, obloquy, and rage. Although owning slaves was long a source of prestige and a signal of personal wealth and even importance, it eventually became an embarrassment the world over (Quirk 2011: 65; Hellie 1982: 690; Tise 1987). "All the world sees," Helper gleefully noted, is "that in a commercial, mechanical, manufactural [sic], financial, and literary point of view, we are as helpless as babes" (1860: 23). The vast majority of people, nations, and religions are now ashamed of being associated with forced labor as it is now seen as an indication of cultural, economic, and political backwardness, a perception that could negatively affect trade, borrowing, and other aspects of international diplomacy. Even if the claims in this chapter are objectively false (though of course they are not), they are subjectively true in the estimation of most people alive today (Quirk 2011: 55, 246; Derrick 1975: 10).

That is good because international peer pressure could be an important tool for neoabolitionists today just as it was important to abolitionists in the nineteenth century. Slavery in the nation's capital and the internal slave trade hurt America's image at home and abroad. By the 1810s, runaway slave advertisements and other traces of slavery in national sheets like the *National Intelligencer* were thought to disgrace the entire country (Mason 2006: 101, 135, 159; Baptist 2014: 27). Slavery in the nation's capital was particularly corrosive, abolitionists noted, because "strangers, foreign ministers, men who reports of us determine our rank in the civilized world, associate with us the enormities of the slave-trade and of slave auctions as among our chief distinctions" (Channing 1839: 15). By 1850, Derby could boldly assert without fear of contradiction (north of the Mason-Dixon line anyway) that "slavery is considered abroad a stigma upon the Union" (p. 14). Even the South tried to distance itself from slavery's worst abuses, like the kidnapping and enslavement of the free born. Despite the efforts of Americans to distance themselves from the peculiar institution, however, slavery in America thwarted reformers in Britain eager to make the Mother Country more like its precocious offspring. After the British abolished slavery, the United States could no longer assert the moral upper hand in diplomatic negotiations (Mason 2006: 94, 102, 168, 219). Abolition in the US and Cuba (1878) placed heavy moral pressure on Brazil's elite. By the early twentieth century, many Indians saw the exportation of indentured laborers as a national stigma that had to be eradicated and it soon was (Schulz 2008: xi; Tinker 1993: 325).

Over the twentieth century, the stigma against slavery waxed ever stronger, inducing many nations to make slavery illegal, as Afghanistan did in 1923, Nepal in 1926, and Iran in 1929. Of course enslavers have incentives to hide their shame without changing their behaviors and slavery remained a serious problem in all three of those places as well as in other societies that emancipated their slaves late and under international duress. Where outright chattel slavery could no longer be practiced due to international scrutiny, slave-like institutions typically appeared (Quirk 2011: 75, 78–81, 191).

In the 1980s and 1990s, the Sudanese government vigorously denied slavery accusations because it felt its national pride was at stake (Jok 2007: 152). Haiti's first popularly elected leader, Jean-Bertrand Aristide, established a restavec hotline but it typically went unanswered or callers heard nothing but a busy signal (Skinner 2008: 17). The first response agency there, the BPM, had only one car and its leader owned restavecs himself. "But I don't rape them," he told reporter Benjamin Skinner when the subject was raised (2008: 24–25).

Some people believed that they were personally responsible for *their nation's* sins. That is why the Quakers were not content just to prevent other Quakers from owning slaves but had to convince Britain to stop the slave trade. Individuals were rewarded or punished in the afterlife but countries received their punishments and rewards on earth, a concept known as Providence (Mason 2006: 12–13, 51: Staudenraus 1961: vii–viii). "It would surely have been more consistent with the avowed principles of Englishmen, both as men and as Christians," the Quakers pointed out, "if their settlement in heathen countries had been succeeded by mild and benevolent attempts to civilize their inhabitants, and to incline them to receive the glad tidings of the gospel" (Anon. 1784: 7). While it is not clear that Providence actually exists (except in Rhode Island), the Quakers were certainly correct in noting that slavery hurt the nation as well as everyone in it. "And wonders within there yet" (Miller 1981: 6; Whitman 1894).

Note

1. Hopkins (1993). Another proverb asserted "you have as many enemies as you have slaves" (Toner 2014: 140, 162).

Bibliography

Acemoglu, D., & Wolitzky, A. (2011). The economics of labor coercion. *Econometrica, 79*, 555–600.

Adamson, A. H. (1972). *Sugar without slaves: The political economy of British Guiana, 1838–1904.* New Haven, CT: Yale University Press.

Akyeampong, E., Bates, R. H., Nunn, N., & Robinson, J. A. (Eds.). (2014). *Africa's development in historical perspective.* New York: Cambridge University Press.

Ali, M., & Wain, J. (1995). *Without mercy: A mother's struggle against modern slavery.* New York: Warner Books.

Anon. (1761). *The annual register, or a view of the history, politicks, and literature of the year 1760.* London: R. and J. Dodsley.

Anon. (1765, August 12). *New York Mercury.*

Anon. (1784). *The case of our fellow-creatures the oppressed Africans, respectfully recommended to the serious consideration of the legislature of Great Britain by the people called Quakers.* London: James Phillips.

Anon. (1811, January 27). *New York Observer.*

Anon. (1835). *Proceedings of the citizens of Charleston, on incendiary machinations, now in progress against the peace and welfare of the Southern states.* Charleston, SC: A.E. Miller.

Anon. (1836). *Narrative of the late riotous proceedings against the liberty of the press in Cincinnati.* Cincinnati, OH: Ohio Anti-Slavery Society.

Anon. (1910a, January 1). What the Cocoa costs the slaves. *Outlook.*

Anon. (1916, December). A new national campaign against 'The last surviving vestige of slavery.' *Current Opinion.*

Anon. (1922a, April 1). White slave found insane from abuse in negroes' hovel. *Philadelphia Inquirer.*

Anon. (1922b, August 11). Woman saved after years of suffering as slave to Chinese. *Idaho Statesman.*

Appiah, K. A. (2007). What's wrong with slavery? In K. A. Appiah & M. Bunzl (Eds.), *Buying freedom: The ethics and economics of slave redemption* (pp. 249–258). Princeton: Princeton University Press.

Appiah, K. A., & Bunzl, M. 2007. What's wrong with slavery? In K. A. Appiah & M. Bunzl (Eds.), *Buying freedom: The ethics and economics of slave redemption* (pp. 249–258). Princeton: Princeton University Press.

Argersinger, A. E. (2016). *The Triangle fire: A brief history with documents* (2nd ed.). New York: Bedford/St. Martin's.

Aristides. (1844, January 12). *The Liberator.*

Ashworth, J. (1995). *Slavery, capitalism, and politics in the antebellum Republic. Volume 1: Commerce and compromise, 1820–1850.* New York: Cambridge University Press.

Atkinson, E. (1861). *Cheap cotton by free labor by a cotton manufacturer* (2nd ed.). Boston: A. Williams & Co.

Bales, K. (2007). *Ending slavery: How we free today's slaves.* Berkeley: University of California Press.

Bales, Kevin. 2012. *Disposable people: New slavery in the global economy*, Rev. ed. Berkeley: University of California Press.

Bales, K., & Soodalter, R. (2009). *The slave next door: Human trafficking and slavery in America today.* Berkeley: University of California Press.

Baptist, E. E. (2014). *The half has never been told: Slavery and the making of American capitalism.* New York: Basic Books.

Barry, R. (1907, March). Slavery in the South to-day. *The Cosmopolitan: A Monthly Illustrated Magazine.*

Basu, A. K., & Chau, N. H. (2007). An exploration of the worst forms of child labor: Is redemption a viable option? In K. A. Appiah & M. Bunzl (Eds.), *Buying freedom: The ethics and economics of slave redemption* (pp. 37–76). Princeton: Princeton University Press.

Bateman, F., & Weiss, T. (1981). *A deplorable scarcity: The failure of industrialization in the slave economy.* Chapel Hill: University of North Carolina Press.

Batstone, David. 2010. *Not for sale: The return of the global slave trade and how we can fight it*, Rev. ed. New York: HarperCollins.

Birney, C. H. (Ed.). (1970). *Sarah and Angelina Grimké: The first American women advocates of abolition and woman's rights.* New York: Haskell House Publishers.

Blackburn, R. (2011). *The American crucible: Slavery, emancipation and human rights.* New York: Verso.

Blackmon, D. A. (2008). *Slavery by another name: The re-enslavement of Black Americans from the Civil War to World War II.* New York: Anchor Books.

Bloch, M. (1961). *Feudal society.* Chicago: University of Chicago Press.

Brenner, R. (1996). The rises and declines of serfdom in medieval and early modern Europe. In M. L. Bush (Ed.), *Serfdom and slavery: Studies in legal bondage* (pp. 247–276). New York: Addison Wesley Longman.

Brown, L. (2000). *Sex slaves: The trafficking of women in Asia.* London: Virago Press.

Buckland, W. W. (1908). *The roman law of slavery: The condition of the slave in private law from Augustus to Justinian.* Cambridge: Cambridge University Press.

Bush, M. (1996). Introduction. In M. L. Bush (Ed.), *Serfdom and slavery: Studies in legal bondage* (pp. 1–17). New York: Addison Wesley Longman.

Cadet, J.-R. (1998). *Restavec: From Haitian slave child to middle-class American.* Austin: University of Texas Press.

Cairnes, J. E. (1862). *The slave power: Its character, career, and probable designs, being an attempt to explain the real issues involved in the American contest* (2nd ed.). New York: Carleton.

Calomiris, C., & Haber, S. (2014). *Fragile by design: The political origins of banking crises and scarce credit.* Princeton: Princeton University Press.

Campbell, R. F. (1899). *Some aspects of the race problem in the South.* Asheville, NC: n.p.

Campbell, G. (2004). Introduction: Slavery and other forms of unfree labour in the Indian Ocean world. In G. Campbell (Ed.), *The structure of slavery in Indian Ocean Africa and Asia* (pp. vii–xxxii). London: Frank Cass.

Carnes, M. E. (2014). *Continuity despite change: The politics of labor regulation in Latin America.* Stanford: Stanford University Press.

Cary, V. (1830). *Letters on female character, addressed to a young lady, on the death of her mother* (2nd ed.). Richmond, VA: Ariel Works.

Cason, C. E. (1928, July 14). Southern slavery revised. *The Independent.*

Chanana, D. R. (1964). *Slavery in ancient India as depicted in Pali and Sanskrit texts*. New Delhi: People's Publishing House.
Channing, W. E. (1839). *Remarks on the slavery question in a letter to Jonathan Phillips, Esq*. Boston: James Munroe and Company.
Childs, D. (2015). *Slaves of the state: Black incarceration from the chain gang to the penitentiary*. Minneapolis: University of Minnesota Press.
Clarence-Smith, W. G. (1993). Cocoa plantations and coerced labor in the Gulf of Guinea, 1870–1914. In M. A. Klein (Ed.), *Breaking the chains: Slavery, bondage, and emancipation in modern Africa and Asia* (pp. 150–170). Madison: University of Wisconsin Press.
Clay, C. (1848). *The writings of Cassius Marcellus Clay: Including speeches and addresses*. New York: Harper & Brothers.
Cochin, A. (1863). *The results of slavery*. Boston: Walker, Wise, and Company.
Commons, J. R., et al. (1918). *History of labour in the United States* (Vol. 2). New York: Macmillan Company.
Conning, J., & Kevane, M. (2007). Freedom, servitude, and voluntary contracts. In K. A. Appiah & M. Bunzl (Eds.), *Buying freedom: The ethics and economics of slave redemption* (pp. 108–140). Princeton: Princeton University Press.
Cook, L. D. (2007). The end of serfdom in Russia—Lessons for Sudan? In K. A. Appiah & M. Bunzl (Eds.), *Buying freedom: The ethics and economics of slave redemption* (pp. 181–199). Princeton: Princeton University Press.
Crothers, A. G. (2001). Agricultural improvement and technological innovation in a slave society: The case of early national northern Virginia. *Agricultural History, 75*, 135–167.
Dalton, M. B. (1950). *Edward Atkinson (1827–1905): Patron of engineering science and benefactor of industry*. New York: Newcomen Society in North America.
Davidson, B. (1961). *The African slave trade*. New York: Atlantic Monthly Press.
Davis, D. B. (1966). *The problem of slavery in Western culture*. Ithaca, NY: Cornell University Press.
Davis, R. C. (2003). *Christian slaves, Muslim masters: White slavery in the Mediterranean, the Barbary Coast, and Italy, 1500–1800*. New York: Palgrave Macmillan.
Derby, E. H. (1850). *Reality versus fiction: A review of a pamphlet published at Charleston, S.C.* Boston: Redding & Co.
Derrick, J. (1975). *Africa's slaves today*. London: Allen & Unwin.
Donald, L. (1997). *Aboriginal slavery on the northwest coast of North America*. Berkeley: University of California Press.
Dower, N. (2004). The global framework for development: Instrumentality or contested ethical space? In C. van den Anker (Ed.), *The political economy of new slavery* (pp. 181–200). New York: Palgrave Macmillan.
Einhorn, R. (2006). *American taxation, American slavery*. Chicago: University of Chicago Press.

Eltis, D. (1987). *Economic growth and the ending of the transatlantic slave trade.* New York: Oxford University Press.

Engerman, S. (2000). Slavery at different times and places. *American Historical Review, 105*, 480–484.

Engerman, S. (2007). Slavery, freedom, and Sen. In K. A. Appiah & M. Bunzl (Eds.), *Buying freedom: The ethics and economics of slave redemption* (pp. 77–107). Princeton: Princeton University Press.

Ericson, D. F. (2011). *Slavery in the American republic: Developing the federal government, 1791–1861.* Lawrence: University of Kansas Press.

Finley, M. I. (1980). *Ancient slavery and modern ideology.* New York: Viking Press.

Fogel, R. (1989). *Without consent or contract: The rise and fall of American slavery.* New York: W. W. Norton.

Foner, E. (1983). *Nothing but freedom: Emancipation and its legacy.* Baton Rouge: Louisiana State University Press.

Gallay, A. (2002). *The Indian slave trade: The rise of the English Empire in the American South, 1670–1717.* New Haven, CT: Yale University Press.

Galloway, C. B. (1904). *The South and the negro: An address delivered at the seventh annual conference for education in the South, Birmingham, Ala., April 26th, 1904.* New York: Southern Education Board.

Gaspar, D. B. (1992). Slave importation, runaways, and compensation in Antigua, 1720–1729. In J. Inikori & S. Engerman (Eds.), *The Atlantic slave trade: Effects on economies, societies, and peoples in Africa, the Americas, and Europe* (pp. 301–320). Durham, NC: Duke University Press.

Geiger, M. W. (2010). *Financial fraud and guerrilla violence in Missouri's Civil War, 1861–1865.* New Haven, CT: Yale University Press.

Goldberg, E. S. (2007). *Beyond terror: Gender, narrative, human rights.* New Brunswick, NJ: Rutgers University Press.

Goodspeed, T. (2015). *Slavery, path dependence, and development: Evidence from the Georgia experiment.* Retrieved August 14, 2016, from Munich Personal Archive. Retrieved from https://mpra.ub.uni-muenchen.de/67202/

Gray, M. (2016). *Why human trafficking is a public health problem.* CNN Freedom Project. Retrieved August 11, 2016, from http://edition.cnn.com/2016/07/11/opinions/human-trafficking-health-margeaux-gray/index.html

Hallgrimsdottir, H. K., & Benoit, C. (2007). From wage slaves to wage workers: Cultural opportunity structures and the evolution of the wage demands of the Knights of Labor and the American Federation of Labor, 1880–1900. *Social Forces, 85*, 1393–1411.

Harris, J. H. (1910, April 14). The cocoa slave-trade. *Herald of Gospel Liberty.*

Hellie, R. (1982). *Slavery in Russia, 1450–1725.* Chicago: University of Chicago Press.

Helper, H. R. (1860). *The impending crisis of the South: How to meet it.* New York: A. B. Burdick.

Hicks, F. C. (1913, August 28). Convict labor in the United States. *The Independent: Devoted to the Consideration of Politics, Social and Economic Tendencies.*

Hochschild, A. (2003). *The unquiet ghost: Russians remember Stalin.* Boston: Houghton Mifflin.

Hopkins, K. (1993). Novel evidence for Roman slavery. *Past & Present, 138*, 3–27.

Houston, A. (2008). *Benjamin Franklin and the politics of improvement.* New Haven, CT: Yale University Press.

Hurmence, B. (Ed.). (1984). *My folks don't want me to talk about slavery: Twenty-one oral histories of former North Carolina slaves.* Winston-Salem, NC: John F. Blair.

Huston, J. L. (2003). *Calculating the value of the Union: Slavery, property rights, and the economic origins of the Civil War.* Chapel Hill: University of North Carolina Press.

Inikori, J., & Engerman, S. (1992). Introduction: Gainers and losers in the Atlantic slave trade. In J. Inikori & S. Engerman (Eds.), *The Atlantic slave trade: Effects on economies, societies, and peoples in Africa, the Americas, and Europe* (pp. 1–24). Durham, NC: Duke University Press.

International Labour Organization. (2014). *Profits and poverty: The economics of forced labour.* Geneva: International Labour Organization.

James, J. A. (1981). Financial underdevelopment in the postbellum South. *Journal of Interdisciplinary History, 11*, 443–454.

Jok, J. M. (2007). Slavery and slave redemption Sudan. In K. A. Appiah & M. Bunzl (Eds.), *Buying freedom: The ethics and economics of slave redemption* (pp. 143–157). Princeton: Princeton University Press.

Jones, J. (2013). *A dreadful deceit: The myth of race from the colonial era to Obama's America.* New York: Basic Books.

Kara, S. (2009). *Sex trafficking: Inside the business of modern slavery.* New York: Columbia University Press.

Kara, S. (2012). *Bonded labor: Tackling the system of slavery in South Asia.* New York: Columbia University Press.

Kilbourne Jr., R. H. (1995). *Debt, investment, slaves: Credit relations in East Feliciana Parish, Louisiana, 1825–1885.* Tuscaloosa: University of Alabama Press.

Kilbourne Jr., R. H. (2006). *Slave agriculture and financial markets in antebellum America: The Bank of the United States in Mississippi, 1831–1852.* London: Pickering & Chatto.

Klein, M. (1992). The impact of the Atlantic slave trade on the societies of the western Sudan. In J. Inikori & S. Engerman (Eds.), *The Atlantic slave trade: Effects on economies, societies, and peoples in Africa, the Americas, and Europe* (pp. 25–48). Durham, NC: Duke University Press.

Klein, M. (1993). Introduction: Modern European expansion and traditional servitude in Africa and Asia. In M. A. Klein (Ed.), *Breaking the chains: Slavery, bondage, and emancipation in modern Africa and Asia* (pp. 3–36). Madison: University of Wisconsin Press.

Kloosterboer, W. (1960). *Involuntary labor since the abolition of slavery*. Amsterdam: E. J. Brill.

Kolchin, P. (1996). Some controversial questions concerning nineteenth-century emancipation from slavery and serfdom. In M. L. Bush (Ed.), *Serfdom and slavery: Studies in legal bondage* (pp. 42–68). New York: Addison Wesley Longman.

Kujala, A. J. (1940, April). An American in Soviet jails. *The Living Age*.

Kumar, D. (1993). Colonialism, bondage, and caste in British India. In M. A. Klein (Ed.), *Breaking the chains: Slavery, bondage, and emancipation in modern Africa and Asia* (pp. 112–130). Madison: University of Wisconsin Press.

Kusimba, C. M. (2004). Archaeology of slavery in East Africa. *The African Archaeological Review, 21*, 59–88.

Leaf, E. H. (1937, March). Oriental miscellany: I. Bootleg slaves in China. *The Living Age*.

Lemon, J. T. (1972). *The best poor man's country: A geographical study of early southeastern Pennsylvania*. New York: W. W. Norton.

Lichtenstein, A. (1996). *Twice the work of free labor: The political economy of convict labor in the New South*. New York: Verso.

Lovejoy, P. E. (2012). *Transformations in slavery: A history of slavery in Africa* (3rd ed.). New York: Cambridge University Press.

Malthus, T. (1817). *An essay on the principle of population: Or, a view of its past and present effects on human happiness* (Vol. 3). London: John Murray.

Manning, P. (1990). *Slavery and African life: Occidental, oriental, and African slave trades*. New York: Cambridge University Press.

Manning, P. (1992). The slave trade: The formal demography of a global system. In J. Inikori & S. Engerman (Eds.), *The Atlantic slave trade: Effects on economies, societies, and peoples in Africa, the Americas, and Europe* (pp. 117–144). Durham, NC: Duke University Press.

Markevich, A., & Zhuravskaya, E. (2014). *Economic effects of the abolition of serfdom: Evidence from the Russian Empire*. Social Science Research Network. Retrieved August 15, 2016, from http://papers.ssrn.com/sol3/papers.cfm?abstract_id=2514964

Markham, E. (1906, November). The hoe-man in the making: Little slaves of the coal-mines. *The Cosmopolitan: A Monthly Illustrated Magazine*.

Mason, M. (2006). *Slavery and politics in the early American republic*. Chapel Hill: University of North Carolina Press.

McKeown, N. (2007). *The invention of ancient slavery?* London: Duckworth.

Meagher, A. J. (2008). *The coolie trade: The traffic in Chinese laborers to Latin America, 1847–1874.* New York: Xlibris.

Meillassoux, C. (1991). *The anthropology of slavery: The womb of iron and gold.* Chicago: University of Chicago Press.

Millar, J. (1771/2006). *The origin of the distinction of ranks: Or, an inquiry into the circumstances, which give rise to influence and authority, in the different members of society.* Indianapolis: Liberty Fund.

Miller, R. M. (1981). The fabric of control: Slavery in antebellum Southern textile mills. *Business History Review, 55*, 471–490.

Mironov, B. N. (1996). When and why was the Russian peasantry emancipated? In M. L. Bush (Ed.), *Serfdom and slavery: Studies in legal bondage* (pp. 323–347). New York: Addison Wesley Longman.

Murphy, L. T. (2014). *Survivors of slavery: Modern-day slave narratives.* New York: Columbia University Press.

Naim, M. (2005). *Illicit: How smugglers, traffickers, and copycats are hijacking the global economy.* New York: Doubleday.

Okoye, D., & Pongou, R. (2015). *Sea change: The competing long-run impacts of the transatlantic slave trade and missionary activity in Africa.* Munich Personal Archive. Retrieved August 14, 2016, from https://mpra.ub.uni-muenchen.de/66221/

Olmsted, F. L. (1856). *A journey in the seaboard slave states: With remarks on their economy.* New York: Dix & Edwards.

Otis, J. (2015). *The collected political writings of James Otis.* R. Samuelson (Ed.). Indianapolis: Liberty Fund. Retrieved August 15, 2016, from http://oll.libertyfund.org/titles/2703#Otis_1644_665

Ovington, M. W. (1910, May 26). Slaves' reminiscences of slavery. *The Independent: Devoted to the Consideration of Politics, Social and Economic Tendencies.*

Owen, R. D. (1864). *The wrong of slavery, the right of emancipation and the future of the African race in the United States.* Philadelphia: J. B. Lippincott & Co.

Parker, T. (1854). *An address delivered by the Rev. Theodore Parker before the New York City Anti-Slavery society at its first anniversary.* New York: American Anti-Slavery Society.

Patterson, O. (1982). *Slavery and social death: A comparative study.* Cambridge: Harvard University Press.

Pelteret, D. (1995). *Slavery in early mediaeval England: From the reign of Alfred until the twelfth century.* Rochester, NY: Boydell Press.

Quirk, J. (2011). *The anti-slavery project: From the slave trade to human trafficking.* Philadelphia: University of Pennsylvania Press.

Rajan, R., & Ramcharan, R. (2008). *Landed interests and financial underdevelopment in the United States.* National Bureau for Economic Research. Retrieved August 15, 2016, from http://www.nber.org/papers/w14347

Ransom, R., & Sutch, R. (2001). *One kind of freedom: The economic consequences of emancipation* (2nd ed.). New York: Cambridge University Press.

Reid, A. (1993). The decline of slavery in nineteenth-century Indonesia. In M. A. Klein (Ed.), *Breaking the chains: Slavery, bondage, and emancipation in modern Africa and Asia* (pp. 64–82). Madison: University of Wisconsin Press.

Resendez, A. (2016). *The other slavery: The uncovered story of Indian enslavement in America*. New York: Houghton Mifflin Harcourt.

Rihll, T. (2008). Slavery and technology in pre-industrial contexts. In E. D. Lago & C. Katsari (Eds.), *Slave systems ancient and modern* (pp. 127–147). New York: Cambridge University Press.

Rogers, C. A., & Swinnerton, K. A. (2007). Some simple analytics of slave redemption. In K. A. Appiah & M. Bunzl (Eds.), *Buying freedom: The ethics and economics of slave redemption* (pp. 20–36). Princeton: Princeton University Press.

Rosengarten, T., & Rosengarten, D. (Eds.). (2002). *A portion of the people: Three hundred years of southern Jewish life*. Charleston: University of South Carolina Press.

Rowland, D. (1903). *A Mississippi view of race relations in the South*. Jackson, MS: Harmon Publishing Co.

Rubin, P. H. (2002). *Darwinian politics: The evolutionary origin of freedom*. New Brunswick: Rutgers University Press.

Salter, J. (1996). Adam Smith on slavery. *History of Economic Ideas, 4*, 225–251.

Sarich, J. (Ed.). (2012). *Follow up study of slavery and poverty Kukrouthi Village, St Ravidas Nagar District Uttar Pradesh, India*. New York: Free the Slaves.

Scheidel, W. (2008). The comparative economics of slavery in the Greco-Roman world. In E. D. Lago & C. Katsari (Eds.), *Slave systems ancient and modern* (pp. 105–126). New York: Cambridge University Press.

Schermerhorn, C. (2015). *The business of slavery and the rise of American capitalism, 1815–1860*. New Haven, CT: Yale University Press.

Schulz, J. (2008). *The financial crisis of abolition*. New Haven, CT: Yale University Press.

Schurz, C. (1903, January). Can the South solve the Negro problem? *McClure's*.

Sewall, S. (1700). *The selling of Joseph*. Boston: Bartholomew Green and John Allen.

Share, A. J. (1982). *Cities in the commonwealth: Two centuries of urban life in Kentucky*. Lexington: University Press of Kentucky.

Shirley, M. (1994). *From congregation town to industrial city: Culture and social change in a Southern community*. New York: New York University Press.

Simon, K. (1929). *Slavery*. London: Hodder and Stoughton.

Skinner, E. B. (2008). *A crime so monstrous: Face-to-face with modern-day slavery*. New York: Free Press.

Smith, A. (1776/1937). *An inquiry into the nature and causes of the wealth of nations*. New York: Modern Library.

Smith, G. W. (1945). Ante-bellum attempts of Northern business interests to 'redeem' the Upper South. *Journal of Southern History, 11*, 177–213.

Smith, A. E. (1965). *Colonists in bondage: White servitude and convict labor in America, 1607–1776*. Gloucester, MA: Peter Smith.

Smith, J. D. (1985). *An old creed for the new South: Proslavery ideology and historiography, 1865–1918*. Athens: University of Georgia Press.

Smith, R. (2003). *Global human development: Explaining its regional variations*. Social Structural Research Working Paper. Retrieved August 12, 2016, from https://www.ciaonet.org/attachments/8474/upload

Smith, C. F. (2008). *Here lies Jim Crow: Civil rights in Maryland*. Baltimore: Johns Hopkins University Press.

Staudenraus, J. (1961). *The African colonization movement, 1816–1865*. New York: Columbia University Press.

Steele, E. S. (1987). Henry George on chattel and wage slavery: The American social philosopher condemned both forms as immoral, irrational denials of equality. *American Journal of Economics and Sociology, 46*, 369–378.

Stowe, H. B. (1852). *Uncle Tom's cabin: Or, negro life in the slave states of America* (3rd ed.). London: C. H. Clarke and Co.

Syrett, H. C., & Cooke, J. E. (Eds.). (1962). *Papers of Alexander Hamilton Volume IV 1787–May 1788*. New York: Columbia University Press.

Taylor, T. (2001). Believing the ancients: Quantitative and qualitative dimensions of slavery and the slave trade in later prehistoric Eurasia. *World Archaeology, 33*, 27–43.

Temperley, H. (1996). New World slavery, Old World slavery. In M. L. Bush (Ed.), *Serfdom and slavery: Studies in legal bondage* (pp. 144–157). New York: Addison Wesley Longman.

Thornton, J. M. (1978). *Politics and power in a slavery society: Alabama, 1800–1860*. Baton Rouge: Louisiana State Press.

Tinker, H. (1993). *A new system of slavery: The export of Indian labour overseas, 1830–1920* (2nd ed.). London: Hansib Publishing Limited.

Tise, L. (1987). *Proslavery: A history of the defense of slavery in America, 1701–1840*. Athens: University of Georgia Press.

Tomek, B. C. (2011). *Colonization and its discontents: Emancipation, emigration, and antislavery in antebellum Pennsylvania*. New York: New York University Press.

Toner, J. (2014). *The Roman guide to slave management: A treatise by nobleman Marcus Sidonius Falx*. New York: Overlook Press.

Travis, J., Western, B., & Redburn, S. (Eds.). (2014). *The growth of incarceration in the United States: Exploring causes and consequences*. Washington, DC: National Academies Press.

Tucker, C. (1853). *Abbeokuta, or, sunrise within the tropics: An outline of the origin and progress of the Yoruba Mission*. London: James Nisbet and Co.

Turton, A. (2004). Violent capture of people for exchange on Karen-Tai borders in the 1830s. In G. Campbell (Ed.), *The structure of slavery in Indian Ocean Africa and Asia* (pp. 69–82). London: Frank Cass.

van den Anker, C. (2004). Contemporary slavery, global justice and globalization. In C. van den Anker (Ed.), *The political economy of new slavery* (pp. 15–36). New York: Palgrave Macmillan.

Vogt, J. (1975). *Ancient slavery and the ideal of man* (T. Wiedemann, Trans.). Cambridge: Harvard University Press.

Von Plato, A., Leh, A., & Thonfeld, C. (Eds.). (2010). *Hitler's slaves: Life stories of forced labourers in Nazi-occupied Europe*. New York: Beghahn Books.

Washington, B. T. (1901). *Up from slavery*. New York: Doubleday Page.

Whiteley, H. (1833). *Excessive cruelty to slaves. Three months in Jamaica, in 1832: Comprising a residence of seven weeks on a sugar plantation*. Philadelphia: n.p.

Whitman, W. (1894). *Leaves of grass*. Philadelphia: David McKay.

Wiecek, W. (1977). *The sources of antislavery constitutionalism in America, 1760–1848*. Ithaca, NY: Cornell University Press.

Williamson, H. F. (1934). *Edward Atkinson: The biography of an American liberal, 1827–1905*. Boston: Old Corner Book Store, Inc.

Wiseman, T. (2015). *Slavery, economic freedom and income levels in former slave-exporting states of Africa*. Social Science Research Network. Retrieved August 14, 2016, from http://papers.ssrn.com/sol3/papers.cfm?abstract_id=2679098

Wright, G. (1987). Capitalism and slavery on the islands: A lesson from the mainland. *Journal of Interdisciplinary History, 17*, 851–870.

CHAPTER 7

That Which Is Unseen II: Slavery's Hidden Costs

John Quincy Adams, William Lloyd Garrison, William Jay, and some other hardcore abolitionists wanted the *North* to secede from the Union because they believed that slavery was corrupting the entire nation. Their moral intuition was actually quite consistent with the economic reality of the antebellum period. "To enslave is not a power under the Constitution. No officer or department of Government can exercise it" (Owen 1864: 180). To support slavery, Southern enslavers sucked subsidies out of the more prosperous North as well as from poor Southern whites. And in the event of a large slave uprising, they threatened to extract even more subsidies, in the form of federal troops and treasure (Fogel 1989: 324–25; Mason 2006: 160; Channing 1839: 22).

So the South could not abide the likes of Joshua Giddings, who argued that the Constitution should be construed to be neutral on slavery (Fogel 1989: 335–37). "If the Federal Government has no Constitutional right to interfere with slavery in any way" as the southerners claimed, Giddings maintained, then it followed that the federal government "had no constitutional right to support it" (Julian 1892: 134). Like Giddings, the Liberty Party simply wanted to withdraw federal support for slavery, which is the same thing a peacetime Lincoln administration might have done. The mere credible threat of removal of subsidies was enough to spark the South to secede even though the clear consensus, even among abolitionists, was that the federal government could do nothing about slavery where it already existed. Acquiescence was not enough; southern enslavers needed federal

R.E. Wright, *The Poverty of Slavery*,
DOI 10.1007/978-3-319-48968-1_7

subsidies (Wiecek 1977: 17; Magness 2015; Fogel 1989: 281–301; Steele 1987: 371).

By some accounts, Roman landowners moved away from slave labor to *coloni* (tenants) when the state cut back on slave control subsidies, rendering it more profitable to exploit free farmers and eventually tie them to the land as serfs. According to social historian Robert Brenner, serfdom was also only viable where it was supported by centralized monarchical states that distinguished the free from the unfree and that enforced tax and immobility laws (McKeown 2007: 59, 74–75; Brenner 1996: 250–51, 258–63). As historian Marc Bloch made clear, the royal authority of medieval Britain was strong enough to track down runaway serfs and punish those who had helped them. Where the government would not, or could not, aid in the return of runaway slaves, mass defections undermined the institution. After every one in five of Korea's enslaved *nobi* began to run away each year, the system quickly petered out. Slavery also waned in the Sudan, although unfortunately temporarily, in the late nineteenth and early twentieth centuries after slaves ran away from their masters en masse and the government proved unable to return them. In 1902, a similar mass desertion also toppled slavery, for a time, in northern Nigeria (Bloch 1961: 271; Kim 2004: 161; Klein 1993: 182; Lovejoy 2012: 245, 265).

The public subsidization of slavery helps to explain the widespread belief that governments were proslavery and that they should compensate enslavers for emancipation. Jamaica planter Aaron Bang, for example, argued that he "did not plant slavery. I found it growing and flourishing, and fostered by the Government" (Hall et al. 2014: 164–65). George Hibbert, who had been compensated by the government after passage of the West India Dock Act injured some of his property interests, argued that "both the slave-trade and slave-ownership had been sanctioned and legislated for by the British Parliament" so restitution was due, just as with the dock act (Hall et al. 2014: 214).

Some public subsidies were subtle, but important nonetheless. Slaves in the US South and elsewhere, with their masters' firm approval, supplemented their diets by hunting, fishing, and foraging on land that was public or that belonged to non-enslavers. (Tramps, those itinerant slaves without masters, did so too, and even grew gardens on public land.) NGOs in Italy give sex slaves condoms and abortions but while helping the slaves they inadvertently subsidize their captors, who encourage their slaves to get the abortions so they can avoid the expense themselves and the condoms, which they seize and sell (Foner 1983: 65; Hurmence 1984: 10, 82, 89–90; Wright 1993: 59; Higbie 2003: 25–65; Kara 2009: 84).

Enslavers always rely on massive public subsidies because the costs of controlling slaves, and the costs of protecting slaves, enslavers, and non-slaves in a slave society are enormous and multifaceted. Once a society discovers how costly slavery is, it must then expend more resources to end it and to restore victims and governments to some reasonable semblance of their former or potential selves. Describing those costs and showing how large they are is the goal of this chapter.

The Costs of Protecting Slaves, Non-Slaves, and Enslavers from Themselves and Each Other

"They become formidable to the state; and it is requisite that they should be strictly watched" (Millar 1771/2006: 254). Slavery begets brutality, an economic "bad" that people will pay to avoid. Violence, or the potential for it, suffuses slave societies: masters against slaves; slaves against masters; slavers against non-slave potential slaves; non-slaves against slavers; slaves against non-slaves; non-slaves against slaves; masters against non-slaves; non-slaves against masters; slaves against other slaves or themselves. Nobody wants to bear the costs of protecting themselves from these vectors of violence so they try to offset as much of it as possible onto the broader society, which typically entails subsidies from local, state/provincial, and national governments. As shown in Chap. 6, enslavers and slavers (slave traders) tend to control government so they tend to receive the bulk of the subsidies. Slaves and non-slaves bear the brunt of the costs as shown below.

Most governments rightly feel that they must protect their non-slave denizens from slavery (Chanana 1964: 93–94). Nobody wants to be enslaved, and some, like an anonymous Sitka woman, believe "it is just as well to die as to be enslaved" (Donald 1997: 82). So most governments enact and enforce laws against kidnapping or enslaving non-slaves. The penalty for enslaving a fellow Athenian, for example, was execution (Rihll 2008: 105 n.83). Medieval Britain also tried to protect non-slaves from enslavement, though not always successfully. Irish traders in Bristol, for example, were known to suddenly raise anchor and sail away with unwary visitors on board who would then be sold to pagans abroad. States in the antebellum US North also tried, with varying degrees of success, to prevent the kidnapping of escaped slaves but especially free-born African-Americans and even Euroamericans who, it was claimed, were sold into slavery after having their appearances altered (Pelteret 1995: 74, 78; Mason 2006: 101, 138–42, 180; Schermerhorn 2015: 180). In 1803, Philadelphia merchant Thomas P. Cope claimed that "perhaps not a day passes but free blacks are stolen by force or decoyed by the most wicked artifices from the Northern & Middle States & sold for slaves in the Southern" (Harrison 1978: 137). There were at least 25 cases of free African-Americans living in Philadelphia being abducted and sold into slavery between 1825 and 1827 alone. In the postbellum South, the federal and sometimes the state governments tried, usually unsuccessfully, to prevent the coercion of freedpersons by their former masters. In 1868 in Greene County, Alabama, for example, hundreds of ex-slaves sued landowners for unpaid wages. The latter responded by burning the courthouse and all its records (Baptist 2014: 190; Blackmon 2008: 19)!

When enslavement threats are external, many governments will prepare for war to protect their denizens from the clutches of slavers. Well-constructed walled villages appeared in the Sudan to thwart slave raiders. Along North America's Northwest Coast, where anyone could fall prey to a rival tribe's slave raiding parties, local rulers expended considerable resources to protect themselves and their tribe members. The young United States fought a second war for independence partly over the kidnapping of American sailors for service on British warships. Contemporaries considered impressment into the British Navy a form of slavery worse than that practiced by the Barbary pirates, who at least did not force their slaves to fight their own countrymen (Klein 1992: 32; Donald 1997: 33–34; Mason 2006: 88–90). In New Jersey, free blacks enlisted armed watchmen to counter the incursions of slave catchers. "Every strange white man," one of them explained, "had to give a good account of himself or leave" (Gigantino 2014: 423).

Discerning who is slave, who is eligible for enslavement, and who is non-slave is another costly endeavor. In the sixteenth century, the Spanish assigned specific courts to hear the pleas of slaves who claimed freedom for meritorious service. In colonial Boston, slaves sued for their freedom on the grounds of natural rights. Maryland courts also used public resources to free slaves who could prove European ancestry. In 1795, Virginia tamped down on freedom suits by passing a law that penalized anyone who assisted a slave in an unsuccessful suit (Davis 1966: 265; Franklin and Moss 1988: 65; Deane 1886: 31; Mason 2006: 19; Fogel 1989: 249). In Philadelphia in October 1850 a federal court freed a reputed slave when the alleged owner could not provide proof of ownership. The decision caused "Great excitement among" the crowd, requiring "a large Police force" to restore "Order" (Harrison 1978: 602). Manumitted slaves and indentured laborers who managed to outlive their contracts had to carry freedom papers with them lest they be mistaken for slaves and sold. Every negro in Barbados, for example, was assumed to be a slave unless he could prove otherwise. The freedom papers were created and verified by public officials at some expense (Harrison 1978: 10; Barzel 1977: 10; Tinker 1993: 191–94).

Slaves had to be protected from themselves. Slaves would sometimes attack each other out of jealousy or desperation (e.g., riots pitting Chinese against Indian indentured laborers) but most of the time they mutilated or killed themselves or their offspring. Many jumped off slave ships, preferring death to dishonor. In Washington, D.C. a slave named Anna jumped from a fourth story tavern window to her death rather than be dragged to slavery in the Deep South, just one of many slaves to take her own life. It was nary impossible for an enslaver, even with public support, to prevent slave suicide, so in some places, like Sao Tome during the troubles of 1875–1876, it became a favorite form of slave resistance. The best that could be done was to postpone the day of death by physically restraining a depressed or melancholy slave or force feeding a slave on a hunger strike (Payne 1912: 48; Bailey 1992: 223; Mason 2006: 137; Clarence-Smith 1993: 167).

By contrast, enslavers could do many things to protect their slaves from non-slaves, slave raiders, and themselves, and government aid played a large role. Stealing slaves from their masters was a major crime in most places, as was raping or murdering another's slaves (Pelteret 1995: 74, 166; Chanana 1964: 94).

Governments also helped to reign in enslavers, who, as discussed in Chap. 6, were often petty despots, and keep them from injuring their own interests in a Simon Legree-like rage. In Rome and those nations that followed Roman law, like Spain and Portugal, enslavers could not lawfully kill their slaves. That law actually had some teeth as some masters were exiled or heavily fined for murdering their chattels. Roman courts also protected male slaves from castration, which increased their market value but made them more dangerous. They also tried to protect slaves from other forms of ill treatment at the hands of their masters or other free persons, with partial exceptions for self-defense and adultery. (A male slave caught having sex with a free woman was to be burned alive while the woman was to be executed too, though more humanely.) Of course the restrictions were put in place to reduce the possibility of a major insurrection rather than out of any regard for those enslaved (Klein 1986: 190–91; Buckland 1908: 2, 29; Davis 1966: 49; McKeown 2007: 88).

The Roman legal code related to slavery was enormous, running to hundreds of pages of intricate detail. Because they were legally property but in fact sentient beings, slaves caused all sorts of legal conundrums that drove jurists batty. Children, parentage, runaways, and the *peculium* (the quasi-property of Roman slaves) raised all kinds of sticky legal issues. Could slaves owe their masters money and vice versa? Could a slave own slaves? The possibility of inadvertently marrying a slave, slave manumissions, and numerous other issues also swelled the legal code and, of course, administrative and legal costs (Buckland 1908: vi, 10, 21–31, 187–238, 598–601).

In Spanish Mexico, government inspectors made surprise visits to ensure that slaves were not being mistreated and, importantly, they brought masters who violated the laws into court. Even in Imperial Russia, officials occasionally chastised enslavers who did not maintain minimal living standards for their serfs (Fogel 1989: 39; Markevich and Zhuravskaya 2014: 3).

In the Anglo-American world, enslavers sometimes allowed the passage of laws that constrained their own worst impulses. In the British West Indies, for example, enslaver-controlled legislatures passed laws that established minimum food requirements for slaves. Later, abolitionists were able to pass more stringent laws, which included the inspection of slave huts and medical records, ultimately paid for by taxpayers (Fogel 1989: 132, 230).

Today, enslavers often murder their slaves or their friends, family members, or neighbors (Kara 2009: 94; Murphy 2014: 122). In 2004, one quarter of all murders in Italy were of foreign women, almost all trafficked by Albanians. Governments of course expend considerable resources trying to combat homicide but, lamentably, law enforcement officials may not expend as much trying to bring the slave killers to justice. In season two of HBO's critically acclaimed series *The Wire*, the Baltimore police department does everything in its power not to investigate the murder of a dozen women trafficked into the city's port via a shipping container. Although ostensibly a fictional story, *The Wire* was so realistic that nobody who saw it was the least bit surprised by the police brutality exposed in 2015 following the tragic death of Freddie Gray.

Non-slaves and enslavers also had to be protected from slaves, and once again most of the costs, which were enormous, fell on the public. While historians now understand that slaves resisted their enslavement in numerous ways, many still downplay violent forms of resistance (Davis 1966: 128; Finley 1980: 38, 113–15). In fact, slaves rebelled frequently and effectively enough that enslavers lived in constant fear of servile insurrection, the "nagging apprehension," as Thornton termed it, "which had the potential for blossoming into genuine alarm in response to objective evidence, however slight" (1978: 312–13). Even the kindest, most paternalistic master believed that if his own slaves would not slit his throat, his neighbor's slaves would be more than happy to do so, especially in slave societies like the Leeward Islands in the early eighteenth century, where slaves outnumbered enslavers and non-slaves two, three, and even six to one (Gaspar 1992: 302–3).

Of course the belief that his own slaves would not murder him under the right conditions was self-delusion, as the owner-rapist of Celia discovered in 1855. (The state executed her at public expense [Gross 2015: 77].) As Augustin Cochin noted, "if the slave lets his master sleep tranquilly, it is not to the credit of the master, but of the slave" (1863: 82). All of the costs of violent slave resistance are of course rightly chargeable to the account of the enslavers and not their victims, who after all were merely asserting their natural rights to self-defense and self-ownership.

From the earliest times, everyone realized that slavery was inimical to the security of enslavers, society, and the government itself. Most enslavers would not trust slaves with militia service, so at best, slaves constituted just more people to be protected during wartime. Loyal slaves could be used to cow or defeat government forces or, more likely, disloyal slaves could aid foreign foes. Knowing that, enslavers might side with the enemy right off (Blackburn 2011: 138; Davis 1966: 62, 397; Lovejoy 2012: 179; Blackburn 1996: 162; Pelteret 1995: 248–49; Mark 1940: 13, 52–56). Any way you slice it, as Robert Owen put it, "slavery is an element of military weakness" (1864: 171). Slave societies therefore spent enormous sums on self-defense, well aware that they were not so much surrounded by enemies as infused with foreign sleeper cells that could strike any night. Although slaves found it difficult to create true communities because their populations turned over so rapidly through sale, death, manumission, escape, and so forth, they often rebelled, or at least credibly plotted to do so (Blackburn 2011: 256; Davis 1966: 137; Miller 2008: 92–93). Without resorting to what French historian Olivier Petre-Grenouilleau called the "cliché of the always rebellious slave" (2008: 246), one can still reject the docility of slaves as a myth and see that slave resistance was and remains an ever present threat to enslavers, their families, and their societies.

The first known slave revolt and maroon community is so old, the seventh century BC, that it comes to us as a legend, though one undoubtedly rooted in actual events. Aristomenes led a revolt of helots (slavish serfs/serfish slaves) against Sparta. They won their freedom at first with help from Sparta's enemies, but later were betrayed by their ostensible allies. They kept up the fight from Mount Eira, raiding Sparta for over a decade. Xenophon discussed a mass desertion of slaves in the mines at Decelea in 413 BCE. Other slave rebellions and maroon communities with populations numbering in the low hundreds were common in ancient Greece and Rome (Sandomrisky 1997; Taylor 2001: 32; Finley 1980: 113–14; Vogt 1975: 78–80).

Over a 70-year period, Rome fought three servile wars that culminated in the defeat of Spartacus in 71 B.C. Inspired by the desire for personal freedom rather than a broader abolitionist agenda, which simply did not exist, hundreds of thousands of slaves in Sicily rallied around a Syrian slave who called himself King Eunus of Antioch. Very little is known about the rebellions, even their precise dates, but each started small before snowballing. Civilians not useful to the rebels were killed, not just cruel masters. (Weapons makers and agriculturalists who agreed to help the rebels were spared.) Each rebellion established what were essentially large, sophisticated maroon communities replete with their own coinage and kings. Aristonicus and Spartacus even had properly equipped troops under their command, including cavalry. Other rebel leaders fought guerilla campaigns. Roman troops eventually snuffed out all three insurrections, crucifying some 6000 slaves in the suppression of Spartacus alone (Phillips 1996: 75; Vogt 1975: 39–40, 56–59, 73–75; Roberts 2011: 163; Bradley 1983; McKeown 2007: 46l; Finley 1980: 98).

Roman masters also feared being killed in their sleep so the law declared that all the slaves in a household where a master was killed by a slave were to be crucified by the state. The idea behind this practice, called *senatus consultum Silanianum*, was to induce slaves to protect their masters from assassination and to limit the incentives of heirs to kill the master to inherit his slave wealth. The law was upheld and if the slave executions caused riots, the government put them down and carried out the sentence, as Nero did, even on large numbers of slaves who could not have known about or stopped the murder (Hopkins 1993: 4; McKeown 2007: 67; Finley 1980: 102, 117–18).

Asia also reeled under an early major servile war, which raged from 133 to 129 B.C. The Zanj revolt in present day Iraq (869–83 A.D.) was perhaps the most successful slave rebellion of all time, though it was not technically slave-led. In the ninth century, a slave assassinated Abu Sa 'id al-Jannabi, the *Madhi* (religious leader) of Bahrayn Qarmati, a quasi-republican welfare state kept afloat by the labor of some 30,000 slaves. According to one of the leading historians of the subject, many others enslaved by Muslims also engaged in flight, murder, rebellion, and sabotage (Vogt 1975: 39; Clarence-Smith 2006: 5; Campbell 2004: xxi; Blackburn 2011: 9).

Major peasant and serf rebellions hit Western Europe in 1358, 1377, 1381, 1524–1525, and 1549. Serfs also erupted in Eastern Europe, in places like Bohemia, Poland, Silesia, Russia, and Hungary, in 1525, 1594–1597, 1626, 1646–1648, 1679–1680, 1766, 1768, 1775, and 1780. The African slave kingdom of Futa Jallon was also rocked by a series of slave rebellions in the 1780s and 1790s (Bush 1996b: 201, 208–9; Lovejoy 2012: 114).

African slaves rebelled in Spain's New World empire as early as 1522. In 1537, Mexico City was also shook by servile insurrection. Between 1540 and 1542, a major insurrection involving 15,000 Amerindians broke out across western Mexico. Only with the help of Indian allies was Spain able to dislodge the disaffected from their mountain strongholds and reassert control. In 1567, northern Mexico erupted in the Chichimec Wars, which saw many Spanish and mestizoes captured and enslaved by nomadic Indians fearful of being themselves enslaved. Ironically, the rebellion was used by Spanish slavers to justify the working incarceration of Chichimec warriors for periods of 6–20 years. By 1576, more than 6000 Chichimec were enslaved in central Mexico. Only by incentivizing soldiers with the prospect of slaves could Spanish authorities raise enough troops to put down the rebellion (Klein 1986: 207; Davis 1966: 129; Resendez 2016: 70, 87–93).

In the eighteenth century alone, more than a dozen slave revolts rocked Jamaica (including Tacky's Rebellion in 1760), which was also home to numerous maroon colonies that carried on guerilla warfare. Slaves also rebelled in Antigua in 1728–1729 (Blackburn 2011: 128; Davis 1966: 138; Gaspar 1992: 316–17).

Slave rebellions also struck the British mainland North American colonies with some regularity. Bacon's Rebellion witnessed a coalition of indentured servants, Indians, slaves, and oppressed free men. Many of the early Indian wars in the South were so intimately intertwined in the Indian slave trade that they can be understood as uprisings of potential slaves. New York City suffered a rebellion of its African slaves in 1712, and South Carolina was hit in 1739. The very next year in both those places plots were uncovered.

Those opposed to allowing slavery in Georgia argued that the institution would endanger the colony's military security and burden its inhabitants with patrol duty (Jordan and Walsh 2007: 69–70, 205–12; Gallay 2002: 58–59; Davis 1966: 139, 147).

Chattel slaves killed their masters or other non-slaves with some regularity in colonial Virginia, spurring calls to curb the slave trade. Slave plots were especially common during the French and Indian War but they continued long afterwards. In early 1767 in Loudoun County, for example, overseer Dennis Dallis was killed and three slaves hanged in retaliation. That same year in Fairfax County, four slaves were executed and then beheaded for poisoning an overseer. Others deadly incidents also took place in Frederick and Stafford counties (Holton 1999: 68–70, 137–39).

During the American Revolution, slaves throughout the new nation met secretly to discuss how to react, especially after the British, who had a habit of making common cause with the slaves of enemies, offered them freedom. Numerous plots and actual rebellions occurred in Virginia in 1775 and South Carolina's war effort was seriously stymied by slaves, like Boston King, yearning to be free (Holton 1999: 140–43; Jones 2013: 50–51, 57, 59).

About the only consolation to enslavers was that no slave rebellion in the New World was successful in the sense that it succeeded in overthrowing a government. But then a major slave uprising in Haiti proved successful and, worse, lasting. The 1792 image of a white baby skewered and held aloft on a rebelling slave's pike must have sent shivers up the spines of every enslaver of Africans who saw it, but what really frightened slaveholders was that Haiti, while hardly a happy place, continued to be independently governed and hence burned like a beacon of hope. Northerners let it be known that they would not interfere if the South were thrown into chaos by a Haiti-like rebellion and warned that the violence there would be repeated because all humans yearn to be free. Little wonder that enslavers freaked when the lieutenants of Gabriel, the chattel of Thomas H. Prosser of Henrico County, Virginia, spoke of rights, vengeance, the liberty of man, and so forth during a slave rebellion in the summer of 1800. In 1805, the free blacks of Philadelphia were still treated so much like slaves that a hundred or so of them marched in military formation in Southwark, pummeled some Euroamericans who got in their way, and made ominous remarks about servile insurrection (Foner 1983: 40; Blackburn 2011: 347; Mason 2006: 17, 31, 117–18; Ignatiev 1995: 56).

Maroon communities also offered slaves the prospect of freedom. They cropped up on the edges of slave societies, like Sao Tome and Principe off the coast of Africa. Maroons in St. Christopher hid in the rocks and mountains, emerging at night to rob their former oppressors. Numerous maroon communities cropped up in East Africa and elsewhere throughout the Indian and Pacific Oceans. Even in the tiny Mascarene Islands, runaways called foxes lived by theft and cunning. On Reunion Island, maroons raided plantations provoking a regime of organized retaliation, runaway slave hunting, and punishment. Jamaica was home to not one but two tough maroon communities. When the governor of Dominica put a price on the head of Quashee, a maroon chief, Quashee reciprocated in kind! Maroons in Brazil, Cuba, Venezuela, Colombia, Mexico, and elsewhere were often so difficult to defeat that governments eventually recognized some of their communities on their promise that they would return new runaways to their owners. One of the Brazilian maroon *quilombos*, Palmares, boasted some 20,000 inhabitants and waged war against Dutch and Portuguese enslavers for decades (Clarence-Smith 1993: 153–54; Gaspar 1992: 308–9; Miers 2004: 4; Alpers 2004: 52–65; Blackburn 2011: 124, 128; Price 1979; Klein 1986: 202; Genovese 1972: 590).

Maroon communities also appeared on mainland North America and continued in Louisiana, South Carolina, Georgia, and Florida into the 1810s. The First Seminole War was as much about destroying Florida's maroon communities, including the so-called Negro Fort on the Apalachicola River, and returning runaway slaves to their masters as it was about Indian removal (Mason 2006: 17, 109, 160; Cairnes 1862: 111).

The biggest slave rebellion in American history took place in Louisiana in January 1811. Followed by their leader, Charles Deslondes, slaves marched on New Orleans, pillaging along the way for a few days before they were put down by Wade Hampton's federal regulars. The American troops beheaded some of the rebels right on the field, and executed others by firing squad after a trial. They then beheaded the corpses and placed the heads on poles. The government killed at least 45 slaves. All told, about 100 slaves lost their lives over the three-day rebellion compared to maybe two dead Euroamericans (Wright 1993: 99–100; Mason 2006: 107, 126; Baptist 2014: 57–65).

During the War of 1812, 300 former slaves in the employ of the British helped to burn Washington D.C. Insurrections in Virginia were narrowly avoided in 1813, 1814, and 1816 and actually occurred in South Carolina in 1822 (Denmark Vesey) and Virginia in 1831 (Nat Turner). Slave revolts also struck Cuba in 1812 and 1844, Barbados in 1816, British Guiana in 1823, and Jamaica in 1831–1832. A great slave uprising also took place in the Bahia region of Brazil in 1835. None of those were trivial affairs but the one in Jamaica was especially frightening because it looked much like a repeat of Haiti at first when some 30,000 machete-armed slaves deserted their plantations at Christmas and began demonstrating for freedom. Initially facing only feeble resistance from the local militia, the rebels burned houses, fields, and sugar mills, and killed several enslavers before British troops arrived. Martial law ended on February 8, 1832 after hundreds of slaves had been executed. In response to those and other uprisings, southern states like Alabama, Louisiana, and Virginia permanently stationed troops in their capitals and other important cities and built armories and gunpowder magazines in places where they would be more effective suppressing slave rebellions than expelling foreign invaders (Mason 2006: 5, 88, 107–8, 160; Blackburn 2011: 231, 278–79, 286, 297; Harrison 1978: 281; Clarence-Smith 2006: 149; Fogel 1989: 226; Thornton 1978: 314; Ashworth 1995: 112; Holton 1999: 144). That all prompted one Virginia slaveholder-turned-abolitionist to argue that slavery was akin to raising tigers, something the state certainly had an interest in arresting, even if it was "a very *lucrative* business." Virginians would not be allowed to raise "the far-famed Upas tree" ("Tree of Death"), he argued, even if it grew entirely on their own private land (Berry 1832: 5). (George Mason had also likened slavery to a "slow Poison" [Blackmon 2008: vii].)

Slaves also regularly rebelled at sea. The 1826 rebellion on the *Decatur* caused citizens to intercede, trials, and executions, all of which cost the public plenty, as did the *Amistad,* the Dutch warship *Anna Palowna*, on which 85 Balinese soldier-slaves mutinied in 1828, and similar cases. Chinese indentured laborers were also constantly rebelling on ship and even normally staid Indian indentured laborers would rebel if any privileges were pulled away without justification (Schermerhorn 2015: 60–61; Reid 1993: 73; Tinker 1993: 168, 226–28).

After Britain freed its slaves, its Foreign Office at times tried to induce slave rebellions in places like Cuba and Brazil. Slave revolts and mass runaways led to abolition in the latter country in 1888 (Eltis 1987: 114–19; Schulz 2008: xii).

In the United States, a private citizen named John Brown tried to spark a slave uprising by raiding the federal armory in Harpers Ferry. His small forces were repulsed, at considerable public expense, by local Virginia militia and US marines under the command of Robert E. Lee. Even Brown's execution was costly because troops had to be deployed due to fears that other radical abolitionists would mount a rescue attempt. Instead, many Northerners hailed Brown as a Christ-like martyr, which made Southerners fear similar attacks (Baptist 2014: 384–86). Even without the likes of John Brown, by the end of the antebellum period slave insurrections and conspiracies were so numerous, and their effects so palpable, that Southerners were acutely afraid that their own property would kill them as they slept (Fogel 1989: 157) while Northerners like Thomas P. Cope confidently predicted that "should the Slave States withdraw from the Confederacy [i.e., the Union]—they will experience the fate of Hayti" (Harrison 1978: 598). Secession did not lead to massive slave uprisings but the North, as predicted, did turn freed slaves against their former masters during the war to great effect (see, e.g., Greenberg and Waugh 2000).

Just as the Civil War did not end slavery, it also did not end violent servile insurrection. The various types of neo- or quasi-slaves described in Chap. 4 also frequently rebelled. As Frederick Douglass noted, "where justice is denied, where poverty is enforced, where ignorance prevails, and where any one class is made to feel that society is an organized conspiracy to oppress, rob and degrade them, neither persons nor property will be safe" (McKivigan and Kaufman 2012: 134).

Riots took place in St. Kitts, St. Vincent, and elsewhere in response to the harshness of Britain's post-emancipation apprenticeship system. In 1865, nominally free blacks in Morant Bay, Jamaica stormed a courthouse to protest the conviction of squatters by local magistrate-planters. They killed the chief magistrate and 15 others during the ensuing melee. The government executed 400 blacks in retaliation. In 1868–1869, the Ogeechee Troubles struck the rice paddies near Savannah, Georgia, where former slaves armed themselves to protect the rice crop they had harvested from landlords and creditors. The governor pardoned the ringleaders because the "troubles" subsided after creating much angst but no bloodshed (Hall et al. 2014: 139; Foner 1983: 27; Jones 2013: 146).

The Kol people in the Bihar region of India staged bloody revolts in December 1831 and again in 1857. By the mid-nineteenth century, Russia suffered from hundreds of serf revolts *per year*. The Dutch corvee led to rebellions in the East Indies. Colonies that used indentured laborers found it necessary to form militias in order to prevent and quell uprisings. In South Africa, the government equipped farmers with firearms so they could protect themselves against Chinese indentured laborers who deserted their posts en masse. Peruvians also toted firearms to protect themselves from marauding Chinese indentured laborers. To combat its indentured laborer problem, British Guiana was the most heavily policed colony in the British West Indies and after the riots of 1869 its police force was essentially militarized. Soon after, slaves in the Sudan erupted into open rebellion (Skinner 2008: 232; Cook 2007: 190–91; Reid 1993: 74; Tinker 1993: 9–10; Payne 1912: 55; Meagher 2008: 234–36; Adamson 1972: 263; Klein 1993: 182).

In the late nineteenth and early twentieth centuries, industrial "wage slaves" in the United States, especially miners, also frequently rebelled. For some reason, historians usually call their rebellions "strikes," though bombs and bullets were much more frequently employed than picket lines and posters were. Government machine guns, not paper cuts, caused the Ludlow massacre after all and the Battle of Blair Mountain was an actual battle of flying lead, not a metaphorical war of words. Police also found themselves in pitched battles with tramp or hobo "armies" and the government also put down prison riots with machine guns and other deadly violence (Gray 1941: 1:471; Adamic 2008; Harring 1977; Childs 2015: 144).

In the early twentieth century, African-Americans trapped in one of the various forms of quasi-slavery still common in the US South staged sit downs, set fire to mines, and ran away in large numbers, up to 10 percent per year (Lichtenstein 1996: 107–9; Blackmon 2008: 98). Many of the victims were, according to a writer in the *Macon Telegraph*, in "sympathy with communism" and proposed an international congress of the negroes of the world. Some even vowed to join the Red Army (Anon. 1922l: 6). Similarly, India's long-running Naxalite rebellion, which outsiders often describe as Marxist, is really a slave rebellion of sorts. India's brick kiln slaves are also thought to be ripe for rebellion (Skinner 2008: 234–35; Kara 2012: 95–96).

In the 1970s, Detroit autoworkers and others who felt enslaved by the potent combination of major corporations and labor unions, started a series of wildcat strikes, that is, strikes not authorized by union authorities. Upset by mandatory 84-hour work weeks and poor working conditions, the strikers, like slaves of old, broke machines and deliberately produced defective parts (Jones 2013: 242–44, 281).

Public Control Costs

"Slave resistance saddled slaveowners and society with certain costs which were inherent in the maintenance of slavery" (Gaspar 1992: 301). As described in Chap. 4, enslavers do suffer some of the costs of controlling their volatile chattels. For example, enslavers will typically divide their slaves, indentured laborers, peons, and other forced laborers so that they do not know each other's language, customs, and so forth, making it more difficult for the enslaved to unite against the enslaver. Astute enslavers will even induce their slaves to monitor each other formally, as on Parchman Farm, or informally, as in many brothels. Titleholders (chiefs) among the Northwest Coast Indians used their own slaves to control the slaves of their respective subjects. To reduce their control costs, enslavers sometimes prefer female and child slaves. Northwest Coast Indians, for example, preferred to enslave women and children taken in raids, especially because they could breed the females and obtain docile males raised in slavery. The Spanish also paid a premium for women and children Amerindian slaves because they were less threatening and more easily controlled (Dal Lago and Katsari 2008; Tinker 1993: 4–5; Donald 1997: 81–83; Campbell 2004: xiv–xv; Resendez 2016: 6).

Chattel slaves, serfs, and other coerced laborers resist enslavement by shirking work, feigning illness, willfully misconstruing instructions, running away, breaking tools, stealing, spoiling crops, and committing other random acts of sabotage, including arson (Bush 1996b: 207–8; Bush 1996a: 11; Clarence-Smith 1993: 167; Owen 1864: 200; Fogel 1989: 157; Chanana 1964: 51, 58, 61; Hopkins 1993: 18; Donald 1997: 84; Finley 1980: 111; Eltis and Engerman 2000: 128). Slave arson was so common in the US antebellum South that some northern insurance companies refused to underwrite policies in any of the slave states. That means in rural areas the costs of slave arson fell upon the right people, slaveholders, but in urban areas, fires quickly spread and could consume large districts, as in Savannah, Georgia in January 1820 (Mason 2006: 2, 108; Wermeil 2000).

The enslavers who earn the highest profits learn how to limit such resistance, perhaps by being ruthless or perhaps by playing the paternalist and compromising with slaves, as Eugene Genovese described in *Roll, Jordan, Roll* (1972). The total cost of forcing human beings to toil against their will, however, is so high that even the most astute enslavers would soon see their profits evaporate if they had to bear it all themselves (Fogel 1989: 159–60). So they slough off as much as possible onto others, typically governments and NGOs (and hence taxpayers and donors). As shown in the section directly above, governments have expended large sums to protect slaves, non-slaves, and enslavers from themselves and from each other. Enslavers also need government to prevent or return runaways and to punish especially recalcitrant slaves (Phillips 1996: 79).

In late Republic Rome, enslavers could request a public official to torture slaves on their behalf. The governments of the British West Indies and the Dutch East Indies would also punish slaves on behalf of their owners, even corporate owners like the great trading corporations. In Haiti, to this day, the police beat restavecs who steal from their masters and elsewhere police officers are hired to pummel recalcitrant slaves. Such beatings are of course extralegal, but in Jamaica, antebellum Virginia, and elsewhere, the public whipping post was available to chastise the "uppity" slaves of ladies and gentlemen too delicate to swing the lash themselves. Enslavers could also direct patrollers to whip slaves for them. Antebellum governments were so involved in controlling slaves on a quotidian basis that many of the barbarities described by Theodore Weld and the Grimke sisters in *American Slavery As It Is* (1839) were perpetrated by magistrates, legislators, and even governors (Finley 1980: 95; Campbell 2004: xiv–xv; Cadet 1998: 15, 31; Bales 2012: 5; Whiteley 1833: 9; Davidson 2015: 89; Genovese 1972: 619; Fogel 1989: 278).

The cost of creating slave codes, and actually enforcing them, were large. The costs of adjudicating slavery in Muscovy, for example, were significant even though slaves constituted only 10–15 percent of the population. They would have been larger except some slaveholders sought to mete out punishment themselves, to avoid the loss of a valued slave to the justice system. Many slave societies redistributed taxpayer wealth to enslavers whose slaves were executed but the compensation was not always sufficient to cover the value of the slave to the enslaver. When slaves in Antigua, for example, were executed or killed while attempting escape, their owners received public compensation. Almost 100 enslavers received such recompense in the 1722–1729 period alone, an average of twelve per year. The expenditures were never questioned, just whether it was better to execute slaves and pay compensation or to "hamstring" or otherwise maim slaves who dared to resist too vehemently. After 1843, enslavers in South Carolina received $200 of public funds if one of their slaves was executed for assaulting a white woman, a sum that effectively put a floor under the price of prime male hands (Goodell 1853; Engerman 2008: 265; Hellie

1982: 689; Franklin and Moss 1988: 115–16; Gaspar 1992: 307–8, 314–16; *South Carolina Statutes*, December 19, 1843).

Slave patrols, an adaptation of militia service, were another major form of public control. Men enlisted into the service had to pay a fine or spend their nights wandering the neighborhood harassing slaves. In Haiti, slavery was maintained only by force of the militia and the slave-catcher brigade. Governments locked runaway slaves and indentured servants in jails until advertisements could be run and their masters located. Slaves who broke free from the internal slave trade were rounded up and executed by local authorities when needed (Blackburn 2011: 189; Hurmence 1984: 8, 95; Smith 1965: 266; Baptist 2014: 25, 169).

In ancient Mesopotamia, according to the Code of Hammurabi, the government and non-slaveholders had to help catch and return runaway slaves. If a runaway's owner could not be ascertained, the government was charged to investigate. The ancient state was also to put to death anyone who tried to steal a slave. Moreover, the existence of slaves made the legal code longer and more complicated because the laws for slaves differed from those of freedmen. The penalty for a surgeon who accidentally killed a freedman, for example, was loss of occupation (amputation of the surgeon's hand) but the penalty for malpractice on a slave was replacing the slave (Davies 1905: 31–33, 91).

Ancient Rome also enforced many laws dealing with fugitive slaves and their return. Government authorities were to capture and bind those suspected of being runaways and private persons had to report runaways or suffer increasingly stiff penalties (Buckland 1908: 268; McKeown 2007: 69). According to historian M. I. Finley, the penalties for harboring fugitives slaves were ferocious. The Roman government also hired professional slave catchers (Finley 1980: 38, 111–12, 124).

In Tuscany in the medieval period, government officials posted descriptions of runaway slaves in prominent places and declared that every citizen should join the search. The decree of 1452 stated that any person who harbored a slave for more than three days would be executed (Davis 1966: 56). Two centuries later, Barbados required all men of Euroamerican descent "to give wandering slaves with no ticket a sound whipping, and detail them till the owner could retrieve them" (Davidson 2015: 116). The Asante suffered so many runaways that in 1816 they made a treaty enjoining the Dutch to return them post haste (Lovejoy 2012: 248).

In the United States, the fugitive slave acts of 1793 and 1850 imposed significant in kind and monetary costs on US citizens and taxpayers. The acts required every American to become a slave hunter. They also created costly litigation and made it more difficult to prevent the kidnapping of free men, even, some feared, Euroamerican free men. Some contemporaries believed that the 1854 Anthony Burns case cost the US government $100,000. Actually, it "only" cost $14,166 but numerous other cases cost from $25 to $745 apiece. The Thomas Sims and Margaret Garner cases both cost over $20,000 and as much as $40,000 each (Fogel 1989: 249, 342; Blackburn 2011: 319; Mason 2006: 86, 120–21; Dalton 1950: 12).

"No fugitive slave was ever seized in Boston and returned after Anthony Burns," recalled Austin Bearse, because a "Committee of Vigilance" made certain of it, despite the high penalties (6 month imprisonment and $1000 fine per offence) exacted under the fugitive slave act (1880: 13, 16). Elsewhere, though, the federal government spent large sums to prosecute slave rescuers like Shadrach Minkins, Jerry McHenry, Joshua Glover, and June Johnson, among others. State governments also got into the act. Three men thrown in jail in Missouri for aiding runaway slaves published a book about their experience. They were lucky that they did not fall into the clutches of enraged enslavers like those in Florida in 1844, who cast Captain Jonathan Walker into a dungeon and pierced his hand with a hot iron for the crime of aiding a runaway slave (Ericson 2011: 90–91; Thompson 1851; Bearse 1880: 7).

In the 1820s, over 300 South Carolinians tried to enforce legislation banning black sailors from entering their state's ports on the theory that black sailors, whether from the North or the British Caribbean, spread abolition sentiments and help fugitive slaves to escape their masters. They created an association, the South Carolina Association (formed in 1823 and incorporated in 1828), that sought to pass legislation to prevent any "foreign" free blacks from visiting the state by land or water and any domestic blacks from visiting any non-slave state or country (South Carolina Association 1823/2001).

Post-emancipation enslavers also needed government assistance to enforce black codes, vagrancy laws, debtor laws, and the like. If anything, the state became more important to enslavers, who insisted that citizens also enforce black codes and the like. After emancipation in the British West Indies, the courts became the most coercive means of disciplining black laborers. In British Guiana, any recalcitrance constituted a criminal offense so enslavers readily utilized the courts to control indentured immigrants, over 65,000 of whom the courts convicted of breach of contract and other minor offences in the last quarter of the nineteenth century. In Suriname, Jewish settlers were pressed to suppress runaway slaves. After Redemption, the Georgia militia kept the state's former slaves at work against their will. Other enslavers, like the masters of bonded laborers in India, have also used the military and the courts to keep their peons in check. Enslavers in India also used the complicated system of caste rules to keep their laborers on the job. British officials were long happy to help local rulers maintain such customs and the all-important rule of law (Beckert 2004: 1,428; Foner 1983: 24–25, 49, 105–7; Smith 1985: 28–31; Schurz 1903; Faber 1998: 3, 105–7; Skinner 2008: 23, 237–39; Kumar 1993: 114, 119–22).

Indentured laborers were just as eager as slaves to break free of their chains and hence resisted their masters in the same ways. In South Africa, Chinese indentured laborers broke the "coolie" trade by exposing just how high the public control subsidies were. They opposed their employers by refusing to work more than a customary amount. If pressed, they went on massive crime rampages. In the first half of 1906 alone, 8000 of them, out of a population of 50,000, were convicted of offenses including assault, desertion, forgery, rape, robbery, and even murder. By refusing to pay fines or to submit easily to corporal punishment, they forced the government to incarcerate them at great expense. Court costs mounted so high that special, informal, faster, and cheaper ones were created just for indentured laborers but they still busted budgets. When farmers conscripted under fugitive slave-like laws failed to stem the tide, the South African government was forced to increase its police force at great expense (Tinker 1993: 182; Payne 1912: 47–55).

As explained above, law enforcement officials often aid and abet sex traffickers and other enslavers. In many places, police officers know who have been prostituted and arrest them if they try to flee. Police even sometimes escort prostituted women from one brothel to another. Police in Thailand charge 2000 baht for the service. Brothel owners in India arrange for the police to arrest women who they wish to intimidate. They do likewise elsewhere (Skinner 2008: 145; Brown 2000: 124, 202–4).

And of course police officers were on the frontlines of the carceral state. The convict labor system exposes governments as enslavers, slave raiders, slave traders, and/or the lackeys of enslavers (Blackmon 2008: 228; McLennan 2008: 111–12). "Prison officers," historian Rebecca McLennan wrote, describing America's postbellum convict lease system, "often found themselves obliged to assist the contractor and his foremen with clerical work and other tasks that were of service more to the contractor than to the state" (2008: 126). Prison officials also administered shock punishments, like slugging, stringing up, ice bathing, and the like, that tortured prisoners but left them able to recover quickly and get back to work (McLennan 2008: 128).

Convicts resisted their enslavement much like chattel slaves did, including self-mutilation, destruction of tools, escape, killing guards or their families, and so forth, all of which imposed costs on the state (Childs 2015: 116, 134).

Interdiction and Restoration Costs

Interdicting slave trafficking is a costly endeavor. Sending troops into regions of heavy slave trading would be an expensive proposition that could backfire because trafficking rates tend to rise after UN troops enter conflict zones. Soldiers, even US ones, find enslaving a lucrative pursuit (Murphy 2014: 73).

Enslavers are not dumb and there is a lot of money involved, so they adapt to slave trading bans. After banning the importation of slaves into their territories, both British and American authorities had to increase the penalties to discourage slavers from trading under the Spanish flag. Between 1806 and 1824, the British legislature passed at least fifteen acts concerning the slave trade in a desperate attempt to keep up with the loopholes being discovered and exploited by slave traders. David Blair has brilliantly described and explained the cat and mouse game that the British Navy played with slave traders over decades. British interdiction efforts between 1816 and 1865 cost £12.4 million directly, that is, for the African Squadron, treaty costs, commission court costs, compensation for wrongful seizure, and so forth. It also cost British taxpayers another £16 million in indirect costs, including profits lost from sales of manufacturers in African markets, higher domestic sugar prices, and administrative costs. The British also paid large sums to informants like Manuel Fortunat, a Cuban shipbroker based in New York who informed British cruisers of slavers' movements. The British also spent taxpayer funds to create a pro-British, antislavery press, abolitionist societies, and a free labor cotton plantation in Brazil (Brown 2000: 173; Eltis 1987: 55, 83, 91–94, 114–15, 215; Blair 2014; Fogel 1989: 218).

Despite numerous setbacks and the high opportunity costs associated with negotiating and re-negotiating multiple bilateral treaties, the British, with selective help from the United States, France, and other nations, finally stomped out the transatlantic trade, though the Islamic trade continued for some time after on a small scale (Eltis 1987: 85–87). As Rear Admiral Corbett explained in 1880, "the Arab dealers ... embark their slaves in small numbers in three or four *dhows* [small sailing ships] at the same time, and run the gauntlet of our cruisers. One of these *dhows* will often be taken while the others escape, and the dealer, having means of buying cheaply on the mainland, can recoup his losses, and make a high profit out of the slaves which he can land safely. In the Red Sea the trade flourishes, notwithstanding the exertions of our ships" (Anon. 1880). A decade later, the British were still paying and getting little for their efforts. As a writer for *Brotherhood* explained, the British government paid for "a line of steamers between Aden and Zanzibar, and this subsidy is inserted among the items for the suppression of the slave trade. When the matter came to be investigated it was found that the goods which were sent on these boats were brought to the coast by THE EAST AFRICAN COMPANY ... on the backs of slaves. Hence we had this most beautiful state of things: that we subsidized steamers to put down the slave trade in order that the same steamers might carry goods which slave labour transported to the coast. ... This whole business of expensive crusades against slavery by us is well worthy of consideration," the editor continued, when much misery was still to be found at home, like "the seamstress that slaves in the East End garret, or the shopwoman that stands for twelve hours in a West End shop" (Anon. 1890). At the same time, Britain subsidized both the shipment of indentured laborers to its tropical colonies and their repatriation (Tinker 1993: 366).

Of course, the enslaved also paid dearly for interdiction. To avoid capture and condemnation of their ships, some slave traders tossed slaves overboard when being pursued. They switched to faster, smaller ships and carried more women and children than previously. Many of those rescued were sent to Liberia or other not-so-pleasant places rather than being properly repatriated (Eltis 1987: 125–38; Staudenraus 1961: 186).

The more things change, the more they stay the same. The human trafficking trade today also resembles a hydra. Close a big brothel and smaller ones pop up elsewhere, or enslavers start an escort service instead. Arrest slavers along one route and they increase their bribes or switch to a more pliable country. Seal up the border crossings and they start to sneak enslaved girls in over the unguarded areas found along most borders. Where sex with children is prohibited lawfully or socially stigmatized, enslavers keep them out of sight in brothels or discretely deliver them to johns (Brown 2000: 104, 113, 120; Skinner 2008: 150).

Manumitting slaves also created large social costs. Although it was recognized that by giving some hope of freedom to slaves, manumission decreased the likelihood of servile insurrection, running away, and other forms of resistance, some slave societies banned it altogether, while many others heavily regulated the practice, to the point of requiring government preauthorization. Part of this was to prevent probate proceedings but part was to limit the presence of freed slaves and their offspring, especially in racialized societies that did not wish to advertise the humanity of their chattels. Manumission was especially complex in Scandinavia, where full manumission could only occur over several generations (Davis 1966: 54–55, 263; Pelteret 1995: 131–50; Mason 2006: 19).

In the United States, manumission was an especially delicate issue because almost everyone was racist and hence repelled by the notion of black citizenship. The solution, many believed, was repatriation or colonization, or in other words, sending free blacks "back" to Africa. Simply sorting through all of the colonization schemes concocted by antebellum Americans entailed significant costs (Staudenraus 1961: 1–4; Mason 2006: 161–62). Robert Finley may have exclaimed "this scheme is from God!" but the American Colonization Society (ACS) proved to be quite divisive (Staudenraus 1961: 17). Some believed it to be antislavery because it encouraged manumission but others thought it proslavery because it rid slave states of the perceived onus of the proliferation free blacks. The point here is that the ACS was a clear negative externality because it was mostly funded by non-enslavers, especially northern philanthropists and federal and state taxpayers. Numerous other colonization schemes also proved costly (Burin 2005: 1–2, 13–33, 79–99; Tomek 2011: 4–6; Mason 2006: 124; Guyatt 2016: 197–224, 247–80, 307–16).

In addition to the outright subsidies, extensive debates over colonization schemes ate up resources as well. John Quincy Adams argued forcefully that buying land in Africa was unconstitutional and not within the scope of the slave trade act of 1819, which only authorized the federal government to transport Africans smuggled into the United States as slaves back to Africa. But the law was stretched to include non-smuggled slaves. In fact, the Monroe and Adams administration provided the ACS with subsidies to the point that some observers even thought the ACS was part of the US government or at least a part of the so-called American System of national economic development that included tariffs, banks, and federally funded transportation infrastructure projects. The ACS was certainly inefficient enough to have been a governmental entity. By the time that Andrew

Jackson stopped the money tap, the US government had spent $264,710 to "repatriate" only 260 Africans (Staudenraus 1961: 51–53, 178; Burin 2005: 14, 17–18; Tomek 2011: 166; Ha 2009: 82–83).

Thwarted at the federal level, the ACS turned to state governments through state chapters like the Pennsylvania Colonization Society, and private philanthropists. Nat Turner's insurrection in Virginia proved a boon. Thomas R. Dew, a professor at William and Mary College, argued that colonization would cause slave prices to increase, which would induce enslavers to encourage breeding, so the total cost of colonization would prove to be astronomical. Nevertheless, a bill paying $30 per head for each free black actually transported to Liberia, up to $18,000 a year for five years, passed the Virginia legislature. The Distribution Bill would have allowed states to allocate federal money to colonization but Jackson vetoed it. Thereafter, colonization slipped away as a major force although the ACS managed to remain in existence with the help of private donations and state funding (Burin 2005: 19, 83; Staudenraus 1961: 178–84, 187).

The ACS tried and failed to obtain a £100,000 subsidy from the British government, but it did get small sums from Pennsylvania, Virginia, New Jersey, Missouri, and, under Buchanan, the federal government once again. Those funds, plus bequests, allowed it to purchase proper headquarters, a paean to racism, and to remain functioning. The ACS survived the Civil War, and World War II in fact, but it was never again a major force. Abraham Lincoln liked the idea of colonization but not Liberia or the ACS. In 1867, instead of providing it with the $50,000 subsidy that it requested, Congress ridiculed the ACS instead. Between 1817 and 1899, the ACS collected a total of $2.8 million from sources public and private (Staudenraus 1961: 176, 218, 240–46, 251; Tomek 2011: 176; Burin 2005: 32, 160–65, 248–49).

NGOs, including various religious orders like the Trinitarians and Mercedarians, ransomed (purchased them from enslavers for the express purpose of freeing them) Europeans enslaved to the Moors. When ransom pleas swamped the NGOs, governments began to sponsor mass redemptions, which were funded by taxes on money changers, playing cards, hearths, and so forth. Governments also paid for a month-long quarantine to ensure the freed slaves did not carry the plague. In Africa, freed slaves received aid from colonial governments, Christian missionaries, and the Mourides, a religious order and indigenous NGO founded in the 1880s. In an attempt to restore (a.k.a. rehabilitate) the former slaves, the Mourides allowed disciples to work for eight years in return for land and the freedom to marry (Davis 2003: 149–53, 180–84; Klein 1993: 185).

Today, restoration costs are enormous. In one case reported by Skinner, Florida's government paid for medication and five different therapists before a sex trafficking victim turned eighteen (2008: 278). The Italian government provides psychological counseling and health care to ex-slaves who testify against their erstwhile enslavers (Kara 2009: 87). Some of the formerly enslaved will need, according to Lou de Baca, "a support network all their lives" (Bales and Soodalter 2009: 125). Many, like the boys choir from Zambia enslaved by a preacher in Texas, become alcohol dependent. Others require counseling or physical therapy. Others need public assistance, as social worker Mary Burchell discovered as she helped Miriam Ali, who lost two of her daughters to Yemeni enslavers, obtain a house and stipend (Bales and Soodalter 2009: 126; Ali and Wain 1995: 97).

Repatriating victims of trafficking is not cheap, either. In many places, therefore, restoration and repatriation is completely ignored or at lease underfunded. The niggardly approach saves budgets in the short term but tends to lead to re-enslavement and hence higher long-term costs. That is why the great Quaker abolitionist Anthony Benezet argued that freed slaves had to be provided land and education. After the Civil War, the US government failed to provide freedpersons with forty acres and a mule, but federal and state governments and private donors expended over $100 million to educate them. Such expenditures were largely wasted, however, after enslavers seized control of Southern governments once again (Kara 2009: 99, 167; Tomek 2011: 25; Engerman 2008: 273; Campbell 1899: 11; Rowland 1903: 18).

Government regulation of labor markets to ensure that they do not reek of slavery costs society plenty (Tinker 1993: 73, 75). Of course governments (i.e., taxpayers) and private donors should not pay the restoration bill, enslavers should. As explained in Chap. 8, taxpayer money should be spent on interdiction and justice systems. The latter needs to convict enslavers and make them restore victims by paying them back wages, with interest, plus repatriation costs and the cost of any ongoing medical or psychological treatment, times three. In other words, Channing was much too lenient, saying "I claim from my oppressor, not food and clothes, but freedom" (Channing 1839: 29). Prosecution, fines, and asset seizures are the means of ending enslavement once and, one hopes, for all.

Summing Up the Costs

"Even from a money standpoint child labor is a great waste. The earning power of the man who has a well-developed body and a common school education is so much greater than that of the man who has neither of these, that the State can much better afford to take care of the comparatively few families dependent upon the wages of children under fourteen or sixteen than it can afford to lose what these children will be able to produce if they are allowed to become fully developed" (Anon. 1906: 622).

Political scientist David Ericson conservatively estimated that between 1791 and 1861 the US federal government spent $51 million, or 2.8 percent of federal government expenditures, on slavery, including suppressing the slave trade, African colonization, fugitive slave renditions, Texas debt relief, leasing of slave laborers, and so forth. He left out the impact of abolitionist mailings on the post office, federal purchases of shares of internal improvement corporations that used slave labor, and other expenditures that were not line items in and of themselves. So the actual transfers from the public to slaveholders were even larger (Ericson 2011: 91, 165, 189).

The slaveries commonplace around the globe today are not identical to the chattel slavery of antebellum America, the Northwest Coast Indians, or the ancients. Today's slaves are unlikely to remain enslaved for their entire lives or to see their children enslaved. They do lose control over their lives during their period of enslavement, however, and hence they have strong incentives to cause trouble for their putative masters. Because most forms of slavery today are illegal or extralegal, governments do not subsidize them as openly as they supported classical forms of slavery. Nevertheless, governments do continue to help some types of enslavers, including those who use the courts to enforce debt collection or who rely on convict labor. Moreover, many governments do not actively dissuade enslavers either, allowing them to function in underground markets that sap vitality from the formal economic sector. Enslavers, like other criminals, do not pay taxes, or at least their fair share of taxes. They essentially free ride on law abiding non-enslavers (International Labour Organization 2014: 45).

Non-slaves no longer tremble in fear of slave rebellions or marauding maroons but many, even in affluent nations, fear that they or their loved ones could fall victim to enslavers. Such fears serve as a disincentive to invest in human capital (training, education) for fear that the returns will be usurped by others. Moreover, enslavers often fight each other over turf and slaves, leading to homicides, drive by shootings, and other socially disruptive and economically costly activities (Skinner 2008: 145, 188).

The biggest social costs of all, though, might be opportunity costs. What could Mississippi flatboat captain Simon Gray have accomplished were he not enslaved (Davis 1966: 230)? "Whatever of mechanical talent or intellect, capable of illustrating a nation, there is in the three millions of slaves," Cassius Clay noted, "is lost for ever for want of education" (1848: 225). The same could be said for the 5 million white Southerners who saw manual labor as beneath them. Carl Schurz noted that after the Civil War some ex-slaves achieved eminence in literature, medicine, law, math, theology, education, art, and mechanics. "They might have accomplished much more, and that many more such men would have come forth," he argued, "had their environment been more just and the opportunities more favorable" (1903). Freed slaves have gone on to do remarkable things, almost always despite their enslavement, rather than because of it (Murphy 2014: 195).

A deadweight loss is of course created when people are not matched with the jobs that best suit them. Freer individuals can discover the best occupation for themselves, but slaves, including those enslaved today, cannot. In the antebellum US South, slaveholders matched slaves to the jobs they were best suited to on the plantation, but slaves obviously were not matched to the best jobs for them economy-wide (Smith 2008: 55; Fogel 1989: 27–28).

Slavery also creates a broader set of opportunity costs. When an investor decides to become an enslaver by investing in a slave, s/he not only creates the various negative externalities discussed above, s/he also forgoes investment in banks, infrastructure companies, or other networks that create very large *positive* externalities (Wright 2010: 108–9). That was why some northern business interests tried to "redeem" the upper South in the antebellum period by planting factories and family farms there (Smith 1945).

More generally, what would our world look like if there were never any forms of slavery and oppression (Foner 1983: 19)? We can never know, but we can know what a future without slavery will look like. It is good, and it is possible.

Bibliography

Adamic, L. (2008). *Dynamite: The story of class violence in America.* Oakland, CA: AK Press.

Adamson, A. H. (1972). *Sugar without slaves: The political economy of British Guiana, 1838–1904.* New Haven, CT: Yale University Press.

Ali, M., & Wain, J. (1995). *Without mercy: A mother's struggle against modern slavery.* New York: Warner Books.

Alpers, E. A. (2004). Flight to freedom: Escape from slavery among bonded Africans in the Indian Ocean world, c. 1750–1962. In G. Campbell (Ed.), *The structure of slavery in Indian Ocean Africa and Asia* (pp. 51–68). London: Frank Cass.

Anon. (1880, December 18). The slave trade. *Labor League Examiner.*

Anon. (1890, May 10). British inconsistency and hypocrisy with regard to the slave trade. *Brotherhood.*

Anon. (1906, October 6). A present day anti-slavery movement. *Friends' Intelligencer.*

Anon. (1922l, November 27). American Black tells Reds in Moscow of 'Slavery in U.S.' *Macon Telegraph.*

Ashworth, J. (1995). *Slavery, capitalism, and politics in the antebellum Republic. Volume 1: Commerce and compromise, 1820–1850.* New York: Cambridge University Press.

Bailey, R. (1992). The slave(ry) trade and the development of capitalism in the United States: The textile industry in New England. In J. Inikori & S. Engerman (Eds.), *The Atlantic slave trade: Effects on economies, societies, and peoples in Africa, the Americas, and Europe* (pp. 205–246). Durham, NC: Duke University Press.

Bales, Kevin. (2012). *Disposable people: New slavery in the global economy,* Rev. ed. Berkeley: University of California Press.

Bales, K., & Soodalter, R. (2009). *The slave next door: Human trafficking and slavery in America today.* Berkeley: University of California Press.

Baptist, E. E. (2014). *The half has never been told: Slavery and the making of American capitalism.* New York: Basic Books.

Barzel, Y. (1977). An economic analysis of slavery. *Journal of Law and Economics, 20,* 87–110.

Bearse, A. (1880). *Reminiscences of fugitive-slave law days in Boston.* Boston: Warren Richardson.

Beckert, S. (2004). Emancipation and empire: Reconstructing the worldwide web of cotton production in the age of the American Civil War. *American Historical Review, 109,* 1405–1438.

Berry, H. (1832). *The speech of Henry Berry, (of Jefferson), in the House of Delegates of Virginian, on the abolition of slavery.* Richmond: n.p.

Blackburn, R. (2011). *The American crucible: Slavery, emancipation and human rights*. New York: Verso.

Blackburn, R. (1996). Slave exploitation and the elementary structures of enslavement. In M. L. Bush (Ed.), *Serfdom and slavery: Studies in legal bondage* (pp. 158–180). New York: Addison Wesley Longman.

Blackmon, D. A. (2008). *Slavery by another name: The re-enslavement of Black Americans from the Civil War to World War II*. New York: Anchor Books.

Blair, D. (2014). *All the ships that never sailed: A general model of illicit market suppression*. Ph.D. dissertation, Georgetown University.

Bloch, M. (1961). *Feudal society*. Chicago: University of Chicago Press.

Bradley, K. R. (1983). Slave kingdoms and slave rebellions in ancient Sicily. *Historical Reflections/Réflexions Historiques, 10*, 435–451.

Brenner, R. (1996). The rises and declines of serfdom in medieval and early modern Europe. In M. L. Bush (Ed.), *Serfdom and slavery: Studies in legal bondage* (pp. 247–276). New York: Addison Wesley Longman.

Brown, L. (2000). *Sex slaves: The trafficking of women in Asia*. London: Virago Press.

Buckland, W. W. (1908). *The roman law of slavery: The condition of the slave in private law from Augustus to Justinian*. Cambridge: Cambridge University Press.

Burin, E. (2005). *Slavery and the peculiar solution: A history of the American Colonization Society*. Gainesville: University Press of Florida.

Bush, M. (1996a). Introduction. In M. L. Bush (Ed.), *Serfdom and slavery: Studies in legal bondage* (pp. 1–17). New York: Addison Wesley Longman.

Bush, M. (1996b). Serfdom in medieval and modern Europe: A comparison. In M. L. Bush (Ed.), *Serfdom and slavery: Studies in legal bondage* (pp. 199–224). New York: Addison Wesley Longman.

Cadet, J.-R. (1998). *Restavec: From Haitian slave child to middle-class American*. Austin: University of Texas Press.

Cairnes, J. E. (1862). *The slave power: Its character, career, and probable designs, being an attempt to explain the real issues involved in the American contest* (2nd ed.). New York: Carleton.

Campbell, R. F. (1899). *Some aspects of the race problem in the South*. Asheville, NC: n.p.

Campbell, G. (2004). Introduction: Slavery and other forms of unfree labour in the Indian Ocean world. In G. Campbell (Ed.), *The structure of slavery in Indian Ocean Africa and Asia* (pp. vii–xxxii). London: Frank Cass.

Chanana, D. R. (1964). *Slavery in ancient India as depicted in Pali and Sanskrit texts*. New Delhi: People's Publishing House.

Channing, W. E. (1839). *Remarks on the slavery question in a letter to Jonathan Phillips, Esq*. Boston: James Munroe and Company.

Childs, D. (2015). *Slaves of the state: Black incarceration from the chain gang to the penitentiary*. Minneapolis: University of Minnesota Press.

Clarence-Smith, W. G. (1993). Cocoa plantations and coerced labor in the Gulf of Guinea, 1870–1914. In M. A. Klein (Ed.), *Breaking the chains: Slavery, bondage, and emancipation in modern Africa and Asia* (pp. 150–170). Madison: University of Wisconsin Press.

Clarence-Smith, W. G. (2006). *Islam and the abolition of slavery.* New York: Oxford University Press.

Clay, C. (1848). *The writings of Cassius Marcellus Clay: Including speeches and addresses.* New York: Harper & Brothers.

Cochin, A. (1863). *The results of slavery.* Boston: Walker, Wise, and Company.

Cook, L. D. (2007). The end of serfdom in Russia—Lessons for Sudan? In K. A. Appiah & M. Bunzl (Eds.), *Buying freedom: The ethics and economics of slave redemption* (pp. 181–199). Princeton: Princeton University Press.

Dal Lago, E., & Katsari, C. (2008). The study of ancient and modern slave systems: Setting an agenda for comparison. In E. D. Lago & C. Katsari (Eds.), *Slave systems ancient and modern* (pp. 3–31). New York: Cambridge University Press.

Dalton, M. B. (1950). *Edward Atkinson (1827–1905): Patron of engineering science and benefactor of industry.* New York: Newcomen Society in North America.

Davidson, J. O. (2015). *Modern slavery: The margins of freedom.* New York: Palgrave Macmillan.

Davies, W. W. (1905). *The codes of Hammurabi and Moses.* New York: Jennings and Graham.

Davis, D. B. (1966). *The problem of slavery in Western culture.* Ithaca, NY: Cornell University Press.

Davis, R. C. (2003). *Christian slaves, Muslim masters: White slavery in the Mediterranean, the Barbary Coast, and Italy, 1500–1800.* New York: Palgrave Macmillan.

Deane, C. (1886). *The connection of Massachusetts with slavery and the slave-trade.* Worcester, MA: Charles Hamilton.

Donald, L. (1997). *Aboriginal slavery on the northwest coast of North America.* Berkeley: University of California Press.

Eltis, D. (1987). *Economic growth and the ending of the transatlantic slave trade.* New York: Oxford University Press.

Eltis, D., & Engerman, S. (2000). The importance of slavery and the slave trade to industrializing Britain. *Journal of Economic History, 60*, 123–144.

Engerman, S. (2008). Emancipation schemes: Different ways of ending slavery. In E. D. Lago & C. Katsari (Eds.), *Slave systems ancient and modern* (pp. 3–31). New York: Cambridge University Press.

Ericson, D. F. (2011). *Slavery in the American republic: Developing the federal government, 1791–1861.* Lawrence: University of Kansas Press.

Faber, E. (1998). *Jews, slaves, and the slave trade: Setting the record straight.* New York: New York University Press.

Finley, M. I. (1980). *Ancient slavery and modern ideology.* New York: Viking Press.

Fogel, R. (1989). *Without consent or contract: The rise and fall of American slavery.* New York: W. W. Norton.
Foner, E. (1983). *Nothing but freedom: Emancipation and its legacy.* Baton Rouge: Louisiana State University Press.
Franklin, J. H., & Moss Jr., A. A. (1988). *From slavery to freedom: A history of negro Americans* (6th ed.). New York: Alfred A. Knopf.
Gallay, A. (2002). *The Indian slave trade: The rise of the English Empire in the American South, 1670–1717.* New Haven, CT: Yale University Press.
Gaspar, D. B. (1992). Slave importation, runaways, and compensation in Antigua, 1720–1729. In J. Inikori & S. Engerman (Eds.), *The Atlantic slave trade: Effects on economies, societies, and peoples in Africa, the Americas, and Europe* (pp. 301–320). Durham, NC: Duke University Press.
Genovese, E. (1972). *Roll, Jordan, roll: The world the slaves made.* New York: Random House.
Gigantino, J. (2014). 'The whole North is not abolitionized': Slavery's slow death in New Jersey, 1830–1860. *Journal of the Early Republic, 34*, 411–437.
Goodell, W. (1853). *The American slave code in theory and practice: Its distinctive features shown by its statutes, judicial decisions, and illustrative facts.* New York: American and Foreign Anti-Slavery Society.
Gray, L. (1941). *History of agriculture in the southern United States to 1860* (Vol. 2). New York: Peter Smith.
Greenberg, M., & Waugh, C. (Eds.). (2000). *The price of freedom: Slavery and the Civil War. Volume Two, the preservation of liberty.* Nashville, TN: Cumberland House.
Gross, K. N. (2015). African American women, mass incarceration, and the politics of protection. *Journal of American History, 102*, 25–33.
Guyatt, N. (2016). *Bind us apart: How enlightened Americans invented racial segregation.* New York: Basic Books.
Ha, S. (2009). *The rise and fall of the American System: Nationalism and the development of the American economy.* London: Pickering & Chatto.
Hall, C., Draper, N., McClelland, K., Donington, K., & Lang, R. (2014). *Legacies of British slave-ownership: Colonial slavery and the formation of Victorian Britain.* New York: Cambridge University Press.
Harring, S. (1977). Class conflict and the suppression of tramps in Buffalo, 1892–1894. *Law & Society Review, 11*, 873–911.
Harrison, E. C. (Ed.). (1978). *Philadelphia merchant: The diary of Thomas P. Cope, 1800–1851.* South Bend, IN: Gateway Editions.
Hellie, R. (1982). *Slavery in Russia, 1450–1725.* Chicago: University of Chicago Press.
Higbie, F. T. (2003). *Indispensable outcasts: Hobo workers and community in the American Midwest, 1880–1930.* Chicago: University of Illinois Press.

Holton, W. (1999). *Forced founders: Indians, debtors, slaves, and the making of the American Revolution in Virginia*. Chapel Hill: University of North Carolina Press.

Hopkins, K. (1993). Novel evidence for Roman slavery. *Past & Present, 138*, 3–27.

Hurmence, B. (Ed.). (1984). *My folks don't want me to talk about slavery: Twenty-one oral histories of former North Carolina slaves*. Winston-Salem, NC: John F. Blair.

Ignatiev, N. (1995). *How the Irish became white*. New York: Routledge.

International Labour Organization. (2014). *Profits and poverty: The economics of forced labour*. Geneva: International Labour Organization.

Jones, J. (2013). *A dreadful deceit: The myth of race from the colonial era to Obama's America*. New York: Basic Books.

Jordan, D., & Walsh, M. (2007). *White cargo: The forgotten history of Britain's white slaves in America*. New York: New York University Press.

Julian, G. W. (1892). *The life of Joshua R. Giddings*. Chicago: A. C. McClurg and Company.

Kara, S. (2009). *Sex trafficking: Inside the business of modern slavery*. New York: Columbia University Press.

Kara, S. (2012). *Bonded labor: Tackling the system of slavery in South Asia*. New York: Columbia University Press.

Kim, B. R. (2004). Nobi: A Korean system of slavery. In G. Campbell (Ed.), *The structure of slavery in Indian Ocean Africa and Asia* (pp. 155–168). London: Frank Cass.

Klein, H. S. (1986). *African slavery in Latin America and the Caribbean*. New York: Oxford University Press.

Klein, M. (1992). The impact of the Atlantic slave trade on the societies of the western Sudan. In J. Inikori & S. Engerman (Eds.), *The Atlantic slave trade: Effects on economies, societies, and peoples in Africa, the Americas, and Europe* (pp. 25–48). Durham, NC: Duke University Press.

Klein, M. (1993). Introduction: Modern European expansion and traditional servitude in Africa and Asia. In M. A. Klein (Ed.), *Breaking the chains: Slavery, bondage, and emancipation in modern Africa and Asia* (pp. 3–36). Madison: University of Wisconsin Press.

Kumar, D. (1993). Colonialism, bondage, and caste in British India. In M. A. Klein (Ed.), *Breaking the chains: Slavery, bondage, and emancipation in modern Africa and Asia* (pp. 112–130). Madison: University of Wisconsin Press.

Lichtenstein, A. (1996). *Twice the work of free labor: The political economy of convict labor in the New South*. New York: Verso.

Lovejoy, P. E. (2012). *Transformations in slavery: A history of slavery in Africa* (3rd ed.). New York: Cambridge University Press.

Magness, P. W. (2015). *A paradox of secessionism: Slavery and the Confederate security state*. Social Science Research Network. Retrieved August 15, 2016, from http://papers.ssrn.com/sol3/papers.cfm?abstract_id=2639529

Mark, I. (1940). *Agrarian conflicts in colonial New York, 1711–1775*. New York: Columbia University Press.

Markevich, A., & Zhuravskaya, E. (2014). *Economic effects of the abolition of serfdom: Evidence from the Russian Empire*. Social Science Research Network. Retrieved August 15, 2016, from http://papers.ssrn.com/sol3/papers.cfm?abstract_id=2514964

Mason, M. (2006). *Slavery and politics in the early American republic*. Chapel Hill: University of North Carolina Press.

McKeown, N. (2007). *The invention of ancient slavery?* London: Duckworth.

McKivigan, J. R., & Kaufman, H. L. (Eds.). (2012). *In the words of Frederick Douglass: Quotations from liberty's champion*. Ithaca, NY: Cornell University Press.

McLennan, R. (2008). *The crisis of imprisonment: Protest, politics, and the making of the American penal state, 1776–1941*. New York: Cambridge University Press.

Meagher, A. J. (2008). *The coolie trade: The traffic in Chinese laborers to Latin America, 1847–1874*. New York: Xlibris.

Miers, S. (2004). Slavery: A question of definition. In G. Campbell (Ed.), *The structure of slavery in Indian Ocean Africa and Asia* (pp. 1–16). London: Frank Cass.

Millar, J. (1771/2006). *The origin of the distinction of ranks: Or, an inquiry into the circumstances, which give rise to influence and authority, in the different members of society*. Indianapolis: Liberty Fund.

Miller, J. C. (2008). Slaving as historical process: Examples from the ancient Mediterranean and the modern Atlantic. In E. D. Lago & C. Katsari (Eds.), *Slave systems ancient and modern* (pp. 70–102). New York: Cambridge University Press.

Murphy, L. T. (2014). *Survivors of slavery: Modern-day slave narratives*. New York: Columbia University Press.

Owen, R. D. (1864). *The wrong of slavery, the right of emancipation and the future of the African race in the United States*. Philadelphia: J. B. Lippincott & Co.

Payne, E. G. (1912). *An experiment in alien labor*. Chicago: University of Chicago Press.

Pelteret, D. (1995). *Slavery in early mediaeval England: From the reign of Alfred until the twelfth century*. Rochester, NY: Boydell Press.

Petre-Grenouilleau, O. (2008). Processes of exiting the slave systems: A typology. In E. D. Lago & C. Katsari (Eds.), *Slave systems ancient and modern* (pp. 233–264). New York: Cambridge University Press.

Phillips, W. D. (1996). Continuity and change in Western slavery: Ancient to modern times. In M. L. Bush (Ed.), *Serfdom and slavery: Studies in legal bondage* (pp. 71–88). New York: Addison Wesley Longman.
Price, R. (Ed.). (1979). *Maroon societies: Rebel slave communities in the Americas* (2nd ed.). Baltimore: Johns Hopkins University Press.
Reid, A. (1993). The decline of slavery in nineteenth-century Indonesia. In M. A. Klein (Ed.), *Breaking the chains: Slavery, bondage, and emancipation in modern Africa and Asia* (pp. 64–82). Madison: University of Wisconsin Press.
Resendez, A. (2016). *The other slavery: The uncovered story of Indian enslavement in America*. New York: Houghton Mifflin Harcourt.
Rihll, T. (2008). Slavery and technology in pre-industrial contexts. In E. D. Lago & C. Katsari (Eds.), *Slave systems ancient and modern* (pp. 127–147). New York: Cambridge University Press.
Roberts, K. (2011). *The origins of business, money, and markets*. New York: Columbia Business School Publishing.
Rowland, D. (1903). *A Mississippi view of race relations in the South*. Jackson, MS: Harmon Publishing Co.
Sandomrisky, L. N. (1997). Aristomenes. In J. P. Rodriguez (Ed.), *The historical encyclopedia of world slavery* (Vol. I, pp. 47–48). Denver: ABC-CLIO.
Schermerhorn, C. (2015). *The business of slavery and the rise of American capitalism, 1815–1860*. New Haven, CT: Yale University Press.
Schulz, J. (2008). *The financial crisis of abolition*. New Haven, CT: Yale University Press.
Schurz, C. (1903, January). Can the South solve the Negro problem? *McClure's*.
Skinner, E. B. (2008). *A crime so monstrous: Face-to-face with modern-day slavery*. New York: Free Press.
Smith, G. W. (1945). Ante-bellum attempts of Northern business interests to 'redeem' the Upper South. *Journal of Southern History, 11*, 177–213.
Smith, A. E. (1965). *Colonists in bondage: White servitude and convict labor in America, 1607–1776*. Gloucester, MA: Peter Smith.
Smith, J. D. (1985). *An old creed for the new South: Proslavery ideology and historiography, 1865–1918*. Athens: University of Georgia Press.
Smith, C. F. (2008). *Here lies Jim Crow: Civil rights in Maryland*. Baltimore: Johns Hopkins University Press.
South Carolina Association. (1823/2001). Memorial ca. 1823. In L. Schweninger (Ed.), *The Southern Debate over slavery: Petitions to Southern Legislatures, 1778–1864* (pp. 78–83). Chicago: University of Illinois Press.
Staudenraus, J. (1961). *The African colonization movement, 1816–1865*. New York: Columbia University Press.
Steele, E. S. (1987). Henry George on chattel and wage slavery: The American social philosopher condemned both forms as immoral, irrational denials of equality. *American Journal of Economics and Sociology, 46*, 369–378.

Taylor, T. (2001). Believing the ancients: Quantitative and qualitative dimensions of slavery and the slave trade in later prehistoric Eurasia. *World Archaeology, 33*, 27–43.

Thompson, G. (1851). *Prison life and reflections; Or, a narrative of the arrest, trial, conviction, imprisonment, treatment, observations, reflections, and deliverance of Work, Burr, and Thompson*. Hartford: Alanson Work.

Thornton, J. M. (1978). *Politics and power in a slavery society: Alabama, 1800–1860*. Baton Rouge: Louisiana State Press.

Tinker, H. (1993). *A new system of slavery: The export of Indian labour overseas, 1830–1920* (2nd ed.). London: Hansib Publishing Limited.

Tomek, B. C. (2011). *Colonization and its discontents: Emancipation, emigration, and antislavery in antebellum Pennsylvania*. New York: New York University Press.

Vogt, J. (1975). *Ancient slavery and the ideal of man* (T. Wiedemann, Trans.). Cambridge: Harvard University Press.

Weld, T. (1839). *American slavery as it is: The testimony of a thousand witnesses*. New York: American Anti-Slavery Society.

Wermeil, S. (2000). *The fireproof building: Technology and public safety in the nineteenth-century American city*. Baltimore: Johns Hopkins University Press.

Whiteley, H. (1833). *Excessive cruelty to slaves. Three months in Jamaica, in 1832: Comprising a residence of seven weeks on a sugar plantation*. Philadelphia: n.p.

Wiecek, W. (1977). *The sources of antislavery constitutionalism in America, 1760–1848*. Ithaca, NY: Cornell University Press.

Wright, D. R. (1993). *African Americans in the early Republic*. Arlington Heights, IL: Harlan Davidson.

Wright, R. E. (2010). *Fubarnomics: A lighthearted, serious look at America's economic ills*. Amherst, NY: Prometheus.

CHAPTER 8

Real Abolition

As shown in Chap. 4, slavery is clearly illegal yet it persists and even grows (van den Anker 2004: 17). The organized antislavery project, as historian Joel Quirk calls the centuries-long efforts to eradicate coerced forms of labor globally, today concentrates on ending de facto practices that were ended de jure in most parts of the world over a century ago. It can, however, he rightly lamented, be difficult to identify reasons for taking up the antislavery cause in the first place (Quirk 2011: 6–7, 68).

This book, I hope, will spur more people to action—the concrete reforms set forth below—because it makes clear the tremendous economic damage that slavery causes. Ending slavery requires not only realizing that slavery is wrong but also that ending slavery is feasible. The first abolition movement grew out of the Enlightenment, which took progress as an article of faith (Quirk 2011: 28, 244–45). We do not have to go that far, but we do need to minimize the costs of abolition while maximizing the benefits. Understanding that slavery hurts the overall economy rather than helps it is a big step in that direction. Enslavers steal jobs directly, of course, but they also steal them indirectly by reducing the economic growth and development that is the wellspring of new jobs. Ending slavery, as Kevin Bales intuited, would create a *freedom dividend* akin to the peace dividend that aided Europe after World War II and much of the global economy at the end of the Cold War (Bales 2012: xxix).

As Moises Naim exhorts, we must stop using moral indignation as the basis for public policy because it just is not enough (Naim 2005: 238). To get the resources that they need, modern abolitionists must make clear that

R.E. Wright, *The Poverty of Slavery*,
DOI 10.1007/978-3-319-48968-1_8

slavery is both immoral and economically costly. Today, the moral case against slavery is very strong, essentially irrefutable, so neo-abolitionists should always preface their remarks by reminding people that slavery is, was, and shall forever be an abomination. Unfortunately, however, slavery's moral bankruptcy is insufficient to stop enslavers from plying their dastardly craft, and also does not induce governments, or most of their citizens, to fight (i.e., expend resources) to eradicate them. Such folks need to be reminded that slavery is immoral but also told that the peculiar institution impoverishes everyone, including themselves.

The notion that enslaving human beings could help the overall economy, as opposed to the much narrower claim that slavery merely pads the bank balances of enslavers, is pernicious because it appears to align the interests of enslavers with those of non-slaves. More importantly, the notion of slave-driven economic growth is simply empirically wrong. This is not to denigrate the arduous labor performed by slaves throughout history but rather to recognize that slavery, qua slavery, creates significant negative externalities (pollution), the costs of which are borne by the entire society/economy. Those costs vary over time and place but exist wherever coercion exists and in direct proportion to the degree that workers are unfree.

In other words, this book is about what antislavery author Kathleen Simon called in 1929 "the priceless value of human liberty" (p. 260). Morally, no price can be put on human liberty. Economically, human liberty has a value that is finite, but extremely large. Basically, this book, especially Chaps. 6 and 7, has shown that because of the large externalities created by unfreedom, we would all be better off if slavery, in all its dastardly forms, had never existed. We cannot change the past, but we can change the future and finally end the large-scale enslavement of laborers for profit.

Adam Smith once claimed that it was "almost impossible that [slavery] could ever be totally or generally abolished" (Engerman 1996: 35). I think he was *precisely* correct. Slavery, as we saw in Chap. 4, has proven itself remarkably resilient and some poor souls will always be kidnapped and enslaved or killed by psychopaths. But Smith held open the possibility, however slight, that slavery could one day be scotched and that day may be nearly here, if only activists, policymakers, and scholars can get on the same page about slavery's economic causes and effects. "Few scholars, and even fewer activists, have any idea of the history that led to the present situation" (Miers 2003: xiv). As this quotation suggests, knowledge of history can help lead the way.

Merely outlawing slavery never worked ("made no difference in practice" [Bush 1996: 8]) anywhere because enslavers merely shifted their victims into new forms of bondage that were either legal or simply not on authorities' radar (Quirk 2011: 83). "Laws change in vain," an abolitionist historian lamented in 1863 (Cochin: 345). Legislation had little effect in British India, Dharma Kumar noted, because "as masters became aware of the official attitude, they sometimes changed old institutional forms without giving up the substance of dominance" (1993: 121). As Kevin Bales made clear, "making something illegal doesn't make it cease to exist; making it illegal only causes it to vanish from view" (2007a: 2). That is both because the perpetrators hide their activities and because governments, and their constituents, find it too easy to conclude that the case is closed though they should recognize that ending slavery is much harder than outlawing it, just as ending murder, rape, and so forth is much more difficult than merely making it illegal to harm others (Quirk 2011: 7–8, 129–37).

Making an activity illegal does not mean that the activity ends, it just changes the cost-benefit matrix (Ould 2004: 72). If the expected cost of performing the illegal activity does not exceed the expected benefit, the activity will persist (Kara 2009: 40, 200, 205). In the case of slavery, uneven enforcement and light penalties mean that enslavement has only been "delegalized" rather than rendered truly illegal (i.e., the expected costs of enslaving others is made greater than expected benefits [Kara 2009: 37; Kumar 1993: 112]). In Sudan, where slavery was endemic in the late twentieth century, there was, unsurprisingly, never a single prosecution of any slave raider or enslaver (Skinner 2008: 104). In India, some enslavers have been convicted under the Child Labour Act of 1989 but the fines imposed were too pathetically small to have much effect (Kara 2012: 205). "Even with a 100 percent conviction rate," Kara noted, "the exploitation of bonded labor remains a very good business decision" (Kara 2012: 207).

"Governments," wrote Moises Naim in his insightful book on illicit trading activities, "need to drive up the risk and down the reward that traffickers get from the human trade" (Naim 2005: 106). (And they certainly should not be paying enslavers, as the US government did in at least one notorious recent case [Bales and Soodalter 2009: 130].) As historian Joel Quirk put it, if involuntary labor practices are even perceived to enjoy advantages over more enlightened practices, the former will be rendered more difficult to extirpate (2011: 124). Unfortunately laws, even perfectly designed ones, are only as effective as the will to enforce them (Kara 2012:

186). The tendency is to blame a lack of resources instead of the real culprit, a lack of commitment (Quirk 2011: 4). For example, Pakistan ratified CEDAW (Convention on the Elimination of All Forms of Discrimination Against Women) but the government does not enforce it, so it is widely considered "a joke." Similarly, antislavery legislation in Nepal has languished unheeded and unenforced on the statute books for decades (Brown 2000: 187, 190).

It is high time that governments showed enslavers that they are serious about abolition by locking them up and fining them heavily, more heavily than they could ever hope to earn by exploiting anyone (Kara 2012: 215). Enslavement occurs whenever the enslaver's cost of acquiring a slave is less than the expected present value of the slave's future labor minus maintenance, control, and other costs (Manning 1990: 21, 34). Slavery is essentially the economics of theft and should be dealt with as such (Engerman 2008: 273). In other words, governments need to make the expected profits of enslaving others negative, which they can do by raising the conviction rate as well as the criminal and civil penalties associated with slaving. In 1855, "An American" argued that slavery would end only when it became unprofitable, which he thought could be accomplished, given that slavery was still legal, by boycotting the sale of slave-produced goods (1855: 11). Such boycotts, however, rarely worked because of the costs of coordinating them. Contemporary slavery is like a cancer: not only is it growing but its cure depends on the specific type of cancer one is considering. Consumer boycotts make much more sense against multinationals than local brick producers; religious slavery is best combated through education and debate (van den Anker 2004: 3, 16). Sex and most forms of bonded labor are probably best attacked directly now that slavery is illegal in virtually all jurisdictions.

The best direct policy would be to seize enslavers' ill-gotten assets but the simple fact of the matter is that money is too easily laundered, or made to look like it originated in legitimate activities, to differentiate consistently between clean-looking and actually clean assets (Sharman 2011: 5–6, 37–95). The next best alternative is to impose very heavy fines (seizure of assets whether clean or not) and, of course, jail time. This goes for both those doing the physical enslaving but also the real holders and other conspirators (Bales 2012: 238).

One of the reasons that the formal emancipation of chattel slaves (and serfs) never worked to end enslavement is that former slaves never received any compensation (Engerman 2008: 270). "Freeing the Negro without freeing the land," Brazil statesman Joaquim Nabuco (1849–1910) noted, "is but half an abolition" (Foner 1983: 34). England emancipated its slaves, Edward Atkinson argued, but "stopped far short of making them men, leaving them subject to oppressive laws made entirely under the influence of their former owners" (Foner 1983: 42). Benjamin Franklin came to antislavery slowly but he realized that it was "such an atrocious debasement of human nature" that abolition was insufficient. Freed slaves needed education and employment lest they fall again into "misfortune" (Waldstreicher 2006: 183–89; Houston 2008: 222). The same insight holds today, of course, but many freed slaves become re-enslaved because of inadequate post-freedom aid (Bales and Soodalter 2009: 100–1).

Sometimes enslavers received compensation, but all that policy did was to strengthen their advantage over their former bondsmen and/or wreck the economy. Compensation for slaveholders cost Brazil so much, and was botched so badly, that it led in June 1889 to an acute financial crisis that led to end of the monarchy and a decade of political and economic instability (Engerman 2008: 86, 103; Schulz 2008).

Presumably, no enslaver today would dare ask for compensation for freeing their illegal slaves but that is no deterrent given the profits to be made enslaving others. Enslavers need to pay for their crimes and most of what they pay should go to their victims. This idea is not new—Hinton Helper wanted to fine or tax slaveholders $40 plus per year, per slave and to use the proceeds "for the sole advantage of the slaves" (1860: 178)—but no government ever had the will to try it. Assets seized from convicted enslavers, explained Bales and Soodalter, are earmarked for the budgets of law enforcement agencies, not for helping former slaves to rebuild their lives (2009: 264). "Their lives and labor were stolen," the duo correctly noted, "and the criminal slaveholders should pay them back" (p. xvi). Skinner agreed that rehabilitation should be funded out of fines but I would warn against putting fines into state coffers as some of it will end up being spent on other projects (2008: 97). Moreover, governments often come to rely on fines, sin taxes, and so forth, giving them an incentive to keep people parking illegally, smoking tobacco products, and so forth.

Ending slavery should not be conflated with ending the trade in illicit drugs or guns. None of them are really victimless crimes as they all create large negative externalities. But slavery creates direct victims as well as indirect ones. Those direct victims, the enslaved, should be entitled to receive treble damages directly from their enslavers, that is, the difference between their compensation as a slave and what they would have received in a competitive market, plus punitive damages for rape, bodily injury, mental anguish, and other torts. One judge in Florida had the right idea when he fined enslavers $3 million, the sum he estimated that they had earned from their agricultural slaves, but the fines actually need to be higher than what the enslavers make because the conviction rate will never be 100 percent (Bales and Soodalter 2009: 59). (Many ex-slaves remain too traumatized to testify at trial [Kara 2009: 196].) As Dan Werner, the legal director of the Workers' Rights Law Center of New York noted, "we want to make it costlier to use slaves than to hire paid workers" (Bales and Soodalter 2009: 65).

Convicted enslavers who cannot or will not pay should themselves be enslaved, by the state, and the proceeds turned over to their erstwhile victims, or to some sort of NGO or government agency tasked with ensuring that the money is not misspent. The idea is hardly new. Centuries ago, Jean Bodin argued that wise leaders should reduce the number of possible victims of enslavement by providing education and employment for the poor and the formerly enslaved (Davis 1966: 113–14).

Slave traders, from the lowly local recruiter to the largest wholesale distributor, also need to be caught, convicted, and forced to compensate their victims. Capturing slaves is costly and gets more costly as the number of slaves taken increases; the policy goal should be to make it too costly for anyone to capture any appreciable number of slaves (Rogers and Swinnerton 2007: 29).

In addition to compensating their victims, enslavers need to repay society for the negative externalities their enslavement of others created. In other words, they need to pay a Pigouvian tax. In 1832, Charles James Faulkner (1806–1884) of Virginia argued in a speech before the Virginia House of Delegates that slaveholders should forfeit their ownership stakes in their slaves without compensation from the government. The public, he noted, never pays "for property which is removed or destroyed because it is a nuisance, and found injurious to that society" (Helper 1860: 176). But why stop merely at the loss of the value of the slave?

Heavy fines and Pigouvian taxes could help to convince corporations to clean up their supply chains, rendering abolition just plain good business practice (Skinner 2008: 292). Making corporations responsible not only for their own employees but also those of their major business partners would go a long way toward making them more responsible. So, too, would limiting how much they could spend on defense attorneys (Bales and Soodalter 2009: 68). Any funds received from any parties should be entirely earmarked for slavery prevention programs, lest the screams of the enslaved end up funding aircraft carriers or superhighways.

The political will is not there yet, but it is building as the public learns more about the horrors of modern slavery and trafficking. The number of people newly enslaved in the United States exceeds the number of annual murder victims (Bales and Soodalter 2009: 106). There is little to wonder about here as the rewards of enslaving others are greater and the costs lower than murdering them. Fewer than one in 100 enslavers is convicted and most of those, even the enslaver of a woman for 19 years, get light sentences (Bales and Soodalter 2009: 7, 32). The US government spends about $200 million a year fighting slavery compared to the $12 billion a year it expends on combating the trade in illicit drugs (though making an exact division is difficult as enslavers are often involved in a panoply of illicit trades) (Skinner 2008: 113; Bales and Soodalter 2009: 157). America is not alone in this respect as Haiti and many other countries pursue drug traffickers with more zeal and money than they do human traffickers or enslavers. America's anti-trafficking strategy has been compared to a game of whac-a-mole, or rather, whac-a-pimp (Skinner 2008: 113, 283).

The forces of antislavery are somewhat divided. The preoccupation with trafficking focuses attention on trading, especially internationally, rather than on bondage, which of course is the real bane to the economy and the root cause of trafficking (Kara 2009: 4–5). Trafficking also connotes prostitution and border protection, issues that divide neo-abolitionists (Quirk 2011: 216–17). In the United States, anyway, some political leadership on the issue could be helpful. In the late eighteenth and early nineteenth centuries, the Federalist party showed that large numbers of Northerners would vote and even act against slaveholders when they were shown how slavery impinged on their economic and political interests (Mason 2006: 5). Lincoln and the Radical Republicans did likewise in the 1850s and 1860s.

Ending slavery is never easy because enslavers have strong incentives to respond to attempts to squelch them. EU commissioner Anna Diamantopoulou, for example, notes that enslavers "know their business inside and out and respond to changes in the market with a speed unmatched by even the most competitive corporations. Their expertise and ability to exploit the market are surpassed only by their disregard for human life" (Batstone 2010: 154–55).

The good news is that resistance to antislavery is muted and will continue to be so, especially as the word gets out (again) that slavery is not only morally bankrupt it is economically bankrupting. Yes, we are all complicit with slavery, just like Northerners were before the Civil War, and have continued to be complicit to a lesser or greater degree, because we are involved in markets, which are nothing more than economic networks (Farrow, Lang, and Frank 2005). At the same time, though, we are also all victims of slavery due to the large negative externalities that slavery creates. So we should not just feel guilty about slavery, we should be angry that enslavers steal a little bit from us every day.

In the past, enslavers fought abolition politically and militarily and their agglomerated wealth and influence often were enough to stave off legal abolition for decades and even centuries. The good news is that today no society depends on slavery in any significant degree. As a percentage of the world's population, both enslavers and enslaved may be at their historical nadir. (At the same time, slaves are more numerous than ever before because their numbers have been growing, as has the world's population.) Globally, there are only 5 or 6 million slaveholders and they are not a potent political force (Klein 1993: 26; Murphy 2014: 2; Bales 2007b: xii).

If slavery is so economically inconsequential, and if slaves can be bought for a few dollars each, why not finish slavery off by simply buying all the slaves and freeing them? Redemption has a long history. European governments, for example, used to ransom slaves from the Barbary pirates (Davis 2003: 19–20). And who could blame a parent or spouse from ransoming a loved one (Jok 2007: 147; Kellow 2007: 200–206)? As public policy, however, redeeming slaves is not a good idea. For starters, it legitimizes the idea that people can be bought and sold. It also encourages enslavers to seize more slaves and for people to pretend to be enslaved, as during the infamous redemption efforts in the Sudan in the 1990s, so they can split the proceeds with their fake enslavers (Jok 2007: 146–47; Bales 2007b: viii).

Redemption, therefore, should be a tactic of last resort because its overall effects are unclear. It does alleviate the sufferings of the enslaved but not for long if they simply fall back into an enslaver's clutches, which often occurs when liberation is seen as an event instead of as a process, and a long one at that (Appiah and Bunzl 2007: 1–5; Basu and Chau 2007: 42; Bales 2007b: xi). *New York Times* columnist Nicholas Kristof, for example, once bought the freedom of a sex slave for $203 but a year later he found that she had returned to the brothel (Skinner 2008: 35). Redemption, after all, does not get at the root causes of slavery (Karlan and Krueger 2007: 9).

Economists agree that redemption reduces the number of slaves at any given time but also that it increases the total number of people who become enslaved for some period (Karlan and Krueger 2007; Rogers and Swinnerton 2007). Some even argue that the price of slaves may not rise due to the redemption program, and in that case, redemption does not secure freedom for anyone enslaved when the redemptions began (Rogers and Swinnerton 2007: 22). As freed slaves may be damaged for life, assessing the total welfare effects of redemption is difficult (Karlan and Krueger 2007: 10). If enslavement is short and easy, then redemption may increase human welfare on net. If enslavement means rape, torture, and years of imprisonment, however, redemption is almost as bad as slavery itself (Rogers and Swinnerton 2007: 30–32). The key to any successful redemption scheme, Engerman argued, is an effective mechanism to prevent new enslavement (2007: 103). But that, of course, is impossible. A better approach might be to pay slave raiders not to raid (Rogers and Swinnerton 2007: 34).

Another angle of attack is to sever the many connections between the legitimate business sphere and the underworld of slavery as that will make the latter less profitable. Businesses need to be recruited as active abolitionists to induce them to expunge their supply chains, transport and logistics, and finances of slavery. That requires public pressure, and then intra-corporate training and follow up. Many CEOs are still unaware of the scope of the problem. They and their cadre of managers need education, training, best practices instruction, and so forth (Shelley and Bain 2015).

But what activities, precisely, should governments prosecute heavily? The short answer is anything that lowers a worker's score on the freedom index developed in Chap. 2. Many such practices are already illegal in nations that adopted the 1956 Supplementary Convention on the Abolition of Slavery and similar guidelines (Kara 2012: 29). But, as noted above, making an activity unlawful is only the first step toward its eradication.

Brand Whitlock, the erstwhile mayor of Toledo, once asked: "Why is it constantly necessary to do something *to* people? If we can't do something *for* them, when are we going to learn to let them alone" (Anon. 1914: 288)? Robert Dale Owen had it right when he argued that "supply and demand should be left, in all cases, to regulate rates of compensation and places of residence" (Owen 1864: 227). To today's liberals, that may seem cruel, but recall that competitive wages are typically far above the compensation paid to slaves. Our goal should not be to create a world without constraints, which is impossible to achieve, but rather to create enough competition among employers that laborers receive the full value of their marginal product (Conning and Kevane 2007: 110–11, 120, 124–25). "Only the producer-exploiter suffers in a scenario of fair and competitive labor agreements that are reinforced by the rule of law and more equitable bargaining power," Kara correctly noted (2012: 14).

Former slaves no longer need 40 acres and a mule, but they sure could use a fair shake. Ending political slavery, the diminution of civil liberties by autocratic states, would go a long way toward ending labor slavery by drying up supply. As a student from Africa studying at Augustana University in the United States put it, people in poor countries like his cannot do much about combating slavery when they are worried about their next meal. Increasing political liberty will improve economic conditions, decreasing the number of vulnerable people at the bottom, and increasing the willingness and ability of those with higher incomes to help combat trafficking (Bernstein 2004). If places like Moldova or Nigeria, where the life expectancy is 43 years and per capita income is only $1154, could improve their economies, the large supply of potential slaves would dry up (Kara 2009: 67, 90).

Economic uplift has helped to reduce slavery in the past. Indian indentured laborer immigration, for example, petered out before the Great War because they were needed to work in an Indian economy that was experiencing some growth and development (Tinker 1993: 301). Once per capita incomes increase, people in poor countries will start to birth fewer children. Before that demographic transition occurs, birthrates may be reduced with educational campaigns. Cracking down on slavery will help speed the transition by decreasing incentives for having more children (Skinner 2008: 30).

Governments that do not do their part can be sanctioned and/or shamed more effectively than hitherto (Skinner 2008: 195–96). Model growth, antislavery, and anti-trafficking laws can be quickly imposed on many countries in much the same way that anti-money laundering (AML) laws were foisted on most nations in a very short period after the terrorist attacks on the United States in September 2001. Blacklisting, ranking and rating, socialization of government officials, and other soft power techniques were so successful in spreading AML laws that even Nauru, a tiny island nation of just 11,000 people with no domestic financial industry, passed state-of-the-art AML statutes. Despite its numerous more pressing problems, including a debt to GDP ratio of 1600 percent and the world's highest rates of obesity and type 2 diabetes, Nauru pays officials to type zeroes and N/As into surveys and reports and to prepare themselves for the day the country might harbor its first financial institution (Sharman 2011: 1–2, 7–9, 99–164).

Some blame global poverty on globalization but poverty is actually on the wane in no small part due to globalization. What holds many economies back also increases the supply of slaves, that is, conflict, corruption, and caste. Doing away with the last named institution in South Asia, along with the notion that debts should be intergenerational, would go a long way toward halving the number of slaves worldwide (van den Anker 2004; Firmo-Fontan 2004: 91–92; Upadhyaya 2004).

Other reforms that appear like they would be helpful include the establishment of so-called john schools where the customers of prostitutes caught by the police pay a fee and attend classes regarding prostitution and its ill effects. Such schools cost taxpayers nothing and reduce recidivism (Bales and Soodalter 2009: 86–87). The formation of networks of freed slaves should also be encouraged so that the formerly enslaved can help each other, just like former slaves used to help newly freed slaves in antebellum Boston (Baptist 2014: 315). Microfinance institutions could help to reduce slavery by keeping people out of debt to traffickers or employers. Anything that reduces income inequality could help as well. One reason slavery is still common in India is because individual Indians are either wealthy or impoverished so the former can take advantage of the latter (Tinker 1993: xii).

Perhaps the greatest financial mind of the late twentieth and early twenty-first centuries, Yale economist Robert Shiller, has proffered interesting ideas, hitherto largely ignored, that would ensure sufficient aid is brought into poor regions after famines, floods, earthquakes, tsunamis, and so forth (2003). Too often in the past, catastrophes have led already vulnerable populations directly into debt peonage and worse (Campbell 2004: xxiv). Shiller's plan would not stop catastrophes from happening but it would go a long way toward ensuring speedier recoveries (Tinker 1993: 39).

Technology can also help to end human enslavement. In 1908, a newspaper editor extolled the coming end of "animal slavery" as machines replaced horses, mules, oxen, and so forth. The story featured a probably apocryphal little girl from the countryside exclaiming "Oh, look, mamma at that naughty man. He's making horses pull the trolley car" (Anon. 1908: 329). Animal slavery is, indeed, largely a thing of the past. According to Jean Francois Mouhot and others, we now enslave fossil fuels instead (2011). They certainly produce massive negative externalities but the point here is that technological change can render slavery obsolete. Just as machines now pick cotton, why could not sexbots alleviate the pain of millions of enslaved girls? In fact, advanced sexbots would probably already exist if there were not so many vulnerable young women available for enslavement (Gurley 2015).

Bibliography

An American. (1855). *Cotton is king: Or the culture of cotton, and its relation to agriculture, manufactures and commerce.* Cincinnati, OH: Moore, Wilstach, Keys & Co.

Anon. (1908, February 6). Animal slavery. *The Independent: Devoted to the Consideration of Politics, Social and Economic Tendencies.*

Anon. (1914, April). The futility of the white slave agitation as Brand Whitlock sees it. *Current Opinion.*

Appiah, K. A. (2007). What's wrong with slavery? In K. A. Appiah & M. Bunzl (Eds.), *Buying freedom: The ethics and economics of slave redemption* (pp. 249–258). Princeton: Princeton University Press.

Appiah, K. A., & Bunzel, M. (2007). What's wrong with slavery? In K. A. Appiah & M. Bunzl (Eds.), *Buying freedom: The ethics and economics of slave redemption* (pp. 249–258). Princeton: Princeton University Press.

Bales, K. (2007a). *Ending slavery: How we free today's slaves.* Berkeley: University of California Press.

Bales, K. (2007b). Foreword. In K. A. Appiah & M. Bunzl (Eds.), *Buying freedom: The ethics and economics of slave redemption* (pp. vii–xii). Princeton: Princeton University Press.

Bales, Kevin. 2012. *Disposable people: New slavery in the global economy*, Rev. ed. Berkeley: University of California Press.

Bales, K., & Soodalter, R. (2009). *The slave next door: Human trafficking and slavery in America today.* Berkeley: University of California Press.

Baptist, E. E. (2014). *The half has never been told: Slavery and the making of American capitalism.* New York: Basic Books.

Basu, A. K., & Chau, N. H. (2007). An exploration of the worst forms of child labor: Is redemption a viable option? In K. A. Appiah & M. Bunzl (Eds.), *Buying freedom: The ethics and economics of slave redemption* (pp. 37–76). Princeton: Princeton University Press.

Batstone, David. 2010. *Not for sale: The return of the global slave trade and how we can fight it*, Rev. ed. New York: HarperCollins.

Bernstein, W. J. (2004). *The birth of plenty: How the prosperity of the modern world was created.* New York: McGraw-Hill.

Brown, L. (2000). *Sex slaves: The trafficking of women in Asia.* London: Virago Press.

Bush, M. (1996). Introduction. In M. L. Bush (Ed.), *Serfdom and slavery: Studies in legal bondage* (pp. 1–17). New York: Addison Wesley Longman.

Campbell, G. (2004). Introduction: Slavery and other forms of unfree labour in the Indian Ocean world. In G. Campbell (Ed.), *The structure of slavery in Indian Ocean Africa and Asia* (pp. vii–xxxii). London: Frank Cass.

Conning, J., & Kevane, M. (2007). Freedom, servitude, and voluntary contracts. In K. A. Appiah & M. Bunzl (Eds.), *Buying freedom: The ethics and economics of slave redemption* (pp. 108–140). Princeton: Princeton University Press.

Davis, D. B. (1966). *The problem of slavery in Western culture*. Ithaca, NY: Cornell University Press.

Davis, R. C. (2003). *Christian slaves, Muslim masters: White slavery in the Mediterranean, the Barbary Coast, and Italy, 1500–1800*. New York: Palgrave Macmillan.

Engerman, S. (1996). Slavery, serfdom and other forms of coerced labour: Similarities and differences. In M. L. Bush (Ed.), *Serfdom and slavery: Studies in legal bondage* (pp. 18–41). New York: Addison Wesley Longman.

Engerman, S. (2007). Slavery, freedom, and Sen. In K. A. Appiah & M. Bunzl (Eds.), *Buying freedom: The ethics and economics of slave redemption* (pp. 77–107). Princeton: Princeton University Press.

Engerman, S. (2008). Emancipation schemes: Different ways of ending slavery. In E. D. Lago & C. Katsari (Eds.), *Slave systems ancient and modern* (pp. 3–31). New York: Cambridge University Press.

Farrow, A., Lang, J., & Frank, J. (2005). *Complicity: How the North promoted, prolonged, and profited from slavery*. New York: Ballantine Books.

Firmo-Fontan, V. (2004). Responses to sexual slavery: From the Balkans to Afghanistan. In C. van den Anker (Ed.), *The political economy of new slavery* (pp. 91–106). New York: Palgrave Macmillan.

Foner, E. (1983). *Nothing but freedom: Emancipation and its legacy*. Baton Rouge: Louisiana State University Press.

Gurley, G. (2015, April 16). Is this the dawn of the sexbots? *Vanity Fair*.

Helper, H. R. (1860). *The impending crisis of the South: How to meet it*. New York: A. B. Burdick.

Houston, A. (2008). *Benjamin Franklin and the politics of improvement*. New Haven, CT: Yale University Press.

Jok, J. M. (2007). Slavery and slave redemption Sudan. In K. A. Appiah & M. Bunzl (Eds.), *Buying freedom: The ethics and economics of slave redemption* (pp. 143–157). Princeton: Princeton University Press.

Kara, S. (2009). *Sex trafficking: Inside the business of modern slavery*. New York: Columbia University Press.

Kara, S. (2012). *Bonded labor: Tackling the system of slavery in South Asia*. New York: Columbia University Press.

Karlan, D. S., & Krueger, A. B. (2007). Some simple analytics of slave redemption. In K. A. Appiah & M. Bunzl (Eds.), *Buying freedom: The ethics and economics of slave redemption* (pp. 9–19). Princeton: Princeton University Press.

Kellow, M. M. R. (2007). Conflicting imperatives: Black and white American abolitionists debate slave redemption. In K. A. Appiah & M. Bunzl (Eds.), *Buying freedom: The ethics and economics of slave redemption* (pp. 200–212). Princeton: Princeton University Press.

Klein, M. (1993). Introduction: Modern European expansion and traditional servitude in Africa and Asia. In M. A. Klein (Ed.), *Breaking the chains: Slavery, bondage, and emancipation in modern Africa and Asia* (pp. 3–36). Madison: University of Wisconsin Press.

Kumar, D. (1993). Colonialism, bondage, and caste in British India. In M. A. Klein (Ed.), *Breaking the chains: Slavery, bondage, and emancipation in modern Africa and Asia* (pp. 112–130). Madison: University of Wisconsin Press.

Manning, P. (1990). *Slavery and African life: Occidental, oriental, and African slave trades.* New York: Cambridge University Press.

Mason, M. (2006). *Slavery and politics in the early American republic.* Chapel Hill: University of North Carolina Press.

Miers, S. (2003). *Slavery in the twentieth century: The evolution of a global problem.* New York: Rowman & Littlefield.

Mouhot, J.-F. (2011). *Slavery, fossil fuels and climate change.* Paris: Editions Champ Vallon.

Murphy, L. T. (2014). *Survivors of slavery: Modern-day slave narratives.* New York: Columbia University Press.

Naim, M. (2005). *Illicit: How smugglers, traffickers, and copycats are hijacking the global economy.* New York: Doubleday.

Ould, D. (2004). Trafficking and international law. In C. van den Anker (Ed.), *The political economy of new slavery* (pp. 55–74). New York: Palgrave Macmillan.

Owen, R. D. (1864). *The wrong of slavery, the right of emancipation and the future of the African race in the United States.* Philadelphia: J. B. Lippincott & Co.

Quirk, J. (2011). *The anti-slavery project: From the slave trade to human trafficking.* Philadelphia: University of Pennsylvania Press.

Rogers, C. A., & Swinnerton, K. A. (2007). Some simple analytics of slave redemption. In K. A. Appiah & M. Bunzl (Eds.), *Buying freedom: The ethics and economics of slave redemption* (pp. 20–36). Princeton: Princeton University Press.

Schulz, J. (2008). *The financial crisis of abolition.* New Haven, CT: Yale University Press.

Sharman, J. C. (2011). *The money laundry: Regulating criminal finance in the global economy.* Ithaca, NY: Cornell University Press.

Shelley, L., & Bain, C. (2015). Human trafficking: Fighting the illicit economy with the legitimate economy. *Social Inclusion, 3,* 140–144.

Shiller, R. J. (2003). *The new financial order: Risk in the 21st century.* Princeton: Princeton University Press.

Skinner, E. B. (2008). *A crime so monstrous: Face-to-face with modern-day slavery.* New York: Free Press.

Tinker, H. (1993). *A new system of slavery: The export of Indian labour overseas, 1830–1920* (2nd ed.). London: Hansib Publishing Limited.

Upadhyaya, K. (2004). Bonded labour in South Asia: India, Nepal and Pakistan. In C. van den Anker (Ed.), *The political economy of new slavery* (pp. 118–136). New York: Palgrave Macmillan.

van den Anker, C. (2004). Contemporary slavery, global justice and globalization. In C. van den Anker (Ed.), *The political economy of new slavery* (pp. 15–36). New York: Palgrave Macmillan.

Waldstreicher, D. (2006). Capitalism, slavery, and Benjamin Franklin's American Revolution. In C. Matson (Ed.), *The economy of early America: Historical perspectives and new directions* (pp. 183–217). University Park: University of Pennsylvania Press.

Bibliography

Acemoglu, D., & Wolitzky, A. (2011). The economics of labor coercion. *Econometrica, 79*, 555–600.

Adamic, L. (2008). *Dynamite: The story of class violence in America*. Oakland, CA: AK Press.

Adamson, A. H. (1972). *Sugar without slaves: The political economy of British Guiana, 1838–1904*. New Haven, CT: Yale University Press.

Akyeampong, E., Bates, R. H., Nunn, N., & Robinson, J. A. (Eds.). (2014). *Africa's development in historical perspective*. New York: Cambridge University Press.

Alexander, J. (2001). Islam, archaeology and slavery in Africa. *World Archaeology, 33*, 44–60.

Ali, M., & Wain, J. (1995). *Without mercy: A mother's struggle against modern slavery*. New York: Warner Books.

Allen, R. B. (2004). The Mascarene slave-trade and labour migration in the Indian Ocean during the eighteenth and nineteenth centuries. In G. Campbell (Ed.), *The structure of slavery in Indian Ocean Africa and Asia* (pp. 33–50). London: Frank Cass.

Alpers, E. A. (2004). Flight to freedom: Escape from slavery among bonded Africans in the Indian Ocean world, c. 1750–1962. In G. Campbell (Ed.), *The structure of slavery in Indian Ocean Africa and Asia* (pp. 51–68). London: Frank Cass.

Ames, K. M. (2001). Slaves, chiefs and labour on the northern northwest coast. *World Archaeology, 33*, 1–17.

An American. (1855). *Cotton is king: Or the culture of cotton, and its relation to agriculture, manufactures and commerce*. Cincinnati, OH: Moore, Wilstach, Keys & Co.

R.E. Wright, *The Poverty of Slavery*,
DOI 10.1007/978-3-319-48968-1

Anderson, B. (2004). Migrant domestic workers and slavery. In C. van den Anker (Ed.), *The political economy of new slavery* (pp. 107–117). New York: Palgrave Macmillan.

Anon. (1761). *The annual register, or a view of the history, politicks, and literature of the year 1760.* London: R. and J. Dodsley.

Anon. (1765, August 12). *New York Mercury.*

Anon. (1767). *The commercial conduct of the province of New York considered.* New York: n.p.

Anon. (1784). *The case of our fellow-creatures the oppressed Africans, respectfully recommended to the serious consideration of the legislature of Great Britain by the people called Quakers.* London: James Phillips.

Anon. (1802–1864). Negroes miscellany. Society Miscell. Collection, Box 11A. Historical Society of Pennsylvania, Philadelphia, PA.

Anon. (1811, January 27). *New York Observer.*

Anon. (1835). *Proceedings of the citizens of Charleston, on incendiary machinations, now in progress against the peace and welfare of the Southern states.* Charleston, SC: A.E. Miller.

Anon. (1836). *Narrative of the late riotous proceedings against the liberty of the press in Cincinnati.* Cincinnati, OH: Ohio Anti-Slavery Society.

Anon. (1838, March 18). The hill indentured laborers: A new slave-trade. *Weekly True Sun.*

Anon. (1846, October). Slaves and slavery. *United States Magazine and Democratic Review.*

Anon. (1848). *Regulations to be observed by all persons employed by the Lawrence Manufacturing Company.* Lawrence, MA: Lawrence Manufacturing Co.

Anon. (1880, December 18). The slave trade. *Labor League Examiner.*

Anon. (1890, May 10). British inconsistency and hypocrisy with regard to the slave trade. *Brotherhood.*

Anon. (1903, July 16). The new slavery. *New York Observer and Chronicle.*

Anon. (1904a, April). The Congo 'slave' state. *Baptist Missionary Magazine.*

Anon. (1904b, April 6). Is England establishing a new slavery? *Christian Observer.*

Anon. (1906, October 6). A present day anti-slavery movement. *Friends' Intelligencer.*

Anon. (1908, February 6). Animal slavery. *The Independent: Devoted to the Consideration of Politics, Social and Economic Tendencies.*

Anon. (1909, November 6). The slave traffic in America. *Outlook.*

Anon. (1910a, January 1). What the Cocoa costs the slaves. *Outlook.*

Anon. (1910b, June 11). Slavery emancipation in China. *Outlook.*

Anon. (1911, July 15). The punishment of a white slave trader. *Outlook.*

Anon. (1913a, February 20). What is slavery? *The Independent: Devoted to the Consideration of Politics, Social and Economic Tendencies.*

Anon. (1913b, August 28). What is white slavery? *The Independent: Devoted to the Consideration of Politics, Social and Economic Tendencies.*

Anon. (1913c, November). Is white slavery nothing more than a myth? *Current Opinion.*

Anon. (1914, April). The futility of the white slave agitation as Brand Whitlock sees it. *Current Opinion.*

Anon. (1916, December). A new national campaign against 'The last surviving vestige of slavery.' *Current Opinion.*

Anon. (1917, September 20). A worse thing than slavery. *Life.*

Anon. (1919, April). The enslavement of the professor as Veblen sees it: A protest against the commercialization of our universities. *Current Opinion.*

Anon. (1921, December 10). Where is slavery? *Indiana Farmer's Guide.*

Anon. (1922a, January 11). Girls lured into slavery. *Kansas City Star.*

Anon. (1922b, February 18). Are we ready for industrial slavery? *The Independent and the Weekly Review.*

Anon. (1922c, February 19). Stronghold of slavery: Innocent refugee girls enticed by promises of work into traps set by procurers. *Morning Oregonian.*

Anon. (1922d, April 1). White slave found insane from abuse in negroes' hovel. *Philadelphia Inquirer.*

Anon. (1922e, April 6). Offers self as slave for funds to save mother. *Columbus Daily Enquirer.*

Anon. (1922f, April 14). Only slave country. *Bellingham Herald.*

Anon. (1922g, May 14). Slave days are recalled by baseball dealings. *Duluth News Tribune.*

Anon. (1922h, August 11). Woman saved after years of suffering as slave to Chinese. *Idaho Statesman.*

Anon. (1922i, August 14). Girl bares drug ring: Revival of white slave traffic revealed. *Morning Oregonian.*

Anon. (1922j, August 28). Child 'Farm Slave' says death threat kept her prisoner. *Philadelphia Inquirer.*

Anon. (1922k, October 20). White slavery charges facing state leaders. *Fort Worth Star Telegram.*

Anon. (1922l, November 27). American Black tells Reds in Moscow of 'Slavery in U.S.' *Macon Telegraph.*

Anon. (1922m, December 1). Held on white slavery charge in county jail. *Aberdeen Daily News.*

Anon. (1922n, December 3). Woman flees after three years' 'Slavery'. *Philadelphia Inquirer.*

Anon. (1922o, December 15). Police probe white slave ring in state. *Fort Wayne News Sentinel.*

Anon. (1922p, December 19). Girl accused in shoplifting blames woman: White slave activity here is suspected. *Fort Worth Star Telegram.*

Anon. (2015). Roundtable of reviews for The Half Has Never Been Told. *Journal of Economic History, 75*, 919–931.

Appiah, K. A. (2007). What's wrong with slavery? In K. A. Appiah & M. Bunzl (Eds.), *Buying freedom: The ethics and economics of slave redemption* (pp. 249–258). Princeton: Princeton University Press.

Argersinger, A. E. (2016). *The Triangle fire: A brief history with documents* (2nd ed.). New York: Bedford/St. Martin's.

Aristides. (1844, January 12). *The Liberator.*

Armes, W. D. (Ed.). (1903). *The autobiography of Joseph Le Conte.* New York: D. Appleton and Co.

Ashworth, J. (1995). *Slavery, capitalism, and politics in the antebellum Republic. Volume 1: Commerce and compromise, 1820–1850.* New York: Cambridge University Press.

Atkinson, E. (1861). *Cheap cotton by free labor by a cotton manufacturer* (2nd ed.). Boston: A. Williams & Co.

Austen, R. A., & Smith, W. D. (1992). Private tooth decay as public economic virtue: The slave-sugar triangle, consumerism, and European industrialization. In J. Inikori & S. Engerman (Eds.), *The Atlantic slave trade: Effects on economies, societies, and peoples in Africa, the Americas, and Europe* (pp. 183–203). Durham, NC: Duke University Press.

Bailey, R. (1992). The slave(ry) trade and the development of capitalism in the United States: The textile industry in New England. In J. Inikori & S. Engerman (Eds.), *The Atlantic slave trade: Effects on economies, societies, and peoples in Africa, the Americas, and Europe* (pp. 205–246). Durham, NC: Duke University Press.

Bales, K. (2007a). *Ending slavery: How we free today's slaves.* Berkeley: University of California Press.

Bales, K. (2007b). Foreword. In K. A. Appiah & M. Bunzl (Eds.), *Buying freedom: The ethics and economics of slave redemption* (pp. vii–xii). Princeton: Princeton University Press.

Bales, Kevin. 2012. *Disposable people: New slavery in the global economy*, Rev. ed. Berkeley: University of California Press.

Bales, K., & Soodalter, R. (2009). *The slave next door: Human trafficking and slavery in America today.* Berkeley: University of California Press.

Baptist, E. E. (2014). *The half has never been told: Slavery and the making of American capitalism.* New York: Basic Books.

Barrow, J. H. (Ed.). (1838). *The mirror of Parliament for the first session of the thirteenth Parliament of Great Britain and Ireland, in the first and second years of the reign of Queen Victoria.* London: Longman, Orme, Brown, Green, & Longmans.

Barry, R. (1907, March). Slavery in the South to-day. *The Cosmopolitan: A Monthly Illustrated Magazine.*

Barry, K. (1979). *Female sexual slavery*. New York: New York University Press.

Barzel, Y. (1977). An economic analysis of slavery. *Journal of Law and Economics, 20*, 87–110.

Bastiat, F. (1850). *That which is seen, and that which is not seen*. Retrieved August 11, 2016, from http://bastiat.org/en/twisatwins.html

Basu, A. K., & Chau, N. H. (2007). An exploration of the worst forms of child labor: Is redemption a viable option? In K. A. Appiah & M. Bunzl (Eds.), *Buying freedom: The ethics and economics of slave redemption* (pp. 37–76). Princeton: Princeton University Press.

Bateman, F., & Weiss, T. (1981). *A deplorable scarcity: The failure of industrialization in the slave economy*. Chapel Hill: University of North Carolina Press.

Batstone, David. 2010. *Not for sale: The return of the global slave trade and how we can fight it*, Rev. ed. New York: HarperCollins.

Baumol, W., Litan, R. E., & Schramm, C. J. (2007). *Good capitalism, bad capitalism, and the economics of growth and prosperity*. New Haven, CT: Yale University Press.

Bearse, A. (1880). *Reminiscences of fugitive-slave law days in Boston*. Boston: Warren Richardson.

Beckert, S. (2004). Emancipation and empire: Reconstructing the worldwide web of cotton production in the age of the American Civil War. *American Historical Review, 109*, 1405–1438.

Beckert, S. (2014). *Empire of cotton: A global history*. New York: Knopf.

Benezet, A., & Wesley, J. (1774). *The potent enemies of America laid open: Being some account of the baneful effects attending the use of distilled spirituous liquors, and the slavery of the negroes*. Philadelphia: Joseph Crukshank.

Berlan, A. (2004). Child labour, education and child rights among cocoa producers in Ghana. In C. van den Anker (Ed.), *The political economy of new slavery* (pp. 158–180). New York: Palgrave Macmillan.

Bernstein, W. J. (2004). *The birth of plenty: How the prosperity of the modern world was created*. New York: McGraw-Hill.

Berry, H. (1832). *The speech of Henry Berry, (of Jefferson), in the House of Delegates of Virginian, on the abolition of slavery*. Richmond: n.p.

Bingham, T. A. (1911). *The girl that disappears: The real facts about the white slave traffic*. Boston: Richard G. Badger.

Birney, C. H. (Ed.). (1970). *Sarah and Angelina Grimké: The first American women advocates of abolition and woman's rights*. New York: Haskell House Publishers.

Bishop, R., & Robinson, L. S. (1997). *Night market: Sexual cultures and the Thai economic miracle*. New York: Routledge.

Blackburn, R. (1996). Slave exploitation and the elementary structures of enslavement. In M. L. Bush (Ed.), *Serfdom and slavery: Studies in legal bondage* (pp. 158–180). New York: Addison Wesley Longman.

Blackburn, R. (2011). *The American crucible: Slavery, emancipation and human rights*. New York: Verso.

Blackmon, D. A. (2008). *Slavery by another name: The re-enslavement of Black Americans from the Civil War to World War II*. New York: Anchor Books.

Blair, D. (2014). *All the ships that never sailed: A general model of illicit market suppression*. Ph.D. dissertation, Georgetown University.

Bloch, M. (1961). *Feudal society*. Chicago: University of Chicago Press.

Boas, F. (2014). *Neanderthals*. Quite Interesting. Retrieved October 9, 2014, from http://qi.com/infocloud/Neanderthals

Bodin, J. (1606). *The six bookes of a commonweale* (R. Knolles, Trans.). London: Impensis G. Bishop.

Bradley, K. R. (1983). Slave kingdoms and slave rebellions in ancient Sicily. *Historical Reflections/Réflexions Historiques, 10*, 435–451.

Brass, T. (2013). Debating capitalist dynamics and unfree labour: A missing link? *Journal of Development Studies, 50*, 1–13.

Brenner, R. (1996). The rises and declines of serfdom in medieval and early modern Europe. In M. L. Bush (Ed.), *Serfdom and slavery: Studies in legal bondage* (pp. 247–276). New York: Addison Wesley Longman.

Bromberg, E. (1942). Wales and the mediaeval slave trade. *Speculum, 17*, 263–269.

Bronner, M. (1922, July 27). Unsettled conditions result in resumption of terrible traffic. *Wilkes Barre Times Leader*.

Brougham, H. (1807). *A concise statement of the question regarding the abolition of the slave trade* (4th ed.). London: Longman, Hurst, Rees, and Orme.

Brown, L. (2000). *Sex slaves: The trafficking of women in Asia*. London: Virago Press.

Buckland, W. W. (1908). *The roman law of slavery: The condition of the slave in private law from Augustus to Justinian*. Cambridge: Cambridge University Press.

Burin, E. (2005). *Slavery and the peculiar solution: A history of the American Colonization Society*. Gainesville: University Press of Florida.

Burke, E. (1775/2000). Mr. Burke's speech on moving his resolutions for conciliation with the colonies. In D. Browich (Ed.), *On empire, liberty, and reform: Speeches and letters of Edmund Burke* (pp. 66–134). New Haven, CT: Yale University Press.

Bush, M. (1996a). Introduction. In M. L. Bush (Ed.), *Serfdom and slavery: Studies in legal bondage* (pp. 1–17). New York: Addison Wesley Longman.

Bush, M. (1996b). Serfdom in medieval and modern Europe: A comparison. In M. L. Bush (Ed.), *Serfdom and slavery: Studies in legal bondage* (pp. 199–224). New York: Addison Wesley Longman.

Cadet, J.-R. (1998). *Restavec: From Haitian slave child to middle-class American*. Austin: University of Texas Press.

Cairnes, J. E. (1862). *The slave power: Its character, career, and probable designs, being an attempt to explain the real issues involved in the American contest* (2nd ed.). New York: Carleton.

Calomiris, C., & Haber, S. (2014). *Fragile by design: The political origins of banking crises and scarce credit.* Princeton: Princeton University Press.

Campbell, R. F. (1899). *Some aspects of the race problem in the South.* Asheville, NC: n.p.

Campbell, G. (2004). Introduction: Slavery and other forms of unfree labour in the Indian Ocean world. In G. Campbell (Ed.), *The structure of slavery in Indian Ocean Africa and Asia* (pp. vii–xxxii). London: Frank Cass.

Carnes, M. E. (2014). *Continuity despite change: The politics of labor regulation in Latin America.* Stanford: Stanford University Press.

Cary, V. (1830). *Letters on female character, addressed to a young lady, on the death of her mother* (2nd ed.). Richmond, VA: Ariel Works.

Cason, C. E. (1928, July 14). Southern slavery revised. *The Independent.*

Chanana, D. R. (1964). *Slavery in ancient India as depicted in Pali and Sanskrit texts.* New Delhi: People's Publishing House.

Channing, W. E. (1839). *Remarks on the slavery question in a letter to Jonathan Phillips, Esq.* Boston: James Munroe and Company.

Childs, D. (2015). *Slaves of the state: Black incarceration from the chain gang to the penitentiary.* Minneapolis: University of Minnesota Press.

Clarence-Smith, W. G. (1993). Cocoa plantations and coerced labor in the Gulf of Guinea, 1870–1914. In M. A. Klein (Ed.), *Breaking the chains: Slavery, bondage, and emancipation in modern Africa and Asia* (pp. 150–170). Madison: University of Wisconsin Press.

Clarence-Smith, W. G. (2006). *Islam and the abolition of slavery.* New York: Oxford University Press.

Clay, C. (1848). *The writings of Cassius Marcellus Clay: Including speeches and addresses.* New York: Harper & Brothers.

Cochin, A. (1863). *The results of slavery.* Boston: Walker, Wise, and Company.

Cohen, D. (2006). From peasant to worker: Migration, masculinity, and the making of Mexican workers in the U.S. *International Labor and Working-Class History, 69,* 81–103.

Collins, J. C. (Ed.). (1904). *Sir Thomas More's Utopia.* Oxford: Clarendon Press.

Commons, J. R., Saposs, D. J., Sumner, H. L., Mittelman, E. B., Hoagland, H. E., & Andrews, J. B. (1918). *History of labour in the United States* (Vol. 2). New York: Macmillan Company.

Conder, J. (1833). *Wages or the whip: An essay on the comparative cost and productiveness of free and slave labour.* London: Hatehard and Son.

Conning, J., & Kevane, M. (2007). Freedom, servitude, and voluntary contracts. In K. A. Appiah & M. Bunzl (Eds.), *Buying freedom: The ethics and economics of slave redemption* (pp. 108–140). Princeton: Princeton University Press.

Cook, L. D. (2007). The end of serfdom in Russia—Lessons for Sudan? In K. A. Appiah & M. Bunzl (Eds.), *Buying freedom: The ethics and economics of slave redemption* (pp. 181–199). Princeton: Princeton University Press.

Crothers, A. G. (2001). Agricultural improvement and technological innovation in a slave society: The case of early national northern Virginia. *Agricultural History, 75*, 135–167.

Dal Lago, E., & Katsari, C. (2008). The study of ancient and modern slave systems: Setting an agenda for comparison. In E. D. Lago & C. Katsari (Eds.), *Slave systems ancient and modern* (pp. 3–31). New York: Cambridge University Press.

Dalton, M. B. (1950). *Edward Atkinson (1827–1905): Patron of engineering science and benefactor of industry*. New York: Newcomen Society in North America.

Darity Jr., W. (1992). British industry and the West Indies plantations. In J. Inikori & S. Engerman (Eds.), *The Atlantic slave trade: Effects on economies, societies, and peoples in Africa, the Americas, and Europe* (pp. 247–282). Durham, NC: Duke University Press.

Davidson, J. O. (2015). *Modern slavery: The margins of freedom*. New York: Palgrave Macmillan.

Davies, W. W. (1905). *The codes of Hammurabi and Moses*. New York: Jennings and Graham.

Davies, W. (1996). On servile status in the early Middle Ages. In M. L. Bush (Ed.), *Serfdom and slavery: Studies in legal bondage* (pp. 225–246). New York: Addison Wesley Longman.

Davis, D. B. (1966). *The problem of slavery in Western culture*. Ithaca, NY: Cornell University Press.

Davis, R. C. (2003). *Christian slaves, Muslim masters: White slavery in the Mediterranean, the Barbary Coast, and Italy, 1500–1800*. New York: Palgrave Macmillan.

Dawson, E. C. (1930). *Missionary heroines of the Cross*. London: Seeley, Service & Co.

Deane, C. (1886). *The connection of Massachusetts with slavery and the slave-trade*. Worcester, MA: Charles Hamilton.

Delaye, K. (2004). Slavery and colonial representations in Indochina from the second half of the nineteenth to the early twentieth century. In G. Campbell (Ed.), *The structure of slavery in Indian Ocean Africa and Asia* (pp. 129–142). London: Frank Cass.

Derby, E. H. (1850). *Reality versus fiction: A review of a pamphlet published at Charleston, S.C.* Boston: Redding & Co.

Devereux, C. (2000). 'The Maiden Tribute' and the rise of the white slave in the nineteenth century: The making of an Imperial construct. *Victorian Review, 26*, 1–23.

Doerflinger, T. (1986). *A vigorous spirit of enterprise: Merchants and economic development in Revolutionary Philadelphia*. Chapel Hill: University of North Carolina Press.

Donald, L. (1997). *Aboriginal slavery on the northwest coast of North America.* Berkeley: University of California Press.

Dower, N. (2004). The global framework for development: Instrumentality or contested ethical space? In C. van den Anker (Ed.), *The political economy of new slavery* (pp. 181–200). New York: Palgrave Macmillan.

Dublin, L. I. (1927, January 27). Are ants civilized? *Youth's Companion.*

Dyer, C. (1996). Memories of freedom: Attitudes towards serfdom in England, 1200–1350. In M. L. Bush (Ed.), *Serfdom and slavery: Studies in legal bondage* (pp. 277–295). New York: Addison Wesley Longman.

Edwards, L. (1998). The problem of dependency: African Americans, labor relations, and the law in the nineteenth-century South. *Agricultural History, 72,* 313–340.

Einhorn, R. (2006). *American taxation, American slavery.* Chicago: University of Chicago Press.

Eltis, D. (1987). *Economic growth and the ending of the transatlantic slave trade.* New York: Oxford University Press.

Eltis, D., & Engerman, S. (2000). The importance of slavery and the slave trade to industrializing Britain. *Journal of Economic History, 60,* 123–144.

Emmett, R. B. (2014). *Malthus, the slave trade, and the civilizing effect of the preventive checks.* Social Science Research Network. Retrieved August 11, 2016, from http://papers.ssrn.com/sol3/papers.cfm?abstract_id=2449035

Engels, F. (1894). *Anti-Duhring* (E. Burns, Trans.). Leipzig: n.p.

Engerman, S. (1996). Slavery, serfdom and other forms of coerced labour: Similarities and differences. In M. L. Bush (Ed.), *Serfdom and slavery: Studies in legal bondage* (pp. 18–41). New York: Addison Wesley Longman.

Engerman, S. (2000). Slavery at different times and places. *American Historical Review, 105,* 480–484.

Engerman, S. (2007). Slavery, freedom, and Sen. In K. A. Appiah & M. Bunzl (Eds.), *Buying freedom: The ethics and economics of slave redemption* (pp. 77–107). Princeton: Princeton University Press.

Ericson, D. F. (2011). *Slavery in the American republic: Developing the federal government, 1791–1861.* Lawrence: University of Kansas Press.

Ex-Slave. (1932, April). White-collar slavery. *Forum and Century.*

Faber, E. (1998). *Jews, slaves, and the slave trade: Setting the record straight.* New York: New York University Press.

Fahrenfort, J. (1960). Foreword. In W. Kloosterboer (Ed.), *Involuntary labor since the abolition of slavery: A survey of compulsory labour throughout the world* (p. vii). Leiden: E. J. Brill.

Farrow, A., Lang, J., & Frank, J. (2005). *Complicity: How the North promoted, prolonged, and profited from slavery.* New York: Ballantine Books.

Feeny, D. (1993). The demise of corvee and slavery in Thailand, 1782–1913. In M. A. Klein (Ed.), *Breaking the chains: Slavery, bondage, and emancipation in modern Africa and Asia* (pp. 83–111). Madison: University of Wisconsin Press.

Finley, M. I. (1980). *Ancient slavery and modern ideology*. New York: Viking Press.

Firmo-Fontan, V. (2004). Responses to sexual slavery: From the Balkans to Afghanistan. In C. van den Anker (Ed.), *The political economy of new slavery* (pp. 91–106). New York: Palgrave Macmillan.

Fishback, P. (1989). Debt peonage in postbellum Georgia. *Explorations in Economic History, 26*, 219–236.

Fitzhugh, G. (1857). *Cannibals all! Or, slaves without masters*. Richmond: A. Morris.

FJ. (1918, December 14). Slavery. *Indiana Farmer's Guide*.

Fogel, R. (1989). *Without consent or contract: The rise and fall of American slavery*. New York: W. W. Norton.

Fogel, R., & Engerman, S. (1974). *Time on the cross: The economics of American negro slavery*. New York: Little, Brown and Company.

Foner, E. (1983). *Nothing but freedom: Emancipation and its legacy*. Baton Rouge: Louisiana State University Press.

Franklin, J. H., & Moss Jr., A. A. (1988). *From slavery to freedom: A history of negro Americans* (6th ed.). New York: Alfred A. Knopf.

Frankopan, P. (2016). *The silk roads: A new history of the world*. New York: Alfred A. Knopf.

Freedmen's Bureau. (1870). *Reports of Generals Steedman and Fullerton on the condition of the Freedmen's Bureau in the Southern states*. Washington, DC: n.p.

Gallay, A. (2002). *The Indian slave trade: The rise of the English Empire in the American South, 1670–1717*. New Haven, CT: Yale University Press.

Galloway, C. B. (1904). *The South and the negro: An address delivered at the seventh annual conference for education in the South, Birmingham, Ala., April 26th, 1904*. New York: Southern Education Board.

Garrett, M. A., & Xu, Z. (2003). The efficiency of sharecropping: Evidence from the postbellum South. *Southern Economic Journal, 69*, 578–595.

Gaspar, D. B. (1992). Slave importation, runaways, and compensation in Antigua, 1720–1729. In J. Inikori & S. Engerman (Eds.), *The Atlantic slave trade: Effects on economies, societies, and peoples in Africa, the Americas, and Europe* (pp. 301–320). Durham, NC: Duke University Press.

Geiger, M. W. (2010). *Financial fraud and guerrilla violence in Missouri's Civil War, 1861–1865*. New Haven, CT: Yale University Press.

Genovese, E. (1972). *Roll, Jordan, roll: The world the slaves made*. New York: Random House.

Georgia Negro Peon. (1904, February 25). The new slavery in the South—An autobiography. *The Independent: Devoted to the Consideration of Politics, Social and Economic Tendencies*.

Giddings, G. W. (1892). *The life of Joshua R. Giddings*. Chicago: A. C. McClurg and Company.

Gigantino, J. (2014). 'The whole North is not abolitionized': Slavery's slow death in New Jersey, 1830–1860. *Journal of the Early Republic, 34*, 411–437.

Goderich, L. (1831). *Papers relating to the emancipation of Crown slaves in the colonies*. London: House of Commons.

Goldberg, E. S. (2007). *Beyond terror: Gender, narrative, human rights*. New Brunswick, NJ: Rutgers University Press.

Goodell, W. (1853). *The American slave code in theory and practice: Its distinctive features shown by its statutes, judicial decisions, and illustrative facts*. New York: American and Foreign Anti-Slavery Society.

Goodspeed, T. (2015). *Slavery, path dependence, and development: Evidence from the Georgia experiment*. Retrieved August 14, 2016, from Munich Personal Archive. Retrieved from https://mpra.ub.uni-muenchen.de/67202/

Gray, L. (1941). *History of agriculture in the southern United States to 1860* (Vol. 2). New York: Peter Smith.

Gray, M. (2016). *Why human trafficking is a public health problem*. CNN Freedom Project. Retrieved August 11, 2016, from http://edition.cnn.com/2016/07/11/opinions/human-trafficking-health-margeaux-gray/index.html

Greenberg, M., & Waugh, C. (Eds.). (2000). *The price of freedom: Slavery and the Civil War. Volume Two, the preservation of liberty*. Nashville, TN: Cumberland House.

Gross, K. N. (2015). African American women, mass incarceration, and the politics of protection. *Journal of American History, 102*, 25–33.

Grubb, F. (2011). *German immigration and servitude in America, 1709–1920*. New York: Routledge.

Gurley, G. (2015, April 16). Is this the dawn of the sexbots? *Vanity Fair*.

Guyatt, N. (2016). *Bind us apart: How enlightened Americans invented racial segregation*. New York: Basic Books.

Ha, S. (2009). *The rise and fall of the American System: Nationalism and the development of the American economy*. London: Pickering & Chatto.

Hall, C., Draper, N., McClelland, K., Donington, K., & Lang, R. (2014). *Legacies of British slave-ownership: Colonial slavery and the formation of Victorian Britain*. New York: Cambridge University Press.

Hallgrimsdottir, H. K., & Benoit, C. (2007). From wage slaves to wage workers: Cultural opportunity structures and the evolution of the wage demands of the Knights of Labor and the American Federation of Labor, 1880–1900. *Social Forces, 85*, 1393–1411.

Harring, S. (1977). Class conflict and the suppression of tramps in Buffalo, 1892–1894. *Law & Society Review, 11*, 873–911.

Harris, J. H. (1910, April 14). The cocoa slave-trade. *Herald of Gospel Liberty*.

Harris, J. H. (1920). *The chartered millions: Rhodesia and the challenge to the British Commonwealth*. London: Swarthmore Press.

Harrison, E. C. (Ed.). (1978). *Philadelphia merchant: The diary of Thomas P. Cope, 1800–1851*. South Bend, IN: Gateway Editions.

Heeren, A. (1824). *Reflections on the politics of ancient Greece* (G. Bancroft, Trans.). Boston: Cummings, Hilliard & Co.

Hellie, R. (1982). *Slavery in Russia, 1450–1725*. Chicago: University of Chicago Press.

Helper, H. R. (1860). *The impending crisis of the South: How to meet it*. New York: A. B. Burdick.

Herder, J. G. (2004). *Another philosophy of history and selected political writings* (I. D. Evrigenis & D. Pellerin, Trans.). Indianapolis: Hackett Publishing Company.

Hicks, F. C. (1913, August 28). Convict labor in the United States. *The Independent: Devoted to the Consideration of Politics, Social and Economic Tendencies.*

Higbie, F. T. (2003). *Indispensable outcasts: Hobo workers and community in the American Midwest, 1880–1930*. Chicago: University of Illinois Press.

Higgs, R. (2009). *Depression, war, and Cold War: Challenging the myths of conflict and prosperity*. Stanford, CA: Independent Institute.

Hochschild, A. (2003). *The unquiet ghost: Russians remember Stalin*. Boston: Houghton Mifflin.

Hodkinson, S. (2008). Spartiates, helots, and the direction of the agrarian economy: Toward an understanding of helotage in comparative perspective. In E. D. Lago & C. Katsari (Eds.), *Slave systems ancient and modern* (pp. 285–320). New York: Cambridge University Press.

Hogendorn, J., & Lovejoy, P. E. (1992). Keeping slaves in place: The secret debate on the slavery question in northern Nigeria, 1900–1904. In J. Inikori & S. Engerman (Eds.), *The Atlantic slave trade: Effects on economies, societies, and peoples in Africa, the Americas, and Europe* (pp. 49–76). Durham, NC: Duke University Press.

Hopkins, K. (1993). Novel evidence for Roman slavery. *Past & Present, 138*, 3–27.

Houston, A. (2008). *Benjamin Franklin and the politics of improvement*. New Haven, CT: Yale University Press.

Hurmence, B. (Ed.). (1984). *My folks don't want me to talk about slavery: Twenty-one oral histories of former North Carolina slaves*. Winston-Salem, NC: John F. Blair.

Huston, J. L. (2003). *Calculating the value of the Union: Slavery, property rights, and the economic origins of the Civil War*. Chapel Hill: University of North Carolina Press.

Ignatiev, N. (1995). *How the Irish became white*. New York: Routledge.

Inikori, J. (1992). Slavery and the revolution in cotton textile production in England. In J. Inikori & S. Engerman (Eds.), *The Atlantic slave trade: Effects on economies, societies, and peoples in Africa, the Americas, and Europe* (pp. 145–181). Durham, NC: Duke University Press.

Inikori, J., & Engerman, S. (1992). Introduction: Gainers and losers in the Atlantic slave trade. In J. Inikori & S. Engerman (Eds.), *The Atlantic slave trade: Effects on economies, societies, and peoples in Africa, the Americas, and Europe* (pp. 1–24). Durham, NC: Duke University Press.

International Labour Organization. (1930). *Forced Labour Convention, No. 29.* Retrieved August 11, 2016, from http://www.ilo.org/dyn/normlex/en/f?p=NORMLEXPUB:12100:0::NO::P12100_ILO_CODE:C029

International Labour Organization. (2014). *Profits and poverty: The economics of forced labour.* Geneva: International Labour Organization.

James, J. A. (1981). Financial underdevelopment in the postbellum South. *Journal of Interdisciplinary History, 11*, 443–454.

Johnsen, D. B. (2006). A culturally correct proposal to privatize the British Columbia salmon fishery. In T. L. Anderson, B. L. Benson, & T. E. Flanagan (Eds.), *Self-determination: The other path for Native Americans* (pp. 94–133). Stanford: Stanford University Press.

Johnson, W. (2013a, March 31). King Cotton's long shadow. *New York Times.*

Johnson, W. (2013b). *River of dark dreams: Slavery and empire in the cotton kingdom.* Cambridge: Harvard University Press.

Jok, J. M. (2007). Slavery and slave redemption Sudan. In K. A. Appiah & M. Bunzl (Eds.), *Buying freedom: The ethics and economics of slave redemption* (pp. 143–157). Princeton: Princeton University Press.

Jones, N. T. (1990). *Born a child of freedom, yet a slave: Mechanisms of control and strategies of resistance in antebellum South Carolina.* Middletown, CT: Wesleyan University Press.

Jones, J. (2013). *A dreadful deceit: The myth of race from the colonial era to Obama's America.* New York: Basic Books.

Jordan, D., & Walsh, M. (2007). *White cargo: The forgotten history of Britain's white slaves in America.* New York: New York University Press.

Kara, S. (2009). *Sex trafficking: Inside the business of modern slavery.* New York: Columbia University Press.

Kara, S. (2012). *Bonded labor: Tackling the system of slavery in South Asia.* New York: Columbia University Press.

Karlan, D. S., & Krueger, A. B. (2007). Some simple analytics of slave redemption. In K. A. Appiah & M. Bunzl (Eds.), *Buying freedom: The ethics and economics of slave redemption* (pp. 9–19). Princeton: Princeton University Press.

Kellow, M. M. R. (2007). Conflicting imperatives: Black and white American abolitionists debate slave redemption. In K. A. Appiah & M. Bunzl (Eds.), *Buying freedom: The ethics and economics of slave redemption* (pp. 200–212). Princeton: Princeton University Press.

Kilbourne Jr., R. H. (1995). *Debt, investment, slaves: Credit relations in East Feliciana Parish, Louisiana, 1825–1885.* Tuscaloosa: University of Alabama Press.

Kilbourne Jr., R. H. (2006). *Slave agriculture and financial markets in antebellum America: The Bank of the United States in Mississippi, 1831–1852.* London: Pickering & Chatto.

Kim, B. R. (2004). Nobi: A Korean system of slavery. In G. Campbell (Ed.), *The structure of slavery in Indian Ocean Africa and Asia* (pp. 155–168). London: Frank Cass.

Klein, H. S. (1986). *African slavery in Latin America and the Caribbean.* New York: Oxford University Press.

Klein, M. (1992). The impact of the Atlantic slave trade on the societies of the western Sudan. In J. Inikori & S. Engerman (Eds.), *The Atlantic slave trade: Effects on economies, societies, and peoples in Africa, the Americas, and Europe* (pp. 25–48). Durham, NC: Duke University Press.

Klein, M. (1993). Introduction: Modern European expansion and traditional servitude in Africa and Asia. In M. A. Klein (Ed.), *Breaking the chains: Slavery, bondage, and emancipation in modern Africa and Asia* (pp. 3–36). Madison: University of Wisconsin Press.

Knight, M. (1704/1825). Entry of October 7. In S. K. Knight & T. Buckingham (Eds.), *The journals of Madam Knight and Rev. Mr. Buckingham* (pp. 35–46). New York: Wilder & Campbell.

Kolchin, P. (1993). *American slavery, 1619–1877.* New York: Hill and Wang.

Kolchin, P. (1996). Some controversial questions concerning nineteenth-century emancipation from slavery and serfdom. In M. L. Bush (Ed.), *Serfdom and slavery: Studies in legal bondage* (pp. 42–68). New York: Addison Wesley Longman.

Kujala, A. J. (1940, April). An American in Soviet jails. *The Living Age.*

Kulikoff, A. (2000). *From British peasants to colonial American farmers.* Chapel Hill: University of North Carolina Press.

Kumar, D. (1993). Colonialism, bondage, and caste in British India. In M. A. Klein (Ed.), *Breaking the chains: Slavery, bondage, and emancipation in modern Africa and Asia* (pp. 112–130). Madison: University of Wisconsin Press.

Kurten, B. (1980). *Dance of the Tiger.* New York: Random House.

Kusimba, C. M. (2004). Archaeology of slavery in East Africa. *The African Archaeological Review, 21*, 59–88.

Kvach, J. (2013). *De Bow's Review: The antebellum vision of a new South.* Lexington: University of Kentucky Press.

Larsen, C. (1995). Concluding remarks. In L. Beck (Ed.), *Regional approaches to mortuary analysis.* New York: Plenum Press.

Lazarus, R. M. (1827/1977). Letter to Maria Edgeworth, January 6. In E. E. MacDonald (Ed.), *The education of the heart: The correspondence of Rachel*

Mordecai Lazarus and Maria Edgeworth (pp. 109–114). Chapel Hill: University of North Carolina Press.

Leaf, E. H. (1937, March). Oriental miscellany: I. Bootleg slaves in China. *The Living Age*.

Lemon, J. T. (1972). *The best poor man's country: A geographical study of early southeastern Pennsylvania*. New York: W. W. Norton.

Lichtenstein, A. (1996). *Twice the work of free labor: The political economy of convict labor in the New South*. New York: Verso.

Lichtenstein, A. (2015). Flocatex and the fiscal limits of mass incarceration: Toward a new political economy of the postwar carceral state. *Journal of American History, 102*, 113–125.

Locke, J. (1690/1952). *The second treatise of government*. New York: Macmillan Publishing.

London, J. (1907). *The Road*. New York: Macmillan.

Lovejoy, P. E. (2012). *Transformations in slavery: A history of slavery in Africa* (3rd ed.). New York: Cambridge University Press.

Lyttleton, D. E. (1924, November 19). The League's big little jobs. *Outlook*.

Magness, P. W. (2015). *A paradox of secessionism: Slavery and the Confederate security state*. Social Science Research Network. Retrieved August 15, 2016, from http://papers.ssrn.com/sol3/papers.cfm?abstract_id=2639529

Malthus, T. (1817). *An essay on the principle of population: Or, a view of its past and present effects on human happiness* (Vol. 3). London: John Murray.

Manning, P. (1990). *Slavery and African life: Occidental, oriental, and African slave trades*. New York: Cambridge University Press.

Manning, P. (1992). The slave trade: The formal demography of a global system. In J. Inikori & S. Engerman (Eds.), *The Atlantic slave trade: Effects on economies, societies, and peoples in Africa, the Americas, and Europe* (pp. 117–144). Durham, NC: Duke University Press.

Mark, I. (1940). *Agrarian conflicts in colonial New York, 1711–1775*. New York: Columbia University Press.

Markevich, A., & Zhuravskaya, E. (2014). *Economic effects of the abolition of serfdom: Evidence from the Russian Empire*. Social Science Research Network. Retrieved August 15, 2016, from http://papers.ssrn.com/sol3/papers.cfm?abstract_id=2514964

Markham, E. (1906, November). The hoe-man in the making: Little slaves of the coal-mines. *The Cosmopolitan: A Monthly Illustrated Magazine*.

Martin, D., & Frayer, D. (1998). *Troubled times: Violence and warfare in the past*. New York: Routledge.

Marx, K. (1846). Letter to Pavel Annekov, 28 December. *Marx & Engels collected works* (Vol. 50). London: Lawrence & Wishart.

Mason, M. (2006). *Slavery and politics in the early American republic*. Chapel Hill: University of North Carolina Press.

McDougall, E. A. (2007). Dilemmas in the practice of *rachat* in French West Africa. In K. A. Appiah & M. Bunzl (Eds.), *Buying freedom: The ethics and economics of slave redemption* (pp. 158–178). Princeton: Princeton University Press.

McKeown, N. (2007). *The invention of ancient slavery?* London: Duckworth.

McKivigan, J. R., & Kaufman, H. L. (Eds.). (2012). *In the words of Frederick Douglass: Quotations from liberty's champion.* Ithaca, NY: Cornell University Press.

McLennan, R. (2008). *The crisis of imprisonment: Protest, politics, and the making of the American penal state, 1776–1941.* New York: Cambridge University Press.

Meagher, A. J. (2008). *The coolie trade: The traffic in Chinese laborers to Latin America, 1847–1874.* New York: Xlibris.

Meillassoux, C. (1991). *The anthropology of slavery: The womb of iron and gold.* Chicago: University of Chicago Press.

Meriwether, E. A. (1881, August). Are women slaves? *Shaker Manifesto.*

Miers, S. (2003). *Slavery in the twentieth century: The evolution of a global problem.* New York: Rowman & Littlefield.

Miers, S. (2004). Slavery: A question of definition. In G. Campbell (Ed.), *The structure of slavery in Indian Ocean Africa and Asia* (pp. 1–16). London: Frank Cass.

Mihalopoulos, B. (2011). *Sex in Japan's globalization, 1870–1930: Prostitutes, emigration and nation-building.* London: Pickering & Chatto.

Miles, R. (1987). *Capitalism and unfree labour: Anomaly or necessity?* New York: Tavistock Publications.

Millar, J. (1771/2006). *The origin of the distinction of ranks: Or, an inquiry into the circumstances, which give rise to influence and authority, in the different members of society.* Indianapolis: Liberty Fund.

Miller, K. (1905). *As to the leopard's spots: An open letter to Thomas Dixon, Jr.* Washington, DC: Hayworth Publishing House.

Miller, R. M. (1981). The fabric of control: Slavery in antebellum Southern textile mills. *Business History Review, 55,* 471–490.

Miller, J. C. (2008). Slaving as historical process: Examples from the ancient Mediterranean and the modern Atlantic. In E. D. Lago & C. Katsari (Eds.), *Slave systems ancient and modern* (pp. 70–102). New York: Cambridge University Press.

Mironov, B. N. (1996). When and why was the Russian peasantry emancipated? In M. L. Bush (Ed.), *Serfdom and slavery: Studies in legal bondage* (pp. 323–347). New York: Addison Wesley Longman.

Moore, J. H. (1988). *The emergence of the cotton kingdom in the old Southwest, Mississippi, 1770–1860.* Baton Rouge: Louisiana State University Press.

Morgan, E. (1975). *American slavery, American freedom: The ordeal of colonial Virginia.* New York: W. W. Norton.

Mouhot, J.-F. (2011). *Slavery, fossil fuels and climate change*. Paris: Editions Champ Vallon.

Movement for Black Lives. (2016). *Reparations*. Retrieved August 11, 2016, from https://policy.m4bl.org/reparations/

Murphy, L. T. (2014). *Survivors of slavery: Modern-day slave narratives*. New York: Columbia University Press.

Naim, M. (2005). *Illicit: How smugglers, traffickers, and copycats are hijacking the global economy*. New York: Doubleday.

Neff, E. (1924). *Carlyle and Mill, mystic and utilitarian*. New York: Columbia University Press.

Negro Nurse. (1912, January 15). More slavery at the South. *The Independent: Devoted to the Consideration of Politics, Social and Economic Tendencies*.

Nevinson, H. W. (1906). *A modern slavery*. New York: Harper and Brothers.

Nizan, R. (2004). Child labour in Latin America: Issues and policies in Honduras. In C. van den Anker (Ed.), *The political economy of new slavery* (pp. 137–175). New York: Palgrave Macmillan.

Noem, K. (2014). *Argus Leader: Social media factor in driving sex trafficking, speakers say*. In the News. Retrieved August 11, 2016, from http://noem.house.gov/index.cfm/2014/2/argus-leader-social-media-factor-in-driving-sex-trafficking-speakers-say

Noyes, A. (1917, January 24). 'The Lion of Flanders': The true history of the slave raids in Belgium. *Outlook*.

Okoye, D., & Pongou, R. (2015). *Sea change: The competing long-run impacts of the transatlantic slave trade and missionary activity in Africa*. Munich Personal Archive. Retrieved August 14, 2016, from https://mpra.ub.uni-muenchen.de/66221/

Olmstead, A. L., & Rhode, P. W. (2008). *Creating abundance: Biological innovation and American agricultural development*. New York: Cambridge University Press.

Olmsted, F. L. (1856). *A journey in the seaboard slave states: With remarks on their economy*. New York: Dix & Edwards.

Oshinsky, D. M. (1997). *'Worse than slavery': Parchman farm and the ordeal of Jim Crow justice*. New York: Simon & Schuster.

Otis, J. (2015). *The collected political writings of James Otis*. R. Samuelson (Ed.). Indianapolis: Liberty Fund. Retrieved August 15, 2016, from http://oll.libertyfund.org/titles/2703#Otis_1644_665

Ould, D. (2004). Trafficking and international law. In C. van den Anker (Ed.), *The political economy of new slavery* (pp. 55–74). New York: Palgrave Macmillan.

Ovington, M. W. (1910, May 26). Slaves' reminiscences of slavery. *The Independent: Devoted to the Consideration of Politics, Social and Economic Tendencies*.

Owen, R. D. (1864). *The wrong of slavery, the right of emancipation and the future of the African race in the United States*. Philadelphia: J. B. Lippincott & Co.

Parker, T. (1854). *An address delivered by the Rev. Theodore Parker before the New York City Anti-Slavery society at its first anniversary*. New York: American Anti-Slavery Society.

Patterson, O. (1982). *Slavery and social death: A comparative study*. Cambridge: Harvard University Press.

Patterson, O. (2008). Slavery, gender, and work in the pre-modern world and early Greece: A cross-cultural analysis. In E. D. Lago & C. Katsari (Eds.), *Slave systems ancient and modern* (pp. 32–69). New York: Cambridge University Press.

Pauketat, T. R. (2005). The forgotten history of the Mississippians. In T. Pauketat & D. Loren (Eds.), *North American Archaeology* (pp. 187–211). Malden, MA: Blackwell Publishing.

Payne, E. G. (1912). *An experiment in alien labor*. Chicago: University of Chicago Press.

Peck, G. (1996). Reinventing free labor: Immigrant padrones and contract laborers in North America, 1885–1925. *Journal of American History, 83*, 848–871.

Pelteret, D. (1995). *Slavery in early mediaeval England: From the reign of Alfred until the twelfth century*. Rochester, NY: Boydell Press.

Petre-Grenouilleau, O. (2008). Processes of exiting the slave systems: A typology. In E. D. Lago & C. Katsari (Eds.), *Slave systems ancient and modern* (pp. 233–264). New York: Cambridge University Press.

Phillips, W. D. (1996). Continuity and change in Western slavery: Ancient to modern times. In M. L. Bush (Ed.), *Serfdom and slavery: Studies in legal bondage* (pp. 71–88). New York: Addison Wesley Longman.

Pierson, H. W. (1870). *A letter to Hon. Charles Sumner, with 'statements' of outrages upon freedmen in Georgia*. Washington, DC: Chronicle Print.

Pigou, A. (1920). *The economics of welfare*. London: Macmillan and Co.

Postma, J. (1992). The dispersal of African slaves in the West by Dutch slave traders, 1630–1803. In J. Inikori & S. Engerman (Eds.), *The Atlantic slave trade: Effects on economies, societies, and peoples in Africa, the Americas, and Europe* (pp. 283–299). Durham, NC: Duke University Press.

Pound, R. (1909). Liberty of contract. *Yale Law Journal, 18*, 454–487.

Powderhorn Food Community Co-op Records. (1974–1995). *Minnesota Historical Society*. Minnesota: St. Paul.

Prakash, G. (1993). Terms of servitude: The colonial discourse on slavery and bondage in India. In M. A. Klein (Ed.), *Breaking the chains: Slavery, bondage, and emancipation in Modern Africa and Asia* (pp. 131–149). Madison: University of Wisconsin Press.

Price, R. (Ed.). (1979). *Maroon societies: Rebel slave communities in the Americas* (2nd ed.). Baltimore: Johns Hopkins University Press.

Quirk, J. (2011). *The anti-slavery project: From the slave trade to human trafficking*. Philadelphia: University of Pennsylvania Press.

Rajan, R., & Ramcharan, R. (2008). *Landed interests and financial underdevelopment in the United States.* National Bureau for Economic Research. Retrieved August 15, 2016, from http://www.nber.org/papers/w14347

Ransom, R., & Sutch, R. (2001). *One kind of freedom: The economic consequences of emancipation* (2nd ed.). New York: Cambridge University Press.

Reid, A. (1993). The decline of slavery in nineteenth-century Indonesia. In M. A. Klein (Ed.), *Breaking the chains: Slavery, bondage, and emancipation in modern Africa and Asia* (pp. 64–82). Madison: University of Wisconsin Press.

Resendez, A. (2016). *The other slavery: The uncovered story of Indian enslavement in America.* New York: Houghton Mifflin Harcourt.

Rihll, T. (2008). Slavery and technology in pre-industrial contexts. In E. D. Lago & C. Katsari (Eds.), *Slave systems ancient and modern* (pp. 127–147). New York: Cambridge University Press.

Roberts, B. (1913). History of the Mormon Church. *Americana, 8*, 57–98.

Roberts, K. (2011). *The origins of business, money, and markets.* New York: Columbia Business School Publishing.

Robinson, J. (1933). *The economics of imperfect competition.* London: Macmillan & Co.

Rockman, S. (2006). The unfree origins of American capitalism. In C. Matson (Ed.), *The economy of early America: Historical perspectives and new directions* (pp. 335–361). University Park: University of Pennsylvania Press.

Rogers, C. A., & Swinnerton, K. A. (2007). Some simple analytics of slave redemption. In K. A. Appiah & M. Bunzl (Eds.), *Buying freedom: The ethics and economics of slave redemption* (pp. 20–36). Princeton: Princeton University Press.

Rosengarten, T., & Rosengarten, D. (Eds.). (2002). *A portion of the people: Three hundred years of southern Jewish life.* Charleston: University of South Carolina Press.

Rowland, D. (1903). *A Mississippi view of race relations in the South.* Jackson, MS: Harmon Publishing Co.

Rymer, N. (1873, November 8). An English slave market—A relic of barbarity. *Miners' Advocate and Record.*

Saller, R. (1996). The hierarchical household in Roman society: A study of domestic slavery. In M. L. Bush (Ed.), *Serfdom and slavery: Studies in legal bondage* (pp. 112–129). New York: Addison Wesley Longman.

Salter, J. (1996). Adam Smith on slavery. *History of Economic Ideas, 4*, 225–251.

Sandomrisky, L. N. (1997). Aristomenes. In J. P. Rodriguez (Ed.), *The historical encyclopedia of world slavery* (Vol. I, pp. 47–48). Denver: ABC-CLIO.

Saradamoni, K. (1973). Agrestic slavery in Kerala in the nineteenth century. *Indian Economic Social History Review, 10*, 371–385.

Sarich, J. (Ed.). (2012). *Follow up study of slavery and poverty Kukrouthi Village, St Ravidas Nagar District Uttar Pradesh, India.* New York: Free the Slaves.

Sato, S. (2004). Forced labour mobilization in Java during the Second World War. In G. Campbell (Ed.), *The structure of slavery in Indian Ocean Africa and Asia* (pp. 97–110). London: Frank Cass.

Sawyer, L. P. (2013). Contested meanings of freedom: Workingmen's wages, the company store system, and the *Godcharles v. Wigeman* decision. *Journal of the Gilded Age and Progressive Era, 12*, 285–319.

Scheidel, W. (2008). The comparative economics of slavery in the Greco-Roman world. In E. D. Lago & C. Katsari (Eds.), *Slave systems ancient and modern* (pp. 105–126). New York: Cambridge University Press.

Schermerhorn, C. (2015). *The business of slavery and the rise of American capitalism, 1815–1860*. New Haven, CT: Yale University Press.

Schottenhammer, A. (2004). Slaves and forms of slavery in late imperial China (Seventeenth to Early Twentieth Centuries). In G. Campbell (Ed.), *The structure of slavery in Indian Ocean Africa and Asia* (pp. 143–154). London: Frank Cass.

Schulz, J. (2008). *The financial crisis of abolition*. New Haven, CT: Yale University Press.

Schurz, C. (1903, January). Can the South solve the Negro problem? *McClure's*.

Sewall, S. (1700). *The selling of Joseph*. Boston: Bartholomew Green and John Allen.

Share, A. J. (1982). *Cities in the commonwealth: Two centuries of urban life in Kentucky*. Lexington: University Press of Kentucky.

Sharman, J. C. (2011). *The money laundry: Regulating criminal finance in the global economy*. Ithaca, NY: Cornell University Press.

Shelley, L., & Bain, C. (2015). Human trafficking: Fighting the illicit economy with the legitimate economy. *Social Inclusion, 3*, 140–144.

Shiller, R. J. (2003). *The new financial order: Risk in the 21st century*. Princeton: Princeton University Press.

Shirley, M. (1994). *From congregation town to industrial city: Culture and social change in a Southern community*. New York: New York University Press.

Simon, K. (1929). *Slavery*. London: Hodder and Stoughton.

Skinner, E. B. (2008). *A crime so monstrous: Face-to-face with modern-day slavery*. New York: Free Press.

Smith, A. (1776/1937). *An inquiry into the nature and causes of the wealth of nations*. New York: Modern Library.

Smith, A. (1896). *Lectures on justice, police, revenue and arms*. Oxford: Clarendon Press.

Smith, G. W. (1945). Ante-bellum attempts of Northern business interests to 'redeem' the Upper South. *Journal of Southern History, 11*, 177–213.

Smith, A. E. (1965). *Colonists in bondage: White servitude and convict labor in America, 1607–1776*. Gloucester, MA: Peter Smith.

Smith, J. D. (1985). *An old creed for the new South: Proslavery ideology and historiography, 1865–1918*. Athens: University of Georgia Press.

Smith, R. (2003). *Global human development: Explaining its regional variations.* Social Structural Research Working Paper. Retrieved August 12, 2016, from https://www.ciaonet.org/attachments/8474/upload

Smith, C. F. (2008). *Here lies Jim Crow: Civil rights in Maryland.* Baltimore: Johns Hopkins University Press.

South Carolina Association. (1823/2001). Memorial ca. 1823. In L. Schweninger (Ed.), *The Southern Debate over slavery: Petitions to Southern Legislatures, 1778–1864* (pp. 78–83). Chicago: University of Illinois Press.

Spooner, L. (1845). *The unconstitutionality of slavery.* Boston: Bela Marsh.

Starna, W., & Watkins, R. (1991). Northern Iroquoian slavery. *Ethnohistory, 38*, 34–53.

Starr, C. (1958). An overdose of slavery. *Journal of Economic History, 18*, 17–32.

Staudenraus, J. (1961). *The African colonization movement, 1816–1865.* New York: Columbia University Press.

Stauffer, J. (2007). Frederick Douglass and the politics of slave redemptions. In K. A. Appiah & M. Bunzl (Eds.), *Buying freedom: The ethics and economics of slave redemption* (pp. 213–222). Princeton: Princeton University Press.

Steele, E. S. (1987). Henry George on chattel and wage slavery: The American social philosopher condemned both forms as immoral, irrational denials of equality. *American Journal of Economics and Sociology, 46*, 369–378.

Steinfeld, R. J. (1991). *The invention of free labor: The employment relation in English & American law and culture, 1350–1870.* Chapel Hill: University of North Carolina Press.

Steinfeld, R. J. (2001). *Coercion, contract, and free labor in the nineteenth century.* New York: Cambridge University Press.

Stone, A. H. (1908). Some problems of Southern economic history. *American Historical Review, 13*, 779–797.

Stowe, H. B. (1852). *Uncle Tom's cabin: Or, negro life in the slave states of America* (3rd ed.). London: C. H. Clarke and Co.

Syrett, H. C., & Cooke, J. E. (Eds.). (1962). *Papers of Alexander Hamilton Volume IV 1787–May 1788.* New York: Columbia University Press.

Taylor, C. C. W. (1983). A note on ancient attitudes towards slavery. *Analysis, 43*, 40–43.

Taylor, T. (2001). Believing the ancients: Quantitative and qualitative dimensions of slavery and the slave trade in later prehistoric Eurasia. *World Archaeology, 33*, 27–43.

Taylor, J. E. (2014). The Great Depression and its aftermath. In R. E. Wright & T. Zeiler (Eds.), *CQ Press Guide to U.S. Economic Policy* (pp. 45–60). Washington, DC: Sage.

Teackle, L. (1817). *An address to the members of the legislature of Maryland, concerning the establishment of a loan office for the benefit of the landowners of the state.* Annapolis: n.p.

Temperley, H. (1996). New World slavery, Old World slavery. In M. L. Bush (Ed.), *Serfdom and slavery: Studies in legal bondage* (pp. 144–157). New York: Addison Wesley Longman.

Theiss, L. E. (1908, November 5). Loan slaves and their emancipation. *The Independent: Devoted to the Consideration of Politics, Social and Economic Tendencies.*

Thompson, W. G. (1833, May 26). The black and the white slave. *Weekly True Sun.*

Thompson, G. (1851). *Prison life and reflections; Or, a narrative of the arrest, trial, conviction, imprisonment, treatment, observations, reflections, and deliverance of Work, Burr, and Thompson.* Hartford: Alanson Work.

Thornton, J. M. (1978). *Politics and power in a slavery society: Alabama, 1800–1860.* Baton Rouge: Louisiana State Press.

Tiffany, J. (1849). *A treatise on the unconstitutionality of American slavery.* Cleveland: J. Calyer.

Tinker, H. (1993). *A new system of slavery: The export of Indian labour overseas, 1830–1920* (2nd ed.). London: Hansib Publishing Limited.

Toledano, E. (1993). Ottoman concepts of slavery in the period of reform, 1830s–1880s. In M. A. Klein (Ed.), *Breaking the chains: Slavery, bondage, and emancipation in modern Africa and Asia* (pp. 37–63). Madison: University of Wisconsin Press.

Tomek, B. C. (2011). *Colonization and its discontents: Emancipation, emigration, and antislavery in antebellum Pennsylvania.* New York: New York University Press.

Tomlins, C. (2006). Indentured servitude in perspective: European migration into North America and the composition of the early American labor force, 1600–1775. In C. Matson (Ed.), *The Economy of Early America: Historical Perspectives and New Directions* (pp. 146–182). University Park: University of Pennsylvania Press.

Toner, J. (2014). *The Roman guide to slave management: A treatise by nobleman Marcus Sidonius Falx.* New York: Overlook Press.

Travis, J., Western, B., & Redburn, S. (Eds.). (2014). *The growth of incarceration in the United States: Exploring causes and consequences.* Washington, DC: National Academies Press.

Tuchman, B. (1984). *The march of folly: From Troy to Vietnam.* New York: Ballantine Books.

Tucker, C. (1853). *Abbeokuta, or, sunrise within the tropics: An outline of the origin and progress of the Yoruba Mission.* London: James Nisbet and Co.

Turley, D. (1996). Slave emancipations in modern history. In M. L. Bush (Ed.), *Serfdom and slavery: Studies in legal bondage* (pp. 181–196). New York: Addison Wesley Longman.

Turton, A. (2004). Violent capture of people for exchange on Karen-Tai borders in the 1830s. In G. Campbell (Ed.), *The structure of slavery in Indian Ocean Africa and Asia* (pp. 69–82). London: Frank Cass.

Union Nations. (1926). *Slavery convention*. Office of the High Commissioner. Retrieved August 11, 2016, from http://www.ohchr.org/EN/ProfessionalInterest/Pages/SlaveryConvention.aspx

Upadhyaya, K. (2004). Bonded labour in South Asia: India, Nepal and Pakistan. In C. van den Anker (Ed.), *The political economy of new slavery* (pp. 118–136). New York: Palgrave Macmillan.

Van Bueren, G. (2004). Slavery as piracy: The legal case of reparations for the slave trade. In C. van den Anker (Ed.), *The political economy of new slavery* (pp. 235–247). New York: Palgrave Macmillan.

van den Anker, C. (2004). Contemporary slavery, global justice and globalization. In C. van den Anker (Ed.), *The political economy of new slavery* (pp. 15–36). New York: Palgrave Macmillan.

Vogt, J. (1975). *Ancient slavery and the ideal of man* (T. Wiedemann, Trans.). Cambridge: Harvard University Press.

Von Plato, A., Leh, A., & Thonfeld, C. (Eds.). (2010). *Hitler's slaves: Life stories of forced labourers in Nazi-occupied Europe*. New York: Beghahn Books.

Waldstreicher, D. (2006). Capitalism, slavery, and Benjamin Franklin's American Revolution. In C. Matson (Ed.), *The economy of early America: Historical perspectives and new directions* (pp. 183–217). University Park: University of Pennsylvania Press.

Walker, J. E. K. (1983). Pioneer slave entrepreneurship—Patterns, processes, and perspectives: The case of the slave Free Frank on the Kentucky Pennyroyal, 1795–1819. *Journal of Negro History, 68*, 289–308.

Wallace, G. (1760). A system of the principles of the laws of Scotland. In *The annual register, or a view of the history, politicks and literature of the year 1760* (3rd ed., pp. 263–265). London: R. and J. Dodsley.

Waln, N. (1764). To Richard Waln Jr., January 8/18. Waln Papers, Family Correspondence, Box 7. Historical Society of Pennsylvania, Philadelphia, PA.

Warren, J. F. (2004). The structure of slavery in the Sulu zone in the late eighteenth and nineteenth centuries. In G. Campbell (Ed.), *The structure of slavery in Indian Ocean Africa and Asia* (pp. 111–128). London: Frank Cass.

Washington, B. T. (1901). *Up from slavery*. New York: Doubleday Page.

Way, L. (1848). *The practical sugar planter: A complete account of the cultivation and manufacture of sugar-can according to the latest and most improved processes*. London: Smith, Elder and Co.

Weld, T. (1839). *American slavery as it is: The testimony of a thousand witnesses*. New York: American Anti-Slavery Society.

Wergeland, A. M. (1916). *Slavery in Germanic society during the Middle Ages*. Chicago: University of Chicago Press.

Wermeil, S. (2000). *The fireproof building: Technology and public safety in the nineteenth-century American city*. Baltimore: Johns Hopkins University Press.

Whartenby, F. (1977). *Land and labor productivity in United States cotton production, 1800–1840*. New York: Arno Press.

White, S. (2014). Freedom's first con: African Americans and changing notes in antebellum New York City. *Journal of the Early Republic, 34*, 385–409.

Whiteley, H. (1833). *Excessive cruelty to slaves. Three months in Jamaica, in 1832: Comprising a residence of seven weeks on a sugar plantation*. Philadelphia: n.p.

Whitman, W. (1894). *Leaves of grass*. Philadelphia: David McKay.

Wiecek, W. (1977). *The sources of antislavery constitutionalism in America, 1760–1848*. Ithaca, NY: Cornell University Press.

Wiener, J. (1979). Coming to terms with capitalism: The postwar thought of George Fitzhugh. *Virginia Magazine of History and Biography, 87*, 438–447.

Wilbur, C. M. (1967). *Slavery in China during the former Han Dynasty 206 B.C.—A.D. 25*. New York: Russell & Russell.

Willey, P., & Emerson, T. E. (1993). The osteology and archaeology of the Crow Creek massacre. *Plains Anthropologist, 38*, 227–269.

Williamson, H. F. (1934). *Edward Atkinson: The biography of an American liberal, 1827–1905*. Boston: Old Corner Book Store, Inc.

Wiseman, T. (2015). *Slavery, economic freedom and income levels in former slave-exporting states of Africa*. Social Science Research Network. Retrieved August 14, 2016, from http://papers.ssrn.com/sol3/papers.cfm?abstract_id=2679098

Wright, G. (1987). Capitalism and slavery on the islands: A lesson from the mainland. *Journal of Interdisciplinary History, 17*, 851–870.

Wright, D. R. (1993). *African Americans in the early Republic*. Arlington Heights, IL: Harlan Davidson.

Wright, G. (2006). *Slavery and American economic development*. Baton Rouge: Louisiana State University Press.

Wright, R. E. (2008). *One nation under debt: Hamilton, Jefferson, and the history of what we owe*. New York: McGraw-Hill.

Wright, R. E. (2010). *Fubarnomics: A lighthearted, serious look at America's economic ills*. Amherst, NY: Prometheus.

Wright, R. E. (2014). *Corporation nation*. Philadelphia: University of Pennsylvania Press.

Wright, R. E. (2015). *Little business on the prairie: Entrepreneurship, prosperity, and challenge in South Dakota*. Sioux Falls, SD: Center for Western Studies.

Wright, R. E. (2017). Financing U.S. economic growth, 1790–1860: Corporations, markets, and the real economy. In P. L. Rousseau & P. Wachtel (Eds.), *Financial systems and economic growth: Credit, crises, and regulation from the 19th century to the present*. New York: Cambridge University Press.

Zaborney, J. (2012). *Slaves for hire: Renting enslaved laborers in antebellum Virginia*. Baton Rouge: Louisiana State University Press.

Zeuske, M. (2012). Historiography and research problems of slavery and the slave trade in a global-historical perspective. *International Review of Social History, 57*, 87–111.

Index

R.E. Wright, *The Poverty of Slavery*,
DOI 10.1007/978-3-319-48968-1

B

C

F

N

T

U

X

Y

Z

www.ingramcontent.com/pod-product-compliance
Lightning Source LLC
Chambersburg PA
CBHW050522240926
51846CB00003B/652
9783319489674